4/24

D1337983

SHELLEY

SHELLEY

Also Known as Shirley

SHELLEY WINTERS

GRANADA
London Toronto Sydney New York

Granada Publishing Limited
Frogmore, St Albans, Herts AL2 2NF
and
3 Upper James Street, London W1R 4BP
Suite 405, 4th Floor, 866 United Nations Plaza, New York, NY 10017, USA
117 York Street, Sydney, NSW 2000, Australia
100 Skyway Avenue, Rexdale, Ontario M9W 3A6, Canada
PO Box 84165, Greenside, 2034 Johannesburg, South Africa
61 Beach Road, Auckland, New Zealand

Published by Granada Publishing 1981

Grateful acknowledgment is made to Paramount Pictures Corporation, Columbia
Pictures, Twentieth Century-Fox Film Corp., Universal City Studios, Inc., Metro-
Goldwyn-Mayer Inc., Warner Brothers, United Artists Corporation, and American
International Pictures for the use of still photographs. The credits and copyright
notices for all photographs are listed on page 509-511 which are hereby
incorporated by reference and made a part of this copyright page.

Portions of this book were previously published in *Ladies' Home Journal*.

Grateful acknowledgment is made for the use of lines from "Richard Cory" by
Edwin A. Robinson which is fully protected by copyright. Used by permission of
Charles Scribner's Sons.

ISBN 0 246 11496 7

Printed and bound in Great Britain by
William Clowes (Beccles) Limited, Beccles and London

Granada ®
Granada Publishing ®

For Blanche
who has always made my reach exceed my grasp

Have ye leisure, comfort, calm,
Shelter, food, love's gentle balm?
Or what is it ye buy so dear
With your pain and with your fear?

—PERCY BYSSHE SHELLEY

ACKNOWLEDGMENTS

I wish to thank especially my good friends of twenty years, Jan and Robert Lowell, who now live in Rome and came back to the United States for six months to help me organize, collate, punctuate and "grammaticize" my memories. Principally, they instilled in me the discipline to write this book.

My special thanks to Ellis Amburn, my editor at William Morrow, who for a year and a half helped me get my past in order. Now, if only he would do the same for my future!

And to Helen Darvall, my friend and associate, who kept things calm amidst the mental and physical chaos of this Work.

SHELLEY

BOOK ONE

My All for Art . . . and Money

CHAPTER 1

Who is Shirley Schrift? What happened to her, and what metamorphosis took place that changed her into Shelley Winters, movie star?

Adolescence is the time when most children struggle with their identity. I have come to feel that when adolescents are forced by circumstances to change their name, for whatever reason, they somehow bury part of that identity and for much of their adult life are compelled to try to reclaim and rejoin it into a unified feeling of a complete self.

So it was with me. At about fifteen, I was in the office of the Group Theatre in New York to read for an understudy in a play called *Retreat to Pleasure* by Irwin Shaw. I didn't have a clue what kind of part it was. I only knew I had to have it. The secretary asked me my name.

"Shirley Schrift."

She wrote it down on a little card, then asked me if I was registered with Equity.

I quickly replied, "I don't want to rush things."

"Shirley Schrift isn't a very good name for an actress," she told me. "Let's see if we can figure out another one. . . . What's your mother's maiden name?"

"Winter," I told her.

She wrote it down. "Do you like 'Shirley'?" she asked.

"God, no, there's millions of Shirleys all over Brooklyn, all named after Shirley Temple."

"Well, wouldn't you like a name that sounds like Shirley in case someone calls you?"

I thought for a moment. "Shelley is my favorite poet, but that's a last name, isn't it?"

She wrote it on the card in front of "Winter." She looked at it. "Not anymore it isn't. Shelley Winter. That's your name."

She handed me the card, and I looked at it. It felt like me. Half poetic and half cold with fright. "Okay," I told her. "Send it in."

Years later, in their infinite wisdom, Universal Studios added an S to "Winter" and made me plural.

13

* * *

My grandfather in St. Louis would sit me on his lap, and while I played with his watch chain, he would say: "Shirley, learn this for all your life. A wise man, Hillel, said, 'If I'm not for myself, then who am I for? But if I am only for myself, what am I? And if not now, WHEN?'" I believe this was my first clear memory. I think I was about three.

He looked at me with his beardless Santa Claus face and twinkling blue eyes and said, "Do you understand me?"

"Zayda, that's too hard."

"Yes, babyla, but if you really come to understand that, you'll have the answers to all the things that happen to you."

My life, like maybe everyone else's, has been many forks in the road. Yearly. Monthly. Weekly. And depending on my personal needs at any given moment and/or my feelings of responsibility to my fellowman, I have often wanted to scurry back to the fork and take the other road. Sometimes I've even tried to do it, and it's caused me a lot of grief.

So if you will take my hand, we will go down the rocky road that leads out of the Brooklyn ghetto to: one New York apartment, two Oscars, three California houses, four hit plays, five Impressionist paintings, six mink coats, ninety-nine films and a liberated lady with a smog-stricken palm tree.

One of Colette's characters in *Cheri*, says, "The longer you wear pearls, the realer they become." And so it is with my family's legends and often the memories of my old friends, with slight variations and different colorings. But what follows is how *I* remember it.

It seems to me that my mother and father were third cousins. (The only figure I am absolutely sure of is 10 percent, 'cause that's what the agent gets.) Both sides of my family seem to have come from a little town called Grymalow, about 200 miles from Vienna, which had a peculiar habit of changing countries. The only ancestor I ever heard about was Katie Schratt, a great-aunt who was Emperor Franz Joseph's mistress . . . she must have converted.

My father's mother had seven children. Aunt Zisel, her oldest, brought thirty-five cousins from Europe by flicking chickens—removing the feathers. Two Uncle Bens, one rich and one poor one. Uncle Heinrich, who ran a restaurant in Budapest, Uncle Yakel who was a butcher in Austria, Uncle Sharkey, who owned a barbershop on Delancey Street, and my father, Jonas.

My father's fate was decided for him. In fact, the marriage contract was drawn via the mails, so he was destined for St. Louis,

Missouri, where my mother had been born. He came to New York at the age of thirteen by way of the "regulation steerage sweatshop route" and started looking for the streets paved with gold. He was dazzled by the American dream and immediately set out to become a millionaire. When he was eighteen, he went to St. Louis, and he and my mother, who was sixteen, met for the first time at their engagement party. They fell in love—or so they said—and were married.

According to the law in those days, my mother lost her citizenship by marrying an alien. When my father was twenty-one, he took out his citizenship papers and became a naturalized American. My mother never believed that she had lost her citizenship since she'd been born in the United States. Many years later, in California we went to get her passport so as to go to England, where I was to make a film—the passport man told her that she was not a citizen.

She looked at him with contempt and said, "Listen, mister, I've been voting and working for the Democratic Party all my life. Okay, deport me back to St. Louis."

My mother's name was Rose, Rose Winter Schrift, source of my strength, talent, *chutzpah* and ingenuity, and the lady I clung to no matter how many times I left home or got married. I even fought Death for her, unable to accept the fact that anyone or anything would take her away from me. Until finally, in the intensive care ward after her third heart attack, when they were readying her for a pacemaker operation, she pulled all the needles out of her arm, looked at me and said, "Baby, it's time you let me go. Don't forget you're an artist. You did it for both of us. Now I have to go join My Partner."

She is buried beside my father in a plot next to Al Jolson's elaborate tomb. They always loved his records. It was a beautiful cemetery back then in 1966; now there are miles of freeways crisscrossing around it.

In 1925 Jonas Schrift was not only an expert patternmaker and cutter for a large men's clothing manufacturer—he designed the loafer coat—but he was also their chief salesman for the midwestern territory. He dressed impeccably, his tie always matching his pocket handkerchief and his socks. He had a gold collar pin with two little blue stones on each end and a stickpin with a matching blue stone. And he always washed and waxed our blue Essex on Sundays.

After considerable nagging, I would sometimes get him to take me along on a selling trip. Early in the morning I would sit on the front steps, all dressed up, waiting for him to get his sample cases

ready and his clothes just so. My mother had dressed me in a blue
outfit to match our Essex, while my older sister, Bappy (I couldn't
say Blanche), glowered. I would go with Daddy to St. Joe or Kan-
sas City on sweltering summer mornings, but I loved it because of
his stories about all the things we would do when he became a
millionaire.

At that time we lived in a three-room ground-floor apartment in
a four-story tenement on Newstead Avenue, where I had been born.
I slept in a crib in the living room until Bappy, who was five years
older, would allow me to join her on the convertible divan. She
resisted this arrangement for years as I was a periodic bedwetter.
Cribs must have been larger in those days.

My father was very careful with a buck, of course, because he
was saving up to be that millionaire. There were always vicious
arguments when my mother wanted to buy us winter coats or shoes
or foolish things like that. All our other clothes she made herself.

Somehow she saw to it that we had music lessons. Bappy was
very good at piano, but I was so-so at my singing. I wouldn't learn
to read music (I'm still sorry about that); I liked to make up my
own songs. In kindergarten it drove the teacher crazy when all the
children put their hands over their hearts and sang "My Country
'Tis of Thee" and I imitated an Al Jolson record, singing "America,
I Love Thee." My first counterpoint.

Each year St. Louis holds a celebration—the Veiled Prophet—and
part of the celebration is a pageant. I was to be the little fairy who
led onto the stage all the other characters, dressed in costumes from
every corner of the world. My mother made me a green tulle tutu
trimmed with ropes of silver tinsel and a silver wand with a tinsel
star. I had only soft ballet shoes on, but somehow, despite the pain,
I danced on my toes. I sat downstage right and, making up my own
dialogue, started the pageant by announcing, "Commence!" Then,
with a wave of my wand, I introduced each act.

At the end of the evening the mayor of St. Louis came up on the
stage, picked me up in his arms and said, "Baby, you're a natural."

"I know," I replied. I guess I was about four.

When we were good and my father felt a little flush, we would
join the entire Winter family, including Zayda and Bubba, and
drive out to Crabapple Farm. It had a freshwater lake, and we'd all
go swimming. I couldn't swim yet, but that didn't faze me. There
was a big slide that went into the deep water. Undaunted, I would
zoom down it, swallowing half the lake, and frantically dog-paddle
to shallow water.

Later, with my zayda and bubba silently disapproving, we all would eat the most glorious pork spareribs that had been barbecuing in a hickory pit; the smell would keep us salivating all afternoon. With them we had huge sour pickles, homemade root beer and real beer that came out of barrels. My grandparents brought a chicken and roasted it carefully over the fire so they could have a kosher dinner.

There is a terrifying Jewish superstition. My grandmother would take a chicken, chop off its head and swing the carcass over me and Blanche so that any evil or disease that might attack us would go into the chicken instead. This is called *schlug kapores*.

When a polio epidemic broke out in St. Louis, my grandmother would let us swim only in lakes fed by freshwater streams. She also tied camphor in little bags around our necks. There must have been something to it; none of the Winter kids got polio (apologies to Jonas Salk).

A kind and patient man, Zayda was the only person I've ever known who really knew how to listen to little children and treat them like people. My zayda instilled in all of us the sense that human life is precious and holy and that there is some glorious design and purpose in nature and to our existence.

I remember the lovely holiday when my grandfather built a long, narrow sukkah, a wood-frame structure covered with luscious purple grapes and leaves. All the grandchildren sat at the sukkah and ate raisins and almonds and drank seltzer with a little homemade wine in it. Zayda sat at the head of the table, my little bubba at the foot, and he told us wonderful stories of the old country and the Old Testament. For many years I was mixed up about my real relatives and my biblical ancestors. I was so glad that "Uncle Abraham" didn't kill "Cousin Isaac" and that God intervened and sent the ram. But sometimes at Temple on the High Holy Days, my real cousin Isaac would tease and torment me, so I was secretly sorrier for the ram.

My grandmother was four feet ten and weighed about eighty-five pounds. She had steel gray hair; it never got white. I never remember her sitting down. It seemed nothing for her and my mother to cook a Passover dinner for one hundred relatives, and the entire service was read with the different ritual foods. It took about five hours, all the young children would fall fast asleep, and we would wake up in the morning in my Bubba's feather bed—the greatest security blanket since Linus's.

In those days it seemed as if I rarely woke up where I went to sleep. As a result, to this day, first thing in the morning I have to study the furniture for a couple of minutes to make sure where I am. The gypsy nature of my film life hasn't helped me resolve this disturbing sense of musical beds.

For instance, sometimes in St. Louis when it was unbearably hot, my parents would pick us up in our pajamas, take a thermos of cold lemonade, cookies and blankets to lie on, and drive somewhere in cool Forest Park Highland to sleep. In the morning I would wake up with squirrels nibbling at the cookies around me and the humming birds attacking the flowers and the cardinals screaming because we had violated their territory.

Forest Park Highland also had a terrific amusement park with a terrifying roller coaster. One Fourth of July my sister took me on it many times. I held onto her, screaming with terror and delight. She was ten; I was five and her constant responsibility—maybe she was hoping I'd fall off.

There were lots of fireworks and sparklers, and my mother and father warned me not to touch anything. Naturally I grabbed a sparkler, unfortunately from the wrong end, and my hand was badly burned. I was so frightened because I'd disobeyed that I darted across the parkway. I had a navy blue dress on, and it was night, and a car hit me, knocking me about twelve feet.

I woke up in the hospital. Bappy was in hysterics. My father was shaking her because she hadn't watched me, and my mother just stood there in frozen fear. Miraculously nothing was broken, and there was no serious concussion, but the doctors gave me a tetanus shot and treated my hand. When the policeman asked me why I was running across the road right in front of the traffic, Bappy said in her firm little voice, "She was so scared she'd get a beating because she disobeyed and burned her hand—that's why she ran away." My parents shriveled.

The policeman said, "Well, Shirley, you're all right. You just dented the man's bumper a little bit. Don't do it again. You were lucky you weren't killed."

He took my mother and father out in the hall to talk to them. Blanche sat on my bed, and I said in a scared voice, "Bappy, what's 'killed'?"

She hesitated. "Stop thinking about it. It looks like every time Daddy starts worrying about money, he hits *us*." She held my other hand until I went to sleep. It took a long time, and I dreamed of "killed," whatever that was.

Death is a difficult thing for young children to cope with, and

I think they should be helped to understand it. I wasn't. My father
was so often driven by money worries he became cruel and my
mother was so distraught and angry that Bappy and I felt secure
only at our grandparents' house. My beloved Zayda died suddenly
of diabetes which was diagnosed too late. My grandmother followed
him three months later. I don't know what she died of; I think
she just stopped living. When I saw my Zayda at the funeral parlor
with the coffin open, I couldn't understand why he was sleeping in
that box. When they closed the box and put him in the ground,
I became frantic, believing he was just sleeping and it was a terrible mistake. I screamed and hit out at everyone until I had to be
taken away.

I wouldn't eat and became quite skinny. I was even mean and
nasty to my mother, despite her grief. "You'll be sorry, Shirley,"
she told me. "When my time comes, you'll look for me in every
corner and you'll give everything you own for a glimpse of me."
She was right. When she died, I wore her nightgowns for years
and used to walk around our apartment, hoping I would catch a
glimpse of the electric image she must have left on this earth.

My mother was a beautiful coloratura soprano and had once won
a St. Louis Municipal Opera contest. A rich St. Louis shoe lady
wanted to finance her musical education in Italy, but my mother's
parents felt they'd used all their resources to get away from the
old country, and they weren't about to let their beautiful red-
haired daughter go back under any circumstances. And in those
days young girls just didn't do things like that.

I remember her singing beautiful soprano selections on summer
nights on the front porch and my sister and me walking down to the
neighborhood bakery, with the fireflies flickering and the smell of
lilacs everywhere, and hearing her sing "Indian Love Call" off in
the distance so that we wouldn't be scared. Then we all would sit
on the porch and eat hot jelly doughnuts and drink ice-cold lemonade, and she would sing many beautiful soprano selections for us.
In fact, for all the neighbors, who were also sitting on their porches
because it gets *hot* in St. Louis in the summer. No air conditioning,
just an occasional fan, but we never noticed.

It was the Depression, and I guess we were poor, but nobody
told Bappy and me. We had so much love, and fights, and responsibility for each other. When Bappy had to have her tonsils taken
out, I had to have mine taken out. It was cheaper for two of us. I
remember waking up in the middle of the night, frightened and
croaking, and Bappy getting up and slipping me little pieces of ice

to suck on from the ice bag around her throat. I was too young to have my own bag. The night nurse came rushing in, and they had a terrific argument, but Bappy croaked a promise she would stay awake and watch me so I wouldn't strangle myself. I guess Blanche was a little nurse even then.

Despite the pain and arguments, there were lots of good times. We were surrounded by the huge Winter family, one for all, all for one and all very musical. My mother was the only girl, and Uncle Irving was a one-man band. Uncle Al could only play the horses but could read music. He disgraced himself by marrying a beautiful *shiksa*; he and my Aunt Helen are in their seventies now, still happily married and still playing the ponies. My Uncle Joe was a violinist and the true musical genius of the family. He was concert-master of the St. Louis Municipal Orchestra in the summer, and I used to love to sit on the floor and listen to him practice. In the winter he was the first violinist at the Ambassador Theater, and one of my earliest memories is that of being held in his arms while watching and listening to Al Jolson in *The Jazz Singer* and not being able to differentiate between the vaudeville performers and the people in the movie. During the early thirties the Skouras brothers begged him repeatedly to move to California and head the Music Department of their budding motion-picture studio, Twentieth Century-Fox, but Uncle Joe didn't want to uproot his family. He was a wonderful father, and the whole family was devastated when he died very young of pneumonia during a miserably cold St. Louis winter.

Bappy and I would often dress up in the pongee dresses that our mother had carefully smocked, sit on magazines on the front steps and wait for our father to come home. He might appear at any time of the day or night and would phone when he was close to home. We were afraid to move for fear of getting dirty. It's odd how I remember myself during this period as being an ugly, skinny child, although in an early photo I'm blonde and cute and a little plump.

When my father received a promotion, we moved to DeTonty Street, then in a suburb near Shaw's Botanical Gardens. We still had only three rooms, but it seemed to me that we had moved to the country, with empty lots full of wild flowers. We were taken to the Ambassador Theater every Saturday because Uncle Joe got us in free. Mother would drop us and sandwiches off at ten in the morning and pick us up after shopping—a minimum of six hours— and we would see *Buck Rogers, Flash Gordon, Movietone News*, a vaudeville show, and sometimes two pictures. My sister swears I never moved; my eyes would stay riveted to the stage and the screen. In fact, it was a constant battle to get me to go to the ladies' room every couple of hours, and our whole section of the theater would become embroiled in the struggle. I was so afraid I would miss something I preferred ruining my coat, my dress and the seat.

The Ambassador Theater had a Major Bowes Amateur Hour one Saturday. Our laundress, Delia, used to sing as she did the laundry in the basement, and I learned her songs by heart. In the middle of the Major Bowes contest, *sans* introduction, I ran up on the stage with Bappy in hot pursuit, but I got there first and sang innumerable verses of "Short'nin' Bread" until they had to give me a prize.

My father was bringing the boss home for supper one evening to discuss a partnership, and my mother made a big banana cream pie and two small ones. She put them out to cool on a newspaper on a high windowsill and told me not to touch them while she took a shower. I sat and looked at those pies, it seemed to me, for hours. Finally, I took a stool and climbed up on the sink and tried to reach my little pie. They *all* fell out of the window and into the alley. My mother called from the bathroom, "Shirley . . . what are you doing?"

"Killing myself," I replied, and fled. I hid in an empty lot about a block away until it was night and I was starving. I finally sneaked home, whereupon I got the worst beating of my life. Blanche had already had hers for not watching me. To this day she has not forgiven me, and whenever anyone mentions banana cream pie, an argument follows.

Despite his boss's offer of a junior partnership and a raise to $100 a week my father was sure he could only become a big capitalist by going to New York. My mother wanted very much to stay in St. Louis with her family or at least for my father to go there first and find a job and an apartment. He refused . . . he wouldn't leave my mother alone. After weeks of fights all night long, my mother capitulated, suddenly grabbed a scissors and began to tear up the old leather sofa. "Our bed!" we screamed.

"You want to go to New York?" she yelled, tearing away. "Let's stop the discussions and go."

We who of course had never seen New York could not understand his obsession with it, but my father broke up our little home. We left our family and headed east on the railroad train with all our belongings in twelve barrels. When my large crib was being packed, Blanche looked at my parents in true surprise and said, "You mean we're going to take *her* with us?" All the Winter relatives came down to the train station to see us off, and little did any of us imagine that the next time we saw each other they would be watching me make a personal appearance on the stage at the Ambassador Theater and starring in a film on that screen.

CHAPTER 2

"Look at the prices," my father whispered, but I managed to get in a cherry Coke, a hamburger and a banana split on the train to New York. I also managed to throw it all up as we were undressing in the berth. It was a relief to the entire crew of the Twentieth Century Limited when we got off at Grand Central.

We were greeted by multitudes of Schrifts. My father's family had formed an organization called Our Cousins' Family Circle—250 strong—whose purpose was to get newly arrived immigrants settled, find them jobs, find husbands for pregnant girl cousins and put boys through college. Especially those who wanted to become doctors, lawyers or accountants. They all were waiting for us, eager to see the redheaded singer whom Jonas had married way out in the Middle West and his two practically *shiksa* daughters. Out we tumbled, including our twelve barrels of china, silver, pots, pans, candlesticks, feather beds, wedding presents, toys and food.

Blanche was immediately accepted—she looked just right, dark and cute. But that perky little blonde must be a throwback to some Polish Cossack. The family, twelve barrels and all, took the subway to Brooklyn. I looked carefully out the windows and, never having been in a subway before, figured we were hurtling through people's cellars and asked where the jars of canned fruit were.

Our new home was in that section of Brooklyn known as East New York—one lovely room for all of us over a kosher butcher shop. Aunt Zisel was married then to her third husband (they kept dying on her). The present one was named Max Bloom, a huge Polish butcher who could speak seven languages, none of them intelligibly.

The butcher shop with its bloody meat terrified me, and I immediately got locked in the huge refrigerator by mistake when I followed Uncle Max in. He was so tall and I was so small that he didn't notice me. While I was busy staring at a dead little lamb, he closed the door. I wasn't strong enough to open it, and it must have been at least ten minutes until he had to come back into the refrigerator, and there I was, scared and shivering. My Aunt Zisel grabbed me up, gave me a hot bath and some whiskey and put me in her bed and covered me with a gigantic Polish *iberbedt* (feather bed), with a hot-water bottle at my feet.

My father immediately realized that despite the lovingness of Aunt Zisel and Uncle Max, four of us in one room would never do. He went into some strange business with my Uncle Abraham, Aunt Fanny's husband, in the Bronx. I think it was a cigar store, but I suspect they sold something else. LIKE BOOZE. Under the counter. He must have made a financial killing because he decided to take the summer off—the first and only vacation of his or my mother's life—and we all moved to Coney Island.

By now I was a bit of a loner. Mother was playing Mah-Jongg; Father was playing handball with Blanche and pinochle with the uncles and discussing the millions he would make after the Depression. Blanche was in summer school, and I—every chance I got—was at the movies. I adored the movies. I would sneak in, crawl up fire escapes and even pay in a pinch. I followed Mae West, Clark Gable and Jean Arthur all over Brooklyn, seeing each picture at least twice.

When autumn came, I had to go to school. Blanche squealed that she had a younger sister. They didn't know whether to put me in kindergarten or the third grade. I had taught myself to read in St. Louis. I was a secret reader and read newspapers, magazines and everything from *The Bobbsey Twins* to *Son of the Sheik*.

One day, just when I was beginning to get used to school discipline, I suddenly doubled over in pain and fell to the floor. I was taken by ambulance to the Coney Island Hospital, where an exploratory operation was performed immediately. The anesthetist gave me a spinal block, and despite the screen that was supposed to block my view, I cunningly watched the entire operation mirrored in the brass cover of the big overhead operating light. The surgeon removed a large tumor from my left side, and while he was in there, he took out my appendix for free. Then I must have passed out.

As I was coming to, I heard the doctor say to my mother, "She has infantile development, and we had to remove her left ovary. I doubt that she'll ever be able to have children."

His words were engraved on my soul for many years; even after two abortions, a miscarriage and, finally, a beautiful baby, I carried with me the feeling that I was not a complete woman. Maybe this helped my acting, but it played hell with my life. I feel that most actresses who allow themselves to be exploited as sex objects have something like that in their backgrounds. I know Marilyn Monroe did. You have been made to feel so sexless and unwomanly that you have to present to the world an image that is one hundred times more womanly than any other woman's.

When I was finally released, the hospital bill was such that I was taken to Uncle Sharkey's to recuperate. One of his three daughters, Eleanor, was a sweet skinny little girl exactly my age. The family lived in a railroad flat in a wonderful place, the Lower East Side. Eleanor and I slept in the back room overlooking the air shaft. We would get up very early and run across everybody's beds to the front room to sit on the fire escape and watch the action on Delancey Street: the pushcarts, the police trying to establish some sort of order, the smells of all the wonderful ethnic foods cooking (later we would get free samples), and the displays of every item imaginable. Later, in Uncle Sharkey's barbershop, Eleanor and I would have to swallow cod-liver oil, for which he would give us each a quarter. The rest of the day would be spent in finding ways of spending all this money.

Eleanor was my first bosom friend, and we loved each other dearly and never had a single fight. Then suddenly, when she was about eight, she died. My beloved Zayda had been old, but Eleanor was young and little—how could the same THING take both of them away? I never forgave anybody. Years later Uncle Sharkey tried to tell me Eleanor had died of kidney failure. I didn't believe him— I guess I needed to believe she was skinny and so had been blown away by the cold autumn winds.

Without consulting any of us, my father rented a store in Jamaica, Long Island. He stocked and fixed up a haberdashery shop that he loved. Now he was his own boss, "A Capitalist." To me Jamaica Avenue was the cat's meow. It was a step up for us, even though we were back on a convertible in the kitchen section in the so-called apartment in back of the store.

We had lived there about six months when one terrible morning my father took me with him to the Bank of the United States to get some change for the day's business. The bank doors were locked firmly, and there were mobs of people in front. The Depression had arrived with a vengeance. All I could hear was the angry murmuring of people saying, "They're only paying five cents on the dollar." I looked up at my father's face, which had gone very white, and he took my hand and led me back to our store. The bank opened a few weeks later, but my father never quite lost that strange, desperate look.

Soon my mother forced my pop to get us a real apartment. No more living over butcher stores or fighting off the rats in the back of the haberdashery. It was only two rooms and a kitchenette, but it had an elevator and a little green lawn in front. I now did my homework to the tune of *Mert and Marge* and Ed Wynn.

Around Christmastime my father gave away souvenirs of matches in little leather holders with every $2 purchase. Late one night a policeman knocked on our apartment door and told us that our store was burning . . . the rats had gnawed on the sulfur matches stored under the counter and caused a fire.

Can you imagine firemen in a men's haberdashery store at Christmas? By the time we got there the little fire was out, but the showcases were smashed, and most of the stock was gone. My father's lovely store was destroyed. And so was my childhood. The actual fire took up no more space than a small closet.

In spite of the fact that my father had hidden $400 under the cash register, he was indicted for arson because of the $5,000 worth of insurance on his shop. He and my mother hired a Schrift relative recently out of law school to take the case. They all were convinced the charge was ridiculous. Why would an arsonist set such a small fire? All my father wanted was the $5,000 worth of stolen stock to be replaced. Because we didn't have the money to raise the bail, he was taken to The Tombs. When I heard that word, I was convinced he was buried alive like my Zayda, so I was very surprised to see him alive at the trial.

Our lawyer was less than brilliant, even if he was a Schrift. The lawyer for the insurance company was older, experienced and skillful, but all I can recall is the judge banging his gavel and saying, "Guilty. Ten to twenty years." And then my mother screaming. A welfare worker took her away to give her a sedative, and my sister and I sat on the courthouse steps, crying. Blanche held me on her lap, trying to reassure me that both our parents would be back in a little while. I knew differently.

My father spent only a year in Sing Sing, but while he was there, he was stabbed by another prisoner and almost died. My mother took me to Ossining, New York, to visit him just once. He stood behind a screen, caged like an animal, with a guard watching, and I flew into a panic, screamed and hit out at the guards so was never taken there again. My sister never went up there . . . never.

My mother spent the next year begging and borrowing money, and while she was carrying on her legal battles with the State of New York, we were forced to move back over Tante Zisel's butcher shop. Everyone seemed to disappear, and I felt abandoned. My mother got a job at Lerner's dress shop working ten hours a day, twelve on Saturdays. My sister refused to transfer from Jamaica

High School, so I almost never saw her. She spent her adolescence on the subway system doing her homework.

I was about nine years old and money was so scarce that I sold magazine subscriptions from door to door. I did well and finally won a pair of longed-for roller skates. I then proceeded to skate all over Queens and Brooklyn, fantasizing as I went. I developed a whole fantasy world during my childhood; reality was too unbearable. This ability to fantasize has been a powerful tool in my acting. But it used to play hell with my real life. Even later in my life I often refused to see things as they really were, and would fantasize them into something nicer.

But at that time fantasy was necessary to my lonely ghetto existence. I would sit at the bus stop on the corner by the butcher shop on Glenmore Avenue, remembering the happier times in St. Louis when we were all together. I'd count the headlights of passing cars and try to decide at which "magical" number Mother would come home from Lerner's. At the tenth car—the fiftieth—the hundredth— the thousandth. I was usually wrong in my magical wagering, but she always came home.

I was going to P.S. 149 and was the most undisciplined kid in the school and failed everything. It was no doubt a relief to the teachers whenever I played hookey. At long last, on a block that was roped off for roller skating, I met a little Italian girl named Lucy. She was the only girl in a family of eight boys. Somehow they had found out about my family history and for a while they became my surrogate family. I began to eat with them almost every night. They were Neapolitan and had a strong Italian love and family closeness. I was always aware of being watched over and guarded and fed all kinds of succulent pasta dishes. Maybe this accounts for my later affinity for all things Italian.

In the summer Lucy and I stayed up as late as we wanted to as long as we played on her stoop. We used to play jacks, stoopball and Ringalevio. The anger I felt about what had happened to my father turned me into a tomboy who would fight at the drop of an imagined insult, and I could beat up any boy my age. I didn't bother with other girlfriends. Lucy and I used to play constantly, sometimes dangerous games, such as climbing over fences, running over abandoned building foundations and hanging off the backs of moving buses. One afternoon my mother came home unexpectedly and caught me at it. She didn't hit me; she just cried. I wished she'd hit me.

After that she made me stop wearing overalls, bought me a couple of dresses and on Saturday afternoons had me work with her at Lerner's as a checker. I had to check how many dresses women took into the changing rooms with them and how many they took out. I couldn't have been very good at it because I didn't care if they stole the whole damned store. That lousy Lerner's store was keeping my mother away from me all the time.

She finally found enough money to hire a powerful lawyer who managed to force a new trial. There was a state committee at that time called, I think, the Lefkowitz Investigation Committee and at the second trial my father was completely exonerated.

Twenty years later I sat in a limousine with Eleanor Roosevelt and Governor Herbert Lehman, waiting for John Kennedy to appear at a rally near Ninety-second Street and Broadway (which was near my Central Park West apartment). Suddenly I burst into tears and began to tell off Governor Lehman about the judicial system in New York State. "It's crooked and it stinks," I cried out while he stared at me in astonishment. But Mrs. Roosevelt somehow understood. She took my hand in hers and said, "Shelley, in a democracy the judicial system is our basis of freedom, but since human beings aren't perfect, mistakes sometimes happen." How intuitive and wise she was.

When my father finally came home from prison, he was a destroyed man. He was always in a quiet rage and would suddenly throw small objects out of the window. His dream of becoming a millionaire had vanished. Instead of suing the city, as Our Cousins' Family Circle wanted him to, he just sat in a corner dressed in an old wine-colored bathrobe. He couldn't get dressed or go out. I hardly recognized him. My dapper young father had been sent away to prison; they seemed to have sent back an old and different man. Neither Blanche nor I could talk to him, and he didn't seem to want to talk to us. He wouldn't look for a job and would fly into a rage at any suggestion to do so. It was a year before he went to work again and then only through the help of the ACWU (Amalgamated Clothing Workers Union). He felt such deep shame at what had happened to him I guess he thought everyone was talking about him . . . "the criminal."

In grammar school a beautiful young dark-haired teacher taught English composition and penmanship. She didn't get very far with my handwriting or my adverbs, but every composition I wrote for her got an A. I seemed to be able to describe from an almost political viewpoint everything I saw in the slums of Brooklyn, and even at that young age the inequalities of the distribution of the good things of the world angered me. My teacher tried to encourage me to become a writer or a lawyer and to concentrate on studying. But she had no idea of the conditions in my home. The only quiet place I had to study was the stairwell near the roof. Bappy stayed at school as late as possible and studied there.

The following summer my mother magically came up with $10 to enable me to get a season pass to the glorious Liberty Swimming Pool. I managed a great dog-paddle, and I was a fearless diver, but the lifeguard realized very quickly that I needed formal lessons, or I would drown the moment he turned his head. One day they put up a notice inviting kids to take swimming lessons and be trained to become Red Cross junior, then senior lifesavers. Without knowing exactly what that meant, I put down my name, and the following Saturday guess who showed up to coach us but JOHNNY WEISSMULLER—Tarzan himself. He taught us the crawl and the backstroke as well as lifesaving techniques. He was making a tour of the ghetto swimming pools to teach kids to swim. One day Tarzan put his arm around *my* shoulder and said, "You have a very strong kick, Shirley, and if you practice your backstroke and kick, you just may make the junior Olympic team." I can't describe the ecstasy I felt, and from that moment on I was in the water from the minute the pool opened at 9:00 A.M until it closed at 8:00 P.M., practicing. My skin got all shriveled. I never made the Olympic team, but I won races and became a junior lifeguard, and all that swimming gave me broad shoulders and long, straight legs. I am thankful to Johnny Weissmuller for that to this day.

One evening I returned from school to find no one home as usual, and as I began to change my school clothes to do the cleaning chores, I noticed a large stain of blood on my gym bloomers. We didn't have a telephone for me to call anyone, so I just lay down on the bathroom floor and waited to die. I thought it had something to do with the operation I'd had. When my mother came home at ten that evening, she seemed happy over the whole thing and ex-plained to me the whys and wherefores of "The Curse." To this day I don't think she had it straight either.

P.S. 64—Birmingham Junior High—was an integrated school, but we didn't know it. No one ever told us we had to be; we just were. It was a melting pot of children of all nationalities and races who had fun together and beat up on each other regularly. I decided to write a play and called it *Alive in the Kitchen* starring twenty-five kids as pots, pans, steaming kettles and other utensils. The success of the show led me to realize where my strength lay in the student hierarchy. Kids began stopping me in the hallways to ask for parts in my plays. But no boys asked to walk home with me. I wasn't pretty enough.

One day I took a long, hard look at myself in the mirror and saw the big mole on the bridge of my nose, the warts on the back of my neck, the thick blonde eyebrows that practically met over my brow, the kinky dirty blonde hair and a pair of overlapping eyeteeth. Not wanting to bother my mother with these little problems, I managed to save up a few dollars from my Saturday afternoon checking job at Lerner's, and located the name of a clinic attached to the Brooklyn Hospital. For $2 the doctor removed the mole and the warts with an electric needle. It hurt like hell, but I didn't let out a peep. At the dental clinic I asked the dentist to take out my right eyetooth because there wasn't any space for it. He refused, pointing out that I needed orthodontia, which would cost three or four hundred dollars. He might as well have asked for $3,000. I told him that if he wouldn't do it, I would tie a string to a doorknob and yank it out myself.

So he did it. What else he did was to place his hand on my left breast, the son of a bitch. But since I hadn't any breasts yet to speak of, I was just humiliated and frightened. I paid him his $2 and bled all over his jacket accidentally on purpose.

For the rest of the school year I sat in class and did my own orthodontia work. With my thumb I pushed my left eyetooth into a small space made larger by my fingers. We could never afford to have Bappy's teeth fixed, so she has had buckteeth all her life. Never mind, so has Gene Tierney. And Bappy is just as beautiful. Inside as well as out.

Those were the days of three items for $1 at most local beauty shops, so I got my kinky hair cut into curls like Elissa Landi, whose photograph I'd cut out of a movie magazine. Then I had my eyebrows tweezed. That last operation hurt so much that they had to give me a shot of gin, and I had to come back again to have the job finished, one eyebrow a day. But it was worth it—the butterfly had to come out of the cocoon.

I was now as tall as Blanche, though still quite skinny, but all the swimming I'd done had made me lanky and I think graceful, and Blanche taught me how to walk around the house with a heavy book balanced on my head to improve my posture. If only I could grow breasts.

I was beginning to hear about the nationwide search for a girl to play Scarlett O'Hara in the film *Gone with the Wind*. Having read that enormous book several times, I decided there was only one person to play Scarlett. *Me*. It didn't take long to find out that David Selznick, George Cukor and MGM's talent scout Bill Grady were interviewing people at the Grand Central Building on Park Avenue. I got myself done up in Blanche's high-heeled shoes and a huge straw hat of my mother's with real pink flowers picked from the empty lot across the street pinned under it—a regular southern belle. I wobbled into the building, found the office and in my best southern Brooklynese announced to the secretary, "Ah'm heah to play Scarlett O'Hara."

There were at least twenty actresses waiting in the office, but the secretary must have figured her bosses needed a laugh, so she sent me right in. With complete self-confidence I slithered in to see the film moguls. They stared at the sight before them—a tall, skinny teenager in a pastel violet dress, an off-the-shoulder bargain-base ment special, with a black ribbon tied around my neck and three powder puffs stuffed in each bra cup. I managed to croak, "Lawdy, folks, I'm the only goil to play Scarlett."

David Selznick and Bill Grady began to laugh hysterically, but Mr. Cukor shut them up. He invited me to sit down, ordered me a Coke and interviewed me about my aspirations. He then seriously explained that I should study acting and try to become known on the New York stage. He also suggested that I study speech and graduate from college first, which seemed to me a peculiar idea since there wasn't time or money for all that. I needed their money now.

But I walked out of that office on air. I didn't get the part, true, but Mr. Cukor made me feel as though I had—he was the first person to treat me as if I were really an actress.

After that interview my mother began bringing home pretty dresses from Lerner's "seconds" rack for me. A beauty contest was announced at the Liberty Swimming Pool. That year I paid for my ticket with $10 I'd saved. There were prettier girls with far better figures in the contest, but with the determination I inherited from Rose Schrift I decided I would win that cup displayed in the glass case in the front office. I began my campaign.

First I made friends with the lifeguard who was to conduct the contest by running errands for him. Then there was a fat little boy who used to follow me around and whose father was in the bathing suit business. I told him I would let him take me to the movies and give him a kiss if he would get me one of those new white satin elastic bathing suits which had just come into style. I think he went down to his father's showroom on a Saturday morning and stole one. After that I got the lady who ran our local beauty parlor to make me up, on credit. Then I bought a pair of Kitty Kelly high-heeled white shoes and bought six fluffy new powder puffs from Woolworth's, three for each side. Then the final coup. At my mother's insistence two years before I had joined the Girl Scouts (despite the fact I considered it a sissy thing to do) and at last it paid off. I made sure that my troop and our brother Boy Scout troop, complete with brass band, would be at the Liberty Pool on the day of the contest.

Fifteen girls paraded across that ramp, and as the lifeguard held his hand over each girl's head, various degrees of applause rang out. When he held his hand over mine, not only did my friends and Girl Scout companions applaud vigorously, but so did the whole Boy Scout troop, and the brass band went crazy. After all, it was their ugly duckling who was turning into a swan, and if it could happen to me, it could happen to anybody. In utter amazement—because there were some really beautiful girls of seventeen or eighteen in the contest—the lifeguard was compelled to award me, a fourteen-year-old, the cup since the rules were that it would go to the contestant who received the loudest applause. Shaking with excitement, I ran the two miles to my house and up the four flights of stairs and proudly displayed it to my family. My father looked at it and said, "Shirley, where did you steal that?" For years I hated him for that. I resolved that someday he would be forced to admit that I was beautiful.

That summer I developed beauty-contest fever. *Sans* my scout claque, I began entering beauty contests in Rockaway, Far Rockaway, Coney Island, Sea Gate, Jones Beach, Brighton Beach and at any swimming pool in the Bronx, Brooklyn, Manhattan or Staten Island you could reach by subway for a nickel. With my newly acquired Mae West walk, I managed to place third or second or even, a couple of times, *first*—but you should have seen the competition those two times. My family figured that the whole city had gone crazy. But I had to prove that I was no longer ugly, even if I still felt ugly inside.

CHAPTER 3

Miss Viola Speer directed the dramatic program at Birmingham Junior High. She soon realized that I, a potential juvenile delinquent that other teachers rejected, had to be guided into something I cared about. After two auditions that I pretended were unimportant, I got the lead in *Good News*. The song "Just Imagine" made me love that show; it seemed to be about my life.

Miss Speer not only personally gave me a program on how to become an actress but she helped civilize us Brownsville kids, inviting us for dinner to her house, where we saw elegant antiques and she subtly made us realize what knives and forks were for. Viola Speer—a spinster teacher with a fractured hip who taught in the toughest section of Brooklyn—taught firm discipline with love and gave us a strong sense of beauty. She opened up the limited world of ghetto children.

After the huge success of *Good News* it came to my attention that there were matinee performances on Saturday and Wednesday afternoons in Manhattan. I was never again seen in school on Wednesday afternoons. I would go to every matinee as well as Friday and Saturday nights. Once I'd seen all the plays—about fifty of them in those days—I would start all over again from the ABCs in the *Daily News*. This didn't include the shows I managed to see on the Subway Circuit, the Ninety-second Street YMHA, Jones Beach, union halls, churches, synagogues and the Jamaica Jewish Center.

I had a photographic memory and would fascinate Blanche by telling her the plays word for word. If it were a play I'd sneaked into during the first intermission, I'd make up the first act. She never knew the difference (I think). I used to sneak backstage or hang around stage doors to get a glimpse of the Lunts, Luther Adler, Stella Adler, Franchot Tone or Paul Muni. I never bothered them for autographs. I just stood as close to them as possible and stared for as long as I could. I was hoping that their talent was catching.

My work in school was improving, and boys began to notice me. I learned to dance the Lindy and Peabody in social clubs in cellars of one-family houses around Brownsville. They'd started out as athletic clubs but ended up *very* social. Some of the boys I knew then were later to become members of Murder, Inc. But others became

33

judges and politicians, big factory owners and even movie stars. My favorite friend was chubby little Joey Kirkland. His young parents were divorced—an unusual thing for that time—and he helped his mom run a lucrative liquor store near Sheepshead Bay. His mother would take care of the store, which was part of her alimony settlement, until Joey came home from school. Sometimes he had thousands of dollars stashed in the refrigerator along with the ice cubes. About once a month he'd bring a bulging briefcase to school and at lunchtime run to the bank and make a deposit. Joey took me to any Broadway show I wanted to go to, with the best house seats, and he took me on my first restaurant date. It was at the Russian Bear, and Joey had to pay in advance because they didn't believe kids like us could afford such a place. He was in love with me, yet I can't remember his ever kissing me. I was in love with an Italian boy by the name of George de Lalla. He was tall with broad shoulders and wore a white knit sweater all the time, and I think he was in love with a beautiful Italian girl with long black hair and an arm withered from polio. She used to sing "It's the Talk of the Town" at assembly, while Joey would hold my hand and cry, I would hold George's hand and cry and George would try to look indifferent.

My mother forced Blanche to let me stay home for her sweet sixteen party. The kids were all dressed up and dancing to Paul Whiteman records. Then the boys began discussing how, when they graduated, they were going to go to Spain in the newly formed Abraham Lincoln Brigade and help the Loyalists. As I listened intently to their passionate speeches, my father chose this moment to march in his BVDs from the bathroom, through the party to his bedroom. Blanche crumbled in mortification, and as a distraction I started to pop all the balloons with a pin.

For graduation from Birmingham Junior High, my mother got me a white chiffon dress, and Joey gave me a corsage of white gladiolas somehow fixed up to look like orchids. Our Cousins' Family Circle took me by taxi to Moskowitz and Lupowitz, a restaurant in Manhattan where important family events were celebrated.

At Thomas Jefferson High, my next erratic educational stop, a short stocky Mr. Wallach told me at the end of my first term of geometry, "Shirley, I could pass you with a C, but you really don't understand the concept of geometry, do you?" I admitted I didn't. "You have a very good mind," he continued, "and I think it's important that you develop it. Perhaps I ought to fail you and have you take the course again, give you special attention and make sure you understand the power and beauty of mathematics. It's going to be important in the coming world." He paused and looked at me from behind his gold-framed eyeglasses. "What do you think?"

I thought. "Mr. Wallach, I think you should fail me. For some nutty reason I have to pretend to be dumb when I know I'm not."

So he failed me, and the following term he taught me how to make use of my perfectly good mind and learn what geometry was all about. What we both didn't understand was my terrible need to write my strengths in sand. I felt safer if people, especially boys, thought I was dumb.

By now Blanche had graduated from high school and started nurses training school. She wanted so much to attend college and major in pre-med studies, but it was just too expensive. I was just fourteen, the right age for working papers, but my mother wept when she signed the permission blank. In shame, my father finally pulled himself together and got a better job as a shop steward. I went to work anyway, at Woolworth's on Chester Street and Pitkin Avenue near Jefferson High, in the hardware department—I wasn't pretty enough for the candy counter—from one in the afternoon until ten at night and from ten to ten on Saturdays . . . for which my take-home pay was $14 a week. There were two rest periods a day and two toilets in the ladies' rest room. The superclean floor lady had a lock on one of them for her own personal use, leaving one toilet for twenty-five girls to use in fifteen minutes.

At Christmas Woolworth's stocked Christmas tree lights and bulbs from Germany. We all had become aware of "Hitler's Germany," so I helped organize an interesting project with my co-workers. For every bulb we sold we broke one. It's amazing how many ways you can think of to break Christmas tree bulbs accidentally on purpose. Our Simon Legree floorlady was going crazy. On New Year's Eve she ordered us all to stay and take inventory, and our dates had to wait outside. That was it! My girlfriends and I organized our own personal strike. Our boyfriends helped out with signs reading: UN-FAIR! UNFAIR! And as we marched, we sang:

"Priscilla Picket Line . . . Priscilla has a line . . . a killer
Stores just couldn't do no sellin'
When Priscilla starts in yellin'
UNFAIR! [beat-beat] UNFAIR! [beat-beat]"

No one went into the store, and we very effectively shut down Woolworth's in that neighborhood mostly because it was a working-class neighborhood. About the third day of my strike I decided I'd better get some professional help. I looked up the CIO in the yellow pages, and in a tiny voice I said, "Hello. This is Shirley Schrift. I've had the Chester Street Woolworth's out on strike for the past three days and no customers are going in. What should I do now?"

"You've got what?" The man on the other end was stunned. "We've been trying to organize retail workers for years. Don't do a thing, Shirley. We'll be down there in a minute."

The strike lasted for three months. The union's demands were: (1) unionization of all the Woolworth stores in the five boroughs; (2) higher wages; (3) a limitation on working hours; and (4) restrictions on child labor. We won all our demands, but negotiators for Woolworth's headquarters in Wall Street insisted that *I* not be allowed to return to work. The union wouldn't hold still for that, but by this time I'd gotten a high-paying job as a model in the garment center at $75 a week—my father was making only $76—and didn't care. "Settle," I told them, "as long as that Fascist floorlady is fired, too." And that's how they settled the strike.

I went to work in the garment center when I was fourteen by telling my various employers—Jantzen, Catalina, Kalmer Evening Dresses and Ceil Chapman among others—that I was eighteen.

So often in my life I've felt like Alice in Wonderland eating from one side of the mushroom to grow tall, then from the other side in order to grow small. When I was twelve, I was pretending to be fourteen, and when I was six, I was pretending to be four. When I wanted to get into junior high school because I hated grammar school and didn't have the proper papers from St. Louis, I managed to make myself a year or two older. Later, on Broadway and in Hollywood, I would lie about my age according to the requirements of the part I hoped to get. Sometimes much older, sometimes much younger. For *A Place in the Sun* I convinced George Stevens I was only sixteen when I was about twenty-one. Ten years later, when I longed to play the role of Mrs. Van Daan in *The Diary of Anne Frank*, I convinced him I was thirty-five and old enough to pass for fifty.

Because of my father's insistence that I "get that diploma," I made a pass at going to high school at night. I enrolled at New Lots Evening High along with Vince Edwards, who was pushing a heavy fabric hand truck in the garment center during the day. That high school was so crowded that there were classes practically around the clock: 7:00 A.M.–1:00 P.M., 1:00–6:00 P.M., and night school, 7:00–11:00. It proved too much for me and even for husky Vince. I had to get up at six, looking chipper, so I used to fall asleep at my desk. As it turned out, I left regular high school in a blaze of notoriety.

The day session and the evening one each had its own huge orchestra. (Brooklyn parents, then and now, go hungry so their kids can take music lessons—if they're talented it's one of the few ways out of the ghetto.) I got the part of Katisha in the senior class production of *The Mikado*. On opening night, the teacher conductor came down with pneumonia, and a student took over for him, conducting the day and evening sessions' orchestras together for the first time. Katisha's opening aria is very close to grand opera, and I worked very hard on my voice, acting, villainy, costumes, makeup and long false fingernails. My first singing line was: "Alone and yet alive! Oh, sepulchre/ My soul is still my body's prisoner!/ Remote the peace that Death alone can bring./ My doom, to wait!/ my punishment, to live!" *Fortissimo*. I thought I was singing loud and good, but the two student orchestras who had never played together before were each at a different part of the score from where I was. Of course, Our Cousins' Family Circle and my mother, who had been an opera singer, were all out front. Suddenly I yelled at the student conductor, "*Stop!*" He froze. "Get your goddamned orchestra together, and I'll make my entrance again." Which he did and I did. It must have gone off pretty well this time because I got an ovation. It was lucky I did because my friends from Junior Murder, Inc., were ready to kill the student conductor. George de Lalla knew how hard I'd worked. Many opening nights on Broadway I've wanted to do the same thing but never dared.

My career as a model had barely gotten started when I decided to buy a big feather for my new Greta Garbo hat one day. During my lunch hour I walked east toward the millinery district and accidentally took Thirty-eighth Street instead of Thirty-seventh. Halfway down the block I saw the Labor Stage Theater and a sign: AUDITIONS FOR THE NATIONAL COMPANY OF PINS AND NEEDLES.

I stopped dead and forgot all about the feather, my modeling career and even my current boyfriend, whom I was mad about. I went inside determined to get into the professional theater. They were holding auditions, and the director, Herman Rosten, looked at the cute and skinny, tall blonde—I had four-inch heels on—and said, "Are you a member of the ILGWU?"

Without missing a beat, I replied, "Of course." He then asked me my name, and I gave the name of a union member, Sonia Epstein, head operator in the sample room where I was the sample model.

When Mr. Rosten asked for my union card, I told him that I had left it at home but would bring it the next day. "All right," he said, "audition."

"What do you want me to play?" the pianist asked as I went up on the stage.

"Do you know any of Katisha's songs from *The Mikado*? In A flat?"

"Not by heart," he said. What he did know was "Tit Willow," the song sung by the male lead. Since I had learned everyone's part in that show, I began to sing all six choruses for them. As I began the last one, Mr. Rosten yelled, "Shut up already! . . . You're in the show."

The next morning I brought Sonia Epstein flowers and some of my mother's strudel and stood as still as a statue while she fitted a dress on me. (I was their worst squirmer.) Finally, she couldn't stand my pleading cocker-spaniel eyes anymore and asked, "Shirley, what do you want from me?" As I told her what had happened, she just stared at me. "*Meshuganah*," she said when I'd finished. "You want to get me kicked out of the union? How can I lend you my union card? If they should find out, we're both dead."

"Please, Sonia," I pleaded. "I'll let Mr. Rosten look at it for only a minute."

"Dumbbell," she said, "my picture is on it!" Sonia had a little dark Wicked-Witch-of-the-West kind of face, but a very sweet nature. I begged and pleaded with her all day, assuring her that I would convince them that I had had my nose fixed and bleached my hair and that I was indeed Sonia Epstein. By six o'clock she had given in and let me have her card. A very courageous act, I realize now in retrospect.

I had three small pictures taken in a Times Square photo machine, pasted one over Sonia's face, then went to meet the director at the Broadway Theater, where *Pins and Needles* was playing. I handed him "my" card and waited while he looked at it, then at me, then back at it.

"Sonia Epstein," he said, "you're forty-one years old?"

"Of course," I replied. "There's a marvelous new plastic surgeon in Brooklyn, where I had my face lifted. The union medical plan paid for it." In those days when I told a fib, I told a *fib*!

Of course, Herman knew it was fishy, but he decided to take a chance anyway because he was having difficulty casting the national company.

Then followed two glorious weeks of rehearsing, during which I learned the lyrics to every single one of the numbers in the show. There was, however, a snake in the Garden of Eden. Someone squealed to the union officials. To get Sonia off the hook, I told the union investigating committee that I had stolen her union card. But I somehow became a lifelong friend of David Dubinsky, president of the ILGWU. I still make commercials for his union to be played over the loudspeakers at World Series games.

Though back then I was devastated. I sat downstairs in the ladies' lounge and cried my eyes out. Finally, Herman came in, took my hand and said, "Shirley, you're talented, and you're going to make it. If not in this show, then in some other. But, honey, I suggest you go to the New Theatre School and learn the theatrical profession in a formal and organized way."

I looked at him through teary eyes and replied, "Okay. Those are the breaks. I'll do as you suggest." Thank God I did. I walked out of the Labor Stage on my spindly legs and headed for the drama school on West Forty-fourth Street near Sixth Avenue—the drama school that was to change my life, my Art, my politics and, I think, my soul.

When I put my foot inside the New Theatre School, it was like Alice going through the looking glass, but through to the right side at last. There was a girl sitting at the desk who looked up and politely asked if she could help. She was easily the most beautiful girl I have ever seen, before or since. She had brown, slanted eyes, dark blonde hair and high cheekbones. She looked somewhat like Madeleine Carroll, but there was an inner beauty about her and a concern for others that I had never seen in any other person except my Zayda. Her name was Constance Dowling. When she said, "Can I help you?" she meant it.

I sat down at her desk and poured out all the agony of my rejection at the Labor Stage and how I hated being a model in the garment center: the indignities and humiliation connected with parading your body all day long and the buyers who touched you as they pretended to feel the material.

A terrible thing had happened to me at work as I had started to rehearse *Pins and Needles.* Up to then I had told no one about it, but somehow I could tell it to this sweet, sympathetic girl. A salesman who had recently returned from Denver where he had unsuccessfully taken the cure for TB had asked me to stay late and show the line to a customer. We were standing alongside the cutting table. It was six-thirty, I'd been working since seven-thirty in the morning and I had to get over to my rehearsal of *Pins and Needles.* When

I refused to work late, pointing out that there were five other girls who could show the line, he spit full in my face. This man was filled with anger and hatred probably because of his illness and impending death. There was a large cutting scissors on the table by my right hand, and I picked it up. The salesman and the other models stood frozen as they waited for me to kill him. There was a strange kind of joy in his face as he stared at me. Here I was, fifteen years old, my life just beginning, and there he was, fifty and condemned. Suddenly, in a flash, I knew why he'd done this thing: to get even with me for my refusals to his constant requests for dates. In his eyes I saw this was his chance to take me with him. I put down the scissors, wiped my face and said, "You must need me very badly." Then he lay down across the cutting table and started to cry and scream like a baby. The other models scattered, and I went into the toilet and scrubbed my face with Lysol, and ran from the building.

I had kept this bottled up inside me for the past month, but in five seconds I was pouring it all out to Constance Dowling. She became my closest and most beloved friend for the next twenty-five years. Connie was a tremendous positive influence for me, and I've always wished I could have been as valuable to her.

At the time Connie was working at the New Theatre School to pay for her acting classes, and when she wasn't working there, we would run around Broadway, trying to get any kind of job connected with the theater. By this time I hated modeling with an all-consuming passion. We auditioned to become Copa Girls. Connie got the job and was a Copa Girl for about a month, then quit. She said it was worse than modeling.

I had gone to the audition with my elastic beauty-contest bathing suit, complete with powder puffs. They asked me to do a time step, a shuffle-off-to-Buffalo and two more time steps in double rhythm. I tried but stumbled and fell. The boss, Signor Perona, a well-known Broadway character, said in Neapolitan, which he didn't think I'd understand, "This one is crazy and has two left feet."

I shot back, "*Non mi frega niente, Signor Stupido.* [I don't give a fuck, Mr. Stupid.]" I could have gotten myself killed, things being what they were in those days and the depth of my insult. But they were so amazed by my understanding Neapolitan that they just stared as Connie hurried me outside before anything violent could happen.

We had similar experiences at other nightclubs and finally ended up as ushers for $1 a performance at the Belasco Theater. It was then the Group Theatre's playhouse. As we stood in the back every night or grabbed empty seats, we had our first experience of watching great actors using the Stanislavsky Method, performing the work of fine new playwrights. Every night the performances seemed to be different and better.

We got our dinners free at Schrafft's, where we occasionally worked the cocktail hour, but for the most part things were gay and nothing was very serious in our young lives. The day's most pressing problem was how to raise enough money to buy a bottle of Opening Night perfume. There was a wonderful cafeteria named Hector's on Broadway, and our entire dramatic school would go there after class at eleven P.M. We developed a system for our late suppers. The rolls and butter, relishes, coleslaw, tea, lemon and water were free, so we would arrive about thirty strong, bang our trays around and buy ten dinners, which we all would share. We ate very well that way. I don't know whether the cashier was confused or compassionate, but during the Depression everybody helped each other.

During the times I was forced to model and was also going to dramatic school at night, I was the only one in our class who was working. So every night I would buy twenty nickel White Castle hamburgers, complete with pickles, ketchup and onions, and leave them in my unlocked locker at school. All my starving fellow students helped themselves. It was my gesture to the Arts, but it made my locker and my rehearsal clothes smell awful.

There was a spirit then, especially in the Theater, of all for one and one for all. We used to help each other get jobs, meeting every day in Walgreen's basement coffee shop to exchange casting tips as well as clothing for auditions. We were genuinely happy when one of us got a job. The alienation of the kids today seems so sad to me. I often moderate classes at the Actors Studio, West and East coasts, as well as at the Strasberg Institute and the Circle Theatre, and the feeling I get from the kids is: "Don't tell anybody anything, especially about casting." And the jealousy, like "I could have done it better," whenever someone else gets a job. I have never been able to understand it. Maybe the politics of the thirties, which was a sort of "Popular-Frontishness," affected our personal behavior. Today, I guess, every country is nationalistic and out for itself, and countries are made up of individuals who accept, unknowingly, I guess, the philosophy of their governments. That's the only reason I can think of to explain the attitudes of the young actors I come across nowadays. In addition, back then we all had the drive to become Legitimate Stage Artists, but now all they want is to become either famous television or film or rock-and-roll stars. The idea of just making a good living in the various media of the entertainment world doesn't even seem to occur to them. It's either you're a superstar or you're a *nothing*. A nonperson, a nobody.

CHAPTER 4

By this time we were living in Flatbush and were comparatively rich because Blanche began working as a graduate nurse and could help with the rent. (Of course, Blanche being Blanche, she took a job as a visiting nurse for the Henry Street Settlement.) She and I even had our own bedroom with *two separate beds*, and our mother had done it in a Mexican motif.

It was also about this time that I discovered SEX, with all its physical needs and romantic implications. I had had various school-girl crushes, especially on Johnny Weissmuller and the Liberty Swimming Pool lifeguard, but I didn't know exactly what you were supposed to do about it. Now my fellow actresses at school began to regale me with a mine of misinformation. The height of it all was when one night going home on the subway to Brooklyn, a pretty Lithuanian actress told me about a date she'd had the night before with a handsome young actor, Alfred Ryder. The conversation went something like this:

"Well, we had Chinese food, and then he took me all the way home to Brooklyn. For some reason he got very angry when he found out I lived with my parents. When we necked in the hall, you know what he did? When he kissed me he put his tongue in my mouth! I knew it wasn't *my* tongue!" In a worried voice she added, "Shirley, do you think I can get pregnant from that?"

I thought it over for a minute, then said, "I'll ask my sister, who's a nurse. She must know.'"

I'm not so sure that Blanche knew because during that period she was a brand-new probationary nurse. The first day that she was in the obstetrical ward, a head nurse handed her razor, soap and a bowl and said, "This woman's ready for delivery . . . prep her."

Blanche only vaguely understood what she meant and began to shave everything in sight. The baby was born with its head shaved right down the middle. Her career as a nurse almost ended before it began. The baby's father wanted to sue the hospital, but since it was a healthy son, after four girls, he forgave my weeping sister and the hospital.

After a few "deep emotional" acting classes, I decided that my lack of life experience was hindering my Art, and I was determined

43

to get rid of my virginity as soon as possible. Also, urged by my Sexual Urges, I began to have more serious crushes. My first one was on Richard Conte, whom I saw on Broadway in his first big role. He was a marvelous actor and a part-time teacher at my drama school. Years later, when I worked with him in one of my first films, *Cry of the City*, I told him about it, and he said, "Oh, yeah, I remember you. You were the cute little blonde who used to stare at me at the stage door. Why didn't you say something? I'd gladly have accommodated you."

I then fell madly in love with a handsomely homely and brilliant young actor whom I shall call George Spelvin. He was one of the younger members of the Group Theatre and was also a part-time teacher at the New Theatre School. He was a lovely person and had only two things wrong with him: He was a bit of an alcoholic and a notorious philanderer. But he seemed to be crazy about me and took me to the rehearsals of his new play. It was by Louise Platt (I can't remember the title), and he outacted Kazan, or so I thought—no mean trick. At the first preview he was so nervous he got drunk before the show, and I spent the entire evening in the wings, pouring black coffee into him every time he made an exit.

Whenever he took me out, I'd try to drink a whiskey sour, but I'd choke on it and ask for a Coke. He told me I was "infantile." That's a dangerous word to use to me, ever since I heard that idiot doctor say it at the Coney Island Hospital when I was coming out of the ether. George Spelvin and I had fun and fights, and we necked and petted and did everything BUT. After a couple of months George issued an ultimatum. "I'm too old for this sort of thing. Either we have an affair, or we stop seeing each other." Whether it was my religious training or my instinctive knowledge that he was not husband material, or my sexual ignorance, or my fear of pregnancy since I had no idea how one avoided it, I just couldn't do it.

I remember leaving his apartment that night, walking alone in the snow and sleet on Eighth Avenue, my heart breaking, the tears freezing on my cheeks. I took the subway home to my safe bourgeois house, snuggled into my bed and tried to figure out why I was so ambivalent about George: (1) I had decided to be a great actress; (2) I was physically, intellectually and artistically mad about him; and (3) almost all the other girls I knew did *it*, so why couldn't I?

For about three weeks I didn't see George. He didn't answer my phone calls and avoided Walgreen's and all the other places I hung out. Somewhere around the third week I landed a job modeling at the Automobile Show along with another girl, both of us in cute shorts and camping outfits demonstrating the convertible bed in the back of the Nash car. The company thoughtfully provided us with a hotel room in which to change into our costumes as there were no dressing rooms at the Grand Central Palace, where the show was being held. We would work until about 1:00 A.M. and then go up to our hotel room to change our clothes.

My co-model in this demonstration was a little Catholic girl who lived in Hoboken. She took the subway and two buses and went home every night. One night I didn't turn in my hotel key but trudged out into the raging blizzard and went to a liquor store, where I bluffed my way into buying a fifth of Southern Comfort, then bought six bottles of Coke and three large bags of potato chips so I wouldn't choke on the whiskey. I took my aphrodisiacs back to the hotel room.

When I was sufficiently brave, I gave the telephone operator George's number, which was a public phone on the ground floor of his rooming house. After a long time he answered, and I started to cry.

"Hello . . . hello," he yelled. "Who is this? What's the matter? Is that you, Mom?"

Very quietly I answered, "No . . . it's me."

"Are you crazy?" he screamed. "There's a blizzard outside, and it's three o'clock in the morning."

"I know," I answered. "I have a room . . . number seven thirty-five in the Lexington Hotel, and I also have a large bottle of Southern Comfort and some potato chips. Do you want to come up and see me sometime? Like right now?"

After a ten-second pause he asked, "Do you mean what I think you mean? I'll kill you if you're playing games with me again."

I swore I was serious about my sexual intentions. He arrived six minutes later. He had an overcoat over his pajamas and was carrying his clothes. I was wearing a slip and by now had drunk a third of the Southern Comfort, and the bed was littered with potato chips. I was also certain that God or Zayda would strike me dead. George was a Catholic, Irish, an actor, a drunkard, and worst of all, he had never told me he loved me.

Through my alcoholic haze I looked up at him. He was laughing. He gently loosened the hold I had on the bottle and the bag of chips and wiped my tear-streaked face. Then he got rid of the broken potato chips in the bed and straightened it. Then he turned off the light. As I listened to the blizzard outside, he reached over and turned on a radio that I hadn't even noticed was there. By the dim light from the radio, he proceeded to make lovely and expert love to me. To the strains of "The Moon Was Yellow," a frightened girl became a fulfilled young woman.

The next morning, when I looked at myself in the mirror, my eyes and cheeks were glowing. We had a bountiful room-service breakfast, courtesy of the Nash Automobile Company, and when George left for rehearsal, I rushed over to school to find Connie and dragged her out to lunch. As we went down the elevator, she looked at me a little sadly and murmured, "You don't have to tell me . . . I know." Over chili she said, "Honey, does he love you?"

"I can tell he loves me a lot," I assured her, "the way he made love to me."

"I'm sure he does," she said gently. Then, in an embarrassed way, she added, "Darling, did you use anything? Or did he?"

"Oh, lots of things," I answered, remembering the whiskey and potato chips. "Why, is there anything wrong?"

She then explained to me that if the affair were to continue, which, of course, I knew it would, I must go to her doctor and get fitted for a diaphragm or some sort of gold button which she had. The diaphragm sounded cheaper.

Alas, I'm afraid Connie's instructions came too late. During the next three months I had a wonderfully happy time with George S. and all his important Broadway friends, but early one Sunday morning I threw up violently in the bathroom. Blanche saw me, waited until I was finished, then, as she wiped my face, got the truth out of me. She would have screamed at me except that my parents were asleep in the other bedroom. "Why did you wait so long?" she demanded.

"Well, if I'm pregnant, he'll marry me, and I can get the hell out of Brooklyn. We'll have an apartment in Manhattan, and I'll take care of the baby."

"You can't take care of a cat. Tomorrow you're going to tell him, you hear?" she said in a low, tense voice. "God forbid he does what you want. You're just going to have your sweet sixteen birthday party, and already you want to set up housekeeping."

The next day while we were having lunch at the Chinese restaurant and George was finishing his second strong rum drink, I laughingly informed him that my sister thought I was pregnant. His fingers froze around the glass.

"By the way," he finally managed to croak, "how old are you?

Really?" I was going to lie as usual because he wasn't saying the right words like "Well, if you are, then we'll get married, darling." I told him I was fifteen and three-quarters. He was silent for a long time. "Do you want me to go to prison?" he finally managed. "Is that what you're doing, jailbait?"

I got up and left, went straight home to Brooklyn and huddled in a corner of my bedroom. My mother, who wasn't working now, knew something was wrong but thought it had something to do with the "acting business." George tried to call me several times. The next morning I took the call, but I didn't give him a chance to say anything. "New Year's Eve is next week," I told him, "and Gene Kelly is giving a big party at the Waldorf. If you get all dressed up and meet me there after your show, I'll do anything you want." "Okay, kid."

I'll never forget that New Year's Eve. I wore a beautiful white strapless dress with multicolored sequined butterflies all over it. I had "borrowed" it from Kalmer Evening Gowns. I went to the Waldorf and danced with all the celebrities, never taking my eyes off the front door, watching for him. By two-thirty I knew he wasn't coming.

I went up to one of the limousines parked out front and asked the chauffeur if he'd please give me a lift to West Forty-sixth Street. When I got there, I walked up the three flights of his crummy boardinghouse with white orchids in my hair, drenched with Opening Night perfume and with murder in my heart. Not to speak of his baby in my belly. I kicked the door open. He was lying on his messed-up bed. "Happy New Year, you bastard."

He looked up at me and said, "You're a beautiful vision."

"Thank you." As I slipped out of my strapless dress I said, "Tomorrow we'll do what you want, but someday I'll get revenge." Some years later, when I was a starlet in California he really fell for me and proposed. "No," I answered. "You're a bit-part actor and a drunk and I'm a potential star." Revenge was not very sweet; in fact I hated myself, and so we became good friends for many years.

George took me to a nice struggling young doctor in New Jersey who refused to perform an abortion when he discovered I had a tubular pregnancy. This sent me into shock because I knew I had only one ovary. I called Connie Dowling, and she came right out and got me. Then, together with Blanche, they got me into the Jamaica Hospital. Blanche lied to my parents, telling them I had an ovarian cyst or something. Connie secured the services of a well-known gynecologist; God knows how she paid him. He operated and saved my one and only ovary. Connie stayed with me throughout the whole traumatic experience. She had been having a long painful love affair with a married director—he couldn't give her up or divorce his wife. It took my beautiful young friend a long time to recover from this experience, it dragged on so. I was luckier.

There's something in upper New York State called the Borscht Circuit, located in the Catskill Mountains and consisting of many hotels and camps. Nowhere else in the world is there an equivalent training ground for actors and entertainers. My first summer vacation from dramatic school I was hired for the staff of Aaron and Pinya Pasher's Lake Shore Chateau, which in no way compared to the fashionable hotels, but the theater—which also was the social hall—was large and well equipped. It far outshone any of the other hotels around "Lake Nishgedaiget" (loosely translated, it means "everything's great, so I don't care").

My salary was $100 for the ten-week season. We had a six-piece orchestra from some high school, a leading man, a leading woman, a girl comedian (me), a boy comedian and a stage manager-director. The weekly program was as follows:

Monday night:	Game Night. Physical ones like Simon Says. (All the weekend husbands had gone home.)
Tuesday night:	Two One-Act Plays, preferably powerful.
Wednesday night:	Dance Contests. All waiters obliged to "mingle."
Thursday night:	An Arty Picture, followed by an intellectual tearing apart of the film along with coffee and danish.
Friday night:	A Serious and Modern Three-Act Play (usually somewhat left, which infuriated the husbands, who were somewhat right, and had just arrived for the weekend). When we did *Waiting for Lefty*, all the wives helped us and got to their feet and yelled, "Strike!," no doubt against their bondage to their husbands and children. It was very effective.
Saturday night:	A Full Musical Revue, score and lyrics borrowed from current Broadway hits,

such as the following sung to the tune of "Bei Mir Bist du Schoen":

If you'd be in style
Wear clothes made of lisle,
Don't buy anything that's Japanese.
Lisle's three times as strong,
Lasts three times as long,
Don't buy anything that's Japanese.
The Fascist forces wage war in conspiracy,
If we refuse to trade with them, we aid
    Democracy . . .
Ta ta ta . . . ta . . . ta . . .
That's why China begs
Keep silk off your legs,
Don't buy anything that's Japanese.

Sunday night: A Concert. Serious records with lecture.

How we managed to do all that in one week was simple. We never slept. The man responsible for this program was Teddy Thurston, who had a beautiful singing voice and was head of the social staff. Incidentally, he came from St. Louis. Also incidentally, I had a big crush on him.

My parents came up for a visit on my birthday, August 18, and immediately noticed that I weighed eighty-nine pounds. Despite the fact that I had just scored a great hit in Lake Shore Chateau's *Pal Joey* and everyone at the hotel was saying, "She's a regular Mary Martin," my parents insisted on dragging me back to Brooklyn and chicken soup, and probably saving my life in the process.

I don't quite remember how I managed it, but the following winter I finally made the move and went to live—part time—with three other girls at the Hotel St. James in Manhattan. Of course, my father didn't know. I would go home to Brooklyn a couple of nights a week and Fridays for roast chicken and chicken soup. My mother and sister aided and abetted my deception.

One Thursday night we had about forty hungry actors in our hotel room, and we cooked spaghetti and meat sauce in the bathroom on a two-burner electric stove and spiked each gallon of cheap wine with a pint of cheaper gin. Some of the boys had recently returned from Spain, where they had fought with the Abraham Lincoln Brigade, and they played guitars and taught us the Loyalist songs. A good inspirational time was had by all.

The remarkable thing about those days was the feeling of comradeship. It's true the world was different then, yet it was in a way simple and black and white. All the problems could be solved. After defeating the Falangists, the Fascists and the Nazis, we believed the whole world would then join hands and march into some brave new era of eternal sunshine and a Swedish-type socialism, and everyone would be good to each other because there'd be freedom from hunger and fear. We would talk until the wee hours of the morning, and there was nothing we couldn't solve with the help of the Popular Front. President Roosevelt had recognized the Soviet Union at long last, and a great new "recognized" economic experiment was going on in the world in which everything would be divided equally among all the people.

About this time I became involved with what must have been the first Off-Broadway production, which was performed in the ballroom of the Hotel St. James. It was very wittily called *Of V We Sing*, the V, of course, signifying Victory. It was a couple of years before the United States entered the war, but England was struggling for its life, and France had capitulated. I had a number in this memorable show in which I had to strip down to a very modest chemise. The lyrics went like this:

> You just loosen the League of Nations, then strip off a section
> of France
> 'Cause you've got to appease with a striptease when Herr
> Hitler is staging the dance.
> Demonstrate that Vichy Twist . . . show them what Herr
> Quisling kissed.
> Do like Laval and Monsieur Pétain; then you bend way down
> and you shake your can.
> Oh, you strip and you strip for the Nazis, with an art that no
> tart could surpass.
> But you've got to appease with a striptease till you get way
> down to your . . .

The song was accompanied by appropriate gestures and not very difficult dance combinations, so I performed it quite well. This anti-Nazi revue brilliantly combined the best of entertainment with good propaganda. *Of V We Sing* opened to huge success and publicity, and we charged $1 admission. Up to that point my mother, sister and I had managed to keep it a secret from my father that I was in show business. For him even a bordello would have been better . . . an honest day's pay for an honest day's work. The third or fourth night the newspaper *PM* printed a full page of pictures of me doing the striptease number. The following night my father came to see the show and in the middle of the number came up on the stage and dragged me, struggling and screaming, up the aisle while the audience called him some colorful reactionary names.

My parents were glad to see me go back to the Lake Shore Chateau the following summer, and Aaron Pasher assured them I would have to do only four shows a week. I managed to wangle several rooms and lots of good things to eat for the boys who had returned from Spain. One of the Pasher brothers was a Wobbly, and he hired many of the returned veterans for the season. Some of them had lost either an arm or a leg, making the Wednesday night dance contests a little bizarre. But none of the wives complained.

It was very important for me to get those boys jobs because a few weeks before I'd had one of the most joyous experiences of my life. I had marched in a May Day parade with the contingent from Actors Equity, wearing the union banner across my chest, carrying an American flag and singing and shouting anti-Nazi slogans and songs. My future, as an artist and an enlightened woman, seemed certain and enthralling.

I got a job in a Shubert show that tried out in Philadelphia and closed in Philadelphia. The only good thing about it for me was that I was able to join Equity. It solved that old problem of "you can't join the union unless you have a job, and you can't get a job unless you belong to the union." It cost $25 for me to join because I was a minor—otherwise, it would have been $50. It might as well have been $500. I'd had no time for modeling what with studying, making the rounds, doing $10 vaudeville gigs in New Jersey and living in two places at once. I'd told the producers of the show that I was a member of Equity, and so I just had to come up with that $25 somehow. One morning I woke up after Blanche had gone off to work, and I found an envelope under my pillow. It contained $25. Where she got it I don't know, but I think she must have sold her blood. Clancy Cooper, an actor, and Sol Burry, a writer, solemnly took me up to the Equity offices, where I became a member. I was a professional at last.

When the 1939 World's Fair opened in Flushing, Blanche and I walked over the Queensboro Bridge from Manhattan to get there— about ten miles. We paid no attention to Billy Rose's Aquacade or all the other countries' technological advances of the past decade; we stood in front of a Soviet tractor in the USSR building. "See," Blanche said to me, "it works. They can build tractors. The System Works!" A pretty Russian girl repeated, robotlike in English, the accomplishments of the various five-year plans since 1928. We gazed at this tractor with awe while she told us about the new world that was being born and built in her country, where each person would have enough, "Each according to his ability and each according to his need." I had seen the slums and death in the Brooklyn tenements, and part of Blanche's training included a period when she was visiting nurse in the Harlem slums. We wrote to our congressman, requesting that Congress immediately pass such a law, with the help of President Roosevelt, of course, to get the same for our country.

The young representative of the USSR was somewhat confused by Blanche's inquiries about whether straightening teeth was free in the Soviet Union and by mine about beauty contests and dramatic training. She gave us some pamphlets, and we walked back home to Flatbush. We had managed only the price of admission. My father, who at this point was a devout ex-socialist, immediately took away our pamphlets and burned them in the stove. He also insisted that they got the tractor from Sweden. "Oh, yeah?" I argued, "What about the Moscow Art Theater and Stanislavsky?"

"They're probably Lithuanian, and they had existed in czarist Russia." Oh, God, he was so dumb then. Funny how much smarter he got as I got older.

One beautiful day that spring I was walking along Forty-fourth Street, and as I passed Sardi's, through the window I noticed a man reading a newspaper. The big black headline caught my eye. HITLER SIGNS PACT WITH STALIN. I can still feel the sensation of physical illness that went through me. I knew by then about concentration camps and the relatives I was missing.

A few weeks previous to this at an Our Cousins' Family Circle meeting that my mother had forced us to attend, a member of the family read off a list of the names of young cousins, uncles and aunts in Germany and Poland who had been rounded up by the Nazis and sent to labor camps. We hoped they could be saved with ransom, and we were trying to buy their lives from the Nazis. Through the Jewish Agency we knew all about the labor camps, but we hadn't yet heard about Hitler's Final Solution. All the relatives, even those with only meager incomes, were donating their pennies and dimes, eager to help save our families—brothers, sisters and little children—who were in such jeopardy.

Later we heard that my father's brother, Uncle Yakel, who still lived in Poland, had come home from work one day to find that his wife and three children had been taken away in a sealed boxcar. His wife was beautiful, and a talented pianist. Their oldest daughter was studying to be an engineer, his son had just had his Bar Mitzvah and wanted to be a doctor and their youngest was an eight-year-old girl. After the war he found out that the boxcar was detached from the train and left on a siding while the people packed inside slowly froze and starved to death. With my actor's sense of identification, this could perhaps be one of the reasons I've often felt so cold and hungry ever since I learned about their fate. Yakel was sent to a labor camp because he had a trade which was useful to the Nazis. Yakel Schrift never believed in their deaths and spent the rest of his life looking for them throughout Europe, Canada, the United States and Israel. He died in his eighties in Israel, hit by a car. Still searching.

Although I had countless people explain the military whys and wherefores of the Soviet strategy, emotionally the Hitler-Stalin pact was somehow never acceptable to me. Even to this day.

I walked around in a daze. Blanche was living in a dormitory at the hospital, and some midnights I would go to the hospital and sneak into bed with her, longing for the old convertible sofa we used to share.

I've since come to understand that a baby must walk in its own good time. If you force it too soon, it becomes bowlegged, or its hips go out of joint. I believe this is what happened to me emotionally. I had skipped the average period of childhood and adolescence because I was aware of the constant need in our family for money. That terrible spring all the idealistic solutions I'd accepted fell apart around me. Even Zayda's first lesson had betrayed me. So I decided that since I wasn't personally able to do anything about the shits of the world, from now on I was going to take care of Number One. Me. The Brand-New SHELLEY WINTER. Idealist Shirley Schrift, who took part in strikes and tried to make the world a better place for everybody to live in, could go get lost.

CHAPTER 5

Now that my new name was firmly entrenched with Equity, I carefully appraised the ladder of success. I diligently read the theatrical gossip columns of Winchell, Leonard Lyons and Earl Wilson. In the *Daily News* there was one full page devoted to such columns. I read them on the subway and studied movie magazines and *Theatre Arts* magazine like textbooks. At home I would spend hours looking into a full-length mirror and used all my know-how and street cunning to figure out the best way for me to escape into the world of "The Theatre," where the money, security, glamor and love must surely be.

I made a lot of decisions. 1. God helps only those who do it themselves; 2. To learn everything I could about makeup; 3. To learn everything I could about acting in the theater, musical comedy and the movies; 4. To buy a bra that pointed upward; 5. To dress as though I were rich; and 6. To have a really serious intellectual affair.

So I went into debt with my first fur coat. It was skunk but dyed to resemble sable. I loved it more than any real sable, mink or chinchilla I ever had later in my life. At the same time I bought a necklace of Majorca pearls—a beautiful imitation of the real thing. I borrowed $300 from the Manufacturers Trust Company and paid it back at the rate of $25 a week plus $50 interest. But those fourteen weeks during which I carried around that damn loan book have made me hate any kind of installment buying to this day, although I realize it's against all American Tradition. I buy cars, houses, apartments for cash. I hate paying interest.

I think I got a job understudying Julie Haydon in *The Time of Your Life*, but the entire experience is a blur. All I remember is sitting out front with George Jean Nathan, watching the play over and over again and never rehearsing. One matinee Julie Haydon broke her ankle but went on anyway that night with her leg in a cast. I didn't show up the next day. Fifteen years later, when I broke *my* ankle during the run of *A Hatful of Rain*, I had the decency to miss three performances so my understudy would have the chance to go on. Besides, my ankle hurt like hell.

After *The Time of Your Life*, I heard in Walgreen's that the musical *Meet the People* was auditioning actors for the national company. Fifteen people were needed, and all had to be able to act in the sketches and sing and dance. I sing fairly well, and because of my Borscht Circuit experience, I was good in sketches, and I can do one dance step at a time just great. It's putting the steps together in any combination that defeats me. But despite this seemingly congenital klutziness, I got into *Meet the People* somehow, along with Jack Albertson, Betty Garrett, Henny Youngman, Joey Faye and some of the original cast. I was in seventh heaven! True, we were going to perform on Broadway for only one week, before we went on the road, but I was at last in a real Broadway musical.

I signed my Equity contract for the run of the play, at the minimum salary of about $65 a week. When I read the fine print, I noticed that the producers had up to five days of rehearsal in which to let you go.

There were lots of songs in the show—solos, duets, group numbers—as well as about four dance numbers and ten or more sketches. With my usual speed I learned every number in the show by watching the Broadway performances every night and arrived at our first rehearsal two hours early to practice with the assistant director. I rehearsed "In Chi-Chi Castenango," "Union Label," "The Bill of Rights" and all the other chorus numbers I was in. I worked tirelessly. Nevertheless, late on the afternoon of the fifth day the director, Danny Dare, called me into the ladies' lounge and said, "Listen, kid, you're wonderful in the sketches, you sing great and you really look lovely up onstage—but you just can't dance." I looked at him blankly. It couldn't be happening TWICE. So the following morning I was back at the theater bright and early, singing "In Chi-Chi Castenango" while going through the tango tap steps endlessly. The assistant choreographer showed up with a hangover at about ten and watched me in confusion. But since I was there, he started rehearsing with us anyway. A couple of stupid-looking, ugly aspiring actresses wandered in, no doubt in answer to some villainous agent's instructions. I'd had the foresight to bring the doorman a bottle of rye and some of my mother's strudel, so he informed them that they were in the wrong theater.

When Mr. Danny Dare showed up around four, I was still rehearsing away like mad. He must have thought I was a little feeble-minded and had failed to understand him the previous day, so again he took me into the wings and said, "Listen, kid, you're wonderful in the sketches, you sing great and you really look lovely up onstage

—but you just can't dance! Understand?" I understood. I also understood about the five-day clause. I thanked him and left the theater, smiling because this was the sixth day and I couldn't be fired.

The next morning I showed up again at eight, and by the time the rest of the cast arrived I knew most of "In Chi-Chi Castenango" and could sing and dance the "Union Label" number very well, provided there was another girl in front of me I could watch. When Mr. Danny Dare arrived—it was the seventh day—he just looked helplessly at the stage manager and said, "Get Shelley fitted for her costumes."

In New York, when the new cast went in, as we did the "Union Label" number, which was accompanied by a small-scale striptease down to bra and step-ins, I was always one garment behind all the other girls, much to the despair of the director and the hilarity of the audience. Getting notes after the performance, I expected Danny Dare to fire me with two weeks' notice. Instead, he said, "Leave it in, Shelley. It's funny." If Gypsy Rose Lee was the Queen of the Striptease, I was the Court Jester.

But I was having the time of my life and getting to know other young artists on Broadway. Among them were Betsy Blair, a lovely redheaded Irish beauty, who was going out with Gene Kelly; Lyn Whitney, who was in *My Sister Eileen;* June Havoc, who was in *Pal Joey;* beautiful Connie Dowling, who was in *Hold On to Your Hats* with Al Jolson; and David Burns, the funniest and dirtiest comedian and sweetest man I've ever met. I was being accepted as their equal! A budding Broadway Star. I didn't walk down Forty-fourth Street anymore; I was flying a foot off the sidewalk.

We used to meet for drinks at Sardi's on matinee days, and sometimes someone with money took us there for dinner. I stepped through the doorway with my right foot as my grandmother had taught me to do upon entering any new venture. We sat there and pretended not to look at Katharine Cornell, Alfred Lunt, Lynn Fontanne, Helen Hayes and Henry Fonda. On Forty-fifth Street there was an exotic Chinese restaurant that served a nine-course meal complete with tea and fortune cookies for thirty-five cents, and next to it was Ralph's, an Italian restaurant where everybody met to flirt and exchange casting news; a complete dinner was fifty-five cents. Next to the Imperial Theatre was Harold's, and Harold was a big man with an enormous beer belly covered by a white apron, a bald head with gray hair on both sides, and he loved actors. All over his restaurant were photos of actors going back to 1901. A complete home-cooked American meal there was sixty cents, but it was actually the cheapest because you didn't have to pay. If you were an actor, you simply signed. I remember the drinks were a quarter. Gene Kelly, who also ate there, went to Hollywood still owing quite a tab. Harold didn't ever remind him; he was so proud of Gene. After all, he was Irish.

At the time Gene was the toast of the town in *Pal Joey*, and his best friend, Dick Dwenger, was a talented young playwright. Dick was broke, as most struggling young playwrights are, so Gene finagled him a job as his dresser. Since the show already had a professional wardrobe man and dresser, Dick didn't do much except sit in a corner of Gene's dressing room and write. For this he received $100 a week. Every now and then he would make a pass at brushing off one of Gene's costumes with his pencil. We had wonderful suppers at Harold's, Gene, Betsy Blair, Dick and I, talking into the wee hours of the morning. Dick was very intelligent and held a master's degree in political science, which awed me no end, yet he never made me feel dumb or ill-educated. He told me which books, magazines and newspapers to read. He bought me my first symphony record. Dick and I cared very much for each other, but at that point in my life I was incapable of anything but platonic relationships. I had yet to get over the trauma of George.

When *Meet the People* was finally rehearsed, we played one whole week on Broadway, then got ready to go out on tour. My parents bought me a secondhand real theatrical trunk—I still have it— and brought it to my dressing room. Dick took me and it to the station, and as I kissed him good-bye, I said, "See you soon, Dick."

He held my hand and looked into my eyes, a very serious expression on his face, and replied, "Little friend, I have a strange feeling we'll never see each other again."

"Don't be silly," I told him. "It's only a season contract."

But he was right. He was killed a few months later when his plane was shot down. For some reason he had enlisted in the Canadian Air Force.

Dick Dwenger was one of the few people I've ever known who put his money where his mouth was. Not many do. My sister is one. She always took the lowest-paying jobs that did the most for other people; when other nurses were getting as much as $100 a day, she would be working for Planned Parenthood or Family Planning groups for $500 a month. When she graduated from nursing school, instead of working in a doctor's office or an expensive private hospital, she became a visiting nurse for the Henry Street Settlement. While working there, she wore a blue uniform and blue hat and carried a small black bag. After her first month we'd never let her take much money with her because she would give it away. That would start another fight between my father and mother, with my father saying he knew that they should never have let her become a nurse. "She's setting up her own 'Schrift Relief Agency,' " he complained.

"It's her own money, and she can do what she wants with it," my mother screamed back at him.

"You're a liar," my father yelled back. "It's you who give her my money."

This family fight never ended until the day my father died. I'm sure he didn't expect to win and was well aware that our Zayda had got to us first and taught us that we were indeed our brothers' keepers.

I was at last on a real theatrical train, part of a show going on tour. Me a professional actress. The only disappointing thing was that Danny Dare had somehow found out my true age, and so Peggy Ryan's mother, who was her chaperone, was to be mine as well. My mother gladly signed this agreement. I had to room with Peggy and her mother, and Mrs. Ryan never let me out of her sight. Some days I was tempted to tell her I was not the sixteen-year-old virgin she thought I was but was, instead, a jaded woman of the world.

In Detroit we had a six-week engagement at the beautiful Shubert Theater. In the alley behind the theater was a well-known gourmet restaurant run by gangsters. The company stayed at the enormous Book-Cadillac Hotel. This was the first time I'd registered at such an important hotel, and Peggy, who was a real theater child, explained to me that room service was free. What a lie!

While her mother was downstairs shopping in the arcade, we quickly ordered from this magical room service a $10 lunch. Considering the fact that I was earning $65 a week, this was a little out of line. As we were gorging ourselves with Eggs Benedict (my first) and banana splits, Peggy's mother returned. Since we had a technical rehearsal coming up in an hour and a performance next after-noon, she quickly got us into the bathroom, made us put our fingers down our throats and throw up our wonderful lunch. Wise woman.

We showered, set our hair and walked through the lobby like the little princesses we were. Detroit loved show people. Someone came up to me and asked if I was Shirley Temple. Maybe it was because I had blonde curls all over my head. I promptly nodded and signed her name. My first autograph request! Peggy Ryan had been in a couple of pictures and really was famous. She was also a sensational tap dancer and then weighed about seventy-five pounds and was four feet ten inches tall. I guess people figured that if she was a movie star, the blonde kid with her must also be one.

This was my first taste of fame and glory, even if only reflected, and God, how I loved it! I glowed so that my skunk coat really became sable. When we arrived at the theater for the light rehearsal, there was my name up on the marquee along with everyone else's, but since the names were listed alphabetically, mine was in last place. Right then I should have changed my name to Shelley Autumn. I think I didn't because I knew that members of the St. Louis Winter family (who knew I was using their name) were driving up to Detroit to see me.

I didn't exactly understand what a technical rehearsal was, and I thought it would prove me to be unprofessional if I asked, so I didn't. Every time we began a number on this new stage and the stage manager would yell, "All right . . . cut to the end," I took it personally. I felt it was a reflection on my performance, so I kept trying harder. Again, whenever we started a number and were a few bars into it, he'd yell, "Cut to the end." I imagined the orchestra was looking at me and thinking I was some sort of klutz who had gotten into the show by mistake, and I was terribly embarrassed. By the time we were doing the fourth or fifth number I burst into tears, ran up to the stage manager, slapped him and said, "Look, if you want to fire me, don't embarrass me in front of the orchestra and the crew." He stared at me in amazement for a minute, then said, "Listen, stupid, this has nothing to do with you, and quit creating scenes, we don't want to go into golden hours. This is a light and technical rehearsal for the crew, and you're just a body out there, so get into your next costume and shut up."

Thank God. After the rehearsal the owner of the gourmet restaurant in the alley invited the cast to dinner, but Mrs. Ryan gathered up the minors in the show and took us back to the hotel, where we ate toast and drank hot cocoa to calm our stomachs. We fell asleep while we were still protesting violently.

The show opened and was a huge success. Detroit was very much a union town in those days, having recently been completely unionized by the AFL and CIO, and they loved our political revue. They loved the music, the lyrics, Virginia O'Brien, Peggy Ryan, Fay McKenzie, Jack Albertson and ME! I'm in debt forever to those critics in Detroit because they erased the gnawing doubt in the back of my mind about my beloved theatrical calling. No matter what any critic ever said about me from then on in any film or play, I believe the Detroit critics and have loved them ever since.

One night the younger members of the Winter family filed into my dressing room and stared in stunned silence at the brand-new Shelley Winter. My Cousin Leatrice whispered in awe, "Well, you told us when you were three that you were going to be a star."

I gave her a kiss and replied, "Honey, I hear by the grapevine that Mary Martin is very worried." We all went out for pancakes, and then they drove home to St. Louis. They were strange with me and I felt a little lonely and lost.

About the third week of the run I got some long-stemmed roses with a nice and intelligent note from a young man whom I shall call Paul Miller. He was a salesman who worked out of Chicago and knew one of my relatives in St. Louis, who had asked him to look me up. He said he was staying at the same hotel, had seen the show and would like to take me to dinner. At last! But how to get out of the clutches of Mrs. Ryan and eat at the fabulous gangster restaurant?

I called Mr. Miller and explained that he'd have to meet Mrs. Ryan first, but I would love to have dinner with him Saturday after the show. He arrived backstage, looking very handsome in a dark sort of way, not unlike my father. He was about twenty-five or twenty-six. After Mrs. Ryan questioned him very closely about our connections in St. Louis and got him to promise to have me back at the hotel by 1:00 A.M.—the show ended at 11:00—she unwillingly agreed.

I wore Blanche's white chiffon graduation dress. Paul bought me gardenias, and I put one in my hair and another on my purse.

"Shirley, where would you like to go for supper?"

I gave him a dirty look as I replied, "That used to be my name; it's not anymore."

"I don't think you're old enough to be a Shelley yet," he told me. "You still look like a Shirley to me, although a very beautiful one."

I laughed and asked him if he knew about the famous gangsters' restaurant in the alley. He did, and that's where he took me. He didn't ask what I wanted; he did the ordering. He had a martini but ordered a Shirley Temple for me, which made me furious. He made up for that by ordering wine with dinner and letting me have a glass. Even though it was a very expensive wine, I hated the taste, and he guessed because he immediately ordered me a Coca-Cola.

Throughout the meal I was a little ill at ease because I'd never known any fellow like him. He was a college graduate and a very successful businessman, and all I could talk about was "The Theatre." Yet somehow we managed. There was an orchestra, and after dinner we danced. He was pretty good at the jitterbug, though not as good as I was. After all, I had won contests in Brownsville.

When he found out that all I'd seen of Detroit was the theater and the hotel lobby, he gave me a moonlight tour of the city in a huge blue car. As we drove out Jefferson Avenue, which is where the rich people lived, we passed a tall apartment building called Alden Park Manor. He looked over at me and said, "See that building, Shirley? Someday we're going to live in it."

I giggled. I thought he was crazy. He then showed me the mansions of the automobile tycoons in Grosse Pointe, then took me through the tenements where the automobile workers lived. He mentioned that without these workers there wouldn't be those big homes for the Ford, Chrysler and General Motors executives. After that remark I promptly fell in love with him.

For the next two weeks, whenever he could, Paul took Peggy, her mother and me to all the interesting sights in and around the city. I know now that Detroit has become a tough and terribly industrialized city, but in 1941 it was quite beautiful, with wide, clean streets, outdoor Polish restaurants with swinging lanterns and lots of concerts in the parks. It was early fall, the parks throughout the city were beautiful and suddenly I wasn't scared of men anymore. Sometimes after my show Paul and I would drive to lovers' lane, but the moonlight necking never got too serious for me.

Once he took me up in a small open-cockpit airplane, and we flew around the field for a half hour for only $5. I loved it. I think it must have been some kind of test for me because he always loved flying and would shortly prove it.

Meanwhile, we were enjoying our rapid romance, and he proposed to me on a plane to Cleveland on a Sunday (my day off), while he was on a sales trip. He slipped a beautiful three-karat ring on my finger. (I still wear it.) While I gasped, he suggested that since I was quite young, I should come to Chicago to meet his family, and as soon as he was able, he would come to New York and meet mine.

This whirlwind romance was the talk of the show. Then one night, when Paul couldn't meet me because he was with a customer, I was getting dressed and suddenly found myself with my head on my arms, weeping bitterly. I took off his ring and put it back in its small black velvet box. Paul was handsome, Jewish, intelligent. He didn't seem to care that I wanted to be in show business. And I knew my parents would adore him. But how could I marry him unless I told him what had happened to me with George Spelvin?

As I sat in that dark dressing room, crying, Jack Albertson, who was late in leaving the theater, came into my dressing room. He must have heard me. "What's the matter, kid? You should be as happy as a lark. What's going on?" I looked up into his comic-intelligent face and told him about the entire George Spelvin episode and my resolve to confess to Paul before continuing our engagement. Jack turned on the lights, straightened me up and said, "I'm going to talk to you as if you're an adult because you're bright. If Paul loves you, he's going to marry you anyway. All you'll accomplish if you tell him is to give him a thorn in his side which will bother him for the rest of his life. The truth is not always the kindest thing. You'll make yourself feel honorable, but what will you be doing to him? As I understand it, he doesn't want you to get married until you're eighteen, so you have over a year to think about it. Forget about the whole thing until then. I'm sure there must be things in Paul's past that he doesn't want you to know about."

I decided to take his advice, and I immediately felt much better. Now, as I rethink it, Jack used much rougher language than that—after all, he was an ex-burlesque comic—but that was the gist of what he said to me that night.

As we approached the fifth week of our run and were looking forward to going on to Chicago and despite the fact that business was very good, the rumors of war seemed to be scaring everybody. Some of the automobile plants were already converting to tanks. Our Saturday night closing notice was put up, I almost fainted. The devastating final Friday night arrived, and no rescinding notice had gone up, and we knew our show would close after tomorrow's evening performance. Then it was over, and I watched with a kind of agony as the stagehands destroyed the sets of *Meet the People,* my first professional show.

Paul suggested that instead of going back to New York on Sunday, I fly with him to Chicago and meet his mother, sister and other relatives. Then he would come with me to New York in a week and meet mine. And that's what we did.

I loved Chicago and found all his relatives very *haimish*. Especially his mother. I didn't care much for his golf club, where he played almost every day we were there. Sometimes thirty-six holes.

Eighteen in the morning and eighteen in the afternoon. While he was so occupied, I read plays and tried to talk to the other Chicago ladies who were waiting for their husbands or boyfriends to finish their eternal golf. It wasn't easy to communicate with them because they treated me as if I were from another planet. This should have forewarned me.

As it turned out, I had to take the train back to New York alone, in the luxury of a roomette, because Paul had to attend a sudden important sales meeting. Before leaving Chicago, I bought two sofas at the Merchandise Mart, which I still have. I've been recovering them ever since.

When I got back to New York, Paul called my parents from Chicago. I had told them all about him and his family. My father checked with our St. Louis relatives. The report must have been great. My mother and father cried with happiness. He was to fly to New York for Christmas, meet my parents, and we'd see some shows. I spent my time looking for another play, going to auditions and working at the New School for Social Research in Erwin Piscator's classes.

On Sunday, December 7, I was sitting in front of our Philco, memorizing *Rocket to the Moon* for drama class, when suddenly the Sunday opera was interrupted by the announcer. Japanese planes had attacked Pearl Harbor and wiped out our fleet. Everyone came running in from various parts of the house, and we stared at each other in stunned disbelief. America had always seemed so strong and invulnerable; how could anyone do that to her? And why were most of our warships in Hawaii?

About four or five that afternoon Paul phoned, finally having got through, and told me he was enlisting in the Army Air Corps. The next day he phoned to tell me he was accepted. He said that since I was so young, we should wait until after the war to get married. I replied that if we did, I would lie about my age and be the first WAC to join up, so he agreed to come to New York and meet my parents.

On the first day of January, 1942, we were married in my family rabbi's study. Paul looked very handsome in his officer's uniform, and I was wearing a white dress with a short veil. I decided not to tell him about George Spelvin; Paul was going away to fight for our country, and I didn't want to add to his problems. We had a reception at Moscowitz and Lupowitz and our honeymoon at the Hotel St. George in Brooklyn. What I remember most about it is holding

Paul in my arms and knowing he was scared, yet he had to be a pilot and avenge Pearl Harbor and the concentration camps we were hearing about. I recall him sending out for champagne and White Castle hamburgers, and this time he let me drink my share of the wine. But I didn't need it. We made lovely and already lonely love.

CHAPTER 6

After our honeymoon we returned to Detroit by way of Niagara Falls, through Canada to Windsor and into Detroit, where Paul got rid of most of his possessions, stored his civilian clothes in mothballs and turned over his accounts to fellow salesmen who were married with children, and who were not yet eligible for the draft. During this period I experienced a sense of *déjà vu*. It was as though I were reliving that time when I was a little girl and my father was a traveling salesman. I was very proud of my husband's determination to help his country wipe out the Nazis, the Fascists, and the Nipponese, and I wanted to do my part in helping him. Physically and I think psychologically I was able to do it a little. But when he wasn't around, I would collapse into being a typical wife whose soldier husband was going off to kill or be killed. I hoped he wasn't aware of my secret desperate feelings; because of my childhood and adolescent insecurities, it seemed that whenever I really loved someone, circumstances would make them abandon me. Suddenly the Air Corps notified Paul to report for basic training, and I had to return to New York alone.

At Walgreen's drugstore someone told me that at the 44th Street Theater Max Reinhardt, the famous German director, was auditioning singers for the English version of the Strauss operetta *Die Fledermaus*. As the Metropolitan Opera had closed because of the war, all of the Met musicians who weren't in the Army were being used, as well as many of the Met Opera singers. Because of my experience as Katisha in *The Mikado*, I figured I might as well go over and audition, too.

It was a beautiful theater, and above it was a tiny jewel box of a theater called the Nora Bayes. (Years later, when I returned from Hollywood for a personal appearance, I found they both had been torn down and transformed into *The New York Times'* garage. When I saw that, I never felt the same about *The New York Times*.) I went backstage, gave my name to the stage manager and peeked into the audience, where I saw Mr. Reinhardt sitting with his son, Gottfried, who was in Army uniform. He was in Special Services and temporarily stationed in Astoria. He had done the translation from the German and retitled it *Rosalinda*. I had a special reverence

for Max Reinhardt because when I was little my father had taken
me to see *The Eternal Road*, which was based on the wanderings of
the Jewish people and was an extraordinary theatrical event. . . .
But I really had no idea of the international importance of this
director.

When my name was called, I came out onto the stage and faced
a huge bright work light. I followed two singers who had beautifully
sung arias from *Butterfly* and *La Bohème*. Max Reinhardt addressed
me from the audience. "Vot is your name, and vot is your experience?"

For some reason I replied, "My name is Shelley Winter, and so
far my life experience has been lousy. But I was a hit in Detroit
in *Meet the People*."

He laughed. "Tell me, Sheeley, are you a mezzo or lyric soprano?"

"My mother is a beautiful mezzo and sang at the St. Louis Municipal Opera. I guess I have a low and high register with not much
in between. But I'm very musical."

I certainly had a loud speaking voice because the producers at
the back of the house could obviously hear me. I was enthralled as
I stood on that stage and gazed out at the crystal chandeliers and
that beautiful theater, not too concerned about whether or not I got
the job. (In later years I read a wonderful line by Clifford Odets:
"There is nothing as beautiful as a waiting dark theatre; it is a night
without a star.")

Mr. Reinhardt's voice interrupted my thoughts. "Sheeley, are
you just going to stand there and admire the theater, or are you
going to sing something for us?"

"Oh, sure," I replied brightly. "What kind of show is this?"

After a moment he spoke. "When you are beginning rehearsal,
you never know what kind of show you have until you open. In
Vienna it was an operetta about a man who disguises himself as
a bat."

I remembered *No for an Answer*, an anti-Nazi show George
Spelvin had been in that I had seen many times. I told Mr. Reinhardt
about it and then sang part of the opening number about a bat,
a cappella.

> There once was a war betwixt the beasts and the birds,
> The birds flew against him, so he went where the beasts were.
> The beasts nearly tore him to pieces . . . and this is what a
> worker must learn
> from the bat.

He'd better know which side he's on . . . and not be torn to
pieces by both
sides.

It was in a minor key and quite powerful. Max Reinhardt said,
"That sounds like Kurt Weill. Is it?"

"No," I replied, surprised at my own theater knowledge. "It's by
a protégé of his. An American called Marc Blitzstein."

"Have you anything else you can sing for me? Something that will
give me more of an idea of your vocal range. After all, this a light
operetta . . . we hope."

I asked the accompanist if he could do anything from *The Mikado*,
preferably one of Katisha's numbers. He shook his head. I just happened to have the sheet music of "In Chi-Chi Castenango" in my
purse, so I handed it to him and told him to play it in A flat. I then
proceeded to sing it and go into all the dance steps that I had
memorized so laboriously. When I had finished, Mr. Reinhardt
applauded. I was stunned. I suppose that after five hours of listening to grand opera, he found my little Mexican number a relief.
"Sheeley," he said to me, "if there is no part in this show for you,
I will write one. The leading comedian is Oscar Karlweis, a very
famous Viennese actor. You will play his coquette."

The stage manager took me by the arm, dragged me off the stage
and told me three or four times that I should report for rehearsal
the following Monday. It wasn't sinking in. I knew I couldn't be
with Paul for another three or four months, but I wanted to join
him as soon as he was finished with Officers' Training School. Thank
God they offered me only a two-week contract instead of a run of
the play. That meant they could fire me with two weeks' notice, but
I could give *them* two weeks' notice whenever I wanted to. So I
began rehearsals of *Rosalinda*.

The music was gorgeous, and Dorothy Sarnoff, who played the
lead, had a tremendous coloratura soprano voice, and the girl who
played Adela had a beautiful lyric soprano. In fact, the entire cast
had beautiful voices, except Oscar Karlweis and me. There were
many times during the next few weeks when I wondered what the
hell I was doing in this show with the best singers in New York.
I used to stand in the wings and listen to the orchestra at every
opportunity. Gottfried Reinhardt must have thought that Karlweis
and I were funny together because our parts kept getting bigger
and bigger during the four weeks of rehearsal.

The producers seemed to like me, and at night I took an intense

course in speech to get rid of my Brooklyn accent and try to sound
at least slightly elegantly European. My zayda and bubba came to
my aid as I could recall a lot of German expressions from my childhood which I sprinkled around. Reinhardt had me skipping all
over the stage, fanning myself coquettishly, and I did my part with
enormous confidence. I didn't realize I was in a million-dollar
show. I just thought it was a sort of tacky Viennese operetta directed
by an out-of-work refugee, even though distinguished. However, I
was having a great deal of fun, and I wrote Paul everything that
happened whether or not he could read it. He finally asked me to
print. His letters had large portions censored, but I gathered he
was somewhere in Texas going through hellish basic training.

During one terrible rehearsal very close to the opening I was
waiting to sing my solo line near the finale of the first act. The
chorus was singing harmony while Gene Barry, who also was in
the show, sang an octave lower, and I was supposed to come in
singing my one solo line. But whenever the conductor, Erich Wolfgang Korngold, pointed his baton at me, I froze. Finally, after
keeping his musicians—at least fifty of them—for two hours on
overtime, he called a ten-minute break.

I went downstairs in tears, unable to believe that it was so impossible for me to harmonize one line. One of the oboe players, a
sweet slight man who sat near the stage in the pit, said to me,
"Korngold is terrifying you, Shelley. Watch me out of the corner of
your eye. I carry your melody, and I will give you your pitch and
first note. When I lean back my head, that is your cue."

We resumed the rehearsal. The oboeist leaned back his head,
and I came right in. Korngold stopped the rehearsal and graciously
admitted that "Even a tone-deaf little Brooklyn idiot can be trained
to harmonize."

Our dress rehearsal was a shambles, with scenery falling down,
the wrong costumes showing up in the wrong numbers and actors
arguing about the staging. But opening night it all came together
magically. I wore a stunning mauve ruffled period costume with a
cape and headdress and long white gloves, and I carried a fan. I
got wonderful reviews and was thrilled. What I didn't realize was
that the leading actors and actresses, although great singers, were
for the most part rather plump, so Mr. Reinhardt kept the spotlight
on me a great deal.

For the first and only time in his long career as a critic, Walter
Kerr had to print a retraction in the New York *Herald Tribune*.
He got my role confused with that of Adela, the second lead, a

small, plain, plump girl with a glorious voice who sang four important arias, and in his review he not only praised my comedic talent
but gave me credit for her beautiful voice. After his retraction
appeared, he wrote me a letter in which he said, "Max Reinhardt
dazzled the audience so much with your blonde and purple beauty
that no one could take his eyes off you for very long, and so that's
why I made that mistake." Adela didn't talk to me for the run of
the show.

All went well until the first matinee, during which my lovely
oboe player jerked his head back a little too far and fell over backward. The musicians, who were packed closely together in the pit,
collapsed like a house of cards. There was a shocked silence; then
the audience roared. The show came to a full stop as the musicians
straightened themselves out and sorted the scattered scores and
music stands and instruments. To say it was bedlam is an under-
statement. The oboe player later said he had fainted and didn't
squeal on me, but despite that, Korngold broke his baton and,
with what could be only some sort of musical intuition, threw
the pieces at *me*.

Not long after that historic moment in the theater, Paul got a
three-day pass after basic training and came to New York. I
eagerly showed him my name, which had just been put up in
lights—last billing, but glowing nevertheless. He insisted we stay
at a fancy hotel, and those three days were strange ones, during
which he treated me differently from before. Not better, just differently. Maybe it was because I was starring in a big Broadway
hit. I did my best to reassure him I was the same Shirley, telling
him I had turned down a run-of-the-play contract in order to be
with him when he finished Officers' Training School. I would be
with him anywhere he could live off base, and I wanted to have
a baby.

His reply was: "You're still a baby yourself. I think we'd better
wait until we're sure our baby will grow up with a father."

I tried not to understand what he meant by that. He seemed
much older than he had when we were in Detroit. It was a bitter-
sweet spring day when I went with him to the train, and we clung
to each other when we said good-bye.

There was a peculiar spirit around New York in those days; it
was almost as if the people who weren't actually fighting the war
were in some strange way enjoying it. Under the guise of patriotism
there seemed to be a general loosening of morals and manners, with

everyone living for that day or that night and to hell with tomorrow. We knew that in Great Britain the theaters were blacked out, and audiences often had to go into bomb shelters when performances were interrupted by the blitz. All we had on Broadway were practice alerts, and I seem to remember that though the lights in Times Square were dimmed, they were rarely turned off. Wouldn't you know that the first time my name was up in lights, they were dimmed and sometimes turned off.

Then one night another and even more terrifying incident occurred during a performance of *Rosalinda*. Near the beginning of the second act Oscar Karlweis was supposed to make his entrance with Adela on his arm, with a group of laughing ballet dancers following them. I opened the act with four lines about expecting the Prince soon and my love for him and his money. Karlweis was the Prince.

I said my four lines—NO PRINCE. I repeated the lines, paraphrasing them slightly in order to sound different. STILL NO PRINCE. The house was packed with 2,000 people. Even Korngold froze. I crossed to the chorus, trying, as I approached them, to involve them in a "period" conversation. They backed away from me. I skipped over to the ballet dancers, fanning myself as I went. They toe-danced away across the stage. STILL NO PRINCE. I looked desperately into the wings—NO STAGE MANAGER!

What had happened was that Adela, in her third-floor dressing room, had not heard her cue bell and was sitting in her tights, writing a letter to her soldier boyfriend. She had lost all sense of time. Oscar Karlweis refused to make his entrance without her, and the stage manager had to run up the three flights of stairs to get her into her costume. Alone on the stage during all this time and since no one would help me, I proceeded to improvise a five-minute monologue about the conditions in Vienna at the turn of the century. Including traffic problems. It began to take on the sensation of a nightmare in slow motion. The ghost of my great-aunt Katie Schratt must have come to my rescue because what the hell did *I* know about Vienna in the 1900s, especially its traffic problems? I guess I was funny because the audience was in hysterics. But it seemed as though I were out there for hours, floating around the stage, staying in character and carrying on about my love for the Prince and Viennese society. Finally, I was about to say, "Audience, go home! I can't think of anything else to say."

At that moment the Prince and Adela made their entrance. His opening line was: "I'm so sorry we're late, Fifi, but the Emperor had one of his parades, and it delayed us."

I turned to the audience and said, "See, I knew it was the traffic."

After the performance I got roses and carnations and candy from everyone connected with the show and an *órchid* from Erich Wolfgang Korngold, which I've kept pressed among the pages of the score and libretto of *Rosalinda*. He came backstage before the following day's performance and said, "I apologize. They raise intelligent, courageous geniuses in Brooklyn, not idiots." Then he kissed my hand gallantly, and from then on when he pointed his baton at me, he smiled. I could sing my line of harmony without the help of the oboeist. But just in case, he still played my first note a bit louder.

On Saturday night after the performance, as I was taking off my makeup, dressed only in my cotton slip, black lisle stockings and flat Mary Janes, who should burst into my dressing room but Harry Cohn, head of Columbia Pictures and creator of Hollywood Sex Goddesses. He looked slightly askance at my outfit, and I quickly slipped into my "negligee" (one of Blanche's medical robes from Brooklyn Hospital).

"Listen, kid," Cohn said, "you're terrific out there. You think you could do the same thing in front of a camera?"

"Well, my father takes pretty good pictures of me with his Brownie."

I guess he thought it was a joke, so he laughed and went on. "How would you like to make a test for me? I'll direct it."

I was stunned. "What would I do?"

"Anything you please."

"Where and when do we do this . . . this test?"

"Tomorrow, Sunday," he replied. "Ten A.M. at Twentieth Century-Fox Studios. Fifty-ninth and Tenth. And do whatever you want. Any funny monologue you know. There'll be a hairdresser and makeup man there." He looked at me for a moment. "And be sure to wear something sexy."

"How long will it take?" I asked. "I have to be back home in Brooklyn in time for dinner."

He looked at me incredulously, and his voice was controlled when he spoke. "Okay. We'll skip lunch. I have to catch a plane to the Coast tomorrow night anyway."

"I'll try to borrow the costume I wear in the show," I said. "Would that be all right?"

"Sure. Whatever you want," he replied. Then he asked me if I would like to go with him to Sardi's for a drink and supper.

"Gee, I'd love to go to Sardi's. I've only eaten there twice. But I'd better talk to the stage manager about using my costume, and then I think I should get to bed early so I won't have rings under my eyes tomorrow."

Whatever Cohn's plans for me that evening were, he appreciated my businesslike attitude. He left me sitting in my dressing room, wondering exactly what I had agreed to. The chorus girl I was sharing the dressing room with hugged and kissed me in her excitement at my good fortune. (She later married Vincent Sardi, and they adopted five children.) After getting the stage manager's reluctant okay to borrow my costume, I hurried home to find something for my test. I decided on Dorothy Parker's "The Waltz." Then I went to the nurses' residence at the hospital, where Blanche cued me until I was letter-perfect. She had to be on duty at seven, so we each had about four hours' sleep.

Early on Sunday morning I packed my makeup, and carefully carrying the box with my costume, I took the subway to Fifty-ninth Street. It was a frosty morning as I walked across to Tenth Avenue, and when I got to the New York studios of Twentieth Century-Fox, I stepped through the doorway with my right foot. There followed a whirlwind two hours during which a man by the name of Eddie Senz did my makeup, sensational eyelashes and then my hair, very glamorously building up my own blonde curls with false hair underneath. I fought with him about putting body makeup on my bosom, shoulders and arms. But he did it anyway.

Finally, I was taken out onto the sound stage and found a modern set which didn't go at all with my period costume. Harry Cohn was there talking to Arnold Picker and Max Arnow. The three of them looked strangely at my costume; then Cohn said, "What are you going to do, Shelley?"

"Well, Harry, the only good thing I could think of is Dorothy Parker's 'The Waltz,' but I need more space than that cluttered-up set. All I need is a chair and a table over on the side. And could I have some music to waltz to?" I had thoughtfully brought along a record of "The Blue Danube," certain that there'd be a record player at the studio.

Cohn screamed, "Strike the set!" and it scared the hell out of me. Some men came in and removed most of the furniture, leaving me the table and chair I'd requested.

"The Waltz" is about an ugly duckling of a girl, a wallflower, sitting at a dance, when some imaginary baboon of a man comes over and asks her for a dance. The monologue consists of what she says to her imaginary partner and what she is really saying sotto voce to herself.

"Show us what you're going to do," Cohn instructed.

"Sure, Harry," I replied. "Could someone play this record for me?"

"Listen, honey, there's been some big development in sound; we can dub in the music later."

I didn't know what he meant. "Harry," I protested, "I need the music for certain cues."

In a thoroughly exasperated voice he yelled, "Will someone go out and get or buy a fucking phonograph?" No mean accomplishment on a Sunday morning. Turning to me, he said, "All right, Shelley, do it for me once without the music until they come back with a phonograph."

"Okay, Harry," I replied. "But could you at least hum 'The Blue Danube' for me?" I had no idea at the time of the fear this man induced in most people.

He turned to Max Arnow and said, "Hum 'The Blue Danube,' Max."

He did, and I proceeded to do my ten-page monologue with an imaginary actor in a modern set and dressed in my period costume. Partway through I stopped and turned to Mr. Arnow. "Max," I said, "could you please hum louder when I'm talking to my imaginary boyfriend and lower when I make the caustic remarks to myself?"

"Yeah, Max, why don't you do that?" Cohn said to him.

All through the test a strange-looking long iron bar which terrified me was following me around and kept me ducking. It must have looked as if I were curtsying, but I was too shy to ask them what it was. I later learned it was the sound boom.

When I finished the monologue, Harry Cohn smiled at me and said, "Okay, Shelley, until they get back with the phonograph, could you sit on that stool and turn your head from side to side and answer the questions I ask you?"

"Sure, Harry, but I'm hungry. How about sending out for a tuna fish sandwich?"

Cohn yelled, "Six tunas on rye toast with tomato coming up." Then he turned to me and asked if I wanted a chocolate milk shake as well.

"How do you know I want that?" I asked in surprise. How could he possibly know that when I was nervous tuna fish sandwiches and chocolate milk shakes had a tranquilizing effect on me?

"I know everything," he replied.

Eddie Senz came over and started in powdering my face and fixing my lipstick, and the hairdresser fussed over my hair. I stopped them after two minutes. To this day I can't stand being fussed over when I'm concentrating on a scene I'm about to shoot.

I then began doing a "personality test," sitting on a stool and turning my head from left to right when Cohn told me to. Never being too sure of left and right to begin with and being nervous as well, I was constantly turning my head in the wrong direction, making the cameraman swivel his camera wildly, trying to stay on me. Cohn solved this problem by getting Arnow to clap his hands in back of the camera in the direction they wanted my head to move. Cohn asked me a lot of personal questions, which I answered truthfully, but when he asked my age, I replied that I was twenty-one. (I thought it had something to do with the legal age of movie actresses. It has.) A few minutes later, when he asked me the year of my birth, I got confused and gave away I think my real age. Then he asked if I had a boyfriend. I stuttered as I admitted that I had a husband. For the next three minutes of film I bragged about Paul until Cohn said, "Shut up already, or I'll sign *him*."

He called, "Cut!" just as the man with the phonograph and the sandwiches and milk shakes arrived simultaneously. We took a break, and I devoured two of the sandwiches while Harry Cohn and Max Arnow ate the others. Then Cohn said, "Hey, kid, if you get a contract, you're going to have to take off some weight."

I was about 105 pounds. I looked at him, aghast. "From where? My elbows?"

He laughed and said, "Okay, Nutsy, let's do your scene now."

The cameraman was a famous New York one, and this part of my test he photographed in color. Very unusual and expensive in those days. What I didn't know was that Cohn was considering me for Rita Hayworth's girlfriend in *Cover Girl*.

Then they forced me to fix my makeup. So, in my mauve nineteenth-century costume from *Rosalinda*, I proceeded to do the very modern "The Waltz" by Dorothy Parker. I don't know how I was, but my imaginary partner was great. He kept standing on my feet and bumping into the furniture, the mauve taffeta bow in my hair kept falling over and the other dancers in the imaginary ballroom were stepping on the train of my bustle. I had no fear of the camera (I developed that later), and since I really wanted to join Paul after he graduated from Officers' Training School, I was as relaxed as if I was in acting class.

When the nine minutes—a full camera load—were up, Cohn again yelled, "Cut!" At that moment I was back at my chair where my clumsy partner had returned me. I kept right on with the scene, taking off my shoe, rubbing my foot, talking and drinking my imaginary wine. Cohn must have taken it personally. "Jesus Christ!" he screamed, "I said, 'Cut,' so why the hell are you still acting?"

"I'm not interested in your technical problems," I answered calmly. "I have to finish my scene, don't I?"

Cohn studied me for a long time, then said something very odd. "I think," he muttered to himself, "I've found a way to get even with Frank Capra."

"Frank Capra? He's the one who made *It Happened One Night*, isn't he? I saw it ten times."

"*I* made it," Cohn roared. "He just directed it. Shelley, don't you ever forget that the executive producer is the most important person on a picture. Never mind the director." Later on I learned that his advice was, in most cases, sad but true.

With great care I took off my *Rosalinda* costume, "forgetting" to return the glamorous eyelashes, then was struck by a sudden thought. "Hey!" I called out through the dressing-room door. "Will my mother and father be able to see the test?"

It was Max Arnow who answered. "No. The film goes off to Hollywood tonight to be developed, and we see it there."

Cohn had already left for the airport, so I didn't even get the chance to say good-bye. I took the subway home, arriving just in time for a late dinner. My father glowered at me and my heavy makeup, but when I told him that I had just made a test for Columbia, his face lit up. "You know," he said, "when I went to St. Louis so long ago, I really wanted to go to California. You can reach your hand out the window there and pick an orange for breakfast. How do you think you did?"

"Terrific, I think." But a cold feeling was inside me. Here I was—the rave of the season in my first Broadway hit—and all my fantasies of becoming another Helen Hayes and doing Shakespeare and Ibsen for the Theatre Guild were suddenly placed in jeopardy.

My father was now making $96 a week. I finished my meal, went into my Mexican bedroom and lay down on the bed with the pillow over my head. Then the comforting thought struck me. Maybe I'd been lousy in the test. After all, I didn't take such great still photos as my nose was too wide, and my bosom was too flat, and my hair was too kinky. I spent an ambivalent sleepless night.

When I arrived at the theater for the Monday night performance, the wardrobe mistress was ready to kill me *and* the stage manager. "You're never allowed to take a costume out of the theater," she screamed. "Now I barely have time to press it for your entrance." But she didn't tell on us to the producers.

About four weeks passed, and I almost forgot about the test. Then two things occurred simultaneously. Paul phoned to say that he was now a second lieutenant and in a couple of weeks he would be in Shreveport, Louisiana, where he would begin training with B-17s, and we could live together off the base. The same day I received a call from the New York offices of Columbia Pictures to come up there with my mother and father. As per usual in my life. when I come to the fork in the road, I try to take both.

I went over to the Columbia office with my parents and was handed a standard seven-year contract with options every six months, starting at $100 a week and going up to $5,000 at the end of the seven years. The entire Schrift family practically fainted. I looked at Arnold Picker, who was vice-president of Columbia, and asked, "Am I sure to get the five thousand dollars in seven years' time?"

"Well, you can be pretty sure about the first year [the second six-month option went up to $200 a week] because it takes that long to train you for the camera. A big studio like ours gives you a lot of publicity and grooms you, and so, if you're good in just one picture, your name becomes a household word all over the world." (This was pre-TV.)

I sat down. My dream of becoming a First Lady of the Theater began to fade before my eyes. I heard my father say to me, "*Nudnik*, sign it. Have you suddenly gone crazy? It's every American girl's dream. A chance like this. Don't you want to be a movie star?" I didn't know.

"There's a small fly in the ointment, however," Mr. Picker said, looking at my parents. "Because of Jackie Coogan and Jackie Cooper, there's a new California law called the Protection of Minors Act, and half of what she earns must be put into War Bonds for her. Also, since she's a minor, one of you will have to go with her to Hollywood."

My mother looked at him aghast, then suddenly said, "My other daughter is a nurse, and she's over twenty-one. Couldn't she go to California with Shelley?"

"How do you know Blanche wants to go to California?" I yelled. "I don't want to disrupt everybody's life."

But my wonderful mother, instead of coming to my rescue, said, "Your sister has been moping around the house ever since that boy she knew got killed in Spain. Besides, I think it would be good for her to practice nursing in California. And I bet medical schools are cheaper out there as well." Mr. Picker quickly assured us that it was so, and Blanche would be a suitable chaperone.

My father and I studied the seven-year Columbia contract, and all of a sudden, like magic, he seemed different, younger and happy. As if all the misery and disillusionment he had suffered in his early manhood were about to be reversed by his daughter's money potential. America WAS the Land of Opportunity, after all. You *could* become a millionaire! In the movies anyway.

Sensing my ambivalence, my mother looked at me, but we both were helpless before my newly important father. He put on his eyeglasses and very carefully read the whole contact, including the fine print, and he got Mr. Picker to change the salary between the third and fourth years from $750 to $1,000 a week. He found other little clauses that drove the Legal Department of Columbia crazy, but they realized that if they wanted me, they had to deal with my father. When the revisions were to his satisfaction, he initialed everything and signed "Jonas Schrift" in his beautiful penmanship. That was followed by an illegible scribble, "Shirley Schrift." Mr. Picker glanced over the six contracts and asked, "Where is Shelley Winter?" I had to hold myself back from replying that I was leaving her on Broadway to become a stage star; instead, I wrote "A.K.A. [Also Known As] Shelley Winter" under my signature.

All this took place on the morning of a matinee day, so I had to rush over to the theater from the Columbia office to make the performance. I didn't tell anyone about my contract but informed the producers that I was giving them my two weeks' notice so that I could join my husband, who was now a lieutenant and soon to be stationed in Louisiana. They were very nice about it and understood my wanting to be with him before he was shipped overseas.

Max Reinhardt came into my dressing room that night and floored me with the following words: "Sheeley, I understand your desire to stay with your husband until he must go and fight. You understand you project a *joie de vivre* over the footlights and a natural comedic talent, and it is this, not the spotlight, that makes the audience watch you. No one can be taught that; an artist of the theater must have it born into him." He paused. "You can come back to the show whenever you want." I swallowed hard. Then he said, "In my next show I will train you carefully, and you will star in it. God willing that I'm still here."

A year later I was in Hollywood, as was his son, Gottfried, and Max Reinhardt was dead. And with him perhaps died my dreams of becoming a great artist of the theater. Perhaps not—I'm still trying.

Two weeks after that I was notified by Columbia to report to its studios in Hollywood for its film *Cover Girl*, and I was given two first-class tickets on the Super Chief for Blanche and me. Without hesitation, I gave Blanche her ticket and put mine in my purse and caught the day coach to Shreveport, Louisiana. I figured I'd call up Cohn and explain why I couldn't be in *Cover Girl*. I didn't know exactly how long I'd be with Paul before he went overseas, so I couldn't make Cohn any promises. . . .

As the wheels of the train made that wonderful sound on the tracks, I kept hearing Max Reinhardt's words over and over again. "No one can be taught that; an artist of the theater must have it born into him."

I got off the train in Shreveport looking like what I thought a lieutenant's wife should look like, complete with white gloves. Paul met me at the train. He was only a second lieutenant, but those gold bars on his shoulders made me feel very important. He was all dressed up for the occasion, too, looking very smart in his officer's pinks.

At first we were very awkward with each other. He didn't know that Columbia had given me a contract on the basis of my test, and I didn't tell him. Living quarters were scarce and terribly expensive in towns close to all Army bases, but Paul had managed to find an apartment over somebody's garage. It consisted of one room with a pull-out bed, a tiny kitchen, and it cost *only* $100 a week. All those "patriotic" landlords were doing their bit for the war effort.

For a while that little apartment was like seventh heaven. With cookbooks from the library plus exact recipes from my mother, I managed to become quite a good cook. Paul would go to the base at 6:00 in the morning and be home in time for a 6:00 P.M. home-cooked meal. One by one, then two by two, he brought his entire crew home to dinner. He wasn't supposed to fraternize with enlisted men, but I think he was proud of me and my cooking ability. I also learned how to shop carefully, using all our food stamps, in addition to those my mother would send, and Paul would often bring home things like steaks or legs of lamb from the commissary.

We were very happy . . . well, as happy as we could be with the knowledge that as soon as he completed his B-17 training, he would be shipped to one of the theaters of war. However, we both decided to ignore the fact and NEVER discuss it. We went to all the movies, to whatever little theater and plays were in and around Shreveport, to sandlot baseball games on Sundays and to dances at the base and the officers' club.

The segregation in the South bothered me a great deal. It was the first time I'd actually seen those signs on rest rooms doors and drinking fountains in the park, stating WHITE ONLY and COLORED ONLY. What really got me was the signs in the restaurant windows which announced that WE RESERVE THE RIGHT TO REFUSE SERVICE TO ANYONE. Since there were many black enlisted men, they must have wondered what they were fighting for. I don't think their wives came to the dances, or at least I don't recall ever seeing them. Paul, of course, wasn't allowed to go into the enlisted men's or NCOs' clubs, but since he'd made the point of bringing his whole crew home for dinners, they all became buddies, helping one another out with personal as well as financial problems. It's possible that this feeling of oneness and cooperation is the reason Paul's plane became the squadron leader during their eighty bombing missions.

Then one day disaster struck. Paul intercepted one of Blanche's letters from Hollywood, in which she told me that the director of *Cover Girl* was getting very annoyed at my not showing up to learn the songs and dances. All the famous models and cover girls from New York were already there rehearsing, and I was making myself infamous by my absence.

Paul and I had a knock-down, drag-out fight. He ordered me to go to Hollywood immediately to fulfill my contract and do this important picture, and I insisted on staying with him until he was shipped overseas. He yelled that I was jeopardizing a lucrative career and that there was no guarantee that he would come back, and I screamed that he was selfish and that I was old enough to make my own decisions, and besides, he wouldn't even let me have a baby like all the other soldiers' wives. The fight got louder and stormier until all the neighbors took sides. It ended up with Paul packing all his gear and moving back to the base, his departing words being "Now you'll have to go to Hollywood like an adult and fulfill the contract you signed."

After drying my face, I went to a phone booth and placed a collect call to Harry Cohn at Columbia Pictures in Hollywood.

When I finally got him on the phone, I said brightly, "Hello, Harry. Remember me? Shelly Winter?"

"Yeah," he growled. "But I'm beginning to forget you. You're supposed to be here rehearsing *Cover Girl*. Where the hell are you?"

I explained the situation to him rapidly, concluding with "What I want you to do, Harry, is call Colonel So-and-So at the Shreveport Air Base—you may have to go through Army Air Force Headquarters in Washington—and ask him to get Lieutenant Paul Miller to the phone. That's my husband. Then you explain to Paul that you don't need me out there until after he goes overseas." Stunned silence. "Listen, Harry, so I won't be a cover girl. But I'll be in a lot of other pictures for you, and I'll behave like a doll. And you don't have to pay me until I get there."

Cohn finally found his voice. "Well, I guess there are a lot of ways of fighting a war, and this is as good a way as any." And then he did exactly as I asked. So by me, forever after, Harry Cohn was a *mensch*.

Late that evening Paul returned to our little room with all his gear as he had been instructed to do by his colonel. He kissed me and said, "Military intelligence could have made great use of you. How in hell did you get Harry Cohn to tell me whenever you decide to arrive at Columbia was okay with him?"

I blinked and smiled demurely. "I sure must have made a great test, huh?"

A funny look came over Paul's face. "You're really serious about all this acting stuff?"

"*Comme ci, comme ça*," I fibbed casually.

We spent a glorious month in our Shreveport seventh heaven. Then, without warning, Paul's squadron was transferred to Blythe, California. Again he tried to get me to join Blanche in Los Angeles, this time saying that I'd be able to visit him on weekends, reiterating that he never knew when they would suddenly send him overseas and I would be left alone. I wouldn't listen.

We arrived in Blythe in the desert heat of August. All Paul could find for us was a wooden shack that seemed to be held together by the wallpaper. It had an outhouse, and we had to bathe in the same tub I washed the clothes in, filled from a garden hose. The average daytime temperature was about 120 degrees, and at night it would cool off to 100. The joke around the base was that if you asked to be transferred to the Pacific from Blythe, you were a coward.

I learned to make cold imitation borscht, using the juice from canned beets, and imitation sour cream by beating buttermilk and adding a little lemon juice. Paul's bombardier miraculously kept the icebox supplied with blocks of ice. Whenever Paul returned from the base, all dirty and greasy, he would find a tub of hot water, green soap and Lux flakes and another tub of ice water ready and waiting for him. And a very cold double vodka martini. I would remove all the oil stains from his face and body with cold cream. He complained that it made him smell like a whorehouse, but I think he liked it anyway and could hardly wait to get home.

He used to bring back little Indian presents for me, I presumed from the reservations they would fly to, and some nights he'd take me in a jeep to the extraordinarily beautiful desert with the sky full of stars. With his sextant he tried many times to explain to me just what a navigator does on a B-17. First he gets a sighting on a star, then figures the ground speed, whatever that is, then the plane's speed and the wind speed from whatever direction it's coming, gets the latitude and longitude, then adds, subtracts and multiplies them all together. In this way he locates his course and his target. Radio silence had to be maintained. Since we all felt at that time that he would be shipped to the Pacific, I had little faith that he could ever find some tiny Japanese island way out there. I couldn't make head or tail of anything he kept patiently explaining to me, but I guess this Air Force system worked because we won the war. When I looked through his sextant, all I saw was a sky full of gorgeous stars. One night under those brilliant stars, he told me, "You'd better not become a famous actress because then you'll make a lot of money and get into tax troubles with the government because you just can't understand math." He was joking, but was he ever right!

Life in Blythe became rather terrifying as the bombing training intensified, the heat in the sweltering airplanes causing some of the boys to die of heat prostration. Some of the fliers forced their wives and babies to go home. I stayed indoors most of the day with ice in front of the electric fan, reading everything I could get my hands on as well as working to improve my speech.

When Paul got a three-day pass, we drove to L.A. in a "borrowed" jeep. We visited Blanche in her rooming house near Cedars of Lebanon Hospital, which was run by a ninety-year-old ex-silent film star. All over the place were hatstands with hats on them and photos of long-forgotten movie stars. Also about sixteen cats, to which I was allergic. I didn't once go near Columbia Studios or even phone. All I did was walk up and down Western Avenue, looking

into the windows of the many furniture stores, and dream of when
the war would be over and Paul would come home. He would have
his firm transfer him to the L.A. area; then we would buy a rose-
covered cottage in the Hollywood Hills, which I would furnish in
Early American. Then we would have a baby, and we would live
happily ever after. Of course, this all would take place in between
my starring in pictures and plays!

Paul suddenly had to drive back to Blythe, and Blanche and I
followed in her car. We drove at night to avoid the heat, but even
so the engine overheated, and we had to stop at every gas station
along the 250-mile route. We discovered there was a leak in the
radiator, so at one point I crawled under the car and plugged up
the hole with an orange. In those days they grew all along the
highways and were free for the taking. When we finally arrived at
the little shack in Blythe, Paul looked very surprised. I think he
hoped I had decided to remain in L.A. and start my movie career.

Blanche stayed for a few days and took Paul's part in every
argument. When at one point she said I wasn't helping him, we
had ourselves a real slapping fight. We weren't too old for that.
Then we both suddenly began to laugh and cry hysterically. She
told me the real reason she'd left New York, and it wasn't to be
my chaperone. She too had had an unhappy love affair and needed
desperately to get away from our mother and father and live on
her own, and that was the only way she could manage it. But all
her friends were in New York, and she was lonely in Los Angeles.
This made me feel even worse, and I did my best to comfort her.

After she returned to L.A., there began a particularly unhappy
period with Paul. I wasn't aware of it, but the crews had been
told that they could be sent overseas on a moment's notice. Paul
wanted very badly to go to the European theater; his personal war
was with Hitler. However, the Army had its own ideas of which
squadrons went where. Then the orders came through for his squadron to proceed immediately to Rapid City, South Dakota, which
Paul knew was the jumping-off point for England. I wanted to
follow him there, and we had another really terrible fight.

The night before he left, Paul brought some food back to the
shack and talked to me in a very serious and adult manner, reminding me of what had taken place at Dunkirk and the sacrifices
being made by our armed forces in the South Pacific. By now he
knew about Auschwitz, Dachau and Belsen, although he didn't tell
me. What he told me was that I had to put my courage where my
mouth was and find ways to fight the Nazi and Fascist forces at

home. He impressed on me the necessity to obliterate forever their idea that some men are born "supermen," superior to their fellows. This could be achieved only by the victory of the Allies. "I have a mathematical mind," he said, "but you have a great deal of natural intelligence and street cunning, plus a deep survival sense. If you put your mind to it, I know you'll find ways to help the war effort."

When he didn't return to our little shack the next night, I knew his squadron had left for South Dakota and England, and the words he had said to me were engraved on my heart.

CHAPTER 7

When I moved in with Blanche in her mad rooming house, the first thing I did was phone Connie Dowling, who was now a Goldwyn Girl. She had a very posh apartment on North Sycamore, which, according to the street map Blanche gave me, looked like a short walk up Hollywood Boulevard. Some short walk! Two miles and on three-inch heels. When I got to Grauman's Chinese Theater, I tried to fit my sore feet into the footprints of some of the stars, just as the other tourists and soldiers and sailors were doing. Connie was very happy to see me and drove me out to MGM. I was amazed that a New York girl like Connie had learned to drive so quickly.

MGM Studios awed me no end, and on my first day in Hollywood I watched Elia Kazan direct. I think it was a test for the upcoming *Sea of Grass*, with Katharine Hepburn and Spencer Tracy. Connie and I had lunch in the commissary, where I gaped at so many stars I forgot to eat. At that time Louis B. Mayer had about 350 stars under contract, and the studio had forty-five sound stages, a huge rehearsal stage, where Gene Kelly's ballet company rehearsed forty weeks a year, and four back lots with every imaginable sort of construction, from the Chinese village of *The Good Earth* to a lake with a barge floating on it from Marie Dressler's *Tugboat Annie*. Not to mention French, Italian, Russian, Indian and African villages.

I had the oddest feeling driving around those back lots; they looked so real. Then Connie explained that the buildings were just fronts; nothing was behind them. We drove around the huge studio, from country to country, century to century, in a few minutes. An eerie sensation. In the years that followed I did many films at MGM, but I never got tired of wandering through the enchanting back lots. Film negative has become much more sensitive now and needs much less artificial lighting, so most pictures are shot on location, but in those days any part of the world would be reproduced right there on the back lot. I still think it was the best system because, as Sam Goldwyn once said, "A rock is a rock and a tree is a tree; what's important is what's in the actor's eyes." It's also a great deal more comfortable working in a studio where the department heads take good care of you which gives you more time to concentrate more fully on your performance.

The next day, after a good night's sleep, I got all dressed up and bravely went to Columbia Studios on Gower Street. I COULDN'T GET IN. The guard at the main gate sent me to the Casting Office; the Casting Office sent me to the Featured Players' gate; the Featured Players' gate sent me to the Cashier's gate, all located outside the studio proper. There this runaround was rewarded when they gave me three $50 checks, three weeks' salary of $100, with half taken out for war bonds. But they still wouldn't let me inside the studio.

I walked up to the Columbia drugstore and phoned Harry Cohn. Virginia, his secretary, was very nice. "Shelley, go back to the front entrance right away, and I'll make sure there's a pass for you. Then report to Max Arnow in Casting."

I bought Mr. Cohn a long-stemmed white rose from a street vendor and once again tried the main entrance of the studio. This time the security guard let me in. I asked the first person I saw where I could find Mr. Cohn's office, and after walking up some small peculiar winding stairs, I presented myself to his secretary Virginia, in his outer office. "You're supposed to go to the Casting Office," she told me. "Mr. Cohn is in the middle of a script conference."

"But I only want to see him for a second. To thank him."

Her eyes fixed themselves on the rose in my hand. "I think," she said softly, "this is a first for Harry Cohn."

She pressed a button under her desk. The door opened, and I walked into an enormous office. There, behind a raised and equally enormous desk, sat Harry Cohn. He was screaming at two other big men, who, I found out later, were Sidney Buchman and Charles Vidor. I approached the desk and said, "Hello, Harry," and gave him a kiss on the cheek. "Paul and I want to thank you for what you did for us, and for God's sake, don't get so excited or you'll have a heart attack. After all, it's only a movie you're talking about, and there's a very serious war going on."

The other two men started to choke, and after a minute Cohn, recovering from his surprise, said gruffly, "Okay, Shelley, so you finally decided to show up. Did you take care of the war before you came to Hollywood?"

"I did my best," I assured him, and handed him the rose. He held it, not knowing what to do with it, then sat down in his chair. He introduced me to the other men, who shook my hand with what

I think was gratitude. It bewildered me at the time. I said, "Well, so long, Harry. See you tomorrow." And I walked out of the office, leaving him sitting there with the white rose held stiffly in his hand.

Virginia gave me detailed instructions on how to find Max Arnow's office. As I wandered through an endless maze of corridors toward where I thought Arnow's office and the sound stages were, I bumped into AL JOLSON! I dropped my purse. He seemed rather sad and dejected. I told him how much I loved his singing and how my mother and father did, too, and that we had all of his records. And that I'd seen his show *Hold On to Your Hats* twenty times ('cause Connie had got me in free), and how much I loved watching him sitting on the edge of the stage after the show was over, with his feet dangling into the orchestra pit, and singing until one in the morning. His face lit up, and he said, "Gee, kid, I wish you'd tell Harry Cohn about that. They're gonna do my life story here, and I'd sure like to play myself."

"Don't worry, Al," I told him. "I'll do it. Harry Cohn listens to me. I'm under contract." I proudly showed him my three $50 checks to prove it.

He personally escorted me over to Max Arnow's office, and as we went down the center street, I realized with my actor's intuition that he was trying to walk with a springy, youthful step. I had also noticed that his hair was dyed black and that he had a deep suntan to hide the lines. A cold chill crept down my spine at my first introduction to the youth fixation of Hollywood. Oh, God, I thought, I'm already eighteen and what have I accomplished?

Putting my right foot firmly through the doorway, I stepped into Max Arnow's outer office. His secretary was also named Virginia, and she was one of the nicest people I've ever met in Hollywood. I had to wait about half an hour before he was able to see me, and when I walked into his office, I greeted him with a "Hi, Max."

He fixed me with a cold stare and said, "My name is *Mr.* Arnow, and you walk over there and stand still." He pointed to the other side of the room, then began to appraise me as though I weren't there, and Virginia filled out a chart as he assessed me. "The hair's too dark blonde and kinky, but we can straighten and bleach it. Forehead too low; we'll take care of that with electrolysis. Eyes slant the wrong way, eyelashes should take care of that. Nose too wide; we may have to operate. . . ."

"Like hell you will."

He ignored me. "Lips too thin; makeup will take care of that.

Teeth crooked, caps needed. Shoulders too broad, bosom too flat, waist not narrow enough, hips too wide, legs knock-kneed, wobbly walk, and speech work needed."

Infuriated, I yelled, "Listen, Mr. Arnow, maybe you made a mistake by signing me to that contract. And before I go back to New York, could I at least see my test?"

"Shut up, and sit down," he ordered. "Here's your schedule for tomorrow. Hairdresser at seven A.M., makeup at nine. Bring some dancing clothes for ballet classes at ten-thirty. And no lunch. Go to the studio hospital, and they'll give you some pills and tomato juice. You'll have to lose weight. Two o'clock acting and speech classes in the schoolhouse; four o'clock singing lessons in the Music Department. The schedule will continue until we have a picture for you, or we decide you're ready for a portrait sitting, or you go on suspension."

"What's that?" I asked, a bit bewildered.

"You get paid forty out of fifty-two weeks," he explained. "Twelve weeks is the period between pictures or if you turn down a picture we want you to do. Then we don't pay you for the length of time the picture takes to shoot."

"So what do I do during that time? Wait on tables?"

He just stared at me. I took my schedule and walked out of his office. Virginia followed me out and stopped me. "Shelley," she said, offering me a chair. I blinked back my tears and sat down. "I saw your test with some executives and important directors," she told me. "You were charming and funny, and Max Arnow needed you to be in *Cover Girl* very badly. I think Mr. Cohn blamed Mr. Arnow that you weren't here. One of Mr. Arnow's jobs is to get blamed."

"Oh," I said.

After leaving her office, I wandered around the lot, amazed at how small it was compared to Metro, but I did notice that all the stages were busy. I was afraid to go into any of them to watch the shooting because they had signs that said CLOSED SET. But I acquainted myself with the general geography of the place, and seeing the studio hospital, I wondered if I could have Mr. Cohn arrange for Blanche to get a job there as a studio nurse so she would have time to go to med school at night. For some reason I went up a flight of iron steps to an iron landing, where I found myself in the Sound and Film Cutting departments. I was entranced. One of the editors who was working at a Movieola let me look in it and showed me how a picture is edited. I was stunned to find out that it was a lot of still pictures put together. Just like the vending machines in Coney Island.

I left the studio through the Cashier's gate, just in case any more checks were waiting for me. There weren't. I walked all the way home and told the slightly drunken silent-movie-star landlady all about my first day at Columbia. She said, "Darling, when you act, always insist on an orchestra. Music helps no end. Whatever the mood is of the scene you're playing pick something that produces the same mood in your own experience." She was batty, but it was good advice, and I've used it. Of course, I never insisted on an orchestra on the set, but I now have a small tape recorder with me, and it's surprising the effects I can get with music from *Madame Butterfly* or *Tosca* or *The Purple People Eater* before they call out, "Roll 'em!"

The next day at 7:00 A.M. I reported to the Hairdressing Department, where they used some kind of bleach on my hair that turned it platinum. Then they put on a chemical to straighten it, and there went all my beautiful curls forever. But since Helen Hunt was the creator of Rita Hayworth's hairstyle, who was I to argue? Then she and the makeup man marked my forehead with a pencil and ripped out the corners of my forehead hairline with hot wax so that my forehead would appear larger, and lo and behold I had a widow's peak. Helen told me I would have to have electrolysis two or three times a week to keep the old hairline from growing back.

Dazed with pain and fear, I was turned over to Fred Phillips, the makeup man. Reluctantly I showed him my chart. Eyes slanted wrong, nose too wide, lips too thin, etc. "Close your eyes," Freddy ordered, "and don't open them until I tell you to."

I must have fallen into an exhausted sleep because it seemed like only minutes later that he told me to open my eyes. I looked into the mirror, and a gorgeous platinum blonde stared back. It wasn't me, but she sure as hell looked sensational. She had high cheekbones, large, wide eyes that slanted upward, long lashes, full, sexy lips and a chiseled nose. How had he performed this miraculous feat?

Freddie smiled. "You're a cinch," he told me. He handed me a card. "Here's the name of a dentist. Go see him tomorrow, and he'll make you a plastic bite retainer. Wear it at night, and in a couple of months your teeth will be straight and perfect." He peered in my mouth closely, then added, "Maybe you'll need a couple of caps on the sides as well." That evening when I walked into the house, neither Blanche nor the landlady knew who I was till I opened my mouth.

The next day, a Sunday, Blanche and I went out apartment hunting. There were NO VACANCY signs everywhere. Way up on Hollywood Boulevard in the residential section was a collection of apartment buildings called Peyton Hall. It's still there. The manager said there was an empty apartment she believed was spoken for, but she'd show it to us anyway. I think she was hinting at key money. The apartment had quite a large living room, a bedroom with twin beds, a large dinette, a kitchen and lots of closet space. The rent was $250 a month, kind of steep for us, but I wanted it and decided to pull a little rank.

I asked the manager if I could use the phone, and she listened while I called Harry Cohn's office. I'd heard he always worked on Sundays. If only we had some of those film-loving bastards running the movie industry today, instead of computers! The manager heard me ask, "Harry, is it okay if you take only twenty-five dollars a week out of my salary for a while because there's a lovely apartment here at Peyton Hall, and it has a great big swimming pool which would be good for my figure and for taking cheesecake photos."

I heard him take a big breath and sigh. "Take it, take it. And stop bothering me. And on a Sunday yet." And he slammed down the phone.

Turning to the manager, I said with an innocent smile, "Are you sure this apartment is taken?"

"Oh, no," she replied quickly. "No, no. We like having young starlets who are properly chaperoned live with us. You know Claudette Colbert owns the place."

We signed the lease and moved in at 6:00 A.M. the next day. Blanche went to work, and since I didn't have to report to the studio until 10:30 for ballet class, I unpacked, then took a dip in the big pool. But only up to my neck because I hadn't removed the false eyelashes or messed my hair since the studio had me done over two days before. In the middle of my sidestroke, with my head sticking out of the water, I suddenly found myself looking straight into the eyes of *Cary Grant!* I almost drowned.

Later, while sipping my morning cup of coffee, I looked out the kitchen window, and so help me God, there was an orange tree. I loosened the screen and picked an orange in honor of my father, and as I did so, I was suddenly overwhelmed with loneliness. Before the age when most girls are ready to leave their parents, I had already starred on Broadway, had a husband fighting somewhere in

Europe and was trying to be tough enough to deal with the moguls of Hollywood.

I had to speak to someone, so I stopped off at Connie's apartment, which was only a few blocks away on North Sycamore. I told Connie about my feelings of homesickness, and she said, "Look, Shelley, don't worry. Nothing's real here so just pretend you're in *The Wizard of Oz*, and you'll be all right."

She asked me if I was still longing for that rose-covered cottage, and I told her I was. "I haven't had a garden since I left St. Louis," I mourned.

"Well, be careful, kid," Connie advised. "There's a saying in California that when you put a seed in the ground, you'd better jump back. Everything here happens very quickly." What did she mean?

In those days there was a wonderful little red streetcar that ran from downtown Los Angeles, along Hollywood Boulevard, then cut through a few backyards and went out to the beach. For a nickel. I took it in the opposite direction to Columbia Studios on Gower Street. This time the guard at the gate greeted me with "Good morning, Shelley," pressed a buzzer, and I was let in.

In my little dressing room I changed into my rehearsal clothes— the plaid romper suit left over from my *Meet the People* days, ankle socks and my flat ballet shoes. An appropriate outfit to rehearse in, I thought.

Then I was sent to Stage 5, where Jack Cole and his assistant, Gwen Verdon, were rehearsing contract players for *Tonight and Every Night*, a film I was to be in. My heart sank. I knew that Jack Cole was a famous modern dancer (and dancing was still not my strong point). When my eyes became adjusted to the dark after the bright sunshine outside, I found that I was surrounded by at least two dozen long-stemmed beauties in high-heeled shoes, short shorts and sexy blouses. I felt as though I ought to get myself a pail and mop and hoped no one would notice me.

In a little while Rita Hayworth came onto the stage. She looked gorgeous, but her lovely black hair was dyed a peculiar red blonde, the like of which I'd never seen in real life. Her sweet face was covered by tons of makeup and long false eyelashes, and a large mouth was painted over her own. She was wearing a sexy rehearsal outfit, but it seemed somehow wrong on her. She needed a Spanish shawl. Noticing me hiding behind the scenery, she came over. "Hi there, I bet you're Shelley Winter. I saw your test and your show in New York. You're funny and a very good actress. I didn't know you were a dancer as well."

"I'm not," I confessed in a whisper, trying to hide my feet under a chair. "But let them find it out themselves."

She laughed and said, "Don't be scared. They need you more than you need them." I knew she was trying to help me, so I immediately felt a lot better. I noticed then that she had the same sad look in her eyes that Connie had.

We began to rehearse, and when Jack Cole took one look at my outfit, he put me in the back line. He was trying to teach us a ballet that was half Balinese and half modern. I had my wedding ring on my left hand so I could tell left from right, but I was still a klutz. So were most of the contract girls, who were ex-cover girls, and poor Jack Cole had only six real dancers to work with. The more we rehearsed, the angrier he got. At the beginning of the second week Harry Cohn marched onto the stage with a big cigar in front of him and his entourage behind. As he passed me, with quiet exasperation he uttered, "Will someone get Shelley a costume to rehearse in?" He didn't look at me or break his stride.

I'd made friends with a few of the other girls, some of whom lived at the Studio Club. It was only a few blocks from Columbia, and sometimes we'd take our lunch break there, having our bologna sandwiches and chocolate milk in the garden. A shy, very pretty blonde girl used to sit in a corner and watch us working actresses at lunch. Her name was Norma Jean Something. She rarely spoke to us, and when she did, she would whisper. We would shout back at her, "What did you say?" and that would scare her more. She always wore halter dresses one size too small and carried around a big library book like a dictionary or encyclopedia.

At Columbia I was getting "acting lessons" from a young man with a British accent who came from the University of Michigan. These cockamamie lessons consisted of pasting Scotch tape on our faces so we would learn to act without moving a muscle and always be pretty for the camera. It's a neat trick to smile without making any lines, and even neater—impossible actually—to register emotion. Our teacher said not to worry about emotion—if we had to cry, the Makeup Department had a glass tube with menthol in it that would blow in our eyes to make them water. This violated everything I had learned in drama school, but I said nothing. So we learned the necessary two expressions he taught.

I became very friendly with three lovely girls: Jinx Falkenburg, a famous model; Dusty Anderson, now a well-known painter; and Adele Jergens, a statuesque blonde. There were about six of us contract players who had yet to work in a movie. There were some very handsome male starlets around, like William Holden, Larry Parks, Lex Barker and Bill Hale, but I was so busy writing to Paul every day that if any one of them even looked as though he were going to ask me for a date, I would inquire, "Why aren't you in the Army?" I must have been a real charmer.

One glorious day the Casting Department notified me that I was going to do a part in a film with Rosalind Russell. When I got the script, I found I was a secretary with one line: "You can't go in there now, miss." The first words I ever spoke in a film. But I said them to Rosalind Russell herself. A year or so later, when this so-called comedy was finally released, there was a private showing of it at the Motion Picture Academy Theater, and my mother went with me to see it. The picture was a good deal less than brilliant. After the showing I introduced her to Harry Cohn, and my mother's classic remark to him was: "You know, Mr. Cohn, you're very lucky to have Shelley in that picture." His reply was: "Yeah, I know. And I see who she takes after."

Finally, *Tonight and Every Night* started. I had no lines, and my ballet was left on the cutting-room floor, but Rita Hayworth saw to it that I stood behind her a great deal, so I got a lot of close-ups, even if a little out of focus; even so, I thought I looked very pretty.

Speech lessons were given to us by a stout, very elegant lady who wore a wig. She'd once been a famous British actress who had gotten even more famous in Hollywood when sound came in. She was trying to develop something in us she called mid-Atlantic speech. (It wasn't until I was in the middle of the Atlantic aboard the *Poseidon* that her lessons seemed appropriate.) But try as she might, she just couldn't teach me to sound like Ina Claire. Eventually she threw me out of the class; that didn't make me too unhappy, but it didn't help my speech problems.

Sometimes I sneaked into the projection room to watch the rushes of the films I had watched being shot, and it never failed to amaze me how the personality of a particular actor who while on the set was no better than any of the others would seem to jump off the screen in the projection room. I guess that's what they mean by screen charisma. The third time I slipped into the darkened projection room, I didn't leave quickly enough, and when the lights went on, Harry Cohn spotted me in the back. He walked up to me, so I just stood still. "If you keep on coming to the rushes of my pictures, I'm going to make you choose the takes."

"Okay, Harry, I'd love to."

"Get out of here, Nutsy," he said, "and go practice dieting."

On our days off, Connie, Blanche and I played a game we called Movieitis. In the daytime the movie houses on Hollywood Boulevard charged only twenty-five cents admission, so from our starting point at Brown's Hot Fudge Sundae Parlor on Sycamore and Hollywood Boulevard, at 10:00 A.M. we would work our way down the boulevard to see which one of us could see the most pictures before the prices changed at 5:00 P.M. Most of the time I won. I think my eyes are paying for it now.

Once when Connie was trying to convince me to go with her to a party Billy Wilder was giving, I kept resisting her efforts because I was embarrassed and besides I had a scene to work on for class. She got exasperated with me and said, "You must understand that young beauty is its own passport to anywhere and anything."

"You're probably right, Connie, but in that case I'm going to have to get myself a regulation passport. I don't have the right bones for beauty."

She laughed and said, "Your bones are very cute, and you're fun to be with."

I began hanging around Schwab's drugstore on Sunset Strip, the one where Lana Turner had been discovered, and I often saw Sidney Skolsky and his chauffeur, Norma Jean Baker. She still wore her halter dresses, and she still whispered. She drove Skolsky around to interviews in her old white car since he had never learned to drive. After lunch one day Sidney took us both to the parking lot behind Schwab's and pointed to a long, low wooden building next to it. "That's the Actors Lab," he told us. "It's the new Hollywood home of the Group Theatre, and some of the best actors in the world teach there." It has since been torn down— sadly, because it was one of the few cultural oases in Hollywood.

We almost knocked the poor man down in our rush to get to the front door. The woman in the office said that they gave classes for beginning actors if we were interested. I said I was an inter- mediate because of my work with Nadia Romanov who I had studied with at the New Theatre School. Norma Jean said nothing. The reason for her silence, I found out later, was that she didn't have the $25 down payment, much less the $50 for the six-month course. So I registered at the Lab, took classes and saw the re- hearsals of some of the finest actors in America—Ruth Nelson, Norman Lloyd, John Garfield, Luther Adler, Morris Carnovsky and Lee Cobb. The acting I saw there had nothing to do with the "acting" I was being paid to learn at Columbia Pictures. This gave me a rather schizophrenic approach to movie acting, but I hope I have since been able to resolve the conflict.

Early one morning Connie phoned me and told me to hurry over to Sam Goldwyn Studios as she wanted me to meet Harry Joe Brown, who was going to direct the film version of Kurt Weill's Broadway musical *Knickerbocker Holiday*, in which Walter Huston had introduced "September Song." I had seen the show in New York and had loved it, so I rushed over. Since Connie had told me to look as young as possible, I covered my platinum hair with a babushka and put on saddle shoes and bobby socks. I sang my all-purpose audition number, "In Chi-Chi Castenango." Mr. Brown stood me next to Connie, who was to play the lead; they were looking for someone to play her younger sister. Then he said the most complimentary words ever spoken to me: "You know . . . you do look enough like her to be her younger sister."

Mr. Brown set up a test for me for the following day. In my excitement I forgot to inform Columbia and Mr. Cohn that I was testing at another studio. When I got to the Goldwyn Studios the next morning, the first thing they did was to dye my platinum tresses back to their natural ash blonde, then make kinky curls with hot irons. Then they dressed me in a Dutch costume. I was handed a page of dialogue from which I gathered that the character was sort of the village idiot. When they yelled, "Roll 'em," I broke into a clog step and warbled "Ach du lieber Augustin," which I remembered from my childhood in St. Louis. Johnny "Scat" Davis, the male comedy lead, and I departed from the scene and broke into a wild improvisation about bundling, with me ending up with my face sticking out from under the bed. Harry Joe Brown not only gave me the part but left that scene in the picture. Connie, who had been cheering me from the sidelines, said, "I didn't know you were Dutch."

I replied coolly, "We're actresses. We're everything."

The next day they called to tell me I had the part, and I dashed over to Harry Cohn's office to let him know that I had landed the second lead in a big Sam Goldwyn musical with Charles Coburn and Nelson Eddy. Before I had a chance to open my mouth, he said, "Shut up and sit down. We've decided to get some film on you. I've cast you in *Nine Girls*." He rattled off eight girls' names— I think Nina Foch, Jeff Donnell, Adele Jergens, Myrna Dell, Earle Gailbraith, Dawn Addams, two Texas blondes and me, all playing war brides or something.

"I gotta tell you something," I began. "Now don't get upset, but I can't do that picture."

"What do you mean, you can't do the picture?" he screamed, his face red.

His Virginia heard the screaming and came running in. I explained to her what had happened. "I didn't know I wasn't supposed to test for other studios. I thought all the studios in Hollywood co-operated. I mean, I'm always reading in the trade papers about loan-outs."

Virginia, who was British and had so far survived the blitz, could stand up to Harry Cohn with complete calm. Acting as my agent, she started telling him the wonderful opportunity Sam Goldwyn was giving me and Columbia with this prized role in a big picture. As she talked, Cohn's face became redder and redder, and when she finished, she rushed over to a hidden refrigerator and got a handful of crushed ice and placed it on his face. She then handed him a couple of pills, which he promptly swallowed.

"Look, Nutsy," he sputtered, "you're far from being an idiot despite the impression you try to give. The first picture we assign you to, *Cover Girl*, you don't show up. Now you may not think that *Nine Girls* is such an important film, but I discovered you, and I want to introduce you in one of *our* films."

"You did *not* discover me," I shouted back at him. "*I* discovered me. At a Brooklyn swimming pool during a beauty contest."

He stared at me, openmouthed. Virginia broke the silence. "Mr. Cohn," she said, "I know it's a little unusual, but you know she'll get a tremendous amount of publicity if you loan her out to Goldwyn and she'll definitely come back a big star."

"What the hell's going on here?" Cohn exploded. "I thought you worked for Columbia. Since when have you become Shelley's agent?" We had the sinking feeling that we were both in danger of being fired. Abruptly he picked up the telephone and growled into it, "Get me Sam Goldwyn."

The ensuing conversation went something like this: "Listen, Sam, do I go around testing your people without your knowing it? What do you mean, who? That nutsy little blonde Shelley Winter-time, that's who. . . . I know she didn't tell you; she didn't tell me. She not only forgets she's under contract, she forgets where the studio is. She thinks it's somewhere in Shreveport, Louisiana, for Christ's sake. If you use her in your movie, you'd better assign a guard to her at all times."

Certain that he had ruined my chances to get into *Knickerbocker*

Holiday, I started to blubber. Cohn interrupted his tirade long enough to say to me, "Wipe your nose, snotnose." Virginia handed me a Kleenex. She was grinning, but I was still crying so hard that Cohn had to interrupt himself again to tell me to shut up as he couldn't hear what Goldwyn was saying. Then I heard him say, "Well, Sam, I'll do you a favor. Twenty-five thousand dollars and one of your male players. How about that new kid, Farley Granger? What do you mean, he enlisted in the Navy? What'd he do that for? Can't you get him out? Ah, they're all crazy nowadays. Who else you got? Okay, I'll take him. What do you mean, twenty-five thousand dollars is too much? We're paying her an arm and a leg. [A hundred dollars a week is a leg?] Okay, Sam, it's a deal. But don't forget you owe me a favor."

I wasn't sure what had gone on, but Virginia was smiling. Cohn looked at us for a long time, then said, "Virginia, take her and her sister out to dinner and explain to them what being under contract means."

"Mr. Cohn," I said, "does that mean I can do *Knickerbocker Holiday*?"

And he had the *chutzpah* to say, "Yeah, but it's costing me money." Then he added, "I'm really doing it to get you off my lot for three months. Sam Goldwyn can have you . . . he deserves you. Let me give you some advice, Shelley. Don't make *any* suggestions. Just do your job and don't try to help anybody. Got it?" (I never got it.)

I thanked him profusely and started out. At the door I got an idea and turned around. "Harry," I said, "at the next vacancy in your hospital could you get my sister a job there as a nurse?"

He sighed and said weakly, "I'll try."

CHAPTER 8

Blanche and I were delirious with joy. She'd suddenly become head nurse on her floor at $450 a month and a promise of a job at the Columbia Studio Hospital where, if she got into the studio union, she'd be making $600 a month. I was about to play a featured role in a big Sam Goldwyn picture, and we had a lovely apartment all *our own*. After years of old convertible sofas and the small Mexican bedroom, we felt like women of the world.

I loved the swimming pool and managed to spend as much time as I could in it. Owing to Blanche's diet menus and all the exercise, I was once again a size eight, which was just right for the little girl I was playing in *Knickerbocker Holiday*. I must have grown some after I was twenty, because I was five feet two then, and I'm five feet five now. Blanche says it's because I'm an actress, and when I need to be tall, I get tall, and when I need to be short, I shrink. And it's the same with weight and age. She kids about it, but there seems to be some truth in it.

We entertained some of the other people in the building, and once even Cary Grant and James Stewart came over after swimming for cocktails on a Saturday. Since we had only white wine and cheese, they didn't stay very long. But it was thrilling, and I wouldn't allow anyone to sit in Cary Grant's chair for weeks. Susan Hayward and her boyfriend Lex Barker invited us over to their adjoining apartments, which was very secret and scandalous in those days. We once had dinner with them and two "middle-aged" producers. I mean they were over thirty. Connie and I and all the other studio starlets entertained at the Hollywood Canteen and did USO shows at hospitals that were within driving distance. There were beginning to be a lot of them from San Francisco to San Diego.

My work on *Knickerbocker Holiday* started out with prerecording the songs, which for me was terrifying, even though I had only two short ones to do with Johnny "Scat" Davis. To prerecord then, you had to stand in a glass booth while a fifty-piece orchestra played outside, which you heard through earphones. This made my experience with Erich Wolfgang Korngold seem like kindergarten. However, the advantage of movies is that they can say, "Cut, take one

. . . take two . . . take three . . ." and then they put the good parts
together. Onstage in the theater, whatever happens, you just have
to keep on going.

As the first day of shooting approached, Connie and I both developed the jitters. After all, what did we know about New Amsterdam and Holland? We did a lot of research in the ill-equipped
Hollywood library and even went to the large one in downtown L.A.
I wanted to suggest to Mr. Cohn that I fly back to the Pennsylvania
Dutch countryside and study the people there, but Blanche said
I'd better not. After all, he'd given me permission to go only to
La Brea and Santa Monica Boulevards, where the Goldwyn Studios
were located. But the research I did then came in handy many
years later, when I played Mrs. Van Daan, the Dutch housewife,
in *The Diary of Anne Frank*, for which I won my first Academy
Award.

We started shooting *Knickerbocker Holiday*, and we all sensed
disaster from the third day. Charles Coburn was a fine actor, but
he wasn't Walter Huston. Nelson Eddy had a beautiful voice, but
he was self-conscious in this role and took on a *Chocolate Soldier*
quality. Also, he didn't want Connie to look into his eyes when they
did a scene and insisted she look at his forehead instead. The
director said it looked the same in the camera. Nothing in her training had prepared her for this unnatural way of communicating with
another actor, and it really threw her.

The logistics of the picture were extraordinary, with hundreds
of Dutch and English soldiers milling around the canals on the
set. During lunch breaks I would go rowing in the canal on the
back lot. The assistants were afraid I'd fall in and ruin my costume
and hold up production. In desperation, Harry Joe Brown gave me
an elegant star dressing room complete with shower and sofa bed.
He also had the assistants bring me a diet lunch and ordered me
to take off my costume and rest during my lunch hour.

Strange things began to happen to Blanche and me. Like dopes,
we'd listed our number in the phone book, and Blanche had a
"breather" calling at all hours, followed by a series of obscene
phone calls; since she sometimes worked in the psychiatric ward at
Cedars, it frightened her. We decided that whenever Blanche
worked the 7:00 A.M. to 3:00 P.M. shift, she would come to the
studio and wait for me, and when she worked the 3:00 P.M. to
11:00 P.M. shift, I would wait for her to pick me up at the studio.
When she worked the 11:00 P.M. to 7:00 A.M. shift, she would take
me home before going to the hospital.

One evening I was napping in my dressing room while waiting for Blanche when a key turned in the lock and the dignified Nelson Eddy stumbled into my dressing room, quite drunk, still in costume and weeping. He made straight for the bathroom and didn't seem to notice me as I sat up. It occurred to me that he thought it was his dressing room since they all looked alike. I had seen him very quiet and depressed on the set lately. He too was on loan-out (from MGM), and he knew this picture wasn't going to do him any good. He was already a big star and had the lead in the film, so he had reason to worry. And the director wasn't helping him much because of the complex logistics of the film.

Suddenly he came out of the bathroom wearing long red underwear just like my father's and muttered, "The rushes were lousier today. I think I'd better go back to the Mounties. Hey, move over." I was stunned. Up to that point in the filming he had been the very proper New England gentleman whom I had never even heard say "darn." Besides, my mother loved his pictures with Jeanette MacDonald and used to drag me to them.

I jumped out of bed, wearing one of Blanche's glamorous old hospital robes. "Mr. Eddy," I yelled, "think of your image! What would Jeanette MacDonald say?"

"Who cares? She slides off her Cs."

I made for the door as he sort of lunged for me and fell on the sofa. I slammed the door behind me and ran down the hall and out of the dressing-room building to the front gate. I stood there, cold and shoeless, shivering and frightened. The guard at the gate didn't ask any questions; he just lent me his coat and let me wait in his little shack until Blanche came to pick me up in the rickety old jalopy we'd bought. I leaped in quickly, shivering with cold and fright.

When we got home to Peyton Hall, even though it was 11:30 P.M. in California—2:30 A.M. New York time—she phoned our parents and told them that we could make our dinette into an extra bedroom and that there was a big garment center in downtown Los Angeles where my father could surely find a job—SOON. Our mother got on the phone and asked, "Are you all right? Is Shelley all right?" Blanche assured her that we were, and my mother said that they would be with us as soon as they could sell the furniture. (They made the trip from New York to California faster than our family trek from St. Louis to New York.)

I was crying by the time Blanche hung up. "Why?" I asked. "We could at least have discussed it."

She looked at me helplessly before replying. "I'm beginning to realize what a crazy town this really is. And my working hours are different from yours." Then she began to cry, too. We were two young girls who desperately needed their mother and father with them in Hollywood. Two young girls, a blonde starlet and a cute brunette young nurse, were targets, and we had just discovered that fact. That night we slept together in the same bed, having first double-locked all the doors and windows.

The next morning at six Blanche left for the hospital. Since I didn't have a work call, I waited until it was light and then took the little red streetcar to Schwab's, where I sat at the end of the counter and ordered a huge breakfast. The hell with the diet . . . I was still scared.

As I was eating, Sidney Skolsky came in with his chauffeur, Norma Jean, who about this time was thinking of changing her name to Marilyn Monroe. They sat and watched as I devoured everything in sight. Finally, Sidney said, "What's the matter, Shell? Aren't they feeding you at Goldwyn's? I thought they have a great commissary there."

As always, I told only the truth to reporters, so I said, "That's not it, Sidney. Something scary happened to me, but my mother and father are coming out in a few days to live with us. We've sent for them."

Marilyn was carefully pouring water on a curled-up straw and making it into a paper snake, then she looked at me and whispered, "Gee, I wish I had somebody to send for."

Sidney put his arms around both of us, and we went out, got into her little white jalopy and drove over to the Farmers Market to have a substantial lunch.

The filming of *Knickerbocker Holiday* went on and on, and my role extended three or four weeks over the guarantee, causing Harry Cohn to collect an extra $15,000 from Sam Goldwyn for my services. Nelson Eddy was his usual reserved, polite self and seemed not to remember the embarrassing dressing-room incident.

The day before my parents arrived from New York, Blanche received a letter from the War Department. She tore it open excitedly, and I watched as she read it. Suddenly she began to weep quietly and locked herself in our bedroom. When she finally came out late that afternoon, she told me that she had been trying to enlist in the Army Nurse Corps since Pearl Harbor, even though she had been losing her hearing in one ear and had had a fenestration operation that I hadn't been told about while I was on the road with *Meet the People*. The letter she'd gotten informed her that she had been definitely rejected by the Nurse Corps as her present job was also essential to the war effort. There was nothing I could do to comfort my darling sister who took such good care of me in every emergency and had been alone through one of the worst crises of her life. I was angry with my parents. Did they think I was some kind of idiot child or delicate flower that had to be protected from any unpleasant thing that happened just because I'd become an actress?

When my parents arrived next day, they were bewildered by my cool reception. As soon as Blanche went off to work and I was alone with them, we had a knock-down, drag-out, and for the first time I really told my father off. They didn't answer. Then I got frightened. In the two years I had been away from them they had gotten much older, or so it seemed. In a calm voice—a first for him—my father explained that it was Blanche's wish and that Uncle Al in St. Louis was also losing his hearing, that it seemed to be a congenital thing with the Winter family. I apologized for behaving like a brat and kissed and hugged them both and welcomed them properly.

We then went out and bought a double bed and a small dresser, setting them up in the dinette, which had louvered doors, and put the dining table in the living room. My parents insisted that the dinette would be their room, and Blanche and I would stay in the bedroom, and when Paul came home, he and I would use that and Blanche would sleep on the couch in the living room until Paul and I could get our own place.

Throughout that entire year I wrote to Paul every day, although I hate writing letters. I carefully printed my V-mail letters and mailed them off every morning from the studio post office. His letters in return often described air battles which he made sound like firework displays. He tried to convince me that he was always covered by fighter plane escort and nothing he was doing was particularly dangerous. I almost believed him until I began talking to Army Air Force men at the Hollywood Canteen who had been over there already.

My father immediately got a very good job with the Peerless Pants Company in downtown Los Angeles. But he loved to sit around the pool after work and on weekends, and play gin rummy and discuss with the agents and out-of-work producers their big deals for after the war.

My mother found some transplanted friends from St. Louis and joined Mah-Jongg and poker clubs. I've always felt that my greatest mistake was not giving my mother $5,000 and turning her loose in Las Vegas. We'd have all ended up billionaires. When you played gin rummy with my mother, she knew exactly what cards you held after you played the first two. She was a whiz at math and had a fantastic memory. This talent skipped my generation completely. I believe my daughter has it.

Early one morning there was a knock on the door, and I opened it to find a darkly handsome young sailor with a seabag at his side. He grinned and his dark eyes flashed. "My name's Bernie Schwarz," he introduced himself. "My mother knows your Aunt Fanny in the Bronx, and she said you should take care of me until I get settled." I invited him in, and he stowed his seabag under the couch, proudly informing me that he was under contract to Universal for $75 a week and had recently been discharged from the Navy, where he'd served as a speed typist and gunner when he couldn't avoid it. Bernie was nineteen. He was eager and sweet, completely without guile and totally starstruck. He also had one of the worst Bronx accents I've ever heard. We became very good buddies, but Blanche and my father never stopped warning me that Paul would be furious if he came home and found Bernie in the house. Yet nothing could have been more platonic, and I, like an older sister, kept fixing him up with dates with young actresses like Ann Blyth, Piper Laurie and Janet Leigh, whom he eventually married.

The Sycamore House was a wonderful, enormous old boarding-house in Hollywood where many of my fellow actors from New York were living. They shared, two to a room, and got breakfast and dinner, for $8 a week; everyone pitched in and helped around the house. They also had a little theater—a small stage and fifty seats—up in the attic, where the young writers who lived there could try out scenes from their plays, the young actors could act in them and the young directors could direct. Joseph Papp was one of the residents. It was great fun and wonderful experience. I managed to get Bernie Schwarz's name on the waiting list, and they promised to give him the first vacancy. After all, he was an ex-fighting man and a New Yorker and, more important, he had a steady income. Meanwhile, Bernie took speech lessons, slept on our living-room couch and typed the scripts I was writing and acting in at the Actors Lab and the little theater in the Sycamore House, as well as the lousy drama class at Columbia.

Universal appreciated Bernie's dark good looks and soon assigned him to *The Prince Who Was a Thief*, a Technicolor epic with Piper Laurie, to be directed by Rudy Maté, a well-known cameraman. Bernie was very nervous on the first day, so I went on the set with him for moral support. The first words he uttered on the screen have since become a sort of classic. As this darkly handsome muscular young Arab prince takes the lovely Piper Laurie in his arms, he points beyond the camera and says, "Yonder lies da castle of my fadder, de Prince."

"Cut!" Rudy Maté yelled, and with a dazed look in his eyes asked in his thick Hungarian accent, "Bernie, is dat how you alvays talk?"

"Sure. And you don't talk so hot yourself."

I jumped quickly into the fray. "Look around the set, Mr. Maté. Everyone is laughing hysterically. If you do the picture straight, it'll turn out to be just another Cornel Wilde-Yvonne De Carlo Persian B picture. But if you let Bernie talk like he does naturally, you'll have a hilarious comedy."

Maté looked at me closely. "Who are you, kid? His agent?"

"No, I'm an actress at another studio. But my aunt knows his mother and his family is Hungarian, same as you."

Maté thought all this over for a minute. "Well, this is only my sixth picture as a director, so if it doesn't turn out, I can always go back to being a cameraman. We'll shoot it like you suggest, and the bosses can decide tomorrow when they see the rushes." The bosses' decision was to continue with the Bronx Prince, and the picture was a huge comedy success.

That night at dinner I started in on him about his name. "You can't be a movie star with the name Bernie Schwarz."

And my mother pitched in with "Why don't you use your mother's maiden name like Shelley did?" After much prodding, he finally gave in, and in that picture his billing was Bernie Curtiz. In the following one he was Bernie Curtis, then he finally gave in to the studio's demand that if he expected to become a leading man, he would have to be Tony Curtis. "Bernies," he was told, were comedians.

He finally got off our living-room couch and moved into the Sycamore House. A week later I received a V-mail letter from Paul informing me that he'd be coming home soon. I had returned to Columbia, but directors weren't beating at Harry Cohn's door to get me in their pictures. The roles I could have done were given to Jean Arthur, and no matter how they tried, the studio departments could never fit me into their mold of the Sex Goddess. I always came out funny. The holidays were approaching, and still no Paul.

It was an accepted fact in Hollywood at that time that Sam Spiegel gave the definitive New Year's Eve party. That meant that if you weren't invited to his party, your entire coming year was ruined as far as your status in the industry was concerned. I received a call from Mr. Spiegel's secretary a couple of weeks before the end of December, inviting me to his famous party, I suspect, at Connie's urging. I explained to the secretary that my husband was still not home from bombing, so I had no one to take me. She explained that Rita Hayworth was legally separated from Orson Welles, and she too had no escort, so the studio limousine that would pick her up would do the same for me.

"It will?"

I was notified by the studio that starting January 5 I would be one of six harem girls in *A Thousand and One Nights*, starring Cornel Wilde and Evelyn Keyes. I think Max Arnow hoped I would turn it down and go on suspension. But I had just bought a pretty little red Pontiac convertible, secondhand, of course, and I had to make the goddamned payments, so I said okay.

Blanche, my father and the California Driving School all tried, but I had to take the test four times before the motor vehicle examiner said to me, "Try to get other people to drive you around as much as possible, Miss Winter. And concentrate while driving, if you must drive." I swore on the flag that I would, and he reluctantly gave me a license.

After a rather lonely Christmas I went to the studio and borrowed a dress from Jean Louis to wear to Sam Spiegel's fancy New Year's Eve party. The studio Publicity Department was very impressed— and nervous—that I was going with Rita Hayworth.

She was in Wardrobe the day I picked out my dress and made me choose something white and pastel and strapless. A very sweet, expensive dress. And she suggested I wear with it a priceless white authentic Spanish shawl, something she'd worn in a film. I resented it a little because I wanted to look like a *femme fatale*, but I knew she was right. *Femmes fatales* were a dime a dozen in Hollywood that year. "Listen, honey," Rita told me, "don't wear too much makeup. And leave your hair the color it is [it was still ash blonde from *Knickerbocker Holiday*], and all the directors in town will be falling all over you."

"For parts?"

She laughed. "Eat something before you go, like Scarlett O'Hara. Because there'll be lots of champagne and the food won't be served until after midnight." She seemed to be having more fun getting me ready for the party than going to it herself.

While we were playing dress-up, Harry Cohn came in with his entourage. For some reason he couldn't stand to see Rita Hayworth enjoying herself. He said something mean about Orson Welles and how lucky she was to be getting rid of him.

"What do you mean, Harry?" I said. "He's an intellectual giant."

"How would you know, Nutsy?"

"Well, when my sister was a student nurse, there were many casualties in her hospital from his *War of the Worlds* broadcast. It was so powerful."

"Christ, don't start in again with your sister. I almost had a strike on my hands when I tried to get her into the union. The nurses in the studio hospitals all have to be wives or mothers of the union officials. And I think it's *my* studio!"

Rita, getting a little guts, said, "Harry, next year we'll run you a benefit."

Cohn glared at her. "So you're becoming a wiseass like her." Rita stopped smiling. Everybody stopped smiling. He went on. "Now listen, Rita. I want you to look gorgeous New Year's Eve because they're planning a very important picture at Fox, and I want them to borrow you again. You've been gone so long having that smart bastard's baby that I want you to come back to the public in something great."

"Yes, Mr. Cohn. Of course, Mr. Cohn."

"Do you want me to take you?" he offered. "My wife's in her eighth month and doesn't want to go out."

"No, thank you, Mr. Cohn. Shelley's taking me."

He gave us a funny look. "Christ. Brooklyn meets Tijuana. They're going to say you're a couple of leses."

Rita, looking right at him, said, "Well, with what's around in the Man Department lately, we could do a lot worse."

I immediately broke into song. "They're either too young or too old . . . what's good is in the Army . . . what's left can never harm me. . . ."

Cohn interrupted and, turning to Jean Louis, said, "See that she wears something fantastic. We have a big investment in her." (I didn't think he meant me.) Then he walked out with his big cigar in front and his entourage behind.

All the joy had gone out of Rita's face. I said, "You want to go with me to Lucey's for lunch? Then afterwards we can go swimming in my pool. It'll be fun." In those days it used to be hot enough in Los Angeles at Christmastime to swim. What happened?

She shook her head sadly and said, "I think I'm too old to have fun anymore, Shelley."

"You're younger than my sister," I protested, "and she's still a kid."

She kissed me on the cheek and murmured, "I got old at twelve, dancing every night in nightclubs with my father."

New Year's Eve arrived, and I began getting myself dressed up. I envied Blanche, who had a date with a handsome art dealer to go to a wonderful party at Zarape's, where the young Mexican kids danced just great. My mother and father were going to a poker party at Moki's apartment—Charles Vidor's mother—on the other side of Peyton Hall. They left before I did, and I sat there all dressed up, alone. My mother hadn't prepared dinner because they were going to eat at their respective parties; I tried to eat a dry cheese sandwich but couldn't manage it. I wondered where Paul was and why he hadn't at least wired me. I was immediately angry with myself; I was so grateful that he was still alive and unharmed.

The limousine arrived, and I draped the priceless white fringed silk shawl carefully around my shoulders. We drove to Beverly Hills, where we picked up Rita. She looked as gorgeous as Harry Cohn wanted her to. Sitting beside me in the limousine, this beautiful sex goddess, whom millions of servicemen worshiped, said, "God, I hate holidays. I think they're the lonesomest times of the year." I reached for her hand and held it while lonely tears ran down our cheeks. We blotted carefully, so as not to mess our makeup.

Sam Spiegel's house had floodlights and flashbulbs all over the place, and a pair of handsome Columbia male contract players materialized out of the woodwork to escort us inside so it wouldn't look as if we didn't have dates, which at that time was the cardinal social crime in Hollywood. This made me mad—suppose Paul somehow saw the pictures.

We got inside and joined hundreds of people, the women loaded with jewels and furs, and Rita was immediately surrounded and disappeared. I couldn't find Connie any place, so I took a glass of champagne from a passing waiter and sat in the corner of a huge living room. I didn't even know what our host Sam Spiegel looked like. I must have sat there for nearly an hour. I was starving. I noticed a tall, very skinny man sitting about half a block away.

Suddenly I looked up, and he was standing over me. "Miss Winter, can I get you something? You look a little lost."

"I'm not lost," I told him, "but big crowds always make me feel lonesome."

"Me too," he said. He introduced himself, but there was so much noise all I heard was "Hugh something."

"I'm so hungry," I said. "When do you think they'll serve the food?"

He smiled. "I bet I can get us some advance snacks."

As he disappeared, I noticed he had on white tennis shoes, and I thought, Jesus, the poor guy must have borrowed someone's tuxedo, because it did look rather old and shiny. It occurred to me that he was a set decorator (they are always tall and lanky so they can reach up into the storage bins) and had crashed the party. But then again, so had I, in a way.

Fifteen minutes later he returned accompanied by a butler carrying a large tray and two plates filled with wonderful food. The butler served us cracked crab with mustard sauce, Caesar salad, very rare roast beef, puffed-up square fried potatoes with air inside and hearts of palm. I had never seen any of these foods before and wondered how they got the hearts out of the palm trees.

Nevertheless, I started eating everything in sight. When I came up for air, I noticed that the nice tall man was just playing with his food. He seemed to be more interested in watching me eat. The party was strangely quiet, and I noticed all eyes riveted, I thought, on me. I was so embarrassed I almost stopped eating. I finished the food on my plate, then, at Hugh's insistence, started on his. The dessert, when it arrived, was nectar and ambrosia.

The stays in my dress were suddenly so tight I couldn't bear them. I whispered in my new friend's ear, "Could you please unzip the back of my dress? Under my shawl so no one will notice. I've eaten so much I can't breathe."

He obliged, and the other hundred people in the room pretended they weren't watching. He was doing pretty well with the zipper until the fringe of the shawl got caught in it. I held Columbia's priceless shawl over my head while Hugh tried to untangle it. I peeked out as our host Sam Spiegel turned up to introduce himself, Connie on his arm, looking at me in a very strange way. I tried to explain what had happened; Connie whispered that I should go to the powder room and not have it fixed in public.

But Hugh held me fast. "I'm enjoying this. I've had many mechanical problems to deal with, but this is one of the most fascinating."

I remembered my mother used candle wax when the zippers on my costumes got stuck. Connie, making peculiar signals to me, whispered, "Who knows? Maybe he has an oil can in his car."

"Be quiet," Hugh ordered. "I'm concentrating."

At exactly midnight he got it untangled, and I threw my arms around his neck and gave him a kiss. He blushed. "You're very handy with your hands," I told him, and sang him a little song left over from my New York days: "My boyfriend's mechanically inclined, he'd rather use his hands than sit and talk. Like mess around with my motor or parts. Anything on wheels."

After about three or four choruses of this double entendre gem, with Hugh laughing a great deal, he asked, "Did you make that up?"

"No," I replied, "it's left over from my Borscht Circuit days." That confused him.

Connie and I excused ourselves and went off in search of the powder room. Hugh assured me that he would wait right there for me. After much wandering around and getting nothing but wrong information from famous stars now drunk, we finally found a beautiful bedroom that had been assigned as the ladies' lounge. Ava Gardner was sitting in a corner, waiting for the time when she could decently go home. Connie said she would leave with her. I thought how ironic it was that two of the most beautiful girls in Hollywood were so sad on New Year's Eve. I asked Ava if she'd seen Rita Hayworth, and she pointed over to the bed piled high with fur coats.

"She's over there," she told me. "She was so lonely and bored she fell asleep. I covered her with the coats so no one will disturb her. When she wakes up, we'll all sneak out the back door and get a limousine to take us home." I went over to the bed to make sure Rita wasn't smothering or hadn't torn her beautiful studio dress. She hadn't, but her hair and face were a mess. She'd been weeping. I carefully covered her up.

As Connie fixed my zipper with safety pins, two gorgeous girls we didn't recognize came into the room, one with long red hair, the other with long blonde hair. They were wearing fantastic designer gowns and were covered with real jewels and sables. We three starlets couldn't keep our eyes off them and were dying with curiosity. Ava asked the redhead, "Haven't I seen you before, dear? Where are you under contract?"

The girl adjusted her diamond necklace, tossed her sable cape unknowingly over Rita and replied, "You're Ava Gardner, aren't you?" Ava nodded. Then the redhead looked at Connie and me. "And you two are new stars, right?" We both happily admitted it.

Then the blonde spoke up. "We've seen your movies on the private executive screening-room circuit. Hey," she said to me, "you're real funny."

Ava couldn't stand it. "Where are you two under contract?" she persisted.

The gorgeous redhead looked at us condescendingly. "Don't be silly. You couldn't catch me getting up at five in the morning to slave at a studio like you girls do for a couple of hundred dollars a week. I'm a call girl." She didn't seem to notice our astonished reaction. "As soon as I get my sixth apartment house, I'm retiring. At twenty-five." With that, she exited. (Sam Spiegel, I heard later, always supplied a couple of dozen beautiful call girls at his New Year's Eve parties for the guys who were still alone.)

The blonde indicated the departing redhead. "I don't do as well as Jackie," she said in a husky voice, "because I'm an important director's private property. He lets me work only when he's on location. But I have the penthouse apartment at the Sunset Towers with my own sauna and a great masseuse. I'd love to have you girls come over when you're not working and use the facilities. I'm alone a lot."

Connie looked strange, then said, "I think we're in the wrong business, kids," and we all started to laugh hysterically. Maybe we really wanted to cry. The blonde's name was Betty, a tall, lovely Swede. I promised to come visit her with my sister. I wasn't exactly sure what a call girl was.

As I sat down at the dressing table and began fixing my hair, Ava said, "I'm glad you took Howard Hughes off my hands, Shelley. He really keeps his women in isolation."

"I did *what?*"

"The only problem is," she went on, ignoring my interruption, "he gave me a new car for Christmas, and something was wrong with it. So I took it out to Hughes Aircraft at his suggestion to have it fixed. When I went to pick it up, I drove it about two miles, and the engine fell out. He had it wired, the son of a bitch. I thought he would be furious when I forced him to bring me tonight and then I ditched him to get even. But he obviously thinks you're so cute that I don't think he's noticed."

Connie got very angry. "What is she talking about, Shelley? You don't need that kind of crap."

"I don't know what either of you are talking about," I replied.

"That nice set decorator and I just had dinner together because I was a wallflower and he was alone, too. The poor guy doesn't even own a pair of shoes. He's wearing his tennis sneakers, for God's sake."

"Honey," Betty said, "that 'poor guy' is Howard Hughes."

"And he's no set decorator," Ava added. "He's a millionaire many times over. Everyone at the party is talking about what a fancy he's taken to you."

Betty shook my hand. "What a score, kiddo. Play your cards right and you'll never have to worry for the rest of your life."

I was furious and jumped onto the bed, no doubt stepping on Rita, and yelled, "Now you girls listen to me. I'm the wife of a war hero who was just made a captain and whom I love very much. He'll be home soon, and I have no interest in playing gin rummy or doing anything with any millionaires."

I jumped off the bed and made a stormy but dignified exit that was spoiled by my having to come back to retrieve the damn shawl. It covered up the pins.

I made my way back to where Mr. Hughes was waiting and sat down beside him, keeping my distance. I gave him a very dirty look, and he asked what was wrong. "Are you a millionaire?" I accused him. "Many times over?"

"Well . . ." he said slowly, "that's a slight exaggeration." Then he took the wind completely out of my sails by adding, "But I do make airplanes like your husband is flying, and I've improved them with new ones. They're safer, faster and more effective."

There was nothing left for me to say. I'd never met a multimillionaire before, so all I could manage was: "Why do you wear sneakers?"

"My feet hurt when I wear shoes," he explained. "When you're as tall as I am, it's very hard on your feet."

"Oh."

"Have you had enough of the party yet?" he asked. I nodded. "Would you like me to take you home now?"

"Sure, if it's not too much trouble. But you know," I added meaningfully, "I'm married to a war hero."

"Everyone in Hollywood knows that," he said. "And you're very patriotic and faithful as well."

"Okay," I said with relief.

We left the party together, thanking our host, Mr. Spiegel, as we went. I expected to be taken home in a limousine, but instead, we walked right past the car valets and halfway up the block until we came to a scratched-up little green Ford, circa 1938. As he opened the door for me, Sidney Sheldon, who was then a screenwriter at Columbia and whom I barely knew, came bounding up to us like a posse in a western. He pulled me back and exclaimed very bravely, "*I'll* see that Shelley gets home, Mr. Hughes."

Hughes smiled and said, "Okay."

I was furious with Sidney for his misplaced protectiveness. Hughes turned to me. "Would you like to go to a movie with me sometime and perhaps have a Japanese dinner?"

"I'd love to, Mr. Hughes."

With that, he got into his old green Ford and it roared away. What an engine! I was so mad at Sidney Sheldon I could have killed him. We got into his lousy rented limousine, and all the way back to Peyton Hall he regaled me with horrible stories about Howard Hughes's sex life. I told him, "Sidney, why don't you put all these sexy stories in a script? I think it's nothing but a lot of malicious gossip. Mr. Hughes is a nice man, and he can't help it if he's a capitalist [where was Shirley Schrift, heroine of the working class?] any more than you can help your vivid imagination. And besides, he builds great airplanes."

At about three o'clock on New Year's Day the phone rang, and a man by the name of Johnny Meyers informed me that Mr. Hughes would like to take me to a movie and dinner that evening. I asked why he didn't call me himself.

"Mr. Hughes doesn't like to talk on the telephone."

"He doesn't?" I exclaimed in surprise. "I love it." Mr. Meyers asked me if I could be ready at six. "What time's the movie?" I inquired.

"Whenever you get there." Then he hung up.

The doorbell rang at six sharp, and Howard Hughes came in. He was dressed in a tweed jacket with leather patches on the elbows, a sports shirt, no tie, baggy old slacks and his tennis sneakers. I introduced him to my mother and father without going into who he was as I still wasn't exactly too sure myself. My father immediately got into an argument with him about some congressional investigations, then suggested that he come down to the Peerless Pants Company, where he could get him a new jacket wholesale. One without patches on the elbows. Later Hughes did just that. Plus a few pairs of slacks. Of course he didn't come himself; he sent Johnny Meyers. Regularly. My father told me the jacket cost $36, and the slacks $12 each, and they were tall man's sizes.

We drove to the beach and stopped at Roland's, a narrow, empty restaurant under a stone bridge on the Pacific Coast Highway, which I've never seen open, before or since. It was there that Hughes took me for a Japanese dinner, and we were served by a Japanese waiter. "But aren't all the Japanese in those relocation camps?" I whispered to Mr. Hughes.

"Almost all," he replied with a smile, "but for you the government let a few out."

We sat in a small dusty red velvet booth, and I figured that the reason there were no other diners was that it was New Year's Day and everyone else must be sleeping it off. Hughes began to talk about films, and he certainly knew what he was talking about. He asked about my career, and I told him that I was about to start a ridiculous picture in which I had to play one of six harem girls.

"It's strange," he murmured, "that Harry Cohn was smart enough to sign you, but isn't smart enough to use you properly."

"Are you in the movie business, too?" I asked.

"I used to be."

"And you switched to *airplanes?*"

He laughed. "That among other things. But after the war I'll probably return to the film industry in some way."

We finished our strange Japanese dinner, though I didn't eat much of the raw fish, and got back into the green Ford. We drove to some small movie house in Santa Monica with a marquee that read CLOSED FOR THE DURATION, but we went in anyway. Hughes waved his arm to a man's head sticking out of the projection booth, and a film I'd never seen before called *Hell's Angels* started. Howard Hughes was listed as the director, and only a part of it was in sound. Jean Harlow was the star, and she was fantastic. It was about a girl who was in love with a flier in the First World War, and I cried so hard during the last part that Hughes had to give me his immaculate white handkerchief.

"Are you the Howard Hughes who directed that film?" I asked as we got back in the car.

"Yes."

"And you haven't directed anything since?"

"No."

"You must not have a good agent. I know a very good director's agent at William Morris who lives at Peyton Hall. Do you want me to talk to him?" He laughed and shook his head. He asked me what I thought of the picture, and I told him I thought it was wonderful, especially Jean Harlow.

"You're the closest thing to her I've ever seen," he said quietly.

"Thank you," I replied. "She died, didn't she?"

He just nodded. "Yes. She was only twenty-six. When the war is over, I just might remake that picture and change it to the Second World War. And you'll do Jean Harlow's role."

"I don't think I'm as beautiful as she was," I said faintly. "But I know I could act it. You'll have to ask Mr. Cohn if you can borrow me."

"If he gives us any problems, we'll just buy his studio. He's in trouble with his stockholders now, and television will probably finish him off." He paused, then added, "Jean had a little wide nose just like yours."

"Honest?"

"Cross my heart," he replied. "You didn't enjoy the Japanese dinner very much, did you?"

"Not terrifically."

"You must be hungry. Would you care to come up to my house and have a turkey sandwich? My houseboy is still awake. And I have a pool in my living room if you'd like to take a dip."

"You have a *what*? Aren't you afraid one of your family or friends might get drunk and fall in and drown?"

His answer really clobbered me. "I don't have any family or friends."

"Hugh, don't be silly. Everybody's got friends."

"I suppose so." He smiled. "I have TWA."

Anyway, I explained to him that I had to get home early as I had to be a harem girl the next morning. At my door he shook my hand. I felt a little strange, as if something had happened and I hadn't noticed it. After the war Hughes bought RKO Studios and made Jerry Wald head of production. Hughes worked only at night; no one ever saw him during the day. And to my knowledge he never again went to another big Hollywood party.

One warm spring day I heard over the radio that Franklin Delano Roosevelt was dead. It was as though my own youth had died with him. He'd served three terms, and I truly couldn't remember any other President before him. One of my earliest memories was Roosevelt's fireside chats. I could hear in his voice true concern for the poor people of this country. Sometimes he seemed to be talking to me personally, like "The only thing we have to fear is fear itself."

During the time I was in grammar school in Brooklyn and hot lunches were unexpectedly served to us as part of the NRA program, we were told that Mrs. Eleanor Roosevelt had arranged it.

I thought she was actually in the school kitchen preparing the food. On cold winter days when my mother was working, that hot soup, meat and vegetables and hot chocolate tasted marvelous. A character in *Born Yesterday* says, "My father's political philosophy is that everybody in the world should have a hot lunch." I personally believe that should be the basis of the United Nations.

On that day I heard that President Roosevelt had died I was beyond grief. I wandered out to the pool area, where several men were playing gin rummy. I shouted at them, as though it were their fault, that Roosevelt had just died, but they didn't stop their playing. I swear that if I'd had a machine gun, I would have mowed them down. I ran back into my apartment and wept on my pillow with the gnawing fear that maybe winning the war wouldn't end the power of all the bad people as I had believed it would. I couldn't bear it.

A Thousand and One Nights started, not with a bang but with a whimper. Every morning at four-thirty we six harem girls had to report to Makeup, where they washed and set our hair. Mine they made a sort of pinkish platinum. Very Persian! This was followed by two hours of face and body makeup; then we'd put on gorgeous harem pants and bras, as nude as the Hays Office would allow. Then they'd *cover up* our hair and faces with veils so only our eyes showed. Typical. We wore shoes with points that curled up in front, making it very difficult to walk. All my years in Hollywood it seems I always have trouble with their expensive shoes. I guess my feet have an A. S. Beck last.

Helen Hunt was taking care of me personally; that really scared me as I realized that nearly everybody now believed I was Howard Hughes's girlfriend. The truth is I didn't see him again for years. I was even assigned a star's dressing room at Columbia which I refused. I was afraid Harry Cohn might have the key. I kept my little contract player's closet.

Every morning at eight o'clock we'd go tripping over to the stage —and I *do* mean tripping—bundled up in our oldest overcoats because we didn't want to ruin our good coats with the body makeup. Day after day we were draped around Cornel Wilde or Phil Silvers like scenery and never got to say or sing a word. Once during a take Phil Silvers put his hand on my head and said, "Oh, beautiful one, where doest thou cometh from?" I couldn't help replying, "Yonder lies de castle of my fadder, the Prince." The director yelled, "Cut!" and Phil said, "Listen, kiddo, I'm the comedian on this picture."

"Oh, yeah? Some day you'll find out I can be funny, too."

"You wanna bet?"

Of course, Phil is a marvelous comedian, and many years later we did a film in Italy called *Buona Sera, Mrs. Campbell.* We played husband and wife with three sons and got wonderful reviews. We really were a great comedy team. Of course, I reminded him of those *Thousand and One Nights.*

When that film was on about its nine hundredth night, I was just getting to bed one night when the phone rang. It was CAPTAIN PAUL MILLER, and he was calling from Chicago. As I talked with him, I wept with happiness. He did, too. He'd just been flown from England and was visiting his mother for two days, and then he would take the train to Los Angeles because he couldn't get a priority seat for air travel. He would meet me at the L.A. station in three and a half days and he would stay with me until he was assigned to the Pacific theater. Then he said something very funny—not funny ha-ha—"Are you tired of this acting nonsense yet?"

"They haven't really given me anything to act yet."

He laughed. "You should let your mother be your agent." He whispered, "I love you," and hung up.

The next three days seemed like months. On the day he was arriving I went to the studio as usual, got my hair and makeup all done and, without telling the assistant director, I left at lunchtime and drove my little red Pontiac to the Los Angeles railroad station. I never again did such a thing while filming.

I parked in a no-parking zone and ran to the platform where the Super Chief would come in. I was wearing a blue suit with padded shoulders, white ruffled blouse, dark net stockings and my pink platinum hair piled on top of my head. When the Super Chief finally arrived, I ran up and down the platform, looking for him. No Paul. I ran back to the first car and asked the conductor if an Air Force captain had gotten off in Pasadena. "No, ma'am."

All the passengers had left the platform by then, and far down at the other end I saw what looked like a rather stooped old man in officer's pinks coming toward me. We stopped about ten yards from each other. He dropped his suitcases and said, "My God, it's Betty Grable."

I recognized his voice, and despite the gray hair and lined, weather-beaten face, I knew it was my husband, safe at last. "Paul? Captain Paul Miller?"

"Shirley? Mrs. Shirley Miller?"

We crossed the interminable years, and he took me in his arms and kissed me. We both were shaking and crying. I said something dumb like: "See, you didn't get killed like you thought you were going to." And he said, "And you didn't become a movie star like you said you were going to, although you sure look like one."

He picked up his suitcases, and we went out to my little red Pontiac, which by now had a ticket on it. Paul looked at it and said, "Give me the keys. They really gave *you* a license?"

"Of course, I have a license. I drive slowly and stay on the right."

"Ain't that a pistol! Well, I've always heard California was a careless state. They really gave you a license, huh?" We were both making jokes, trying not to be so nervous. Then we both grew silent as he drove up Sunset Boulevard. I kept peeking at him. He had taken off his officer's cap, and his hair was still brown on top. He looked more familiar now.

In a flash, I knew that this was a man who was really tougher than Harry Cohn and Howard Hughes put together. And with a sinking heart I also knew he was not about to let me decide where he should work or that we would live in a rose-covered cottage in the Hollywood Hills. And in no way would he let me run around Hollywood trying to be a "Movie Star" while he became "Mr. Winter."

CHAPTER 9

My parents greeted Paul with open arms and pride. They immediately insisted on showing him the pool. My mother decided that Paul was about thirty pounds underweight and started cooking up a storm at every dinner. The arrangements were that Paul and I would take the bedroom, and Blanche went to stay with my new friend Betty who had the penthouse at the Sunset Towers.

Paul asked suspiciously, "Shirley, who the hell is Betty?"

Blushing, I replied, "Well, she's sort of a struggling actress, but she has this penthouse, tax-free."

"I bet. Listen, we're moving to a hotel, and Blanche can have her bedroom," he informed me. Suddenly I was A Private?

For some odd reason, even though I had a license and had been driving for almost a year, he insisted on giving me driving lessons. Paul was very different—silent now. He wouldn't tell me where he'd been or whom he'd bombed during his eighty missions. All I knew was he had his captain's bars and had returned home for rest and recreation—I was the party of the second part.

One night Paul took me to Ciro's with a fellow officer from Chicago, Major Walters, and his new wife. They gave us a front table. After all, I was a starlet, and Paul a returning war hero. The Hollywood photographers popped flashbulbs at us and indulged their favorite sport by asking Paul things like: "By the way, what's *your* name, Captain?" The first couple of times Paul laughed and answered, "Captain Winter." After that: "Shove off."

Paul wanted to jitterbug, so I finally did, but first I had to take off my beautiful three-inch heels. These were a special kind of sandal—tied in front with a bow—that Marilyn and I used to "borrow" from the studio. Giggling, we called them our "fuck-me shoes." They really were the sexiest shoes I've ever seen. Whenever we did pinup photos for the soldiers, we wore them.

I'd had enough champagne to dance barefooted with abandon, and Paul—somewhere over the English Channel no doubt—had somehow become an expert jitterbugger. At one point during our routine he threw me over his back, and suddenly I realized *we* had become the floor show. The spotlight was on us, and Ray Sinatra's band was grooving.

When we returned to the table, we were laughing and happy, and Major Walters said to Paul, "See, you could get to like Hollywood. We could join Hillcrest Country Club, which has a great course, and they have poker games for thousands of dollars. With your mathematical know-how you could make a killing just playing poker."

Paul froze. "There are certain business things I don't expect you to discuss in front of my wife." Lamely he added, "Besides, I've played enough poker in the Army to last me the rest of my life."

I caught on. "Paul, does your friend want you to go into a business partnership with him out here in California?"

Silence. "Darling, I can't make any plans," he explained. "There's still a war going on. If Doolittle goes back to the Pacific, he's going to want me to be his navigator again."

I started to cry right there in front of God and all the columnists. He said, "Come on, don't be silly. Our country's still at war. Soon I'll get to be a major, maybe a lieutenant colonel."

"What the hell's going on here? Are you going to be a professional soldier and stay in the Army all your life?" I screamed.

"Are you going to be a goddamned extra all your life and stand in back of the star, and maybe they give you four lousy lines and you call it a career?"

I stopped crying and stared at him, as everyone else at Ciro's was doing. The major quickly asked for the check, but his wife didn't want to go home; she was having a great time looking at all the movie stars.

"I think it's a good idea before they kill each other," whispered the waiter, presenting the check. "We try to avoid blood on the floor here as much as possible."

Certain moments in life are remembered forever. Those few minutes that we stood in front of Ciro's and waited for the car was one. There seemed to be no more stars in the Hollywood sky. I was holding my silly sandals and feeling very cold. Paul put my little silver fox jacket around my shoulders. He didn't seem so tired and old anymore; even his gray hair seemed to have gotten browner. And there was something new about him, something tough and immovable.

But in bed that night he held me and spoke of the war for the first time. "Shirley, when you're over the target, you drop the bombs. You know they'll kill hundreds of people, maybe thousands. You get sick to your stomach because you may be destroying good people like resistance fighters, along with the ammunition dumps and military targets. It's the same in life. You just have to do what you have to do. Bombs away."

I understood but had no answer. We fell asleep in each other's arms. The next day I told him I was going to the studio, but instead, I went to Griffith Park and sat under a tree and took stock of my life. In some mysterious way, the decision was out of my hands.

I really had no choice. I didn't want the money so much; I didn't need the fame. They are the results if your work is good. But I had to perform. There was no other way I could live. I didn't care so much about living in Hollywood. I really wanted to go back to New York. But I didn't want to go back a failure. I had to do one important film before I could face my teachers and fellow actors. I wanted Paul, and I wanted a baby. Why couldn't he at least bend a little and consider living in New York? He couldn't, I knew . . . he loved Chicago, his job, his friends and his family.

When I returned to the hotel, there was a message from the studio. Mr. Arnow expected me in his office the next day at eleven. When Paul got back from his eternal golf, I told him I was nervous about seeing Arnow alone. He said, "You mean all this time you never got yourself an agent?"

"I still only get half my salary, and if I paid an agent ten percent, I'd be left with practically nothing."

He laughed and said, "Maybe you should have joined the WACS. You'd have made more money." He gave me a kiss and decided we'd both go to Max Arnow's office tomorrow. "He'd better be polite to you," Paul said. "I'll wear my gun."

The next day I dressed and made myself up to resemble Rita Hayworth as much as possible. Paul watched me put on my heavy false eyelashes and asked, "Didn't they ever let you look like *you* in a picture?"

This confused me, and I replied, "After all, Paul, these big shots must know what the public wants. My hair's too kinky, my eyes slant the wrong way, my nose is too wide, my lips are too thin, my shoulders are too broad, my hips are too big and my legs are too skinny. So with their Hollywood magic, they correct all these things."

Paul said, "Yeah, I know. But it doesn't look like you when they finish. Maybe if they let you look like you, the public would like Shirley Schrift."

"Don't be silly. Nobody ever liked her. Except you."

We arrived at Max Arnow's office promptly at eleven o'clock, and his Virginia was thrilled to meet Paul. She gave us coffee, and we waited until eleven-thirty. Paul stood up and said, "Shirley, let's go."

"What?" I whispered.

And Virginia said, "Captain Miller, I'm sure he'll be out in a second."

Paul replied, "Well, Shirley has no more time today. She has to go see a producer at MGM." And he pushed me toward the door.

Virginia must have pressed a secret button at that point because Max Arnow came barreling out of his office. He apologized to Paul —not to me—for making us wait. In his office Paul spotted the racing form on Mr. Arnow's desk and nailed him with: "Who do you like at Hollywood Park today?" Arnow blushed—he'd obviously been talking to his bookie while he kept us waiting.

Paul immediately said, "You people have seen to it that Shelley has had no agent during the year she has been here, so as her husband I've decided to help her with whatever new problem she has at this *little* studio."

"What?" The veins stood out on Max Arnow's forehead. I was scared to death but enjoying it.

He then said, "In that case, Captain, I'm going to be very truthful with both of you. We think we've given Shelley a fair trial, and it's cost us a lot of money to train her."

"You mean the forty thousand dollars you got from Sam Goldwyn didn't cover her training?"

"Captain, this isn't the Army, so *you* listen to *me*. I'm head of the Casting Department here. We've given Shelley some training and quite a lot of publicity."

"And some crappy little parts that nobody could do anything with."

"Listen, *do you* or *do you not* want her to go back to Chicago with you, schmuck?"

Paul started to laugh, and I didn't know what the hell was going on. Arnow tried again. "The board of directors of Columbia, Mr. Cohn and I feel we've given Shelley a fair trial." He paused and looked at Paul, who this time didn't interrupt. Arnow continued, "But Shelley's hair is too kinky, her eyes slant the wrong way—"

"I know the rest of the defects," Paul interrupted. "I married them, and I like them."

With that, Arnow picked up the phone and said, "Get me Harry Cohn. He's not? Well, have him call me as soon as he gets in."

I said, "This is enough. You're telling me I'm not photogenic, right?"

Max Arnow nodded. "All these things didn't hurt you on the stage, Shelley. I have been wrong occasionally, but I don't think you're movie material."

"Well, you're gonna be wrong again. As my mother would say, 'in spades.' You're telling me you're not picking up my option, right?"

Arnow hesitated. "Maybe if you want to stay on here at the same salary for another six months, I can talk to Harry. . . ."

"No!" I shouted. "I wouldn't stay at this crummy studio for another six months for a thousand a week! You get girls up at four-thirty in the morning; you spend three hours fixing their hair, putting on face and body makeup; then you cover them with stupid Arab veils, and the only thing that shows is their goddamned false eyelashes. You make everybody look like hookers."

"What the hell are you talking about?" Arnow demanded.

"Don't think I haven't noticed that you've got a bunch of beautiful girls from Texas here who never do a movie. Their real job is to do cheesecake photos and 'entertain' the visiting exhibitors. Wait till the Screen Actors Guild finds out about it. You'll probably go to jail because half of them are minors."

I ran out of the office, holding back the tears. Paul followed, laughing gleefully. "Is it true, honey?" he asked.

"I think so. But ninety percent of those girls marry producers anyway. Those big shots like beautiful idiots who are great in bed." Full stop. "That reminds me, Paul. Am I good in bed?"

"You'll do." He kissed me and said, "When you're in love, it's terrific. Otherwise, it's just an athletic event."

"Honest?"

"Sure," he kidded. "If Hitler wins, it's probably going to be a special event in the Olympics." He saw my expression. "Don't worry, he's already lost; it's just a matter of time."

In my dressing room I swiped one of Columbia's pillowcases, put all my makeup and junk in it and said, "Okay, let's go. I think they've dropped my option."

"With a thud," Paul said.

I went to the Hairdressing and Makeup Department to say good-bye. Helen Hunt whispered in my ear, "They never gave you a good picture or director. Honey, some of the biggest stars in this business have gotten their start here, but by being loaned out to other studios first. But Cohn always alienated and lost them."

Freddie Phillips, standing close by, said, "I made you up the way Harry Cohn wanted me to, but it isn't right for you. All those glamor girls are made to look like they came out of the same mold, and it's hard to tell them apart. You look like a real person." I kissed him good-bye.

Paul trailed after me as I went up to the Wardrobe Department and said good-bye to Jean Louis and the fitters who had helped me. With his charming French accent Jean Louis told me to remember Sarah Bernhardt's advice to all young actresses: "Keep your figure." I don't think I heard him clearly, damn it. I was too upset. God, how I wish I had.

I said good-bye to the guys in the Music Department and went into the adjoining rehearsal stage. Rita Hayworth was rehearsing a number from *Gilda*. She stopped and came over, and I introduced her to Capt. Paul Miller. She kissed his cheek and said, "God, some girls have all the luck." Then she kissed me and went back to her strenuous rehearsal.

After leaving the stage, Paul stood stock-still and suddenly became like a little boy. "Wow!" he said. "Ain't that a pistol! Rita Hayworth just kissed me."

"Shut up, or I'll hit you."

We walked past the cutting rooms. All the music cutters and film editors were starting their lunch break, and they all seemed to know I was leaving the studio. I blew them kisses, and as I passed the shoeshine boy in front of the barbershop, he said to me, "Honey, you don't know it yet, but you just got yourself a ride on the Freedom Train."

Al Jolson and Larry Parks were talking in the corridor, and Sidney Buchman came up behind them. Larry said, "Don't forget about unemployment insurance."

Jolson said, "You can go to the track any day and sit in my box."

Sidney Buchman, in front of my husband, kissed my hand and then kissed me full on the lips and said, "If Frank Capra was still here, you would be a star." I started to cry. Paul gave him a dirty look.

It took the guard a long time to press the button to release the door to let me out—the same one who had been so reluctant to let me in a year ago. As we went out the front door into the daylight, Harry Cohn was climbing out of his limousine. He took a look at the pillowcase in my hand and said, "That's Columbia Pictures property, Shelley." He followed that with: "I haven't met your husband, although I've talked to his colonels and generals."

Reluctantly I introduced him to Paul and hastily wiped my nose and eyes on the property of Columbia Pictures. They talked about the goddamned war. Then Cohn turned to me as if suddenly remembering I was there. He pulled me over under a tree about twelve feet on the other side of the entrance. I was so angry I could hardly look at him.

He said, "Listen, Nutsy, I know you're mad at me, but you don't fit into our Love Goddess image. In fact, you don't fit into any image that I know of. And besides, I'm afraid in another year you'll be running *my* studio. I want to give you some serious advice because I know you're really smart. You can stay out here in Hollywood, and some good director sooner or later is going to find the right part for you. But you've got a great guy there. He's smart, with balls and guts, and he doesn't look the kind who's going to leave his wife when she's forty-five, for some twenty-year-old chick, like I did. But my first wife couldn't have children, and I wanted a son. If you stay married to him, you'll have a beautiful life with lots of children and grandchildren who will love you. One way or another he's going to be a rich man. He's what the postwar world is all about.

"If you stay out here, you'll have a few years as a leading character actress, and then you'll end up on a hill with your Oscars. Be smart. This town really is made of tinsel."

Blubbering, I said, "Oh, go stick your advice up your ass. You yanked me from a starring career on Broadway, you stuck me in a lot of crappy pictures and treated me like an extra and you always think you know everything."

Smiling, he said, "Shelley, I do know almost everything. Just don't end up on that hill with your Oscars."

He said it again, the son of a bitch. He really said it.

"I think it's time you learned the value of a good double vodka martini," Paul said, and we headed for the Brown Derby. He told me to go to the ladies' room and fix my face and that he'd put the pillowcase in the trunk of the car. I washed my face and threw Columbia's false eyelashes down the toilet and ripped the false hair out of my pompadour to join the eyelashes. I took off my Adrian suit jacket with the padded shoulders but couldn't take off the fuck-me shoes because I didn't have any others. I found a rubber band on the floor and pulled my hair back into a ponytail. For the first time in more than a year Shirley looked back at me from the mirror.

When I walked out of the ladies' room, I felt as if everyone in the restaurant was watching me. Paul was waiting at the booth, and I took a piece of ice out of the water glass, wrapped it in his handkerchief and put it on my swollen eyes. The waiters stopped serving. The headwaiter walked over with a bottle of champagne and said, "With the compliments of the Brown Derby for Captain and Mrs. Miller."

Paul held my hand as we waited for our double martinis. They came and not only calmed me down but made me so euphoric that by the end of the meal my arms were around Paul's neck and I was saying, "I want to buy you a cashmere jacket at Sy Devore's. You buy me so many presents. Please let me get you something."

He blushed and said, "Okay. I've always had a secret fantasy about being a gigolo."

We went across to Sy Devore's, and Sy himself waited on us. He also lived at Peyton Hall and used to play pinochle with my father. He waited on Paul as if he were a five-star general. He showed us one of the most beautiful navy blue cashmere blazers I've ever seen, and it fitted Paul as if it had been made for him. Sy said, "I made this jacket for Keenan Wynn for a film that was canceled. All I'd have to do is lengthen the sleeves a little." In a quavering voice I asked how much it was, reminding Sy we were neighbors. He replied, "For you, a hundred dollars." The jacket was worth at least twice that. Paul also bought a pair of gray flannel slacks, and Sy promised to bring them and the jacket to Peyton Hall that night. As we left, he said to Paul, "Captain, I'm proud to put you in your first civilian clothes. Shelley's father has told me everything you were doing during the last year. I have relatives in concentration camps."

Paul said, "Maybe they'll make it, Sy. Don't give up."

Back in the Pontiac, Paul asked, "Why did you want to buy me these civilian clothes?"

"Oh, just for a present." I secretly was hoping that if he put on civilian clothes, they wouldn't send him to the Pacific, as I knew he was itching to get into the new B-26s.

I would drag Paul to the beach every day and rack my brain for things to keep him occupied. One day my girlfriends decided to give Paul and me a party at Peyton Hall and invite all the young contract players from Columbia and the other studios, our neighbors and about six of Paul's friends. The decision to have this party came about in a rather odd way. Columbia's Credit Union held a raffle on a huge live turkey, and even though I was no longer there, I won it. Adele Jergens (I think) brought it over to my house on a leash, assuring me that she had been a farm girl and knew how to kill it, pluck its feathers and clean, stuff and roast it. My father and mother put their bed in the basement, and Blanche made the bedroom look like a den. We figured that about seventy-five people could squeeze into the apartment if some of them stayed out on the patio. They decided to have cocktails at six and dinner at eight, and Dusty was getting the booze wholesale. The plan was that Paul and I were to stay at our hotel, get all dressed up and arrive at the party at seven, pretending to be surprised. The whole thing seemed loony, but my ex-fellow contract players wanted to do it, so I agreed.

In the middle of these preparations Paul got a notice from the Army Air Force in Washington to report to Chicago to teach navigation at a base in Illinois. They informed him that at thirty he was too ancient to fly. You'd have thought they'd told him he was going to be busted, and my captain went into a deep depression. And I mean deep. He sat on the beach all day, looking over the Pacific as if he could will himself to the other side. He put a war map on the wall of our hotel room with colored pins indicating which islands were Ours and which were Theirs. He also began to drink rather heavily. I tried to keep up with him, but the booze made my stomach hurt.

The day of the party arrived, and I got all dressed down with my hair in a ponytail, flat shoes and simple makeup. I'd sneaked back into Columbia to have Helen Hunt ash-blonde my hair so that it could grow back in its natural color. I wore a dress that Paul had bought for me in Chicago and my silver fox chubby even though the weather was warm. He wore his civilian clothes, which he referred to as his yachting outfit—I think he secretly hated them and yearned to be back in his officer's pinks.

We arrived at the party at seven, acted properly surprised and were handed some lethal punch. The Andrews sisters, who lived at Peyton Hall, were on the record player as well as at the party. Paul's friends in uniform had gathered out on the patio with the starlets, while the handsome young actors sat in the living room. I finished my one drink, and then something occurred to me. I searched out Adele and asked, "How come I don't smell the turkey cooking?"

"Oh, my God!" she screamed. "I forgot! I killed it and plucked it, then put it in the Frigidaire this morning, but I had to work so I completely forgot to cook it." We dashed to the kitchen, opened the Frigidaire door, and a naked turkey walked out. Alive. With no feathers. It ran around the place, gobbling and biting the guests. It seemed that Adele had gotten hold of some chloroform from the studio hospital, chloroformed the turkey and wrung its neck. Then she had put it in the Frigidaire. Obviously she hadn't wrung its neck hard enough, and the cold had revived it. After terrorizing the guests, the turkey ran out of the house and down Hollywood Boulevard with Paul, his friends, the male starlets and me ĉhasing after. One drunken major actually took out his gun and was going to shoot it but was dissuaded by a screaming and hysterical me. I was afraid he'd miss the turkey and hit one of my guests. This crazy chase lasted about two blocks until a dog coming from the other direction frightened the poor turkey so that it ran into some shrubbery. Paul caught it and very efficiently broke its neck.

"You killed it," I wailed.

"Well, what the hell did you expect me to do?" he yelled back. "Get it a cashmere jacket? It had no feathers. Did you want it to die of overexposure?"

"I don't know, but you could have been a little gentler even if it was a mercy killing." For a minute I thought he was going to wrap the dead turkey around *my* neck or swing it around my head the way my grandmother used to do.

It was getting dark, and Major Walters said, "Come on, let's get the damn thing back to the pool and give it a decent burial."

"You mean we're not going to eat it?" I shouted. "Then why did you have to kill it?" Somehow I sort of identified with that poor naked turkey. I was crying bitterly by that time. Everything that had happened to me during the past month seemed to be embodied in the bird when it woke up terrified and featherless in a freezing Frigidaire and then ran around, looking for help, only to end up strangled in the street.

When we got back to Peyton Hall, everyone was blotto and cutting up. Paul's Army buddies gave the turkey a full military funeral with a burial at sea. They dumped it into the pool. My father was sure we would be evicted, but Michael St. Angelo, a young actor under contract to Warner's, jumped in fully dressed and pulled the limp turkey out of the pool and put it into the incinerator in the alley. I closed my eyes during the cremation.

When I got back to the party, everyone was laughing uproariously at what had happened. My parents and Mrs. Vidor were certainly out of place with that crowd. The great designer Orry-Kelly was in a terrible snit. He couldn't believe what he'd seen. "That was the most brutal thing I've ever witnessed," he announced, "and this is the most inelegant party I've ever been to in Hollywood." He was wearing Connie's babushka.

My sister suggested we send out for Chinese food and was unanimously cheered for the suggestion. Paul was quite drunk by now, having used my Liberty Swimming Pool beauty cup to drink out of. Without warning he went over to the front door, opened it wide and announced in a loud voice, "All right, everybody . . . out! I didn't do eighty bombing missions in order to have a bunch of fairies in my house!"

Everybody froze and quickly sobered up. Orry-Kelly handed Connie back her scarf and started to leave. I walked up to Paul and said, "Listen, Captain Marvel, this is my house, not yours." I was really furious. "These people are all good friends of mine and have been very nice to me." Orry-Kelly and Jean Louis quietly left and were followed by all the young actors while the girls sneaked into the kitchen. My parents and Connie's mother and Blanche went out to the pool, followed by all of Paul's soldier friends. Paul and I were alone.

"So," he said in a low voice, "this is your house only, is it?"

"Yes, it is, and how dare you throw my friends out like that?"

"Your friends? I've seen the likes of them in the Army." What the hell was he talking about? He went on. "If it was up to them, there wouldn't be any more children."

"Well, if it were up to you, there wouldn't be any either." I think if he'd had his gun with him, he'd have shot me. He took off the jacket I'd bought him and threw it on the floor just as my father came into the room.

"Listen," my pop said, "you're both drunk and angry, and you've gone through a lot of hell in the past couple of years. You're both miserable, and you won't admit it to yourselves. Go back to your hotel, and get some sleep. Everything will look different in the morning."

Paul picked up his jacket. "You want to go back with me?" he asked. I was still shaking with anger and disappointment at his behavior.

"No," I replied, "I'll sleep here with my sister."

"We'll all have breakfast together in the morning," my father said. "Nothing is forever in the morning."

I went out to the pool and lay down on a canvas lounge chair. I was angry at Paul and knew he was just as angry at me. Maybe his anger was what made him say things he didn't really mean. Had he yelled at my friends because he couldn't yell at me? The real and unspoken issue was: Could I go back with him and be a housewife in Chicago while he taught navigators? Would I be able to make a life and career in Chicago? The answer was NO, I couldn't. I knew I had to be an actress—not a movie star, but an artist. I had to work at my art. There was no choice.

As dawn lit up the Hollywood Hills, Paul came out to the pool, completely sober. He lay down on a chair next to me. There's some kind of night-blooming flower in Southern California that has a sickly sweet odor, and the smell of it was all around the pool. Paul took my hand and held it. "You can't come back to Chicago and be a suburban housewife, can you?" he asked softly, making it easy for me.

"No," I replied as softly, "I can't."

"You know, it's funny, but I've always known it in a way."

"I'm sorry," I whispered.

"So am I. And will you please apologize to your friends for me? You know I'm not an intolerant bastard like that. I'm getting the kick in the stomach now."

"I'll tell them."

We stayed there until the pool man came at nine o'clock to clean, then we went inside. We told my parents that we'd decided to end our marriage and that it had nothing to do with the party the night before. We just couldn't live in the same place. My father cried bitterly, but somehow my mother understood. She took me into the bedroom and said, "Paul's a wonderful man, honey, but a woman has a right to a career and life, too. I think I'm such a good cardplayer because my parents didn't let me sing."

It didn't seem to make sense, but I understood that what she was trying to tell me was that she'd spent her life cooking and cleaning and having children and sneaking into the rehearsals at the Metropolitan Opera House. And whenever she had a few cents to spare, she'd buy a ticket to the gallery. Perhaps if Fate had dealt her a different hand, she might have been up there on the stage instead.

When we came out, my father had dried his tears and walked right past me into the bedroom. He didn't talk to me for a year. Later in the week I called Jerry Giesler because that was the only lawyer's name I'd heard in Hollywood. Paul and I went to see him and explained our problem. Giesler, that smart lawyer who had helped defend Clarence Darrow (when Darrow was tried and acquitted of bribing a juror while defending the men accused of bombing the Los Angeles *Times*), tried for an hour to talk us out of dissolving our marriage. Paul finally shut him up with "We love each other, but we can't have a marriage while living in different

Grymalow, Poland, but somehow
near Vienna. The beautiful woman
in the middle is my Aunt Zisel—
the one who brought 35 people to
America flicking chickens.

St. Louis—my mother's mother and
father, Zayda and Bubba

My father, Jonas Schrift

My mother, Rose Schrift

Me and my sister Blanche in our
smocked pongee dresses made by
Mom

Newstead Ave., St. Louis. Shirley's
entrance into the world obviously
pleased Blanche.

ABOVE: Blanche ("Bappy")—honor student at Jamaica High School

LEFT: Shirley—hookey player extraordinaire

Shirley Schrift and chums—Berriman Junior High School (P.S. 64, Brownsville)

Shirley Schrift—the summer she got
beauty-contest fever

The only *goil* to play Scarlett O'Hara

The worst model on Seventh Avenue—I was studying scenes at dramatic
school instead of the style numbers and prices.

Detroit, the alley of the Shubert Theater—a professional at last. My false eyelashes were so thick I could hardly see.

The first off-Broadway show ever (I think), *Of V We Sing*

Meet the People—Detroit

LEFT: *Rosalinda*—
my first hit show
on Broadway. With
Oscar Karlweiss
and company

BELOW: California
at last—practicing
cheesecake at
Peyton Hall

Rita always made sure I was near her, even though the scene was full of famous models. *Tonight and Every Night*

The 999th night of *A Thousand and One Nights*

My lovely friend Connie Dowling helping me to be funny with Johnny "Scat" Davis in *Knickerbocker Holiday* on loan-out to Samuel Goldwyn

Entertaining at the Hollywood Canteen—with Lee Tarloff, Betty Garrett, Lisa Kirk, and Peggy Ryan

Shirley's Holding On, but the Glamorous Shelley Is Winning in Every Department

ABOVE LEFT: The femme fatale

ABOVE RIGHT: The lovely sweet young thing

RIGHT: The famous "FM" shoes

OPPOSITE PAGE

LEFT: My Columbia dancing lessons. Later, Harry Cohn ordered a new rehearsal costume for me, including high heels.

RIGHT: Signing my Columbia contract with ambivalent feelings. Note: I'm wearing Paul's wings.

BELOW: *Ladies of the Chorus*— Marilyn Monroe is in the center, Adele Jergens is to her right. I was somewhere off to the right (I think).

In Scott Fitzgerald's *The Great Gatsby*

If you wear a leopard coat in a black-and-white picture, that's all the audience will look at. (With Richard Conte)

RIGHT: My first day and first scene on *A Double Life* when I set a Hollywood record and went 96 takes

BELOW: The horn-rimmed glasses made me feel Robert Walker's intellectual equal.

Ronald Colman—the first of my
leading men to give me the statue
of his head

The scene was too realistic but I was afraid to yell "Cut!"

The only time Liberace looked at me in *South Sea Sinner*. He was too nervous to take his eyes off the keys.

Errol Flynn used this photo as a bookmark in his first-edition copy of *The Great Gatsby* (which I never returned).

A pack of villains—from the artist's collection. Lawrence Tierney, better known as Dillinger, is in the center.

RIGHT: Around the time of
The Great Gatsby, when my
figure was finally fulfilling

BELOW: The only picture of
Burt Lancaster I have left
since Marlon Brando threw
all the others down the
incinerator.

ABOVE: Doing *The Taming of the Shrew* all over California with John Ireland, especially in Anaheim, Azusa, and Cucamonga.

RIGHT: A decade later, Burt and I were polite to each other doing *Scalphunters* in Durango, Mexico. (With Sidney Pollack, directing and holding his breath)

ABOVE: Jimmy Dean, who often played with knives on and off the screen

LEFT: "Bud"—Marlon Brando—about the time I was doing *Oklahoma!* on Broadway and he was doing *A Streetcar Named Desire*

BELOW: My Mom and Dad attending the Academy Awards when I was nominated Best Actress for *A Place in the Sun*

cities two thousand miles apart. So will you please tell us the quickest way we can end our marriage?"

Mr. Giesler turned to me and asked, "Shelley, are you sure you're not making a mistake?"

"Maybe," I told him. "But I can't do anything else."

He sighed. "What community property is there?"

"I have two thousand dollars," Paul said.

"And I have a red convertible Pontiac, a silver fox chubby and a three-karat diamond engagement ring, which I can give back."

Paul glared at me. "Try to give that back, and I'll strangle you; then we won't need a divorce. And let's not have a fight like we did in Blythe."

Giesler interrupted: "How do you think the community property should be divided?"

"Well," I said, "he's a salesman and needs a car, and you can't get any now."

"I'll be living on the base, so I won't need one," Paul protested.

"They might muster you out all of a sudden, and you'll have to have a car." Before he could protest again, I went on quickly, "And I think you should get four new recapped tires for the trip back to Illinois."

"Okay," he gave in, "but as soon as I can buy a new car, I'll send it back to you. Do you think one thousand dollars will be enough until you get yourself a job?"

"More than enough. My father's paying the rent."

Then, after a long silence: "If you ever need anything, you call me, you hear?"

"Likewise," I answered.

He looked at me distrustfully. "I'll have Major Walters check up on you every month and make sure you're okay."

"That won't be necessary."

"Then I won't take the car."

"How do I put all this in a legal document?" Giesler asked.

"You're the big shot lawyer," Paul told him. "You must know how to arrange things." By this time we were all crying—Giesler, too.

Paul went on. "We just want to get this over with fast. I don't want her sitting home at night like she's been doing for a couple of years. I know how much of this movie business depends on the publicity you get going out to premieres and parties."

"We'll be in Family Court by next Monday," Giesler assured us, and we left his office. It was Thursday. That weekend Paul and I stayed at the Las Tunas Motel in Malibu in the zebra room over-looking the ocean. With all those red lights around the pool, Paul said the place looked like a whorehouse. We made love every day, and every night, sad and strangely erotic love for us middle-class types.

Monday morning we showed up at the L.A. courthouse. For some strange reason we weren't exactly in a courtroom, but at a table with Jerry Giesler and the judge, while listening to all the reasons why the marriage of Capt. Paul Miller and Shirley Schrift should be dissolved. The reasons given, the judge proceeded to do his job. To this day I don't know if it was a dissolvement, an annulment or a divorce. Giesler must have gotten the papers, but I never asked him for them.

Paul gave the clerk $10 to cover the court costs, and when we were out in the hall, he asked Giesler how much he owed him. "You don't owe me a thing," Jerry told him. "I feel a great miscarriage of justice has been done, and with all my legal training I didn't know how to prevent it."

Paul's clothes were already in the trunk of the car, so we drove directly to Peyton Hall, but he didn't get out of the car when we got there. He didn't want to say good-bye to my parents. He said he'd write to them. He took ten $100 bills from his wallet and put them in my purse. I felt nothing.

"Go in," he said. "And tomorrow put the money in the bank. Okay?"

"Okay."

He kissed me, then drove away in the little red Pontiac, and I didn't see him or speak to him again for thirty years.

Thirty years and two wars later, I was in Milwaukee, trying out a wonderful play by Paul Zindel called *The Effect of Gamma Rays on Man-in-the-Moon Marigolds*. It had been done Off Broadway, and I was hoping to take it to Broadway after this tryout. It was a remarkable production with a marvelous cast and was directed by Robert Livingston. The Pelman Theater was in the round, and we were a huge success during the eight-week run, weekends playing to 500 people, which was far more than the theater's capacity. Students would sit on cushions around the stage, and after the performance we held symposiums. The play is about the position of poor women in our society and the terror of old age and poverty and about a brilliant child's scientific experiment which enables her to escape the fate of her mother and sister. It is a very powerful play.

Before our last Saturday matinee I noticed there were about 100 or so kids hoping to get standing room at the evening performance. When I asked the stage manager where all those people came from, he replied that the North Side of Chicago was only forty-five minutes from Milwaukee, and a large percentage of our audiences came from there.

When I got back to the hotel to rest for the evening performance, I picked up the phone and asked the Chicago operator for the number on the North Side of Chicago, and in a couple of minutes I had it. Paul Miller. I hoped there weren't two of them. I took a deep breath and dialed. A woman answered.

"Is Paul there?" I asked.

"Who is this, please?"

"Shelley Winters."

There was a muffled thud like when a telephone is dropped; then the lady said, "He's out playing golf, but he should be back in a little while."

"I'm doing a play in Milwaukee," I told her, "and I thought that he and his family would like to come and see it."

"Thank you," she replied. "I'll give him your number and have him call you when he gets home."

He called me at midnight, not long after I got back from the theater. "Hello," he said, "who the hell is this?"

"Paul? This is Shelley."

"Shelley . . . are you sick? Are you in trouble?"

"No, I'm fine. But tomorrow is our last performance, and since I just found out that Glencoe is so close to Milwaukee, I thought you would like to come and see it with your family."

He replied, after a pause, "We've seen the play with Irene Dailey. But I've seen everything else you've ever done."

That surprised me. "Even *A Hatful of Rain* and *The Night of the Iguana* on Broadway?"

"Of course. I saw *A Hatful of Rain* twice. It was a brilliant play, and you were magnificent in it. And I've seen all your films. In fact, I took my youngest daughter to see *A Place in the Sun* just last month. It's a classic. I'm sure that Theodore Dreiser would have been grateful to you for bringing his factory girl to life like that. My kid is studying Dreiser in school, and she just got through reading *An American Tragedy*, and when I told her that I was once married to you, she was very impressed. I once saw you in a play in Cleveland while John Kennedy was campaigning there. You were also on the platform with him making speeches. Walters' brother was head of the Chicago Republican Party, and he almost had a stroke."

"Paul," I said, "how come you never came backstage to talk to me?"

In his husky, still youthful voice he replied, "What was there to talk about, Shirley?"

BOOK TWO

If This Is Stardom, I'll Take Vanilla

CHAPTER 10

Here I am, not yet in Chapter Eleven and already figuratively and literally bankrupt. No husband, no baby, no contract, no agent and practically no home. My father not speaking to me. My mother staying out of the house as much as possible. Dinner was a silent meal, and everyone managed to make me feel like a leper.

One day I was sitting out at the pool, staring at the water, when suddenly Moki Vidor ran out, weeping and shouting, "It's over! He's dead! The monster is dead! The Nazis have surrendered!" I didn't feel anything. Since about 1936 I had understood what Hitler was. All the anti-Nazi plays I had taken part in and the husband whom I had been so proud of, who had helped bomb the Third Reich into rubble, the whole thrust of my life had disappeared. I felt like someone else, as if I really had left Shirley Schrift in New York and some sorcery had taken place in California that had changed me into a selfish dumb blonde movie starlet. The aspiring, intelligent and aware artist had disappeared.

I didn't want to talk to anyone, so I started walking west on Hollywood Boulevard. As I got close to Fairfax, a car passed, and two young people yelled back at me. It was Tom Drake, then a young leading man and a fine actor, and Jan Clayton—an MGM star and later Lassie's mother. They stopped the car, and Tom asked, "Where are you wandering to? Didn't you hear the war in Europe is over?"

"Yeah, I heard."

"So why do you look so glum? Were you rooting for the other side?"

I shook my head. They invited me to a "high tea." "Okay, thanks." I preferred to be with casual acquaintances on this day of victory that I had waited for so long.

Mrs. Lawrence Tibbett opened the door and greeted the three of us as if we personally had won the war. She seemed quite happy and a bit drunk, and her speech had become quite British, but I still had problems with my Brooklyn speech, so she sounded great to me. The radio was blaring out the news and music from all the capitals of the Allied countries. While one twin son would pour Mrs. Tibbett a drink, the other would deftly remove it after she'd taken one swallow and slip it to me. They were nice boys who resembled

151

their handsome father. I remembered a picture of Lawrence Tibbett's that my mother had dragged me to, called *Rogue Song*, and cheered up by their mother's rum and Cokes, I suddenly burst into the "Cuban Love Song." After three or four cuba libres I began dancing Spanish fashion to my own music.

A very strong hand across my mouth cut off my music and my breathing. A formidable husky voice whispered, "You're making my headache worse." I poured what was left of my drink on his feet and frantically pointed to his hands, indicating he was smothering me. He let go and whispered, "You won't sing anymore, will you?" The tone of his voice made me look down to see if he had a gun pointed at my ribs. He didn't, but there was something so terrifyingly gentle about his manner and voice, despite his huge height and width, that I was sure he was a real gangster. It turned out his name was Lawrence Tierney, and he had played John Dillinger in the film of the same name and had made a tremendous hit.

My delayed reaction to the end of the war finally took place, and tears of relief started running into my drink. "I didn't think the party was that bad," Tierney said in his terrifyingly gentle voice. I introduced myself and explained briefly that I was at last crying with joy that the war in Europe was over and that I had relatives who were in concentration camps. He told me he felt like crying, too. "I have a brother, Scott, who's in the Navy, and he's decided that if it's so easy for me to become a movie star, he's going to take a crack at it, too. Our father is a New York cop, and he thinks I'm a pimp glorifying gangsters and that I'm going to teach my brother to be a pimp, too."

"My father hates me, too," I said in a teary voice. "I had a husband who was a famous navigator who almost personally destroyed Hitler single-handed, but we got divorced. You know, it was one of those wartime marriages."

He began mopping up my face, and an actor I shall call Jonathan Baker sat down beside me. He was a slight man who played villains quite well. He was quite drunk, too. Baker suggested that we all go to the Cock and Bull restaurant on the Sunset Strip. I'd never been there, so I said why not? It was mostly bar, but at the back of the Cock and Bull they had a great buffet. I had to go to the ladies' room, and the busy maître d' sort of gave me directions. I opened the door of what I thought was the ladies' room, but it was an office, and there, staring at me, was the largest gold-framed picture of Hitler I'd ever seen. So I peed right under Hitler's picture, because I couldn't pee on it.

When I got back to the bar, I interrupted a drunken political discussion and asked Mr. Baker why he had chosen this particular restaurant. He replied, "Food's good here, and I know the owners."

Tierney said to him, "I thought you lived in Bishop, California."

"I do," Baker replied. "I don't want my children contaminated by the Hollywood Jews and niggers."

With that I was sober instantly. So was Tierney. But Baker continued, drunk and loud, "You know why this is such a lousy celebration today? We fought on the wrong side. We should have been fighting *with* the Germans *against* the Russians."

Lawrence Tierney said, "And then today you could have had Louis B. Mayer's job. Right?"

Tierney took one look at my anguished face; then he casually picked up Mr. Baker and threw him down the length of the bar, crashing into all the glasses and beer bottles, just like in a western. Then he grabbed me, and we got out fast, into the parking lot, and got into the car and drove away. (I never entered the restaurant again until it had new owners.)

Tierney stopped at Delores Drive-In for hamburgers and coffee. I sat joyless and shriveled in a corner. He put on the radio, and between the patriotic music there were commentators talking about how glorious the future was going to be now that we had won the war. He quickly turned it off. To make conversation, I said, "Did you only play John Dillinger so far?"

"A couple of other little things. But I've done a lot of public appearances at state fairs and a six-month stretch at the honor farm."

I asked if he had been an actor in New York, and he replied that he'd been a cop in Brooklyn. Then he smiled at me for the first time, one of the sweetest and most naïve smiles I've ever seen. "Would you like to go to a motel with me?"

Silence. "Uh. . . ." Pause.

"It's funny," he whispered, "but since I played Dillinger, I have to beat the chicks off with a stick. Now I meet a nice girl from my hometown, I throw a Nazi sympathizer across a restaurant for her and she's looking at me like I'm a rapist."

The only answer I could think of was: "Would it take long?"

And he replied, "With any luck it shouldn't take too long."

And it didn't. So I spent the night of VE Day after the long war with a strange sad actor sleeping at my side and staring into darkness, wondering what the hell had happened to the idealistic, chaste Shirley Schrift.

* * *

I moped around for a month and then went back to "Go." I began swimming every day and dating—platonically—all the handsome male starlets around the pool. One, a singer, David Street, taught me how to play water polo. After a week we were having wild games in the pool, during which I almost drowned Cary Grant. I had my legs wrapped around his body, pushing his head under with a large rubber polo ball. I was playing ferociously according to "Brownsville stickball rules." Finally, two other boys pulled me off Cary, and he swam to the side of the pool, got out and said, "It's too dangerous around here. I'm putting my face and fortune in danger." I couldn't understand his English gentleman rules. In Brooklyn we played to win.

Early one morning the phone rang, and when I picked it up, somebody said, "This is the King Brothers. Are you Shelley Winter?"

"More or less."

He said, "We're doing a picture called *The Gangster* with Barry Sullivan. Can you sing? Lawrence Tierney says you're great."

"He does? Well, I've sung in musicals in New York."

He asked who my agent was, and lying in his teeth, I said, "I haven't made up my mind which one I want yet."

"Well," he said, "we've got a part this afternoon of a sexy nightclub singer who sings 'Bill' to Barry Sullivan and then has a few lines and then somebody kills her. What size are you?"

I took a deep gulp, thanking God for all the swimming I'd done lately, and said size ten or eight. This charming man then asked, "You got big tits?"

"Who are you? Harry Cohn's brother?"

Taking it as a compliment, he laughed and replied, "Under the skin."

When I got to the little studio, they rushed me into a little canvas dressing room and shoved four pages of dialogue into my hand. I grabbed the assistant and shouted, "Where's the music?"

"You don't sing," he said. "You mouth to 'Bill.' We have to shoot in half an hour."

"You're crazy. I have to put on makeup, comb out my hair, dress, listen to the record and learn the lines."

"Okay, forty minutes," he said. "We'll light the set. It's a crab dolly shot, and you're at the piano."

Thank God I knew the words to "Bill," which had been prerecorded by Anita Ellis. Barry Sullivan took his place at a table, a make-believe orchestra crawled up on the stage and I draped myself over the piano, showing as much of my legs as possible. They started the playback, and I mouthed it perfectly in one take. I had watched Rita Hayworth do this many, many times. The director called, "Cut . . . great!" Everyone applauded.

Between scenes, Barry Sullivan introduced me to an actor named John Ireland, who I think was also in the film, and to Bert Marx, an agent. "Agent?" I asked, my eyes lighting up. "I've just left Columbia because they weren't using me correctly."

Bert said, "Really? You're agentless? Come to my office tomorrow morning, and if you want to sign with me, I'll start taking you around to the other studios' Casting departments."

"And I'll glady drive you around the studios since you don't have wheels," John offered. "I'll be between commitments soon."

"You single?" I asked. He was very handsome, tall and sexy, and had a wide nose like mine. "I just got a divorce," I added.

"Well, I'm legally separated and in the process. Listen, beauty, do your acting fast, and I'll wait for you and give you a lift home."

Bert Marx gave me his card and told me to be in his office the next morning at ten. The assistant director yelled, "Okay, let's rehearse."

I was finished by four o'clock, and since they always shot till eight, they had to scurry around, trying to figure out something else to shoot. I put on my tight skirt and thin silk blouse and stole the King Brothers' black net stockings.

John yelled, "Come on, we'll go have a drink at Lucey's." That was the very "in" thing to do then.

I went outside and got in his car, a long beige convertible with seats upholstered with real imitation leopard skin. The car had all sorts of gadgets, like a luminous cigarette lighter, a radio and fox tails on the aerial. It was a prewar Chrysler with chrome-spoked white wheels and a small silver horse on the hood. Wow!

"Where did you ever get this car?"

"I was on location in Texas and won it in a crap game." I believed him. Later on I found out that even though John was born in Canada, he was very Irish and must have kissed the Blarney Stone at birth. He preferred telling wonderful romantic lies even when the truth was easier.

I felt very strange having a date. Even though John was several years older than I was, he seemed somehow younger, almost like a kid. We tooled around Hollywood with his radio blasting, him play-

ing his musical horn at every streetlight and my blonde curls streaming behind me. I kept my legs crossed in my black net stockings
and sexy shoes. I had also swiped the King Brothers' rhinestone
earrings (Mama King came to get them the next day), and I felt like
a real movie star.

"Do you smoke?" John asked me.

"No," I said, "I never learned how. My father coughs so much
from smoking Between the Acts."

"What are they?"

"Those little brown cigarette-type cigars that come in a tin box.
He's had a hard time getting them during the war."

"Really? There are other little brown cigarettes that you roll yourself, and they are remarkable for relaxation and fun."

"You smoke them even when you're working?"

"I never let work interfere with pleasure." He laughed.

We arrived at Lucey's, and John lavishly tipped the parking lot
attendant as well as the maître d'. Everybody fell all over himself
waiting on us. A young actor named Robert Mitchum was standing
at the bar, looking sleepy. John insisted that he join us in the lovely
green outdoor dining room. The first thing John did was order a
telephone, and they brought one quickly to the table. I'd never seen
that done before. John checked with his service. He had his final
call for work on *The Gangster* the next day. Then he called his agent
and discussed some film called *Red River*, to be directed by Howard
Hawks. Mitchum put his arm around my chair and said, "Listen,
kid, everything John tells you, you divide by half." I looked into his
sleepy eyes and believed him.

We then had Pimms Cups (I loved them, especially the cucum-
ber sticks), and after two of them I felt great. I went to the ladies'
room, and as I looked over my shoulder, I noticed that both young
men were checking out my black net stockings. I was glad I'd gotten all that exercise swimming—obviously they were, too. When I
got back, John and Bob were smoking a smelly little cigarette under
the table and laughing uproariously. John told me some rambling
story about his half-brother, Tommy Noonan, and his comedian
partner, Peter Marshall (now the host of *Hollywood Squares*). The
story didn't seem very funny to me, but they were practically rolling
on the floor.

The table was full of food now. Then, abruptly, Bob got even
sleepier and started to yawn. "Listen, John," he said, "do you mind
if I wrap up a steak and take it home? My wife and kids are expect-

ing me for dinner, except I don't think she's got any money left for groceries." John wrapped the steak in a napkin and slipped a $20 bill into the package as Bob finished our Pimms Cups. "Aren't you doing anything?" he asked Bob.

"Yeah, I'm selling crummy Christmas trees out in the Valley, and I'm testing for a picture called *The Story of G.I. Joe.* It's a great script, but you know they'll give it to some big star. Well, that's the way the ball bounces." Bob thanked John for the steak, gave us a sleepy smile and left the restaurant.

I looked at the laden table. "It's not even dark yet," I wondered aloud, "and we're going to have this big dinner?"

"Well, there are so many better things to do at night. Why waste it eating?"

People were beginning to come into Lucey's from Paramount, Columbia and RKO, which were all nearby, and John knew everybody. He seemed to prefer talking to technical people, such as head gaffers and sound and cameramen, rather than to stars and producers. I recognized several important directors, whom he just gave a quick hello to, but he would spend a lot of time talking with members of the crews. I asked him about that, and he said, "Nobody in this business knows what the hell they're doing except the technical people, the musicians, some of the very good writers and a *very* few of the directors. All the rest of them are just guessing. When you're talented and they hire you, you're doing them a favor and making *them* look good. Don't you ever forget it."

"Christ, you sound just like my mother."

"Yeah? What's her name?"

"Rose."

"Rosie sounds like a very smart lady. They're looking for a new production chief at Paramount. You ought to try to get her the job."

I mentioned the fact that he had been questioning me about myself all day but I knew practically nothing about him. He laughed and just ordered some exotic dessert which had very strong brandy on it, then had to drag me almost forcibly to the car because I was so busy staring at all the big movie stars coming in for cocktails and dinner. It was getting dark as we started to drive up Sunset Boulevard. I put on my dark glasses, hoping someone would mistake me for Lucille Ball or Ann Sothern. John held my left hand (now minus wedding ring) and said, "You wouldn't sleep with me on the first date, would you?"

"I wouldn't sleep with you *ever* unless I was sure we were going to have a meaningful relationship." I can't believe I said that, but I did. I think I had justified Lawrence Tierney as some sort of underground anti-Nazi movement I had taken part in.

He smiled. "Okay then, we'll drive up into the Hollywood Hills and look down over the city and the lights and plan our acceptance speeches for when we get our Oscars."

"I don't expect any Oscars," I told him. "As soon as I get one good part, I'm going back to New York and study to become an accomplished actress in the Legitimate Theater."

John looked over at me. "Yeah? Last year I did a play in New York, and from where I sit, it's pretty illegitimate. You knock your brains out rehearsing four weeks, freeze your ass off touring, and one man on *The New York Times* decides if your play is any good. Who knows? Maybe he had a fight with his wife or a lousy dinner that night. I prefer Las Vegas. The odds are better."

"What's Las Vegas?"

He laughed. "I'll take you there sometime. I love it." I was to learn fairly quickly that at that period John was a compulsive gambler. (I think he secretly hated winning.) He felt high only when he was betting too much, and although he was making very large sums of money at that point in his career, he got rid of it quickly.

We drove up someplace high above the city, and he parked on a cliff. We could see all the lights of Hollywood at about a 360-degree angle encompassing the electric HOLLYWOOD sign and the cross over the Pilgrimage Bowl, the lighted Sunset Strip and the streams of rhinestones down Western, La Brea and La Cienega boulevards. We could even make out the MGM sign in the distance and the faintly lit up lion underneath it. I had never seen this breathtaking view before. John lit a thin little brown cigarette, puffed it and handed it to me. I could see the big yellow man in the moon smiling at me and the stars beginning to twinkle.

I tried to puff his cigarette but couldn't inhale it, so he helped by blowing the smoke in my mouth. I enjoyed the kiss but almost choked to death on the smoke. "Can't we get arrested for this?" I gasped.

"If a cop comes up, I'll swallow it. Go ahead, try it again. It'll make you feel like you've already starred on Broadway."

"I have," I told him. "It was only a small part, but Max Reinhardt thought I was 'An Artist.' "

"I do, too."

I was obviously wasting the reefer, as I couldn't inhale, so he took it away from me and put the roach in his sock. I hoped it was out. He kissed me again. A thrilling, passionate kiss, just like in the movies. I felt as though I were in a movie and any minute a cop would come along and yell, "Cut." The radio was playing "Sentimental Journey," and the moon and stars looked like props. The lighting men had now blurred the lights a little into one big hazy glow. And I was necking with a very handsome, desirable and talented actor. What else could a girl from Brooklyn want?

We must have stayed in the car a long time because the next thing I remember the stars had gone out. I woke John, and he said, "Jesus Christ, I have to be at the studio at seven." He took me back to Peyton Hall; it was about 5:00 A.M. when I sneaked into my twin bed. The next afternoon I told my parents that I'd had to shoot all night. I *think* they believed me.

That evening at six-fifteen sharp I was all dressed up again, even though John hadn't called me. I heard his musical horn sound in front of the apartment, and I dashed out before my parents could ask any questions. They managed to catch a glimpse of the guy in the beige convertible with the leopard seats as we took off. John kissed me as he drove, but I kept my eyes on the road. "How did you know I was going to pick you up?" he asked. "I didn't know your phone number."

"Oh, I'm sure of you."

We went to dinner at the Players Restaurant, a wonderful hangout for writers and directors owned by Preston Sturges. You sat on a big balcony overlooking a then trafficless Sunset Boulevard. Bert Marx, John's friend and I believe his agent during that period, was waiting for us. When we sat down, he said, "I thought you were going to see me today, Shelley."

Blushing, I said, "I've been sleeping most of the day. I was tired."

Bert asked John if he had worked that day. "Sure," John replied, "but when I'm working on a cheapie I sleep mostly."

Bert Marx was a rather frail man with black, kinky hair and big eyeglasses and looked rather like Harold Lloyd. But he seemed very knowledgeable about the film business. "Look, Shelley," he said, "if you were coming from a starring role on Broadway or if you'd done an outstanding small role in an important picture, one of the big agents would probably be better for you than I would. But since you've been dropped by Columbia and none of the Casting departments knows your work, we should have good stills taken of you, we hope by John Engstead, and get you some juicy little roles that could lead to a two-picture-a-year contract. That's what John has, and the rest of the time you can free-lance in films or work in the theater."

"You think you can do that for me?" I asked hopefully.

"Yes. I've got my contract right here." So I signed my first agency contract for one year, which is all that the Screen Actors Guild allows, at the Players Restaurant.

Then started a period where I think I was trying to go back and get the adolescence I'd never had. I ran around like a kid, having fun with John for several months. When he wasn't shooting a picture, we would pick up our weekly unemployment insurance checks —about $55—and we and four other unemployed wastrels would meet at Schwab's drugstore and pick our horses from the daily racing forms, have brunch and speed to the track in John's car. When we didn't go to the track, we went swimming out at Malibu (never Peyton Hall!). I managed to keep John's existence a secret from family for almost six months. How I'll never know. Life was one long holiday. John turned down important pictures if we had an exciting project scheduled and if he had money. In fact, in those days I don't think he ever worked unless he needed money. His philosophy was the exact opposite of what I had been raised on. The purpose of life was to enjoy oneself. All day, every day and in every way. We saw each other practically twenty-four hours a day.

One morning Bert Marx took me to MGM, and Bill Grady, the casting director, put me in a picture called, I think, *New Orleans*. What I remember of the film was that people were supposed to keep mistaking me for Lucille Ball, whom I looked quite a bit like at that time, with my hair up on the side and down in the back and newly tinted reddish blonde. Why, oh, why, does every studio want to change the color of your hair no matter what it is?

The most terrible thing I remember about that picture is sitting around a pool on the back lot for six weeks with five other bathing beauties, like the scenery. Gene Kelly, who was in the picture, assured me every day that the director, Gregory La Cava, was going to have me do a scene. Finally, one day I couldn't stand it anymore, and even though we girls were making $500 a week, I went up to the assistant director and demanded, "Listen, I've been assured that I'm going to play a scene in this picture, so when will it be done?"

He looked at the shooting schedule and said, "My God! You bathing beauties should have been off the picture three weeks ago!

We're finished everything on that side of the pool."

The other five MGM beauties decided to drown me because they all needed the loot. If I hadn't been such a good swimmer, they might have succeeded. The men on the set didn't dare come in and rescue me. I finally got away from my attackers and out of the pool, scratched and practically drowned. But I had left several handfuls of hair floating in the pool, as well as false eyelashes, and two of the girls had black eyes and bloody noses. All Gregory La Cava said was: "Couldn't you girls have waited until I had the camera on you, dammit? We could have fitted it in the picture somehow."

Bill Grady took a dim view of my little fracas, but then he said these astonishing words: "Louis B. Mayer has been watching you in the rushes and would like to meet you and perhaps test you. But he wants you to work with Lillian Burns, who is our speech teacher and acting coach for the big stars at Metro, all three hundred fifty of them. I think she even coached Judy Garland and Lassie."

Bert Marx was waiting for me in the parking lot, and he knew all about everything and happily drove me over to the Selznick Studio, where John Ireland was shooting *Red River* with John Wayne and Monty Clift, directed by Howard Hawks. I couldn't wait to tell John my news. There was a CLOSED SET sign on the door. We ignored it. As soon as I saw John, I inarticulately poured out the whole day's events to him. I didn't notice that he was talking to a tall, distinguished gray-haired man who waited patiently for me to finish. John said, "That's great," then looked at the man in an odd manner and said, "Mr. Hawks, may I introduce you to my friend Shelley Winter." What was this, *friend?* Why not girlfriend?

Hawks was smiling, and in a very courtly manner he bowed and said, "It's a pleasure to meet a young lady with such love and enthusiasm for filmmaking."

John said, "Shelley, we're going to shoot a square dance later; perhaps Mr. Hawks would let you be in it."

Mr. Hawks, looking at John, said, "Yes, I think it would be wonderful if she danced with Monty Clift. Would you like that, Shelley?"

John said, "I thought she should be my partner."

Bert Marx, who was standing nearby, said, "Mr. Hawks, she can't do extra work."

Hawks quickly said, "Oh, she can have a few lines with Monty and get a close-up. And you know my pictures are usually important. Suppose we pay her three hundred dollars, and she'll appear in a lovely period costume."

Bert opened his mouth to object, but I said, "Please, Bert, let me do it."

"Okay." He shrugged. "I'm just the chauffeur."

John unwillingly took me over to meet Monty Clift, whom I had seen on the stage in New York and whom I admired tremendously. He was very shy and spoke in a mumble and sort of reminded me of early Jimmy Stewart. But Monty was beautiful and radiated a kind of spiritual and physical graciousness. He took my hand, looked in my eyes and said, "How *are you*?"

And I answered, "I'm okay *now*."

He and John seemed to be very good friends, although they were so opposite in character. John was outgoing and fun, while Monty was introverted and modest. Before he let go of my hand, he said in a husky voice, "I hope we *really* work together sometime."

"I hope so, too," I replied.

So, if you ever watch *Red River* on the late show, look very closely during the square dance scene and you'll see me pass the camera in close-up with Monty Clift. But look real fast. The dialogue where he asks me to dance ended up on the cutting-room floor.

CHAPTER 11

I adored MGM. They treated their actors like real stars and built a heaven around them. I spent every day there from nine to two being coached by Lillian Burns and taking dancing and singing lessons from Gene Kelly's assistant, Stanley Donen, who is now a famous director. They gave me an exquisite dressing room in the stars' dressing-room building, right alongside Lana Turner's, Clark Gable's and Ava Gardner's. They even paid for my lunches, though they were "gourmet diet" lunches in a special sectioned-off area of the commissary. You would eat lunch surrounded by Myrna Loy, Lana Turner, Katharine Hepburn and Robert Taylor, although most of the stars (when they were actually shooting a film) would eat in their dressing rooms.

John Ireland would sometimes join me for lunch, but around post time he would get very nervous. Then he and Mervyn Le Roy would gulp down their food and take the shortcut across the Metro back lot to Hollywood Park Racetrack.

Right in the middle of my rehearsing at MGM, Bert Marx got me a part at Twentieth in *Cry of the City*. It was a small but juicy role, and all my scenes were with Richard Conte. And they paid me $1,000 a week for three weeks. Three thousand dollars!

My father, who still wasn't speaking to me, told my mother that I must use the money to buy packages (apartment house units). My father had this crazy idea that you could put a pin in the map of Southern California, and if you just held onto the properties, you would become a millionaire. Who could listen to such a crazy idea? Certainly not me! So I'm not a millionaire.

I had to stop rehearsals at MGM to do the film at Twentieth, and John had to go to the track by himself for three weeks. Ben Lyon, Twentieth's head of Casting, was talking term contract with Bert after they saw my first day's rushes, but MGM had the previous option. (Besides, they already had Marilyn under contract by then, as well as Betty Grable and Alice Faye. And I wanted to be a "serious" actress.)

I had noticed that people always stared at the leopard seats in John's car and that they got the most attention no matter who was sitting on them. So through most of the film I insisted on wearing a short sad leopard coat I found in the Wardrobe Department. After all, it was supposed to be New York in the winter. Since the film was in black and white, nobody could look at anything but me and my very blonde hair and leopard spots.

I was a bit player and not supposed to see the rushes (the previous day's work), but I asked Richard Conte if I could bring my mother on the lot one evening and sit in on the rushes in the projection room. "Sure," he said . . . so after seeing the rushes, the three of us walked along the executive hallway at Twentieth, and I saw four important-looking men coming toward us. The only one I recognized was Darryl Zanuck. I suggested, sotto voce, that we jump into an empty office. Nick said, "Just keep walking."

As we passed the four men, one of them said, "Rose? Rose Winter?"

I stood rooted. "Hello, Charlie," my mother greeted him. "By the way, where are my mother's sheets?"

I thought she had gone insane. But Charlie turned to another big man and said, "Spyros, I gave you Rose's mother's sheets to give back to her, didn't I?"

Now Nick and I thought they were all insane. My mother continued. "Now listen. Right is right. Those sheets came all the way from Poland, and they had handmade lace on them."

Whereupon started a big argument about the missing Polish sheets. When it was all straightened out, this was the story:

The Skouras brothers had been busboys in St. Louis and had rented a store next to my grandfather's grocery to be used as a nickelodeon. My mother had swiped her mother's sheets for their screen. She played the piano and sang along with the nickelodeon, and her brother Joe played his violin. The Skouras brothers did very well with their nickelodeon and were on their way to Hollywood with my grandmother's sheets.

I breezed through *Cry of the City*, being very well directed by Robert Siodmak, and it was a very good as well as a successful film.

I continued my preparations for the MGM test. One day I met Louis B. Mayer for five minutes. He patted my cheek and gave me a Catholic prayer—which confused the hell out of me. Unknown to me, he was in the process of converting.

John was offered the part of Petruchio in *The Taming of the Shrew* to play in theaters all over California. He told me I was to play Bianca and understudy Kate. The actress who was playing Kate had a boyfriend who was a millionaire and was putting up the money for the production. We rehearsed at night at the Actors

Lab if there was room or at various rehearsal halls around Yucca and
Highland Boulevards. I had a marvelous time working with Shakespeare's beautiful lines. Tommy Noonan, John's brother, was in
the play, too, and we became fast friends. He was a wonderful
performer and later starred in *Gentlemen Prefer Blondes* with
Marilyn.

The day of my MGM test was approaching, and probably because of the beautiful language of *The Taming of the Shrew*, I
decided I had to do something dramatic and special for it. I was
having my lunches at the Writers' Table in the commissary, and I
met Christopher Isherwood, whom I adored. He introduced me to
Lion Feuchtwanger, Salka Viertel (who had been Garbo's writer
in *Camille*), Dorothy Parker and Thomas Mann. All of them were
kind and patient with me, and I began to try to read good books.
A new world was opening up, and the only thing I really resented
about Metro was that I had just missed knowing Scott Fitzgerald,
who had been fired a few years before. Budd Schulberg gave me
lists of books to read, and I managed about four a week. It was
flashlight time under the blanket. In fact, I had to get reading
glasses from straining my eyes reading in the dim light—motels
never have proper reading lamps. John seemed to regard my education efforts as a reflection on his sexual prowess.

Blanche had a subscription to *PM*, the progressive New York
newspaper that had printed the pictures of me doing the striptease in *Of V We Sing*. One day, while browsing through one of
her copies, I found a prose poem about a woman talking to her
amputee husband who had lost a leg in the war and wanted a
divorce. The poem was one of the most powerful and beautiful
things I've ever read. And it was about love and need. Not about
how much he needed her but about how much, after waiting
through the long war, she needed him with her spirit and her
body. She reminded him how in tune their minds were and how
much they had laughed together; they were just two halves without each other and became a whole human being only when they
were together. This piece of literature had humor and great writing.

When I showed it to Lillian Burns and told her this was what I
wanted to do for my test, she tried to talk me out of it. I stood firm.
If I was going to have another term contract, I wanted to do serious
important films, and I felt that in doing this for my test, I would
be notifying Mr. Mayer of this fact. Otherwise, I wasn't an artist
and wasn't interested in being under contract to MGM to do Andy
Hardy pictures.

The day of my test arrived, and the heads of almost every department at Metro were on the stage. I didn't understand why, but this test seemed important to them, too. George Sidney, Lillian Burns's husband, directed the test. I had a very simple hairdo, and the Wardrobe Department gave me soft, feminine clothes. Mr. Sidney first had me do one of those personality tests, turning from side to side while I answered his questions simply and honestly and I hoped with dignity. I didn't put myself down for a change.

Then I did the scene with an actor lying in bed facing me, while I faced him and the camera. Mr. Sidney had him hold his hand over his eyes and listen. Bert, John and I saw the test early the next morning. I came out of the projection room filled with pride and joy! At last I knew that I was a film actress, and I loved the medium. It didn't matter if my nose was a little too wide or my eyes slanted the wrong way or anything. It was the thinking and feeling that went on inside my eyes that mattered. George Sidney had somehow captured all my beliefs and my heart, and it was on the film. I had unconsciously used my experience with Paul through the entire test. You could see the agony, the fun, the fear and the trying.

As we walked down the hall, Lillian Burns said, "It's wonderful, darling, but *he* won't like it." Meaning Louis B. Mayer.

"I don't care. *I* like it. And someday a director will like that quality in me and put it on film, and the public will like it. So it doesn't matter, does it, Lillian?"

She put her arms around me, gave me a big kiss and said, "I'm proud of you and proud that my husband got that performance out of you."

But I was quaking because I really wanted to work for Metro, the most prestigious studio.

That night John took me to Chasen's for dinner to celebrate. Bill Grady, looking very sour, was seated in the booth with his name on it. "What's the matter, Bill?" John asked. "Didn't L.B. like Shelley's test?"

"Like it? He almost killed me. He went in the projection booth and tore the film up with his bare hands."

The next day was pleasure as usual. We went to the track at Hollywood Park, though we had to leave early to get to rehearsal. John had a tip on the fifth race, so we bet on only that one. Agony for John. He bought two $10 tickets, on the nose on a horse that paid 26 to 1. I forget its name. I've almost blocked out the whole incident. While he was buying the tickets, I wandered over to

Franchot Tone's box to have a drink with him, and he asked me what I liked in the fifth. I told him that John had a tip on such-and-such a horse at 26 to 1.

"Not a chance," he said. "Easy Win has to take it." Then, without even looking at the racing form, he proceeded to tell me what Easy Win's grandmother had had to eat in Virginia fifteen years before and how she and her mother ran on dry or muddy tracks. In fact, he knew so much about horses that I almost began to suspect he was in some way related to one. He then showed me two $1000 tickets he had bet on Easy Win. To win.

I rushed back to our box. John was sitting there, calmly having a beer, our two tickets in his hand. I told him excitedly everything Tone had told me. "Listen, John," I added, "he financed the Group Theatre, and he comes from a rich horse racing family, Anaconda Copper, I think. He's got to know what's what."

This was our last $20 that we'd bet, until next unemployment insurance day. John reluctantly gave me the tickets and said, "Hurry up, and change them at the window. Tell them you gave the ticket seller the wrong horse's number." I got to the window a second before the bell rang and the cashier changed our tickets.

We watched the race through binoculars, I confident, John breathing hard. Easy Win was winning halfway down the track when suddenly John's horse, number 3, developed a jet engine and won easily three lengths ahead. I stood there waiting for John to kill me. We would have won $520. He didn't say anything about the race. He just tore up the tickets, then said, "Come on, we have to make rehearsal."

We got in the car, and I must have had a peculiar look on my face because he suddenly started to laugh so hard tears came streaming down his face. I kept asking him why he was laughing when we were so broke. "What the hell," he said, "it's only money, and we're rehearsing a play by a very good author."

We had just enough gas to get to rehearsal, and I had enough change at the bottom of my purse so that we could stop at Pink's and have two huge hot dogs with onions and pickles and root beer. When we got to rehearsal, Tommy, John's brother, lent him some money after trying to find out what was so funny as we were giggling so hard at having lost $500. The leading lady wasn't there, and I played Kate as well as Bianca, and we breathed the onions from our Pink's hot dogs all over the rest of the cast. But my final speech as Kate had in it all the gratitude I felt toward John for not getting angry at me for touting him off the winning horse.

Sometime in the middle of that night, when I was lying in John's arms, I tried to tell him how sorry I was about the money. He wouldn't even let me finish the sentence. "Listen, baby," he said, "you've brought me nothing but luck. Since I know you, I've been doing only important pictures. I didn't want to tell you because your MGM contract didn't work out, but I saw Lewis Milestone last week, and I have one of the leads in the most important war film to be done to date. It's called *A Walk in the Sun* and I'm getting one hundred thousand dollars for it." (That's like a million today.)

"John, you really have to do this one stone-cold sober. Milestone is a great director, and it's a fantastic opportunity."

"Yesterday I had a very good interview with Robert Rossen for one of the leads in *All the King's Men* when they make it at the end of next year. You'll get your opportunity soon."

"Sure."

John started to shoot *A Walk in the Sun*, and many of my friends from New York and the Actors Lab were in it. I used to go on the set and listen to Milestone quietly and lovingly direct his actors. That's the only thing I was jealous of. John stayed cold sober, and he was brilliant in that picture.

It was a frustrating time for me. Most actors know the experience of looking at the telephone at 5:30 P.M. and wondering whether they dare bother their agent. (You know, calling up very cheerfully, chatting and then saying, "By the way, what's happening?") I've always felt the sweetest words an actor can hear are: "They want you." I had one- or two-day parts in several forgettable pictures. Neither I nor the directors were very good. I soon began to realize that as sweet a man as Bert was, he knew only the heads of the Casting departments. To get a really good role, you had to know the directors or producers.

One day, though, Bert surprised me. He could arrange, he said, for me to meet the head of Casting at RKO to discuss a term contract.

"Bert, you know I don't want another term contract." But by now I was so broke that I said it rather feebly, and I was tired of taking buses and trolley cars and hitchhiking around the vast expanse of Los Angeles. There never was and still isn't a decent public transportation system in the City of the Angels.

Bert explained to me that RKO was developing a lot of new young stars, and I should really reconsider seeing "Mr. RKO." The appointment was made. I didn't mention to Bert that I knew Howard

Hughes, who by then owned RKO. If they wanted me for my acting, okay, but I didn't want to use that kind of pull. Besides, I was a little afraid of the strange rumors about Hughes now. I kept hearing stories that he had girls stashed all over Los Angeles, and nobody ever saw or heard of them again till they stopped being his girlfriends.

When Bert and I entered the Casting Office, we sat in an elegant outer office with white carpets, and the secretary was prettier than I was. She gave us some coffee and then ignored us, so I said, "Is Howard in his office?" With her nose in the air she informed me that Mr. Hughes did not have an office at RKO, his office was at Sam Goldwyn's studio and he had never, to anybody's knowledge, set his foot on the RKO lot. Bert looked at me in a funny way, but we just kept waiting. After half an hour I pulled Paul's trick and said, "Bert, don't we have to go to MGM now? It's getting late." Bert looked bewildered. The secretary began to look nervous and explained that Mr. RKO really wanted to talk to me, but was looking at rushes and would be down in a few minutes.

She showed us into the whitest office I've ever seen. The white rug on the floor seemed to go all the way up the walls and meet in the center of the ceiling. The chairs were white; the desk was white; the "casting couch" was white. The presence of the latter made the corn on my left little toe ache. I had on a pair of new open-toed red patent leather pumps which Blanche had financed. I thought they were more dignified than my fuck-me shoes, but still sexy. Anyway, they were cheap and new and hurt like hell!

I knew that executives always had bathrooms attached to their offices, so I asked the secretary if I could use the bathroom. "Of course," she said, "in there," indicating a white door, and I went into a white marble bathroom. The pressure on my left little toe from the new shoes was agonizing, so I looked in the medicine cabinet, and behold, there was a double-edged razor blade lying on the bottom shelf. I washed it off with soap and water, removed my stocking and cut off the corn. But I must have cut too deep because the damned toe started to bleed all over the place. I tried to stop the bleeding with cold water. I could hear Bert talking to somebody on the other side of the door, so I wrapped my toe in Kleenex, put my stocking and shoe back on, fixed my face and bravely, with my best model's walk, came out of the bathroom.

Mr. RKO said hello to my bosom and asked me to sit down on the couch. I sat down carefully, crossing my legs so he could see them. He began asking me questions about what I had done, and I tried to be very animated and funny and sexy and really sell myself, which I hated doing.

But as I was talking to him, I noticed his eyes, which were looking at my legs, suddenly move down to my feet. Following his horrified expression, I saw blood flowing out of my open-toed red pump, all over his white carpet. The only thing I could think of to do was pretend it wasn't happening. Mr. RKO grabbed the wastepaper basket and stuck my foot in it, yelling, "What the hell's happening to your foot?"

Both men looked stunned as I told them what I had done with his razor blade. Mr. RKO gave me more Kleenex to put in my shoe and said we would have the meeting another day. He then pressed a button for the beautiful secretary to show us out, with me hopping on my right foot. The distance to the outer office seemed like the 220-yard dash, and I could hear the secretary asking, "What happened? Did she stab herself?", and Mr. RKO screaming, "That girl's crazy!"

Bert rushed me to his car and drove me to the Hollywood Emergency Hospital, where they stopped the bleeding. So much for my test at RKO. Did I do it "accidentally on purpose"? Was this my way of rejecting another stultifying term contract or was it really an accident? I'll never know.

John and I had made an arrangement to meet at the Sunset Marquis restaurant the next night as he had to do some dubbing on *A Walk in the Sun*. About 11:00 A.M. my mother woke me up with a strange look on her face and said, "There's a Mrs. John Ireland on the phone who would like to talk to you, and it doesn't sound like his mother."

I rushed to the phone, and a very nice lady's voice said, "Shelley Winter?"

"Yes, what can I do for you?" She said that she would like to meet me for lunch and talk to me and that it was rather urgent. Without thinking, I said, "Of course, where shall we meet?"

"What about the Players Restaurant at noon?"

"Sure, I'll be there."

My mother looked at me strangely, and my father pretended to read the newspaper. I dressed as simply as possible, *sans* makeup, and took the streetcar to the Players.

A very attractive blonde woman of about thirty with a thin face and high cheekbones was waiting for me in a booth. When I sat down, she gave me a very nice smile. "I've been wanting to meet you for a long time," she said. Then, with a rather doubtful look on her face, she added, "You're rather young, aren't you?"

"No, I'm almost twenty-one." I was lying, but it seemed the right thing to say.

We ordered lunch, and for once I don't remember what was ordered. She then took a small calendar out of her purse, which she carefully explained to me as follows: "John Junior goes to his counsellor on Tuesdays and Fridays; Peter goes to his on Mondays and the orthodontist every other Friday. My daughter is eleven next week, and she starts her allergy shots every Monday."

I drank a glass of water and said, "Why are you telling *me* all this?"

She looked puzzled. "Well, you've been seeing John for quite a while, haven't you? So when our divorce is final next month, I assume that you and John will be getting married. I'm interested in art, and I want to go study in Paris for a year and the children are staying with John. Of course, I'll see them Christmas and summer vacations. They know all about this, and they approve. So you'll have to be taking them to their appointments because you know how forgetful John is."

In terror, all I could think of to answer was: "But I don't have a car."

Thank God our lunch came. She seemed to enjoy it immensely and rattled on at how excited she was at the prospect of living in Paris free and alone after fifteen years of housework and children. She was very happy about the whole thing and couldn't wait. After a respectable time I said I had to go to the studio and started to leave. She called me back and put the little calendar in my purse.

I took the streetcar back home. When I got there, my mother took one look at me and said, "Should I call a doctor?"

"No, just go out to the pool, and leave me alone."

As I sat there trying to figure out what to do, the phone rang. It was long distance, some man from the United Jewish Appeal who wanted me to host a charity event in Denver in two days because whoever had promised to do it had gotten sick. I agreed at once and added, "Are you calling from the national office in New York?" He said he was. "Great. I can give you three months. I have no commitments for this period of time. I've got three evening gowns and four cocktail dresses. Is that enough?"

This man obviously thought I'd suddenly gone crazy or else I'd had a message from God. He said, "I'll bring your itinerary and a prepared fund-raising speech that you can say your own way and meet you in Denver tomorrow. A travel agency will bring you your tickets in a couple of hours. Thank you, Shelley . . . we really needed somebody for this next three-month period."

I said, "Thank *you*. What hotel do I go to in Denver? I might fly there tonight."

He told me the name of the hotel and said, "Get there whenever you want to."

My mother looked bewildered, but my father put his arms around me for the first time in more than a year, kissed my cheek and said, "I know I raised a girl with a *goldina* heart." They helped me pack and the tickets arrived about three o'clock. My plane was at five. I've traveled thousands of miles all over the world, but that was the fastest packing I ever did. You would have thought Hitler was in Pomona.

My father got me to the airport driving through the back lot of Twentieth Century-Fox, out the front gate, through the front gate of Metro and out the back gate, as I waved to all the guards, and we got to the airport at four forty-five. My parents waved to me from the field as the pilot spun the propellers, and I escaped into the wild blue yonder.

CHAPTER 12

I don't think John suffered too much because during my tour he got a starring role in that great picture *All the King's Men,* and soon after he married his beautiful leading lady, Joanne Dru. I believe they brought about seven children between them to the marriage, inspiring the Hollywood story "Come quick! My children and your children are fighting with our children!" John certainly couldn't eat dinner at home now. Ever. But there were a lot of things he could do. Just great.

I was expecting the tour to be a real drag, boring and lonely. After that jazzy year of living out my missed adolescence, was I in for a surprise! I discovered that between Los Angeles and New York there were millions of cultured, educated, kind and fun people. Of course, a lot of them were curious about Hollywood, and some ladies wanted to know the latest gossip about Rita Hayworth and other celebrities. But mostly they entertained me in their homes and took me to the local theaters, where there were many fine opera and ballet companies and many national companies of Broadway shows.

Philadelphia presented me with an award, a large gold ruler inscribed with these words: "To Shelley Winter, who is helping America live by the Golden Rule." The Mental Health Organization of Atlanta for some mysterious reason gave me a gold bell inscribed "Let Sanity, Health and Tolerance ring out in the land."

Every place I went, people treated me with dignity and as if I were already an important actress. Some even knew the hit I had made in *Rosalinda* or had seen *Cry of the City* or *Knickerbocker Holiday.* I think that tour did my career as much good as did the millions of dollars the UJA raised for the poor displaced European refugees still living in relocation camps, trying to get to the Promised Land which was in the throes of becoming the state of Israel.

When I returned to Hollywood three months later, my experience with John Ireland seemed like something I had dreamed, a rather sexy dream that had turned into a nightmare, but with my built-in resilience I just wiped it all out.

My contract with Bert Marx had been mutually abandoned, and I decided that I was my own best agent and that perhaps I should go back to New York and work in the theater. I had read about a play that had gotten great reviews, called *Born Yesterday* that a Judy Holliday was starring in, written and directed by Garson Kanin. It was the biggest hit of the season in New York. I had casually met Kanin in Walgreen's basement years before, so I thought: What the hell, I'll take a chance and call him. I didn't want to use the phone at my house because my father hated long-distance phone calls.

I decided to go over and use Connie's phone. When I arrived, she was busy packing to move to Italy and work in Italian films. I was very happy for her because she had been very depressed for the last few months. She'd left Goldwyn where she'd hated being a Goldwyn Girl, and she was finally getting away from Hollywood to a new country where she would meet new friends and have a new career. I told her I'd like to call Garson Kanin in New York and try to get the understudy job in *Born Yesterday*, and get myself back to New York and the theater. I'd had the Hollywood glamor. Connie immediately called John Houseman and got Garson Kanin's number. Because it was long distance, his secretary put Garson Kanin himself on the phone. "Hello, who is this?" he asked.

"Shelley Winter. Mr. Kanin, how's the weather in New York?"

"Pretty good. How's the weather in California?"

"It's fine." Pause. I mean, I really had Garson Kanin himself on the telephone, and it terrified me. I wasn't scared of movie directors, but stage directors were something else. Connie looked at me as if I were an idiot. I was finally able to gulp down my fear and explain to Mr. Kanin that I'd heard about the Judy Holliday role in *Born Yesterday* and if the part of the understudy wasn't cast, I would like to come to New York—by bus—and read for it.

He said, "Oh, Shelley Winter. I remember you in *Rosalinda* and Walgreen's basement. You look very much like Judy. For a minute there I thought you called me for a weather report."

"No, I was scared."

He laughed and said, "Listen, I know you're very talented, but the understudy has already been cast. A girl by the name of Jan Sterling is doing it."

I was about to hang up because I didn't want to run up Connie's phone bill. "Wait a minute," he yelled. "Don't hang up yet. My brother, Mike Kanin, is producing a script of Ruth's and mine called *A Double Life*. George Cukor is directing it at Universal International. There's a part of a waitress in it that is funny and sad, and she has all her scenes with Ronald Colman. I think you'd be wonderful for it."

I said, "Oh, sure," knowing they would give the part to Lana Turner or someone like that.

"I'm not kidding. I'll call George Cukor right now at Universal and ask him to read you for the role tomorrow. What's your phone number?"

I gave it to him halfheartedly. I thought he was just trying to let me down easy. "It was very nice talking to you, Mr. Kanin," I said. "If Judy ever leaves the play, think of me, will you?" And I hung up.

Connie knew Kanin and said, "He wouldn't make that up. I'm sure he'll have you read for Cukor."

"Oh, sure," I said. "They're about to give me a great part opposite Ronald Colman."

"Why not?" asked Connie. "You're a good actress and a terrific comedienne."

I kissed her sad eyes and thanked her for letting me use her phone and said I would pay her when the bill came in. "Forget it," my sweet friend said. "The treat's on me. Listen, maybe lightning will strike."

The next morning at ten the phone rang, and somebody with a "Virginia voice" said, "This is Mr. George Cukor's office at Universal International. Is this Miss Shelley Winter?" I made some inarticulate sound. She went on, "Mr. Cukor has to go look at locations. Mr. Kanin called him from New York last night, and he would like to see you right away. Can you come to the studio?"

I replied, "I'll be there as soon as possible." If I could have grown wings, I would have flown. I told my father what had happened and asked if he would drive me out to Universal. He said, "You know gas is still rationed? *Again* with the movies?" I looked helplessly at my mother, who said, "Go." I put on my tightest girdle, my pointiest bra, swept my hair up with combs, stuck on my false eyelashes, two coats of makeup and those you-know-what shoes. This was my chance to play a sexy waitress opposite Ronald Colman!

The guard at UI directed me to George Cukor's office, which was nestled among the top executive bungalows. I looked in my mirror to make sure everything was in place and walked in with my sexiest walk, swinging my large black patent leather handbag. A very English secretary said, "May we help you, miss?"—using the royal "we," I presume.

"My name is Shelley Winter, and I have an appointment with

George Cukor, arranged for me long distance by Garson Kanin from New York."

I was quite nervous despite my bravado, so my speech was lapsing into Brooklynese the more British the secretary got. She kept staring at my outfit. I thought *she* looked pretty dowdy in her skirt and cardigan set, and she had her hair in a *bun*, for God's sake. She picked up the phone and said, "I think Miss Winter has arrived."

The door opened, and there again stood George Cukor from my Scarlett O'Hara audition days. "Won't you come in my office, Miss Winter?" His manner made me feel like Katharine Cornell, so I recovered somewhat from his British secretary's snooty attitude. All over his office were sketches of different scenes from *Othello* and some from *A Double Life*. Mr. Cukor poured me a cup of tea. He didn't have a desk in his office, not even a casting couch. Just a lot of chairs and small tables and bookcases. But there were large photographs of people like Katharine Hepburn and Cary Grant and Spencer Tracy and Helen Hayes all over the place. I began to shiver inside. I was in very fast company in that room.

There was a wonderful terra-cotta bust of Ronald Colman on a stand. I had never seen such a thing, and it fascinated me. Cukor studied me as I studied Ronald Colman. I had used his records from *Lost Horizon* to try to improve my speech, listening to them over and over. He was such a fine actor and so elegant that I didn't even dare to fantasize about him. He and Alfred Lunt, Fredric March and Paul Muni were the greatest actors I had ever seen. They spoke the language so beautifully that it was almost like listening to music.

Cukor interrupted my reverie. "May I call you Shelley?"

"Of course," I replied. I longed to tell him about the time I auditioned for Scarlett O'Hara, but I didn't dare. I held my breath when he said, "You know, there's something familiar about you. But I can't really tell what you look like in that outfit and with all that makeup. You know, Shelley, this part is a simple waitress who's probably Polish and works in an Italian restaurant in Greenwich Village. She's not a glamorous starlet."

"Who do you want me to look like?"

He smiled and said, "She probably looks like Shirley Schrift. [Were there no secrets in Hollywood?] Would you be offended if I asked you to go into my bathroom and take off that tight girdle that's killing you and the tight bra, comb out your hair and wash your face?" I gave him a funny look, and he added quickly, "And then put your clothes back on, of course."

"What about the shoes?"

"They're okay for now, but we probably can do better if you get the part."

I went into his bathroom and did exactly as he asked, carefully avoiding my toes as I took my stockings off. I put my eyelashes in a little box in my purse and scrubbed my face with soap and water. Then I brushed out my hair and pulled it back on the sides with two little barrettes. I looked in the mirror and thought: Jesus, I don't look like any movie actress I ever saw. But if that's what he wants, I'll give it to him.

I walked back out, and he said, "Walk across the room naturally, and then sit down in that chair." I didn't think I had a natural walk left in me, but I tried. "Garson Kanin says you're a very good actress. Certainly you're the exact type for this role." Was that a compliment? He saw the look on my face and said kindly, "You're very sexy and earthy, but that comes from who and what you are, not the image you're trying to pretend to be." Then he gave me the whole script of *A Double Life* and said, "Are you busy the rest of the afternoon?"

"No," I whispered.

"Well, why don't you have lunch in the commissary? Then read the script carefully and concentrate on the first scene between Ronald Colman's character and the waitress. I should be back from location scouting about three, and we'll read it. Okay?"

He was so nice and kind I suddenly turned to him and said, "Are you from Hollywood?"

He smiled and said, "Well, I've lived out here a number of years, but I was born in Manhattan."

"That's funny, you don't sound like it."

"Don't worry about your speech, Shelley. I like it just fine for this role. You understand?"

I understood, but I could hardly believe it. I carefully carried the huge script of *A Double Life* and dashed out of his office before he had a chance to change his mind. I was so nervous I went into the commissary and got a tuna fish on rye and a chocolate milk shake *to go*—my standard tranquilizer—and ate in the little park across from the commissary as I carefully read the whole script. It was fantastic. Not only was it a wonderful film script, but in my opinion it was fine literature. It dealt with an occupational disease that many actors suffer from. They get very deeply into a role, and the character sometimes starts to take over their personal lives if the show is a hit or the film has a long schedule. For some actors, when you're in a long run, your real life seems make-believe, and the make-believe becomes your reality.

A *Double Life* is about such an actor. Ronald Colman is a stage star playing Othello on Broadway in a long-running hit. The jealousy inherent in the role is beginning to destroy him, and he carries it over into his personal life. Because he cherishes his wife, Desdemona (played by Signe Hasso), and is terrified of hurting her, he starts a casual romance with a waitress he picks up in a restaurant. In her apartment he allows the character of Othello gradually to usurp his real personality, and eventually he strangles the waitress, as Othello does Desdemona. He hardly realizes what he's done as he switches back and forth from playacting to reality.

The role of the waitress was pathetic, funny, sexual, romantic and cunning, but she did not have enough experience to realize the danger of the psychotic actor she had become involved with, and so she perished.

When I finished reading the script, I sat there in the sun, knowing I was born to play this role. Everything in my life had been a preparation for it. Whether Cukor and the executives at Universal would see it, I didn't know. I went back to his office at three-thirty very calm and quiet. He questioned me closely about my reaction to the script and the part. He seemed pleased with my answers. "Shelley," he said, "if you can put your intellectual understanding into this role when we test you for it, you'll get the part, and if it's a good picture, you'll win an Oscar."

"Aren't you going to read me for it?"

"It's not necessary. You'll rehearse tomorrow with Abner Biberman, and the test I think will be next Friday." That was ten days away.

As I rode home on the streetcar, the whole thing seemed impossible. Was I really going to be tested for a lead in an important film opposite Ronald Colman? As I walked up Hollywood Boulevard, I looked at all the footprints of the superstars in the courtyard of Grauman's Chinese Theater, clutching the script of A *Double Life* under my arm and remembering the time when I was a kid and imagined I could be Scarlett O'Hara. The same director had been kind to me then. Maybe he was still just sorry for me.

I spent that night reading and rereading the script, and by midnight I knew it all. I was so excited I couldn't sleep, and I kept

Blanche awake with my reciting of *Othello*. Then I consciously made a decision. I must make the whole thing unimportant and *not possible*, or I would be too terrified to do it.

They notified me to come out and rehearse with Abner Biberman, and when I got there, I realized I was one of six girls testing for the role, including, I think at MGM's insistence, Lana Turner. Wouldn't you know it! I knew they would give the part to her, and there was no use breaking my heart again. I would go along with it and not pin my hopes on it and just practice testing.

I rehearsed with Biberman about three times and got fitted for a waitress's uniform, *sans* girdle and bra, as Cukor wanted. The day before the test Bill Grady at MGM called me and told me there was a one-day part, maybe two, in a picture with Mickey Rooney in which he played a prizefighter. It paid $100 a day, and I would have to be in wardrobe at six-thirty the next morning if I wanted to do it. I thought: What the hell, maybe I'll make enough money to go back to New York by bus and stay with my aunt until I get another show. The test seemed a waste of time.

So I called Abner Biberman and explained to him that I had another job for that day, and I needed the $100. He said, "Well, kid, try to get here by four-thirty. You'll have your makeup on from MGM, and I'll do your test last. The movements are all the same, and you know them from the rehearsals."

The film at Metro was another nothing part. Another girl and I drove up to an outdoor fight ring in a flivver and asked a trainer where the lightweight champ, Mickey Rooney, was. We were his number one fans. Mervyn Le Roy was the director, and it was going rather slowly because Mickey would never shut up between takes. I didn't mind. I was hoping it would go over, and I'd get two days' pay.

We had a lovely box lunch under the trees on the back lot. It was a sunny California day, but all I was thinking about was autumn in New York, Broadway and going to acting classes instead of the races. I mentioned to the other actress that I was supposed to do a test at UI that afternoon. After lunch she went up to Mervyn Le Roy and told him about my test. "Shelley, why didn't you tell me?" he apologized. "We'll do your scene first thing."

I could have killed that girl as I'd been hoping for the extra $100 for another day's shooting. "Thanks a lot," I told her. "You know Universal will never give me the part."

We did our scene quickly, but it was already three by the time I'd changed into my slacks and blouse. I didn't have a car, so I hitchhiked; it was the only way I could get there, and it was safe in those days.

The hitches were few that afternoon, and I was exhausted by the time I got to Hollywood and Highland. It was about five, and I stood there on the island in the middle of the street, waiting for the little red streetcar, and wondered if it was any use for me to go all the way out into the Valley.

Lou Costello stopped at the red light, driving a white Cadillac convertible. He recognized me from the commissary. I told him about my test and how late I was. "Get in," he said, and we sped up Highland, down Lankershim and through the Universal gates, ignoring the lights, speed limits and the studio guard (Abbott and Costello were big Universal stars then).

When I rushed onto the darkened stage, I couldn't see anything for a minute, but I heard Mr. Cukor's voice: "*La Divina* decided to show up."

The electricians were beginning to take down the lights of the restaurant set where the tests had been shot. Biberman told Cukor that I had had a job that day and needed the money. Cukor laughed and said, "Well, take off your eyelashes and get into your costume. And remember, no girdle. Now hurry. We have to be out of here by six or we turn into pumpkins. The front office pulls the plug. No overtime for tests."

He began to rehearse me, Biberman playing Colman's part. It was the waitress's first scene of the film, when he comes into the restaurant. After the third rehearsal I said to Mr. Cukor, "I think I'm ready to shoot."

"You just did. I shot your last rehearsal. I know those magic words 'Roll 'em' terrify actors, so I synchronize the sound and camera without the actors being aware of it. It makes for more spontaneous performances."

"You mean we're through?"

"For now. You were very good and very funny. But from now on it's in the hands of the gods and the executives of Universal."

"And the banks. Right?"

He gave me a kiss on the nose, and as I was leaving, the assistant director gave me some sort of release, which I signed in disgust. As I rode home on the streetcar, I felt as if I hadn't done anything. When my parents asked me how it went, I said that I guessed it was all right, but nothing sensational.

The next day I started to look and call around for other jobs. Glory be, I read in the trades that Lawrence Langner and Theresa

Helburn had arrived in L.A. and were staying at the Beverly Hills Hotel while auditioning replacements for *Oklahoma!* I called Lawrence Langner, who remembered me from *Rosalinda* and said they would audition me on Tuesday. He said, "Shelley, are you sure you're ready to leave Hollywood?"

"Mr. Langner, Hollywood's ready for me to leave."

"Well, next time you come out here you'll come out right. Now you study these songs, "All Or Nothin' " and "I'm Jest a Girl Who Cain't Say No." You won't have to read because we know you're funny, but Rodgers and Hammerstein will want to hear you sing."

By Tuesday morning I hadn't heard anything from Universal, so I figured I hadn't got the part. I knew I wouldn't get it anyway, so I got myself into a cute checkered gingham dress, put a bow in my hair (always wear a getup that's like the part, is my motto) and went to the audition Tuesday afternoon in a studio on La Cienega.

There were about 100 girls there, and they *all* were in checkered gingham dresses. When my turn came, I went into the inner sanctum. Even though this audition meant so much to me, Langner and Helburn, Rodgers and Hammerstein looked so New Yorkish and friendly that I relaxed and sang those two songs as I'd never sung before or maybe since.

Lawrence Langner put his arm around me and said, "Kiddo, in a couple of years Fox is going to make this into a film. I bet you get the part in the film, too." (Gloria Grahame got it.)

"What do you mean, 'too'?" I asked. "Have I got it now?"

He said, "Out of courtesy we have to hear the rest of the girls, but we'll call you by seven, and I'm sure it's yours if you want it."

I took a taxi home and rushed in to tell my parents that I thought I was *singing* in a big hit musical in New York and it was almost 100 percent sure that I had the job.

"We came out here to be with you girls," my father said, "and now you're running back to New York?"

Blanche quickly announced, "Whatever she does, I am not going back to New York."

"I'm over twenty-one," I said. "I can take care of myself."

My mother immediately came up with the solution. "She can live with Aunt Zecil in Brooklyn." Oh yeah? That'll be the day.

We sat and looked at the telephone until seven. At seven-ten it rang. We all jumped three feet into the air. My father got it first. He began negotiating with Lawrence Langner, and I wanted the part so badly I was afraid he would lose it for me. He was saying things like: "I know, Mr. Langner, it's a wonderful opportunity, but she's a very young girl and her family's out here now and she has to have enough money to live in a respectable hotel. . . . No, she's not a minor . . . but she's very naïve [little did *he* know], and we want to be able to protect her. . . . Yes, we'll try to get her a roommate. . . . Well, four hundred dollars doesn't sound right for the St. James Theater. After all, it's such a big theater. . . . Well, she packed them in, in *Rosalinda*; she got more publicity than anyone in the show. . . . You know *Oklahoma!* is going into its fifth year, she could give it a shot in the arm. . . ."

I was writhing on the floor in agony. He wouldn't let me take the phone away from him. I finally heard him say, "All right, five hundred sounds about right." I lay still. My father hung up, looked at me and said, "Listen, *paskcodnyik,* you're getting a second chance. Concentrate on your Art, as you call it. I call it work. And don't go running around with *nogoodniks.* You hear?" I heard and kissed him.

The next day my father and I met the entire Theatre Guild at the Polo Lounge. He carefully read my run-of-the-play contract, and I signed it. They opened a bottle of French champagne, and I agreed to be in New York for rehearsals in three weeks.

As he drove me home carefully, I said good-bye to all the palm trees along Sunset Boulevard. I was happy to be going home to Broadway, where there was no class system, everyone ate in the same restaurants and, if you were a professional actor, your talent and opinions were respected. I vowed that if and when I returned to Hollywood, I would come back a star and be treated accordingly.

The next morning the phone rang, and it was George Cukor calling to tell me that they liked my test and I had gotten the lead opposite Ronald Colman in *A Double Life* and I should report to Wardrobe for fittings.

CHAPTER 13

My mother, who was the only one home at the moment, had heard Mr. Cukor as he told me the news. He was so happy for me he had spoken quite loudly. When he hung up, my mother and I sat on the twin beds and stared at each other. Both jobs were for the same time period. I finally said, "Mom, I have to go out and fit costumes for *A Double Life* and probably rehearse with Mr. Cukor, too."

"Well, take the script, and go do it."

"But tonight I have to rehearse *Oklahoma!* with Mr. Rodgers and Mr. Hammerstein because they're leaving for New York in a couple of days."

"Well, take the score, and go do it!" she repeated.

For some weird reason my mother's logic seemed the only solution. Preparing for *A Double Life* at Universal in the daytime and rehearsing *Oklahoma!* at night. I think we had some crazy mystical idea that we could send Shirley Schrift back to New York to do *Oklahoma!* and Shelley Winter would stay in Hollywood and do *A Double Life*. My father refused to deal with the whole problem since he was very angry at me for signing that little piece of paper at UI without showing it to him first. He was sure it was a financially unfair option for an exclusive seven-year contract, and *he was right*.

The next day at Universal, while rehearsing and discussing the role with Cukor, I burst into tears. "Mr. Cukor, I'm sorry. I can't do the part."

He looked at me in amazement. "Why not, for God's sake?"

"Well, Equity is my first and parent union. . . ." I was crying so hard I couldn't go on.

"That's nice. It's mine, too."

I finally managed to explain that since Universal had taken so long to notify me, I had auditioned to play Ado Annie in *Oklahoma!* on Broadway, and I'd gotten the part. So I'd signed a run-of-the-play contract with the Theatre Guild, and since Equity was my first union, I felt that contract had more validity than the little piece of paper I'd signed for Universal the day I'd made the test.

Mr. Cukor started to laugh. It rather annoyed me, and finally, I asked him please to try to stop because I didn't see anything funny

183

about my not having any decent parts for more than a year and then having two wonderful jobs both taking place at the same time. "Have another Kleenex," he offered, and picked up the phone. "Get me Lawrence Langner at the Theater Guild in New York." I held my breath as he explained to Langner that they both had an actress who signed anything put in front of her. Langner seemed to be laughing, too. After an involved conversation he said, "Thanks very much, Larry," and hung up. He smiled at me. He then asked for William Goetz, one of the heads of Universal. In a very tough voice he explained that the girl he wanted to play the waitress had a previous commitment to do *Oklahoma!* in New York right after filming *A Double Life.* Goetz tried to give him some flak, but Cukor patiently pointed out that this was Universal's most expensive film in several years, and he wanted to "insure" its investment with my performance. I couldn't believe my ears. He reminded Goetz that they had read hundreds of girls for the role. Goetz agreed, I guess. "But why the hell does she want to do that tacky old musical?"

"To learn from a live audience," Cukor replied, and hung up. "Everything's fixed. The Theater Guild has agreed to let you do the film first, and the understudy will play the part on Broadway till you get there. When you're finished with *Oklahoma!*, you'll probably have to report back to UI. But you'd better get a smart agent to renegotiate that option if they pick it up, which I'm sure they will. And don't sign anything again ever until a lawyer has read the fine print."

I wanted to kiss him, but I was afraid to. We continued to rehearse, and his ideas were so original and marvelous that when the rehearsal was over, I went outside and picked some flowers from in front of Mr. Goetz's bungalow. I tied them up with my hair ribbon, and Mr. Cukor's lovely English secretary gave me a silver vase to put them in. When he heard us talking, he came out of his office, looked at the flowers, looked at me and said, "I remember now! Scarlett O'Hara. My thirteen-year-old Brooklyn Scarlett O'Hara!"

I blushed furiously and stuttered, "See? I waited all these years to work for you." He gave me a kiss, and I went home happily on the little red streetcar. When I got my call sheet, I noticed UI had added an *s* to "Winter."

The next week *A Double Life* started. I appeared on the set bright and early the third day of shooting, knowing my lines inside out and upside down. Mr. Cukor introduced me to Ronald Colman.

The legend was flesh; the celluloid image, a human being in three dimensions. He kissed my hand and said in that beautiful voice, "It's a great pleasure to meet you, Miss Winters." I felt knighted and just gazed at him. I couldn't think, move or talk above a whisper.

Cukor didn't notice my reaction and started rehearsing. "Shelley, this is a very simple scene. Ronnie is sitting at a table in the restaurant; you walk up, pour him a cup of coffee and hand him the menu. Then you lean over and pour him a glass of ice water while he looks at your bosom and face. Then take out your pad and pencil while he looks at the menu. Then he says his line, 'How's the chicken cacciatore?' and you say, 'Well, it's your stomach.' You know, just like the test. We need the stage wait because some of the poetry of Othello will be on the sound track as he substitutes your face for Desdemona's in his tortured imagination."

"Yes, sir," I managed to squeak.

The assistant yelled, "Silence, rehearsal."

Would you believe we rehearsed for an hour and I couldn't get it right? Then we did ninety-six—*ninety-six*—takes. Even for those days that was a record. Everything imaginable went wrong.

I stumbled in. I poured coffee on Ronald Colman's hands. I poured coffee in his lap. I dropped my pad. I broke my pencil. I poured the water in the glass, and it overflowed. The next take I broke the glass. I dropped the pitcher. I kept four prop men and the Wardrobe Department cleaning up after me. It wasn't funny; it was a nightmare.

Around Take 60 I realized I just couldn't function, and I think Cukor was beginning to believe he had hired a hopeless klutz. Ronald Colman's presence paralyzed me. It was near lunchtime when I noticed Rufus LeMaire, head of Casting, standing off to the side of the set, and I thought: Oh, my God, I'm costing them too much money, and they're going to replace me. I was quivering with fear when Cukor called lunch—early. Ronald Colman said, "Miss Winters, would you please have lunch with me?" Then he took off his jacket and tie and walked with me to the commissary.

We sat at a corner table, and he asked me gentle questions about myself and my experience in New York. I was still in such awe of him that I could barely answer. Then he told me stories of how he had first come to New York from London—he had lived in a very inexpensive boardinghouse in Brooklyn Heights, and the first jobs he'd had were trying plays out with Florence Eldridge, Fredric March's wife.

"What do you mean, try plays out?"

"Well," he said, "you know, in those days there was no Actors' Equity, so they treated actors any way they wanted to. We would try plays out in New Haven, Philadelphia and Boston. We did the drudgery of rehearsing the lead roles and having them blocked and staged, and then, if the plays were good, the producers would bring in the two stars a week before they came into New York."

The fury of Priscilla Picket Line rose in my breast, and I forgot I was scared. "That's the worst thing I've ever heard of! How could they do that to you and Florence Eldridge? You're great actors!"

Laughing, he said, "Well, in those days we were young and inexperienced and needed the jobs badly."

"I would have killed the producer."

"Once I almost did, accidentally. I presented him with caviar I had received from England. Unknown to me, it was contaminated. He almost died from food poisoning."

By now I was laughing delightedly. "Are you sure it was accidental?"

"Well, perhaps accidentally on purpose."

I pushed away my tuna sandwich and chocolate malt; I didn't need them anymore. "Listen," I said, "how did you get your first break?"

He said, "The star who replaced me in a show was taken drunk on opening night on Broadway. They had to scurry around to find me. I opened the show and got great reviews. My next play, when I was the star, I insisted that Florence Eldridge play opposite me. But we tried out our own plays; the other system is too inhuman to do to fellow actors."

I told him about the orchestra falling down in *Rosalinda*, and he roared with laughter. "Musicals always terrify me," he said. "I was in one once. I can dance quite well, but I can never remember which step comes next."

Amazed, I said, "Me, too. And I've been in a lot of musicals."

During all this the twelve big shots sitting at the executive table were eyeing us strangely.

When we got back to the set, he was still Ronald Colman, but he was also a nice man and my friend. The first take after lunch I did the scene technically perfect, and I think it was quite funny. Anyway, audiences all over the world laughed when I said, "Well, it's your stomach." Everyone on the set crossed himself, and we went on with the scene.

From then on it went wonderfully well, and we got the master shot done by 4:00 P.M., when the whole set sat down to have tea, which Mr. Colman insisted on being served; it was in his contract. He said a tea break was necessary to relax the tensions of the day.

We did our close-ups with renewed vigor, and at five-thirty sharp Mr. Colman got his hat, bowed to everyone on the set and left. As I watched him walk off the stage, I thought of the famous poem "Richard Cory": "And he was always quietly arrayed, and he was always human when he talked; but still he fluttered pulses when he said, 'Good morning,' and he glittered when he walked."

I have always been eternally grateful to Ronald Colman for the way he made me relax at that lunch. He made me feel that I was somehow in his league, thus saving my role in the film and perhaps my career. I will always love him for his kindness and perception. I didn't care if I got an Oscar nomination for this film, but I vowed that I would do everything in my power to see that Ronald Colman got an Oscar. I knew he had never won one in his entire career, although he'd done many wonderful films and had been nominated several times. But this was his most demanding role as an actor.

As I stood looking at the stage door, Cukor came up, put his arm around me and said, "They broke the mold, didn't they?"

I agreed. "There are no actors like him anymore; maybe there never will be again. None of them have the manners and gentle humanity that that man has."

Cukor said, "You two are just great together."

I laughed. "Sure, Coney Island and Cambridge."

"That was what made it so poignant and funny."

I hugged him. "I'm glad you're pleased. I thought for a while this morning that I was going to disgrace you and strike out."

The picture continued day by day in exact sequence. Only a big director can make producers give the actors this gift. I've done at least fifty movies in which you start with the last scene and go backwards. How the hell can you know what you're going to feel or how you're going to behave months after the beginning? Oh, well, all in the name of economy, not quality.

Shooting A Double Life was a joy. Cukor was sensitive, the stage surrounding the set was dark and silent and all the concentration was on our performances. That's what gets exposed to the film, after all.

One day we finally came to the scene where the character of Othello has almost completely taken over the mind of the actor, and Colman strangles me, as Othello does Desdemona. Cukor wanted the murder to have sexual implications, if possible, within the limitations of the Hays Office, the motion-picture industry's self-censoring organization.

I am wearing a satin and lace nightgown when Colman comes to my apartment in the middle of the night (our characters have been having an affair for several months). Although he has taken off his stage makeup, he is still Othello. When I think we are going to make love and ask him if we should put out the light, he grabs my long blonde hair and says, "Put out the light, and then put out the light. . . . Should I repent me; but once put out thy light . . . I know not where is that Promethean heat/That can thy light relume." I felt there was real murder in Colman's eyes and he was going to strangle me, but I didn't dare scream. He edged me toward the bed as Cukor wanted. We found ourselves on my bed with Colman on his elbows and one hand around my throat.

Suddenly a strange voice yelled, "Cut!" Thank God.

Everyone froze. It was Bill Goetz. I thought Cukor was going to knock his and Leo Spitz's heads together. (Mr. Spitz was the financial brains of UI.) They started to argue with Cukor about the scene, and suggested that the Hays Office come down first and see a rehearsal before the scene was shot. I was terrified. I thought Cukor was going to quit.

To distract me, Colman began tickling me, and as I was laughing, my satin nightgown, pasted against my cleavage, pulled away and one of my breasts sort of popped out. Colman gallantly kissed it. Spitz and Goetz almost fainted. They thought it was part of the rehearsal and yelled, "What the hell are we making here? Blue movies?"

When the commotion died down, it was decided to break for lunch until the Hays Office got to the studio and we could show it the rehearsal. That day I had an even lovelier *intime* "lunch" with Ronnie.

The brilliant decision of the Hays Office was that Colman could strangle me on the bed as long as the audience could see one of his feet on the floor.

The picture moved along slowly, four or five pages a day at the most. What a delight! George Cukor never looked through the camera. He knew he had a great cameraman and spent all his time working with the actors. He was funny and kind and sensitive, especially about what a woman thinks and feels. He would always get you to do what he needed for the scene and make you think you had discovered it yourself.

In those days the average printing on a big picture was two or three takes; on *A Double Life* Cukor would print four or five. He insisted I go to the rushes, and we would often have light scotch and sodas in his bungalow after shooting. He would let me sit there while he explained to the editor which take he preferred and then would teach me why I was better in one take than in another. The whole experience was like going to film school; I had the sneaking feeling that I should have been paying UI. But I didn't let the feeling get too strong.

The unit publicity man was giving me a great deal of publicity, and a lot of reporters were visiting on the set. Maybe because she just liked to write nasty stuff and thought the public liked that, Hedda Hopper hated me. Every other day she would print some lie about my love life or my temperament on the set, which was an even bigger lie because I adored every minute of the making of that film. In fact, the only thing I did wrong was to follow Cukor around whenever I could. Once, to get me out of his hair, he finally said, "You love this picture so much that I swear, if I gave you a broom, you'd sweep up the stage."

The Publicity Department arranged a joint interview for me and Gloria Grahame at Hedda Hopper's house one evening after shooting. Gloria was starring in *Crossfire* with Robert Ryan. The article was going to be a big cover story in the Sunday Los Angeles *Times*, about the two new blonde "stars of tomorrow," and would generate a lot of prerelease publicity for *A Double Life*. I agreed to it because I wanted to tell her Ronald Colman was wonderful and should get an Oscar for the film. But I was terrified of meeting Hedda Hopper face to face.

Before the interview I stopped for a drink at the Chinese restaurant across from the studio. Fred MacMurray, sitting at the bar and watching me force down a double martini, asked, "What's the matter, kid? Are you really leading a double life?" I explained to him that I had to meet the UI publicity man at Hedda Hopper's house to do my first interview with her and that I was positive she hated me. Fred MacMurray was a romantic leading man then, not yet the all-American father of TV's *My Three Sons*. He ordered me another double and advised, "Attack is always the best defense. I'll give you some ammunition. I heard that once on a yacht during a very dark night John Barrymore made love to Hedda by mistake, and she's had a secret grand passion for him ever since. Did you ever notice that she never printed anything scandalous about him? And his behavior invented the word." I thanked him profusely,

got back in the car the studio had lent me, sped over Coldwater
Canyon, down into Beverly Hills to Hedda Hopper's house and
rang her bell an hour late. The butler opened the door, and she
was standing in the hallway with one of her famous hats on. Even
in her own house? She said, not welcoming me in, "Oh, the great
New York actress has decided to honor us with her presence."

Gloria Grahame, the two publicity men and photographers were
sitting close by in her den. Taking MacMurray's advice, I demanded
loudly, "Listen, Hedda, cut the crap. I only came over to find out if
John Barrymore was a great lay." She grabbed some shrimp from
the platter the butler was holding and stuffed them into my mouth,
then not so gently escorted me into the den. She asked me what
I was drinking, but it was difficult for me to tell her because she
kept shoving hors d'oeuvres into my mouth. I managed to mumble,
"Vodka." She somehow got rid of the other people, after having
me take a quick picture with Gloria, who whispered in my ear,
"What the hell was that you said to her as you came in?" Hedda
was still shoving things into my mouth, so I couldn't answer. She
told the Paramount and UI publicity men that she'd already interviewed Gloria and preferred to interview me alone.

The UI man was very upset with me and instructed me that
since Miss Hopper had to go to an opening, I should tell her everything about the picture very quickly. As she hustled him out of
the door, she said, "I'll take care of my own openings. I want to
talk to Shelley alone."

She had to wait a couple of minutes until I could swallow the
things she'd been feeding me. When I was finally able to talk, she
glared at me and demanded, "What did you say to me as you
came in?"

A little less feisty, I replied, "I just wanted to know, Hedda, if
John Barrymore was great in the hay. I've always been curious
about him."

She took a long, hard look at me and said, "Why did you ask
me that?"

I answered simply, "Well, everybody knows that you two had
an affair."

The famous gossip columnist gasped, "They *do?*"

"Sure, it's common knowledge in New York. Everybody knows
you were married to De Wolf Hopper, the famous stage star, and
obviously you like to go to bed with famous stage actors, like John
Barrymore, Ronald Colman, etc." (making points, I hoped).

This Wicked Witch of the West transformed into a melting girl right there in front of my eyes. Evidently she'd been waiting for years for somebody to confide in. She dragged me up the stairs to her bedroom, where I saw over her bed a huge and elaborately framed picture of John Barrymore. It was signed "To Hedda, with love and thanks, Sincerely, John Barrymore."

I knelt on the bed, kissed the picture and murmured, "Oh, Hedda, to have known that man. I guess I was just born too late."

She then recounted a second-by-second description of their romantic night on the water under the Catalina moon. I must say that even with her romantic long-distance view, I got the feeling that Barrymore had been very drunk and thought she was Carole Lombard, but of course, I didn't say so. We talked about what a great actor he had been, and then I told her how great Ronald Colman was in A Double Life. Almost as good as Barrymore.

As I got back into the car after six cups of coffee, I felt strangely sad for her despite the fact that I knew she had ruined the lives of so many people with her column. I may have been wrong, but that night it seemed to me that no one, but no one, had ever really loved her.

She printed a fabulous interview about me, saying I was the new combination of Jean Harlow and Jean Arthur. The next Sunday she wrote a glowing article about Ronald Colman. Mission accomplished.

Garson Kanin and Ruth Gordon came on the set, and I thanked them profusely. He replied, "I should thank you. I've seen the rushes." He asked me who my agent was, and I remembered that little piece of paper with my signature on it in UI's vault. I told Kanin I didn't have an agent. He was astonished and suggested I call Feldman-Blum, who were the Famous Artists Agency and handled many important stars. I doubted whether they'd be interested in me until the film was released, but he said he'd call Ralph Blum and put me on the phone.

Mr. Blum remembered me from Knickerbocker Holiday and Rosalinda. "I'll meet you at the Players Restaurant tonight at seven, and we'll talk, and then I'll see your rushes. Perhaps we can find a basis for a good relationship."

I finished a little early, put on my glamor makeup and outfit and got to the Players at six-thirty. With my luck, John Ireland was sitting alone at the bar. With his lovely Irish grin he said, "Sit down. You can at least talk to me now that you're a star."

I shakily complied. "Aren't you engaged to Joanne Dru now?"

He reassured me he was, and ordered champagne to drink to my new career. "See, I told you that all you needed was one good break." Then, with a twinkle, he asked, "Tell me something, that night we were supposed to have dinner at the Marquis, I waited for you at the bar for forty-eight hours. What happened?"

I thought a minute. "I had an attack of charity and went on a terrific tour all over the country, and the plane left at five P.M. that afternoon."

"I'm sure," he said.

With new understanding, I told him that I realized he was a great fiancé, but as for husband material, I had terrifying doubts. He put his arm around me and whispered in my ear, "You may be right, though I hope not. But don't tell Joanne, okay? She's a wonderful mother, and I have to sit with my kids while they eat every night. I can't go out till they're asleep. I'm going crazy."

Ralph Blum rescued me, and I kissed John good-bye. Mr. Blum seated me at a corner table and took out a mimeographed copy of the option I had signed—of course, I didn't have a copy—and asked me why I had signed such an inequitable long-term deal. He sounded like my father. I explained that I was so out of work at the time that I signed anything anybody put in front of me. I explained to him that I had to go to New York when the film was over and do *Oklahoma!* for a season.

"Well," he said, "by the time they have *A Double Life* ready for release perhaps we can get you out of the show, and it's better than running around Hollywood and doing bit parts." Glancing over at John, he added, "And getting into trouble." Then he said, "If they pick up your option, which I have no doubt they'll do, we'll insist you signed this seven-year contract without proper advice from an agent and under pressure because you were testing. I'm sure we can then change it to a free-lance contract with a two-picture-a-year deal." That sounded so familiar I didn't say anything. He continued, "But let's wait until the film starts going around the private executive screening circuit and you're tied up in *Oklahoma!* Then they'll be anxious to have you back and loan you out for a lot of money. They'll better the deal. I'm the top motion-picture lawyer in this city." I knew that was true, and he was a very, very rich one.

Anyway, the words he was saying I could have set to music. I had been so battered by the rejection inherent in being a bit player and was terrified of returning to that status. To this day I feel that getting *A Double Life* was a miracle. So much of a successful career depends on standing on the right corner at the exact right moment. Suppose that girl hadn't told Mervyn Le Roy about the test. Suppose Lou Costello hadn't been driving on Highland Avenue the exact moment he was. I know so many intelligent and gifted actors who spend a lifetime squirming with embarrassment, selling themselves in casting offices, and never get that first lucky break.

Toward the end of my eight weeks we had to do a shot of me in my nightgown going to the door to answer Ronald Colman's knocking and two more shots of me dead on the bed with the police and reporters in the entrance of the little apartment and down the stairway. That was the day Feldman and Blum came on the set with Garson Kanin. They were shooting a medium close-up of me looking in the mirror and then going to the door. I had an attack of Stanislavsky and began improvising. As the camera rolled, I did what Cukor had rehearsed, but I suddenly picked up a bottle of Crêpe de Chine perfume, took out the long glass stopper and dabbed it in my cleavage. I went to the door and let Colman in. He located the perfume immediately, leaned over and kissed the spot.

Cukor yelled, "Cut and print." He walked toward us in slow, measured steps, head bent, and said in controlled tones, "I'm going to print that take, but we have the Legion of Decency in the industry, you know, Mr. Colman and Miss Winters, so would you two *artistes* mind doing the goddamned scene as we rehearsed it, so we can use it in the picture?"

Mr. Colman bowed, and I gave a terrified squeak. "Yes, sir." Cukor removed the perfume bottle from the dresser, and we did the scene exactly as rehearsed.

As Colman and I went to lunch, Cukor said, "What happened to the frightened Shelley of eight weeks ago who went ninety-six takes the first day?"

"George," Colman replied, "you've given her so much confidence, you've stimulated her feminine imagination so, she can't help doing what she does in real life."

Cukor growled something, Colman winked at me and we all went to lunch in the commissary with my two new big shot agents. The little fuss had been funny, but Feldman whispered in my ear, "When you have a director like George Cukor, do *exactly* what he tells you to do. He's smarter than all of us put together. Ask Katharine Hepburn."

The next day was my last day on the film, and all I had to do was play dead on the bed. First the landlady discovered my body, my head at the foot of the bed. It's hard to lie still and not breathe, pretending that you're dead, when the camera is close to you. Especially if you have a friend playing a bit part, as I did—Paddy Chayevsky, in fact—who was trying to raise enough money to buy a secondhand car to drive back to New York and get married and could use the extra $100 for another day's work. Maybe, subconsciously, I didn't want to be finished with the experience of working on this extraordinary film.

When I did this scene with the landlady, I lay very still, and we did it in about three takes. But late in the afternoon, when we got to the scene with the detectives and reporters, I began to twitch and run out of breath during the complicated dolly shot when the reporters were yelling their lines at the detectives.

We didn't get the shot by six o'clock, which is the latest Cukor would work, so everybody had to come back the next morning to do the shot again. I was very embarrassed, but my two or three friends on the picture were joyous that they were getting the additional $100. The next morning we started at ten and by eleven Cukor was ready to *really* strangle me. Suddenly he noticed something peculiar. "Shelley, how come you can lie still and hold your breath until that guy Paddy something says his line? During the last five takes you moved whenever he talked. Shall I take him out of the scene?"

I sat up in bed and blurted, "Please, Mr. Cukor, don't do that. Paddy Chayevsky is a talented young writer, and he's trying to make enough money to go back to New York and get married."

Cukor smiled, took me over to a corner of the set and said gently, "Shelley, I understand the word 'nepotism.' If one of your friends needed some extra money, why didn't you just tell me? I would have used him in another scene, and we could have finished this one last night."

When I stopped blushing, I returned to the bed and lay as still as a mouse, and we got the shot. I had finished *A Double Life.* When I said good-bye to Colman, he kissed me and handed me a large heavy box. He said, "Here's my head, Shelley. You already have my heart." (I waited until I got home to open it. It was the terracotta bust of him that I had admired in Cukor's office the first day.)

I kissed Mr. Cukor good-bye and thanked him for allowing me to attend the George Cukor School of Film Acting. He said, "It's *auf Wiedersehen*, Shelley, because I know you're going to be a tremendous hit in this film, and I'll be using you again. And don't improve on my direction next time." (In *The Chapman Report* with nine other costars, I did exactly as he told me.)

I thanked Michael and Fay Kanin, the producers, and said good-bye to everyone. With that, I ran out of the studio and had to take the little red streetcar because Universal had requested the return of the car it had lent me for the duration of the film.

When I finally got in front of my house, I couldn't believe my eyes. There was my little red Pontiac with a new white convertible top, new seat covers, a new red paint job and brand-new tires. For a minute I didn't know if I was afraid or happy that Paul might have come back. When I went into the house, there was no Paul. But my father told me that the car also had a new engine, transmission, clutch and brakes. He told me that Major Walters, Paul's friend, had driven it from Chicago. "Why in hell didn't he just send you a new car? This job must have cost a lot more."

My mother took one look at my face and said calmly, "Let's finish the packing. You're leaving on the Super Chief tomorrow, and they've made a reservation at a nice hotel in the Fifties, where a lot of respectable English stage actors stay. It's two hundred fifty dollars a month, so maybe you can find one of your nice New York actress friends to share and it would only be one hundred twenty-five dollars each. And watch the phone calls, they're fifteen cents each, so use the pay phone in the lobby."

The next day my family drove me to the station in the red Pontiac with the top down so that my trunk and suitcases would fit in. Blanche lent me her warm sheared beaver coat as I had given away my skunk coat upon going to California when I was so positive that overnight I'd become another Jean Arthur. I told my father to keep the Pontiac, and he said, "No, I'm going to have it put up on blocks and disconnect the battery. My hunch is you'll be back and need it."

With utter conviction I said, "I'm never coming back here. I'm going to be a great theater actress."

CHAPTER 14

My first night back in New York, I saw Julie Harris, already a renowned stage actress, in *Sundown Beach*. The play was being done by a new group called the Actors' Studio, and was staged by Elia Kazan. As I watched the play, I trembled. The acting was a revelation. I had never seen ensemble acting before. I don't know exactly how great the play was, but it moved me deeply. *Sundown Beach* was about veterans with psychiatric problems and their wives and girlfriends, who were quartered in a hotel somewhere in southern Florida while they were being treated. It had a remarkable theme, or so it seemed to me. In war all the soldiers who do the fighting lose, no matter which side wins. Men who have had to kill their fellowman never really recover the ability to enjoy life again and are forever stained with some kind of guilt. That is what I felt the play was really about.

Afterward I stood at the back of the theater, wondering if the anguished behavior I'd seen on the stage had been in Paul too, and he had managed to suppress it. Why else had he talked so much about not actually being in the war, but above it, because he was a flier?

Marty Ritt, a young actor and director I knew from the New Theatre School, brought Elia Kazan over to say hello. Kazan asked me what I thought the play was about, and I told him my thoughts and feelings. He made me feel very good when he said, "You have good insight and a sharp mind for catching the inner themes of a play. You did it, too, when you were a kid and you saw that play I was in by Louise Platt. It was a fascinating play, even if it was a flop. Remember?"

"I remember," I said, and then I thanked him and blushed because he'd become the most brilliant and successful stage director in New York by then.

Kazan told me about the Actors' Studio, which had been formed by the younger members of the Group Theatre and most of the new young talented actors and actresses on Broadway. They met several times a week to experiment with Stanislavsky's theories which later came to be known as the Method. Kazan invited me to be an official observer at the Actors' Studio, where Bobby Lewis,

196

Danny Mann, Marty Ritt and he were the moderators. A few months later, Lee Strasberg, who was a famous director, became head of the studio. I gladly accepted, telling him that I would love to come as soon as I opened in *Oklahoma!* Of course, he had not seen *A Double Life* yet, so his invitation was quite a compliment. "The only requisite," he told me, "is that you work seriously on your speech and body and experiment and expand your acting range. In a few months you'll have to audition, and either you'll become a member of the Studio for life, or we might ask you to do another audition of a different scene, or you could be turned down. But that I doubt."

His last "could" made me an official observer at the Actors' Studio for the next seven years as I commuted back and forth from Hollywood between pictures, never finding enough time to audition.

Will Hare, my date for *Sundown Beach*, took me to Harold's Show Spot. Alas, when we got there it was no longer Harold's but Patsy's, named after the bartender who had bought the place from Harold's children. That kind, actor-loving Irishman had died. I treated Will, who wasn't working, to dinner. Some years later he opened a fancy restaurant in Westport, Connecticut, and practically became a millionaire, but he always remained a member of the Actors' Studio. And many years later when I wrote a play, *One Night Stands of a Noisy Passenger*, that was done Off-Broadway, Will played one of the leads and was extraordinary in it, along with Robert DiNiro, Diane Ladd, Sally Kirkland and Pete Masterson.

At Patsy's I saw lots of theater acquaintances and told them funny stories about my Hollywood adventures (leaving out the sad ones). I was again being treated with respect as a serious actress who was going into a big hit Theatre Guild production. Oh, God, it's a different feeling being an actor in New York than being one in Hollywood. There's a camaraderie among New York actors that doesn't change, even if you're out of work. In Hollywood you're only as good as your last picture or television show.

I told Will I had to get home by 2:00 A.M. because I had to be at the St. James Theater at 10. When he took me back to my hotel and we said good-night, who should be in the elevator but John Gielgud and Dorothy Parker—whom I knew from the commissary at Metro—both a little drunk? She had two Pekinese dogs that seemed like five, and they were winding their leashes around her legs. Ella Logan was in the elevator, also slightly drunk, and she had a large dog. There was also a very fat man and the operator, and it was a very small elevator. Gielgud remained aloof and dignified through it all. Ella Logan lived below my floor, Dorothy Parker lived on my floor and I believe Gielgud had the penthouse. I don't know where the fat man lived because he never seemed to get off the elevator; maybe he was just along for the ride.

As we went up, I realized the operator was also the night doorman. He was newly arrived from Puerto Rico or somewhere and couldn't speak English, and he too was a little drunk. Also, he could stop the elevator *only* between the floors. I think for the next ten minutes Gielgud removed himself astrally from our presence. Even when one of the Pekes nipped his ankle, he remained motionless.

I know I wasn't drunk, as I had had only two Jack Daniel's old-fashioneds, and I had eaten two hamburgers with lots of pickles and onions at Patsy's. I guess I was doing my share of smelling up the elevator, but I wasn't drunk.

Dorothy Parker vaguely remembered me and seemed to know that I had done her "Waltz" for my test at Columbia. She seemed rather irritated about it. I assured her that no one had seen it other than the executives and Harry Cohn. She replied, "But I didn't get paid for it, and it's against my ethics, religion and politics to give Harry Cohn anything free. What I'd like to give him free is this damn elevator, and you know where."

Ella Logan sat down on the floor in order to control her enormous snarling dog, who was hungry and wanted to eat one of the Pekes. She did this by singing him an Irish ballad which I later found out was part of the score of *Finian's Rainbow*.

The fat man just stood there and laughed, "Ho-ho-ho," which really enraged Parker. She turned on this stranger violently. "Christ, it's only October! Can't you at least wait for Thanksgiving to do your fucking Christmas number?" Peering at him closely, she said, "I recognize you. You're the Santa Claus who stands in front of Saks and molests small children when they try to talk to you." That shut him up. Maybe it was the truth.

I tried to reasssure Parker that she was my most favorite author in the world, and I certainly hadn't meant to do anything to offend her. She said, "Well, if I'm your favorite author, then you really must be from Hollywood because that means you're practically illiterate." This really hurt because I'd spent all those nights in the motels in the Valley, under the covers with the flashlight, reading good books, trying to become literate.

Meanwhile, the elevator was jerking from floor to floor, stopping only between the floors, with the operator opening the iron gate every time he was in front of a number on a blank wall. Maybe he was new on the job. When we got to the top, the elevator was stopped automatically by some mechanism; then Gielgud gently pushed the operator aside, moved the elevator back down to the top floor and got off, leaving all of us to the mercy of the confused doorman. I pushed him aside and took control, delivering Ella Logan to her floor. The dog didn't want to get out before he had his dinner, but we pushed him out. I then took Dorothy Parker and me to our floor, and we got off. I closed the gate and left the pilot and Santa Claus to fend for themselves.

The next morning I did have a slight hangover, and although I brushed my teeth five times, I could still taste the onions. I got to rehearsal fifteen minutes late because I couldn't get a cab in the rain. Very New York. I rushed past the St. James Theater doorman and onto the bare stage, tearing off my coat. I was running so fast I almost fell off the stage into the orchestra pit. The stage manager caught me; he was with an assistant stage manager and a rehearsal pianist under a work light. "Miss Winters, I presume," he said. "You're fifteen minutes late; that means you're docked three dollars. A dollar for every five minutes."

That was his opening line to me. Our relationship deteriorated for the next nine months, so you can imagine what his closing line was.

Still trying to establish some kind of rapport, I smiled and said, "That's all right. I'll be making five hundred dollars a week in this show. But from now on I'll be on time."

When I said $500 a week, his face got chalky. He grabbed my arm and whispered tensely, "Don't you dare tell anyone else in the cast that. Lawrence Langner must have lost his mind."

I pulled my arm away, rubbed it and said, "Listen, Mr. Simon Legree, this show has been running for almost five years. Maybe I'll give it a shot in the arm if you don't break *my* arm first."

He replied, "Unfortunately you have a run-of-the-play contract, and the understudy who did just beautifully for the past eight weeks is back in the chorus. I'll be damned if I know why they needed you."

"Charming. Would you like to cut my throat now or later?"

Then started the most peculiar rehearsal I've ever had in my life, before or since. The stage manager held the script and read each line as he wanted me to read it—exactly as Celeste Holm had done it nearly five years ago. I was supposed to imitate him imitating her. Whenever he read my cue, I forgot my line because I have this strange habit of having language come out of my mouth as a result of thought. I had been trained by the New Theatre School and George Cukor to perform this way, even in a musical comedy: *The funniest comedy is when the timing is realistic and natural.*

I tried, I really tried. The chalk marks which indicated the sets confused me, and when we got to the songs, the same thing happened. I knew the lyrics backward and forward, but my efforts to mimic him would make me forget them. The rehearsals were a struggle to the death. I thought I would go crazy. So did he.

I called Equity to find out if this was the way new actors were put into established roles, but Equity said, "We can't make artistic decisions for the producers." But what Equity did do for me was to inform the Theatre Guild office that I was allowed to rehearse only four hours a day and not at all on matinee days. Happily this schedule allowed me to attend the Actors' Studio almost immediately.

Soon the other understudies began to rehearse with me, thank God. I saw the show every night, and although the music and dancing were wonderful, there was a peculiar robot quality to the acting. I was to find out later that when actors stay in a show as long as five years, eight performances a week, the only way they can survive is to develop a technique whereby they literally turn off their minds at eight-thirty and don't wake up again until eleven-fifteen. All the performances are done by rote, and they don't have to even think about what they are saying or doing. Their brains just take a rest.

When we finally got to the dress rehearsal with the full cast, I really tried to imitate Celeste Holm, but I could no more do it than I could fly without an airplane. Langner and Theresa Helburn and Rodgers and Hammerstein watched my miserable strained rehearsal. It really was terrible. Langner asked me afterward what had happened to that performance I had given at the audition, so I told him the truth. "Mr. Langner, I can't imitate another actress. I don't know how. I have to give it my own interpretation and try to stick as close to the character as the author intended. I want this job, but I just can't do it if I have to imitate someone else."

The producers and writers had an artistic huddle, and then Langner said, in front of the whole cast, the chorus, the ballet and the stage manager, "For the last year the show has been looking very tired. The word of mouth has not been good, and business has been falling off. We have a huge company and thirty stagehands, and we need a great deal of publicity to keep the show alive.

That's why we brought Shelley all the way from Hollywood, to try to pep things up. So tomorrow, Shelley, when you go into the show, you do it your way. I'm going to give you another rehearsal with the orchestra, and then I'll take another rehearsal of the scenes you're involved in. And at tomorrow's matinee I want you all to wake up and pay close attention and answer Shelley's line readings because they will be different from what you're used to. And unless you really talk to her, it will throw off your timing." After the two weeks of hellish rehearsals, I wanted to hug and kiss him right there in front of everybody.

Then I put everything else out of my mind, and for the next hour I had a wonderful rehearsal with the beautiful music of *Oklahoma!*, and I sang "I Cain't Say No" in such a funny way that the rest of the cast started to laugh. I think they began to enjoy re-creating their roles, too, because I was different from the girls who had played it during the past five years. Everybody on the stage was enjoying himself.

Rodgers and Hammerstein took me to Sardi's for dinner. Whenever Hammerstein went to the phone or the men's room, Rodgers would tell me that the remarkable thing about *Oklahoma!* was its music and that I must sing out and be sure the audience heard the lovely melodies. I must sing as loudly as I could. Of course, I agreed. When Rodgers went to the phone, Oscar Hammerstein impressed on me how brilliant the lyrics were and that I must enunciate carefully so that the audience could understand all the funny lines or the show wouldn't work. Never mind trying to sing too much, because the orchestra was playing the melodies anyway. Of course, I agreed with him, too.

I went home to my little apartment hotel, confused and tremulous, and wondering what the hell I had gotten myself into. How could I satisfy everybody? Then I remembered what Charles Feldman had whispered in my ear as I was leaving Universal a week before. "When you've got a good director, do exactly as *he* says." Lawrence Langner had been a fine director and had created the Theatre Guild and made it the most distinguished theater company in America. And he had directed me to do it *my* way. I went to sleep content, resolved to obey my director, who in this case was my producer.

The next day I opened in the matinee. The house was packed with high school kids, probably a benefit or on twofers. Agnes de Mille, the show's choreographer, came into my dressing room before the "half hour" and handed me a bouquet of toy oil wells, which, she said, was the state flower of Oklahoma. This made me laugh, and I stopped being so nervous.

The orchestra struck up the overture, a medley of music which by then was adored throughout the world. I made my entrance in a farmyard scene, bumping into a fence which had not been on the chalk marks that the stage manager had drawn on the bare stage at rehearsal. I kicked the fence and said, "Now, who jest put that darned thing there? It weren't there last night when we was spoonin'." And since this was in character for Ado Annie, the audience screamed with laughter. So did the orchestra and the rest of the cast. I was so encouraged by their laughter that I found every comic nuance I could for my "little hot-pants Ado Annie." The show ran five minutes overtime because of the extra laughs.

As I left the stage, I was flying high, exhilarated with the joy of being in front of a live Broadway audience again who obviously loved and enjoyed me. The stage manager was waiting for me. "Listen, you Method actor," he said, using the word as if it were the worst curse word in the language, "we only want laughs where they've been established. And on matinees the curtain is supposed to come down at five-fifteen, not five-twenty. Or else I have to pay the crew overtime."

The producers and Rodgers and Hammerstein came rushing backstage into my dressing room, saying things like: "Shelley, this is the best show we've had since opening night. The audience is milling around the lobby, buying programs and the records."

And Langner said, "The way you did it today, do it every show, and we'll be back doing capacity business in no time." The stage manager slunk out of the dressing room. They all took me to dinner at Sardi's, but I didn't eat much or drink anything, I was so high and happy. I knew I had another performance in a little while, and I wanted to rest and be fresh.

The Cold War was on in Europe, but it was nothing compared to the Cold War that was going on backstage at the St. James Theater. This went on for the nine months I was in the show. Even so, I came to love *Oklahoma!* with its beautiful music and ballet. I would stand in the wings opposite the stage manager and watch the show over and over again, especially Agnes de Mille's ballets.

I began to attend the Actors' Studio as an observer every chance I could, and to see every show on Broadway that played Sundays. (Benefits of hit shows for the Actors Fund are held on Sunday nights, usually around the hundredth performance.)

Every day I didn't have a matinee I would get up at the un-earthly hour of 10:00 A.M. and rush over to the Actors' Studio and take every class I could in improvisation, scene work, sense memory, speech and history of the theater. There were some wonderful actors in Kazan's class, including Marlon Brando, his sister Jocelyn, Maureen Stapleton, Kevin McCarthy, Tommy Ewell and, on occasion, Monty Clift, who was now quite busy in Hollywood, and John Arthur Kennedy, who later changed his name to Arthur Kennedy for obvious reasons. Later on the congressman and the actor became firmly confused in my mind; for a while there I was wondering why John Kennedy was running for the Senate from Massachusetts, when everyone knew he lived somewhere in Connecticut.

And with the other glamored-up girls in the show, I went to parties. It was the postwar world, and everybody was getting rich and giving parties: café society parties out on Long Island, musicians' parties in Greenwich Village, Old Money parties on Park Avenue, parties at El Morocco, parties at the Village Vanguard, ritzy parties at the Sherry Netherland, bohemian theater parties at the Hotel Chelsea.

As Connie had informed me a few years before, a beautiful young girl has a passport to everywhere. And if I wasn't a great beauty, I certainly worked on the illusion. When I and any of the beautiful young ballerinas from the show, dressed to the teeth, made our entrance at El Morocco at eleven-thirty, all heads turned. We usually had dates with the playboys of the Western world, such as Franchot Tone and Cholly Knickerbocker. With Shirley Schrift's values I would try never to look at the check at El Morocco or "21" because I would get nauseated and think: Christ, that's a month's food for a family in Brownsville or Harlem!

Marlon Brando already had quite a reputation among theater people as a brilliant actor because of a small part he'd done in *Truckline Café*, in which he had one scene and flashed across the stage like sexual lightning. He also had another extraordinary reputation, but I figured it couldn't be true because when did he have time? When Marlon began to rehearse *A Streetcar Named Desire*, I asked him if I could watch Kazan direct. He told me to sneak in because even he was scared of Gadge. So I would cover my blonde hair with a black scarf and wear an old black coat and try to look like an usher who had wandered in. I'd sit practically behind a post so Kazan wouldn't notice me, but he talked so softly and individually to his actors that I couldn't hear him. One day after about five rehearsals, during which my post kept getting closer to the stage, Gadge suddenly turned, looked directly at me and said, "Shelley, if you're going to hang around the theater, you can at least go out for coffee for us, and let the stage manager stay on the book." So whenever I didn't have a matinee or a class, I was the gofer for *A Streetcar Named Desire*. I couldn't hear Kazan; even so, the rehearsals were extraordinary. Marlon mumbled and stumbled around, and the other actors fluffed; then he would suddenly spark fire for himself and the others, and you could hear him clearly and articulately in the last row of the balcony. Gadge would rehearse one scene all day, and it seemed painful and agonizing. Then they would have a run-through of the scene at five or six o'clock, and the acting would lift me from my seat. I knew I was watching theater history being made.

I often used to run to the St. James Theater, getting there at 8:05 P.M., and the stage manager would say things like: "Oh, you did decide to show up for your performance tonight." Then he would dock me $1 for every five minutes I was late. Before every performance I would get a flutter of his memos, which *almost* destroyed my performance. In all fairness, I must say he had an unsolvable problem on his hands. Most of the cast had reverted back to robot acting. So when I was doing my spontaneous performance, they'd fall apart, and at some performances the show was a shambles.

The Actors' Studio moved to a large studio somewhere in the Fifties on the west side of Broadway. Marlon invited me to dinner at his and Wally Cox's new apartment one night after my show. There was a New York blizzard raging, and I wore Blanche's sheared beaver coat, two heavy sweaters, tights under my flannel slacks, a woolen snood, a Russian-type hat that came down over my ears, mittens, felt-lined galoshes and a woolen scarf around my face. As I left the theater, Dave Burns, the burlesque comic, asked if I was planning to help the street cleaning crews. "No," I replied, my nose in the air, "Marlon Brando is giving a dinner for me in his home tonight."

" ★*$☆!!★#! " said Dave.

I trudged over to Tenth Avenue through the snowdrifts and climbed up five flights of stairs to their apartment. It was really a *cold*-water flat; there was ice on the *inside* of the windows! Marlon was lifting weights in an untorn long-sleeved gray sweat shirt and asked me to take my coat off. "I'll keep it on," I said.

The apartment consisted of two rooms. The front living room had a double bed and a desk made of orange crates and bricks; in the center of the room was a collection of paint cans and brushes and thinner, encircled by canvas tarps. Marlon and Wally told me they were going to paint their apartment the next day. When I visited them about a year later, the paint cans were still in the middle of the room. All that had happened was about a quarter of each wall had been painted three different colors.

Marlon had a goddamned raccoon in a cage, and I think it was wearing some other raccoon's fur coat, it was so cold in there. And it smelled so bad I immediately told Marlon I couldn't stay unless he put it in the bathroom. Marlon explained that the bathroom was just a toilet and was even colder than the living room, which had the smallest electric heater I had ever seen. I think it was vintage 1900 and one of Edison's few failures. Marlon compromised by putting the raccoon in the small bathtub next to the kitchen sink. He put a wooden door over it; then he put the heater under the sink, aimed at the bathtub to keep the damned raccoon warm.

The kitchen also had a double bed in it, and a round iron kitchen table with four unmatching chairs. I asked why they hadn't gotten any furniture yet, and Marlon said something like: "Listen, Miss Rich Bitch, you're working in a hit Broadway show. I haven't worked in six months, and now I'm just getting rehearsal pay." Wally said he hadn't worked for a year, and if it weren't for unemployment insurance, they would have starved.

Wally and his girlfriend were wearing their coats, too, as they made dinner. I forget her name, but she was a very pretty girl who wore big glasses and had long, straight red hair, which was very bohemian for that time. She was about a size four; just looking at her made me feel fat. When Wally was famous in television as Mr. Peepers, I think she was the girl he married. Years later, when Wally and I both were on *Hollywood Squares*, we used to reminisce about that freezing night. He was so clever and cute and intelligently funny that I sometimes think he was the artistic ancestor of Woody Allen.

While cooking, Wally kept opening the back window to take things out of the tin box attached to the outer windowsill. Everything he brought in was frozen solid: the first frozen food I ever ate.

When they finally served dinner, it consisted of canned tomato soup—I believe made with hot evaporated milk and water and served in broken mugs—cold cauliflower dipped in sour cream, heavy brown rice cooked with nuts, and kasha—practically the only thing I recognized—cooked with raisins and green peppers. Wally announced proudly that this was the first dinner party they'd had in their new apartment.

Marlon asked me again at least to take off my galoshes and put my coat over the back of the chair. The only answer I could think of was: "My family has a peculiar religious custom. When they have dinner for the first time at somebody's house, they keep their coats and hats on."

"Yeah, I know," he said. "I've already researched that."

There were a lot of candles in the middle of the table, stuck in beer bottles. I was grateful for the warmth, but nervous about the flammable paint in the middle of the living room. The others didn't seem cold, but it was like eating outside on Tenth Avenue; I'm sure it was warmer out there. When we got to the main course of rice and kasha, Marlon broke out a gallon of wine spiked with a pint of gin. I realized why nobody was as cold as I was—they'd been guzzling the wine all the time I had been doing the show. I was so hungry I got some of the food down and so cold I drank two water glasses of the spiked wine.

After dinner we had decent coffee made in an electric percolator. Since there were no electric outlets in the apartment, they had to remove the bulb from the overhead fixture to plug in the coffeepot. That was why we ate by so much candlelight.

For dessert Wally took in two frozen grapefruit which he fried on the stove and sprinkled with brown sugar. He explained that Marlon, who was a remarkable physical specimen, was on a diet because he had to be in great shape when his show opened. I knew that was true because during every performance of *Streetcar* he had to throw practically every one of the actors across the stage.

Wally's girlfriend and I washed what dishes there were in the cold water of this cold-water flat. At least my feet got warm from the little heater under the sink. I'd sneakily turned the heater from the direction of the damned raccoon to shivering me. What the hell, I thought, he had on his own fur coat!

Marlon continued his weight lifting as he discussed the experience of working with Kazan. I was curious about what Kazan was whispering to him and Jessica Tandy during rehearsals. He told me that Kazan always got to know his actors' personal histories very well, and in different scenes he would give each actor personal actions which made for interesting conflict. The actors never knew what Kazan told the other actors in the scene.

We talked for what seemed like only a few minutes, but soon it began to get light outside. I looked over my shoulder and noticed that Wally had closed the heavy sliding doors to the living room. I began to shiver with a combination of nervousness and desire. "Marlon," I asked inanely, "why did Wally close those doors?"

"To keep warm, of course. The only way to keep warm in this apartment is to get into bed." Then, intuitively understanding my fear, he gently added, "My body generates a great deal of heat." He was right.

CHAPTER 15

My work in the daytime at the Actors' Studio was becoming more fascinating, while my work with the robots at night at the St. James Theater was becoming more stifling. Marlon was on the road with *Streetcar* for a few weeks, and I couldn't really compete with all his sexual commitments, nor did I want to. I was still looking for a Paul who wanted to be an actor. I had not yet realized those characters are mutually exclusive. My fantasy was that I would someday meet this handsome talented Ph.D. actor and we would marry and have lots of beautiful actor children and we would act into the sunset together.

Lee Strasberg was now teaching at the Actors' Studio. He taught me how to do an Affective Memory exercise, for which I must find a powerful traumatic experience in my own life, remember the sensory details of that moment and with another section of my mind recall them as I acted. It's what makes the playwright's words come out of your own experience. When I finally learned to use this correctly, it became the most powerful tool I ever learned to use in acting.

Connie made another brief flying trip back to New York from Rome and stayed at the Algonquin. She reminded me that I had an intellect, and we started going to museums, using the New York Public Library and seeing good shows again on any afternoons or nights that I could. The new Off-Broadway theater played on Sundays, and that's where most of the new interesting plays were. She was dating old friends from the New Theatre School like Stanley Prager and glamorous *single* postwar novelists and playwrights.

She seemed much happier but totally lacking in personal ambition. In fact, in some strange way she had turned off the whole idea of being an actress. I knew she had done some films in Italy, and spoke Italian very well now. Her sister Doris had just finished a film called *Bitter Rice* with a new Italian sexpot named Silvana Mangano and Raf Vallone, and Connie showed me film stills from the picture. I noticed a handsome dark actor in the stills, who seemed to be the villain in the film. He was very tall for an Italian and I asked her who he was. She told me he was a wonderful Italian stage actor named Vittorio Gassman, who as yet had not done many films and spoke no English. I studied his photo. "He's very interesting-looking and handsome. I bet he'll make it. But why does he seem so familiar?"

"To my knowledge he's never been out of Italy," Connie said, "and you've never been out of Hollywood, so the only place you could have met him was in a dream."

I laughed, and we rushed off to a floating poker game which was getting quite famous around New York because thousands of dollars were being bet. Connie and I just watched and flirted with the Broadway playboys and sports columnists who were the regulars in this high-stakes game.

Of course, I couldn't go to the opening night of *A Streetcar Named Desire* and would have to wait to see it at the Actors Fund benefit. Irene Selznick, the producer, was giving a party after the show, and Marlon said he didn't want to go as he didn't have any clothes. I asked him if he didn't want to hear the applause he was certain to get upon arriving at Sardi's, so why not buy a suit at Bond's?

He said, "No! Christ, I hate the place. Why couldn't they give the party in Chinatown?"

"Because they don't send the reviews from *The New York Times* to Chinatown."

Then he told me they were going to have a special benefit on a Thursday matinee the following week, and I would be able to see it then.

That night I decided to go home and go right to sleep so I'd be nice and fresh for the Actors' Studio in the morning. The next morning I sent out for breakfast, two containers of coffee and the newspapers so I could read all the reviews of *Streetcar*. I had to read them three times to make sure I understood what I was reading. You would have thought it was the Second Coming. One reviewer said, "There has never been, nor will there ever be again, a performance like the one Marlon Brando gave last night."

I couldn't wait to see the play. I called Marlon's stage manager, whom I knew, congratulated him and asked him to make sure I had a seat for the benefit the following Thursday. He told me he'd seen Marlon put one away for me at the box office the day before. "If you want to," he said, "you can sell it for one hundred dollars." And in those days $100 was like $500 now.

"No," I told him, "I have a funny feeling I'm going back to California soon, and I want to see Marlon in Tennessee's play."

When I went to see the special matinee that next Thursday, I completely understood the critics' fever. There was an electrical charge and almost an animal scent he projected over the footlights that made it impossible for the audience to think or watch the other performers on the stage. All you could do was *feel*, the sexual arousal was so complete. I don't believe this quality can be learned; it's just there, primitive and compelling. The only other time I experienced it was when I saw Elvis Presley perform live in Las Vegas; men tell me that Marilyn had it for them.

In all of Marlon's film career he's had only five or six of these great moments when he was able to project this quality from the screen to the audience. Of course, he is a magnificent actor, but these few moments are worth all the millions the film industry has paid him. I believe it is what has kept audiences buying tickets to see even his mediocre pictures over the last thirty years. In my opinion, time has not erased this unique quality he has.

I went backstage after seeing that extraordinary performance. Marlon had a large chorus dressing room to himself on the third floor. (As one of the stars, he was entitled to either a stage or one of the first-floor dressing rooms.) His dressing room was full of barbells and weights, a cot, blankets and other clutter. But no makeup. Just a can of Albolene. If he had makeup in that room, I couldn't see it. I suddenly was so in awe of his genius that I just stared at him.

"Didn't you like the play?" he asked.

It was a funny feeling trying to tell a friend, a sometimes lover and a boy you had seen do not-so-hot improvisations at the Actors' Studio that he was an acting genius comparable to Charlie Chaplin, Laurence Olivier or Alfred Lunt and that he had this remarkable sexual power that none of the others had. I knew that praise from your fellow actors is the sweetest music to an actor's ears. In those days Marlon was a simpler man, and he could be a very sweet and gentle boy, often even incapable of verbally defending himself during critiques at the Actors' Studio.

I stood there knowing that I had seen something I would recall with excitement for the rest of my life. All I could say was an inadequate "Bud, you were really very good tonight." And I stuttered at that.

But he blushed with pleasure and said, "I don't think it was so hot tonight. My energy was low."

SHELLEY / 211

I looked at him amazed and said, "Any more energy and the audience would have gone through the roof."

When he went to shower, I examined all the clutter on his table. Among a Charles Atlas instruction book, about 100 pieces of paper with girls' names and phone numbers and photos (some nude) was a collection of hotel keys from every posh hotel in New York. There were at least a dozen, from such places as the Sherry Netherland, the Waldorf Towers and the St. Regis. When he came out, I said, "Bud, what the hell are you doing? Preparing for a play where you're a burglar?"

Grinning with delight, he told me that every famous woman in films, theater and café society who saw the play would come backstage to congratulate him and "accidentally" leave her key on his dressing table. He told me that during the week of previews he had already managed to use up quite a few of the keys. "While you're performing this play eight times a week?" I asked.

"I know," he told me. "It's exhausting, but I'm doing my best. Some of them are knockouts. And who knows, it's the kind of research I might need sometime when I'm playing something different from Stanley Kowalski."

I looked at the remaining dozen keys and decided to end my physical relationship with Marlon. However, I didn't keep to my resolution. It later resumed in Hollywood under very bizarre circumstances.

That night he had invited me to an early dinner at a cheap Chinese restaurant, telling me he had to eat quickly as he had to sleep before that night's performance. I didn't believe him; I suspected he was using up another of those keys. At the restaurant he said he had dozens of film offers, and I told him, "Don't ever sign a seven-year contract. And only go out there with somebody from your family."

He gave me a strange look and said, "I left home five years ago, but maybe you're right. If I go, I'll take my sister with me, like you did, or live with my grandmother in Silver Lake."

I saw *Streetcar* again a year or so later, when Marlon was beginning to get bored with it. He really did not have much energy every performance, and I was able to concentrate on the magnificent play and the remarkable quality of Blanche DuBois as played by Jessica Tandy. It was breathtaking and somehow a totally different experience than the first time.

❋   ❋   ❋

One of the things that was driving me crazy about playing in *Oklahoma!* eight times a week was that I was offstage for more than an hour in the middle of the show, and I would sit in my dressing room, writing to my folks, reading Stanislavsky or just staring in the makeup mirror examining my defects. But during one matinee, a lovely, sunny, spring Saturday afternoon, I stood at the stage door in my costume and watched them put up the *Allegro* sign on the theater across the street. *Allegro* was a new Rodgers and Hammerstein musical being presented by the Theatre Guild, with an enormous cast and many sets—a heavy show. David Burns, who was playing the peddler in our show, came up behind me and pinched my fanny. I slapped his hand and said, "I wish I could go across the street and see some of *Allegro*."

David took off his watch and gave it to me, threw the stage doorman's sweater over my shoulder and said, "We won't tell anybody, cutie. Get back in fifteen minutes, and you'll have room to spare. I'll tell the callboy where you are."

My whole week picked up, and I ran across the street and into the stage door of the Broadhurst Theater. I stood in the wings behind the stage manager, out of the way of the dancers, and watched some of the enchanting preview of *Allegro*. After a couple of minutes the stage manager looked over his shoulder and saw me standing there in my *Oklahoma!* costume. "What the fuck are you doing here?" he whispered.

"Watching the show," I replied happily. "I have an hour or more when I'm not onstage."

He returned to busily calling the light cues, but one of the old-time electricians whispered to me, "Shirley, you're not allowed to leave the theater once the curtain goes up. You can get in serious trouble."

I scurried back across the street. As I ran in the stage door, there was the stage manager, waiting. I tried to pass him, but he grabbed me and shook me until my teeth almost fell out, screaming hysterically, "You bitch, you're not allowed to leave the theater once the curtain goes up and walk up and down Forty-fourth Street in your costume! I'm going to bring you up on charges at Equity. And they're going to shoot you back to Hollywood with the rest of the trash." I was so shocked I didn't even try to defend myself. I just stood there knowing the man was almost insane. A whole bunch of chorus kids had now come out and grabbed his arms, and one of them said, "The ballet has just ended. Nobody's calling the lights." The stage manager ran to his post.

Later he claimed at Equity that the assistant manager was out on Forty-fourth Street looking for me. Not true. David Burns had told him and the callboy exactly where I was and that I would be back in ten minutes, well before my entrance. But the Equity rule is that once the curtain goes up, you must *not* leave the theater—a rule made in the old days, when actors who had a long wait would sometimes go to the corner saloon and forget to come back.

I rushed back to the hotel, put ice on my lip and drank a shot of whiskey. When I calmed down enough, I called the theater and got David Burns on the phone. He told me to stay home that night and send for a doctor and relate to him exactly what had happened and have him file his report with Equity and the Theatre Guild. When the doctor came, he made sure my jaw wasn't broken. I had bitten my lip and cracked a tooth, and my gums were bleeding. He gave me a shot, and I slept until the next afternoon.

I had turned the phone off, so Lawrence Langner came knocking at my door about 2:00 P.M., bringing fruit and flowers and abject apologies from everyone connected with the management of *Oklahoma!* They understood that I was rather new in the theater and didn't know the rules and in any case would not have been late for my next entrance. He also explained that the tension of keeping a show fresh for almost five years had given the stage manager a small nervous breakdown. They were sending him on a vacation, and I should rest for a couple of days before coming back to the show. The understudy would do my part, although he said it wasn't the same without me.

I smiled, showing my broken tooth, and said, "I hope you're sending him far away."

"As a matter of fact, we're sending him on vacation in Havana."

"That's nice," I said. "Perhaps he'll join Batista's guards."

Before leaving, Langner gave me the name of a very good and fast dentist who would cap my tooth, and the Theatre Guild would pay for it.

I stayed out of the show until the next Wednesday, when the swelling of my jaw had gone down, my tooth had been capped, and my shock had receded.

I called the Famous Artists Agency in California, and Charles Feldman told me that *A Double Life* was being acclaimed on the private screening circuit. He told me I should still go on with the show, and when they found me an important role in a big picture, they would try to get me out of it. "I hope it's soon," I said. "If it wasn't for the Actors' Studio, I'd be under contract to a booby hatch by now."

Feldman said, "The schmucks at Universal haven't read that piece of paper you so hurriedly signed, and we're hoping they don't pick up your option in time." They had had nine months from the time I'd left California to exercise their option. (God, had all these things happened to me in only nine months!)

I meekly interjected, "I hoped they would pick up my option. When I come back to Hollywood, I'd like some security, with a big studio building me up and giving me good pictures."

Ralph Blum was on the other extension and said, "Kid, I know it's miserable in New York, especially in the wintertime, but if we play our cards right, we can better your deal, and Universal doesn't have such good directors. You're a valuable property now, and we can pick up your price and get good directors who will borrow you from Universal, and we can ask for half the loan-out money."

The conversation was getting beyond me. I kept trying to tell them how miserable I was, and they kept talking about money. I tried to tell them that I had learned more of my craft with the Stanislavsky Method at the Actors' Studio, and now I thought I could be good even with a mediocre director in a commercial picture. There was a long pause, and I could tell that now they didn't know what *I* was talking about. Feldman told me Universal's option would expire April 1, and we would decide then what to do.

"Okay," I said, and hung up.

Connie came over from the Algonquin to comfort me. She seemed so much happier and told me that she had been going out with a very famous writer in Italy. She spoke Italian fluently now. I tried to find out if there were any marriage plans in sight with this Cesare Pavese (now recognized, posthumously, as one of Italy's great writers).

She got that sad look on her face again and said, "He's a brilliant man. I think his work will live for a long time, and it's an honor to be with him. But I'm a stranger in a strange land in Italy, and coming back to America, I feel the same here. As if I'm a citizen of nowhere."

I told her to cut it out. She was doing many films in Italy in Italian, had a beautiful apartment, and was meeting all the intelligentsia of Europe—Sartre, Moravia, Hemingway, Somerset Maugham and Robert Capa, and had even met George Bernard Shaw. Her "beauty passport" obviously had more entrée power than mine did.

She smiled her sweet smile and told me that she was going back in a few days. I suggested that she see an Italian psychiatrist, and she reminded me that Italy was a very Catholic country and they didn't have such things there. "That's what they have priests for."

She had to get back to the Algonquin because there was an Italian script waiting that she had to read, immediately, to be shot in Naples. She had to cable the producer a firm yes or no at once.

When Connie left my hotel for the Algonquin, I kissed her good-bye, and she gave me a hug. We recalled that we had known each other since we were fifteen and she was a kid from New York's West Side and I had been a street urchin from Brownsville. She was now an international beauty, and I, if *A Double Life* was a hit, a potential star. Nevertheless, when I walked her to the elevator, we knew that a period of our lives, which had been mostly carefree and happy, was closing with the door of the elevator. I always hate good-byes at elevator doors. They seem so much more final when that steel door closes. In a couple of days my beautiful, intelligent girlfriend flew back to Italy.

The next night I was invited to Sardi's and found the entire Theatre Guild organization, seven strong, sitting at a large table. So was Celeste Holm. They introduced me to her, and I joined them at the table. I was really confused now. She had already won an Oscar for *Gentleman's Agreement*, so she couldn't possibly want to come back to that tacky show. This is what they proposed to me.

As *Oklahoma!* was approaching its three thousandth performance, Celeste Holm and Howard Keel were going to come back to the show for a month. The Theatre Guild asked me to take a vacation in California or Florida, and it would buy the round-trip ticket. Then, after the month of celebration and publicity, I would come back to the show for the rest of my run-of-the-play contract. They had a release ready for me to sign which would allow Celeste Holm to go into the show for thirty-two performances. I signed it cheerfully, saying, "That sounds like it would be very exciting."

Then I ordered the most expensive supper Sardi's had. We all ate, but I noticed Lawrence Langner, his wife and Theresa Helburn kept giving me fishy glances. They kept explaining how important it was for me to get theater experience, that they had seen my *Rosalinda* and that they owned the chic Westport Playhouse and in the summer I should do Molière or Ibsen or Strindberg or Shaw and they would arrange a tour around the country. Not only would I be playing great roles in classics, but I would make a great deal of money. I ate everything in sight and nodded.

The next morning, as soon as Actors' Equity was open, I phoned the Contract Department and told them that I had agreed to let Celeste Holm go in for a month and asked how this affected my run-of-the-play contract. They confirmed my joyful suspicion that it broke it and I was free to negotiate a new contract with the Theatre Guild or leave the play. I couldn't wait for it to be three hours later in California.

Charles Feldman heard all my news and agreed that I had gotten lucky for once with my compulsion to sign things. He was sure the Guild had invalidated my run-of-the-play contract. "But for God's sake, don't sign anything else," he said. "Paramount wants you for one of its very important films next year, F. Scott Fitzgerald's *The Great Gatsby*. A wonderful director and an all-star cast. They would like a five-picture commitment, too. We've got them up to twenty-five thousand dollars for *Gatsby*, but we're not entirely sure of our legal position with Universal yet. When you get back, which I hope will be in two weeks, we'll have a meeting with Spitz and Goetz. We'll try to get them to hold still so that when you get the itch for the theater again, you'll be free to do a limited run on Broadway or this television stuff, which is becoming a very lucrative and important medium."

. I said that I liked radio better. I could form the pictures in my own mind. The little TV box gave me a headache.

He said, "I'm not asking you to watch it, I'm just suggesting you do it occasionally. They're beginning to pay ten thousand dollars to fifteen thousand dollars for a one-hour dramatic show."

"Honest?"

"And it will be more money soon," he told me, "as Madison Avenue is taking over."

I didn't know what the hell he meant, and I didn't want to ask. In a small voice I suggested that I felt I had some obligation to Universal since it had given me that great role in *A Double Life*.

He said these classic words to me: "In show business there are two kinds of people: the successful ones and the ethical ones."

In Mr. Langner's office the next day I found that truth was the easiest and most effective approach. I told him how grateful I was for the chance to be in *Oklahoma!* but how lonely and miserable I was away from my family and about the opportunity that had presented itself at Paramount.

Langner smiled at me and said, "George Cukor has told me about the audience's reaction to you in *A Double Life*. I knew it was going to come. I'll tell you a secret, Shelley. The longer we keep *Oklahoma!* open, the more money Twentieth has to pay us, so we're using every ploy we can think of. We know that we broke your contract, but I'm sure you'll be working for us again, and the more famous you are in films, the more money you'll make for us. I think in your heart of hearts you would like to create your own starring role in a great play, make it a hit and live in a wonderful New York penthouse as a Broadway star should. You deserve it. You're a gifted stage actress."

He had me in tears. At that moment if he'd put any piece of paper in front of me, I'd have probably signed it. Thank God he didn't. I believed that if I got to be a big star in films, I would be sought after on Broadway. Until this day I don't know if my reasoning was correct or not. But the one award I've longed for has always eluded me, the Antoinette Perry Award, known as the Tony, even though seven years later I starred in a great play, *A Hatful of Rain*, got rave reviews and finally saw my name up in lights over the title.

Langner took me to the elevator. He kissed me and said, "You haven't lost your return ticket on the Super Chief, have you?" I assured him I hadn't.

I went back to the hotel, paid the rent on the apartment for six months in advance and told them to forward all my mail to Peyton Hall, Hollywood Boulevard, Hollywood, California. I said good-bye to everyone at the Actors' Studio and asked Mr. Strasberg if my observership allowed me to fly back for sessions between pictures. He said okay, but it would be better if I lived in New York and flew to California for films. I took his advice seven years later when my contract was over.

Celeste Holm went into the show on a matinee. Her real opening took place that night, but I was on the Super Chief with my theater trunk and suitcases, going back to Hollywood the right way, a shining, if slightly tarnished, star.

CHAPTER 16

"Go take that fancy outfit off," my father said, his glasses at the ready. "There's lots of small print in this contract, and it will take me a couple of hours to read it carefully and make notes. You're signing away the most important seven years of your acting life."

Then he did a double take at my new sables and asked me suspiciously where I'd gotten them. He knew they were real natural sables and must have cost $5,000 or $6,000. I told him that Famous Artists had given them to me to welcome me back to California and in celebration of the new contract UI was offering me.

"The day an agent gives a client something for nothing is the day we all go ice skating down Hollywood Boulevard."

Stella Adler was out at the pool and asked me how I was doing. I explained supercasually that my agents had just given me sables and I was going to sign a seven-year contract with UI, starting at $2,000 a week. They were planning a big publicity buildup and were going to make me a big star. She deflated me considerably when she said, "Dumbbell, *A Double Life* has already made you a star. Don't sign a seven-year exclusive contract." I thought she was just being jealous and spiteful. Her sables were old.

I practiced cheesecake poses for an hour and then ran back into the house. My father was on the phone to Ralph Blum, saying things like: "I know that, Mr. Blum, but they can keep all the money when they loan her out . . . and every good director in town wants her now. . . . They'll probably make back every cent they pay her. . . . Well, I think she should keep the loan-out money for at least one picture a year. . . . That's the only condition under which she'll sign an exclusive contract. . . ."

I could hear Mr. Blum yelling through the telephone. Jonas hung up. I screamed at my father, "You've ruined the biggest opportunity of my life. They were going to make me into another Lana Turner."

"God didn't make you into Lana Turner, so how could they?"

I started to cry, and my mother started to yell. "Jonas, this is not the garment industry. What do you know about the motion-picture business?"

He answered, "Business is business, whatever. They put her on

218

film, don't they? Then they put the film in a can, and they sell the can all over the world."

While we all were crying and fighting, the phone rang. I lunged first. It was Mr. Blum telling me that owing to the firm position Famous Artists had taken, they had gotten me one independent picture a year for which I was to keep the money. All I could say was: "Thanks. Does that mean I can keep the sables?"

He cheerfully answered, "Of course," and hung up.

So for the next seven years I was the property of Universal International. Those seven years turned out to be a struggle to the death between me and Messrs. Spitz & Goetz. They kept trying to get me to do their "program pictures," while I kept trying not to do them and to do only good films with good directors. I don't know who won, but my first film under my seven-year contract was *Larceny* and the last was *Playgirl*. They were forgettable films, as was my acting quite often. I think all they wanted me to do was look and act sexy, so I tried to imitate Jean Harlow or Lana Turner, anybody but me. I tried to be sexy—in a vacuum. To this day I've never figured out exactly how one does that. To be sexy, one has to "do it" *at* someone. Often I was so unintentionally funny that I was sure even my longtime one true love, The Mitchell, would laugh. The Mitchell is the name of the camera used throughout the world. He has lasted through adolescence, youth and middle age, through husbands and lovers. He's always been faithful to me, recording on film with the greatest fidelity my most powerful acting moments as well as my phony ones.

In those seven years I did thirty-five films for UI. Leads. Often working from 6:30 A.M. until 8:00 at night, including Saturdays. Most of the distinguished films I did were on loan-out, and I got paid only for five years as I was on suspension for two years for turning down crap. They tried to add those two years to my contract at the end of the seven years, but there was a Supreme Court ruling in the case of Olivia de Havilland and baseball players that any contract over seven years was "human bondage" and against the U.S. Constitution. I know why I love baseball players and Olivia de Havilland.

I hear that I sometimes have a reputation for being temperamental, but how the hell can you be temperamental when you're doing thirty-five crappy pictures and fifteen distinguished films on loan-out to other studios—fifty films in five years? It's impossible to be temperamental while doing all that disciplined work.

Several times I was doing two pictures at once: one for UI in the daytime and another on loan-out at night, sleeping four hours and on my lunch and dinner time. I always had to look beautiful and rested when The Mitchell turned at 8:00 A.M., but after a week or two of this I would get too tired to sleep. I think this erratic intensive work made me a sometime insomniac. But I knew that if I didn't do the quality films, I would somehow be wasting the "seven most important years of my acting life."

In a lot of those UI films I think they just changed the locales, the costumes and the characters' names; the story and most of the dialogue remained the same. Of course, they changed some of the other actors and the name of the picture. I swear if you see *Untamed Frontier* with Joseph Cotten, *South Sea Sinner*—a bastardized version of *Rain*—with Liberace and *Frenchie*—a bastardized version of *Destry Rides Again*—with Joel McCrea, you'll see that they all are the same picture. One in the Wild West, one in the South Seas, and one in a California gold rush town. People must've paid money to see those pictures because the studio kept making them. I would sometimes finish one on Tuesday night and start another on Wednesday morning.

My contract expired in 1955, and I mean expired! That fall I did *A Hatful of Rain* on Broadway. That play was the talk of the town, and people would come back to see it two and three times. I and everyone else in the cast were lionized. Walter Kerr said about one scene that Tony Franciosa and I did that "It was like watching two broken-hearted clowns. You laughed and cried at the same time. An extraordinary feat in the theatre when you can make an audience do that." I am very proud of that play.

One night William Goetz came backstage with his wife, Edy, and William Paley and his wife. As the others complimented me lavishly, William Goetz waited. When they were finished, he came up to me, took my hands and looked into my eyes. He said nothing about *A Hatful of Rain*, just: "You understand, Shelley, that it was my job as president of UI to get you to do all those lousy pictures. That's what the board of directors was paying me for. Those were the kind of pictures they wanted. I finally had to quit, a couple of years after you left. You do understand, don't you?"

Back in 1949, after viewing the rushes of my performance in *Larceny* one night, I felt so awful that I went home and cut off my long blonde hair to about three inches all over my head. I didn't know how the scenes were going to match, and I didn't care. It was either that or kill myself. Every woman understands that action.

When I got to Makeup the next day, Gale McCary, my hair-dresser, and Bud Westmore, the makeup man, just stared. I looked like a blonde poodle. "Don't anybody panic," Gale said. "I'll shape it into curls all over her head. It might even start a new style."

Bud Westmore was two feet off the ground, screaming, "But how in the hell will she match?"

Gale told him they were shooting in sequence, *thank God,* and the director would just have to throw in a line about my having gone out and got a haircut or something. That is exactly what they finally did. I swear that the soft curls all over my head made me act better, and I stopped trying to be sexy and decided to play the character as real as I could. Except at the end of every scene I would give whoever I was acting with an openmouthed smile, whether it was my leading man, John Payne, the dog, or the door-knob.

Marilyn Monroe came over to have lunch with me one day, stayed to watch the rushes and asked me why I smiled like that at the end of each scene. "Well, I have slightly buck teeth," I told her, "and when I smile with my mouth open, you can't tell." Marilyn thought it was very sexy and used that smile forever after because she thought it was sexy, too. I gave it to her with pleasure. I hated it on me.

That Day of the Haircut, when I went to lunch in the commissary, all the other starlets stared at me in horror. They knew I was in the middle of a picture, and the style then was long hair like Rita Hayworth, Linda Darnell and Ava Gardner. I sat down to have lunch, and Spitz & Goetz came over to my table. Gale McCary quickly informed them, "We've decided to give Shelley a new look. I'm sure there'll be lots of publicity about it."

Spitz spit out, "In the middle of a picture?"

And Goetz got in, "She looks like a goddamned chrysanthemum."

But Gale, God bless her, stood her ground. She was one of the most famous hairstylists in the film industry, having been trained by Sidney Guilaroff. She said bravely, "Mr. Goetz, hair is *my* department. We were dissatisfied with the rushes. Shelley was looking like every other studio's blonde sexpot, and this will give her a very unusual look. It's very complimentary to her features on the screen."

"Honest, Mr. Goetz," I added, "it makes my eyes slant up, my nose thinner, my lips fuller and my shoulders narrower. . . ."

"Yeah, and your bosom bigger."

Part of my costumes was a special padded bra, which up to then

I had refused to wear. But the next day, when the studio brass saw the rushes, they were truly amazed that the new hairdo did do all those things. (I had worn the bra.)

Before I started the next picture, appropriately called *Out of the Fog*, with Richard Conte, borrowed from Fox, every important magazine like *Vogue* and *Life* shot a picture story on my new hairdo. It was called the Poodle Cut or the Italian Cut (why the latter I don't know, unless they were precognizant), but ever after Mr. Goetz called it the Chrysanthemum. John Engstead, the photographer, told me that he believes that women freeze their hairdos in the style they wore when they were at their happiest. I think he's right because so far I have almost always used various modifications of that hairstyle. If something else was required, I wore wigs, which I hate and which all Italian directors adore for some mysterious reason.

Despite the artistic troubles I was having, this was one of the happiest periods of my life. At last I was a star! I was the Resident Blonde Bombshell at Universal. It was *my* studio. Spitz & Goetz were men who really wanted to make good pictures, but they were often forced to do commercial ones. But they were far from being the autocrat Harry Cohn had been: they treated my ideas with respect and often took a few of my suggestions.

The Publicity Department was concentrating on me, and I had an interview at lunch almost every day with an important reporter. I figured that the more famous I became, the more likely Universal would be to buy good properties for me and give me good directors. To the delight of the Publicity Department I have always understood that writers have a job to do. It's how they make their living. They weren't out to kill me; they just wanted interesting interviews. So I would do my best to think of funny and interesting things to tell them. I soon became a favorite of the Hollywood Press Corps. I know many actors shrink from the press and just sit there and answer yes or no. But I knew these people could make my name a household word, and I remembered the advice Harry Cohn had given me: "When they buy tickets to see you, only then you're a star and the banks finance your pictures."

Even now when I'm far from being part of the swinging new Hollywood jet set, when a columnist or writer has a deadline to meet, he calls me and says, "Shelley, give me an interview," and I say, "Listen, give me a break. You know everything I've done since I was born." And he answers, "You'll think of something." I say, "Okay," and then take Marlon's advice about imaginary histories, birthplaces, etc., and give them a story that's funny and absolutely contrary to the truth. They don't care. They've got a story, and I guess it adds to "The Winters Tale."

One day in the commissary Yvonne De Carlo, Universal's Brunette Sexpot, came over to me in one of her innumerable harem costumes and said, "Errol Flynn is making a swashbuckling picture on the back lot and was watching you work yesterday. Friday evening he's having an informal dinner party and would like me to bring you. He gives the most elegant small dinner parties. I think Clark Gable will be there, too. Do you want to go?"

DID I WANT TO GO!

In my excitement and confusion, I answered, "What will he serve?"

Yvonne looked at me strangely and replied, "Dumbbell. Wonderful food. And he'll run a new movie."

Trying to speak casually, I said, "Okay, but I'll follow you in my car, in case I want to leave before the end of the picture."

"You won't." She smiled and swished away in all her seven veils.

That Friday, when I went to work at 6:00 A.M., I brought with me a pair of black velvet Capri pants, red satin you-know-what shoes and a tailored white satin shirt. And gold hoop earrings, my first real ones.

At 6:00 P.M. Yvonne was waiting for me in a chauffeured limousine, and we got into quite a fight when I insisted on going in my little red Pontiac and following her. She really got annoyed and said, "Listen, Brooklyn, Errol is a perfect gentleman. Anytime you want to go home he'll send you in his limousine." She finally gave in. "All right, follow me to Shangri-la."

Aunt Fanny in the Bronx had knitted me a beautiful if enormous dark red shawl, which I casually threw around my shoulders, and I followed Yvonne. It was a little involved getting to Flynn's house. We went way up in the Hollywood Hills and finally went through some iron gates, which opened magically.

Mr. Flynn's house was surrounded by a six-foot stone wall, and there was an enormous pool on the front lawn. And guess who opened the car door. CLARK GABLE! I literally fell out of the car. He caught me, and while he was trying to straighten me out, his watch got caught in my shawl. I should have known from that New Year's Eve party never to wear shawls! I just don't have the élan to carry off any kind of shawl.

Gable stood me upright on my three-inch heels, took off his watch, and Yvonne disentangled it from the fringe while I got as red as the shawl. Then Errol Flynn came up, and he was handsomer than in the movies. Yvonne introduced me to both movie idols and another handsome gentleman, who turned out to be Errol's agent, and a beautiful statuesque redhead.

Flynn laughed. "That's one of the greatest entrances I've ever seen. Did you do it on purpose?"

Lying in my teeth, I said, "Of course, Mr. Flynn. At heart I'm a comedienne. I knew Mr. Gable would catch me."

Flynn told me to call him Errol and cautioned me not to depend on Gable's catching ability as he'd already had three double martinis. Gable made some joke like: "I could catch her anywhere, anytime, under any conditions." It wasn't so funny, but that sexy Gable growl made me giggle like a teenager.

We went into the den and sat in deep leather chairs. The butler handed me a double vodka martini in a silver goblet, and I began to feel as though I were in a stylish MGM movie. I noticed for the first time that Yvonne was wearing some gauzy gold harem pants and a sort of bikini top with full sleeves and, I suspected, nothing underneath. She was a knockout. I was a little confused as to who was my date, if it was a date. Both Errol and Clark were equally attentive and charming to all the girls.

We ate at a glass-top table in a sort of outdoor dining room surrounded by flowers and birds, and there were real gardenias floating in the pool. For once I can't remember much of what we ate because I was too intoxicated by the presence of these two men whom, when I was a kid, I had followed in movie theaters all over Brooklyn. I had seen *It Happened One Night* innumerable times in ten different theaters, and *The Adventures of Robin Hood* had thrilled my adolescent heart so that I would watch it until Blanche had to come and drag me out of the theater while Errol was up there swinging from balconies and saving damsels in distress. I looked at them closely, and they both looked as young and vital as they had more than a decade before. I figured they must have some youth secret that the rest of the world's male population didn't have.

While we were having Irish coffee and I was entertaining them with tales of the New York theater, a car drove up. A man who was obviously a doctor with a regulation black bag got out and said, "Hi," and went into the living room. Then, while we were talking and joking, all three men, one by one, went into the living room, and I heard each of them yell "Ouch!" A few minutes later they came back buttoning their shirts and rubbing their right shoulders.

After the second "Ouch!" I excused myself, sneaked down the hallway and peeked through a door into the living room. I saw Errol with his shirt off, and the doctor cut a little flap of skin on the back of his right shoulder, inserted some kind of capsule into it, then took a stitch in the skin, closing it. It seemed very weird, and to this day no regular doctor has been able to explain it to me. But that's what I saw.

I hurriedly got back to the table, beating Flynn by a minute, and lit a cigarette, in order to appear calm and blasé. The waiter filled my glass with rare wine, which I drank down as if it were Coca-Cola. While the gentlemen rubbed their shoulders and I choked on my cigarette, I was wondering how I could get the hell out of there. I had seen the Dracula films, too.

Yvonne hit me on the back and asked why I was smoking when I didn't know how, and I told her that the next film I was to do was Scott Fitzgerald's *The Great Gatsby* on loan-out to Paramount. Alan Ladd and Barry Sullivan would be in it, and Betty Field would play the good rich girl. I was to play the bad poor girl, and I felt it was necessary to learn how to smoke, or how else would the audience know I was a bad girl?

Flynn and Gable started to talk about Fitzgerald, whom they had met in Malibu bars, and Flynn asked me if I had read his books. I explained that I was getting cultural in alphabetical order, and I was only up to Theodore Dreiser, although I had cheated and skipped to the Ws and read all of Thomas Wolfe. Flynn told me he had all of Fitzgerald's first editions, and he would lend me *The Great Gatsby*, as I really ought to be familiar with all of his work before I did that film. He added wistfully, "I wonder why no one ever offers me films like that." I assured him that he gave millions of people delight and enjoyment and thrills. He looked at me shrewdly and said, "Would *you* be content with that kind of career?"

I started to lie a compliment and then stopped. He was too honest and elegant and nice a man. I told him that I felt that the function of films and the theater was to bring joy, as well as to enlighten people's lives. I then quoted something from one of George Bernard Shaw's critiques: "Theatre [or Film] is at its finest when it is an elucidator of social consciousness, a recorder of the mores of its time, a historian of the future, an armory against despair and darkness, and a temple in the ascent of Man."

The table got very quiet, and for a minute I felt as if I had made a gigantic faux pas and brought reality into never-never land. I guess in a way I had. Flynn held my chin in his hand and said, "You've got a lot between your ears beside those blonde curls, haven't you, Shelley?"

I grinned with pleasure and said, "I hope so. I never finished high school, and I'm trying very hard to make up for it, and I'm directing a wonderful play called *Thunder Rock* at the little Circle Theater."

The conversation suddenly turned serious and interesting. Gable asked me if he hadn't seen an English film called *Thunder Rock* with James Mason and Michael Redgrave. I said, "Yes, it was made in England after the Spanish Civil War, and it's about hope."

Flynn's agent asked about the plot—never mind the message. I told him it was a play by Robert Ardrey about a man who takes a job as a lighthouse keeper on an isolated island in the Great Lakes, disillusioned after fighting with the Loyalists during the Spanish Civil War. The democracies had given little help to the Spanish Democratic Republic while the Fascist forces had fully supported the Franco coup.

In the lighthouse the man sees a plaque, dated 1850, with the names of the people sailing from England whose ship went down on the rocks off that island. All the characters from the novel he's trying to write come to life in it, but walk in a slanty, distorted manner and speak in phony, stilted words. Only when the man is shocked into truly looking at his characters is he able to see that these people who were drowned in 1850 really project hope to the audience. There's a woman who has been deported from England for fighting for women's suffrage; a starving child who has escaped from a Welsh coal mine; a Scottish workingman who has been crippled during a strike for a twelve-hour day. Despite the seeming hopelessness at any given moment in world history, when man's future seems lost and hopeless, these characters show that everything they died for, which in their lifetime seemed impossible, came about in less than 100 years. And man's condition improves, and he survives.

I hadn't meant to get on a soapbox, but I was directing the play weekends and nights, and my heart and mind were full of it. Flynn looked at me ruefully and said that he had flown to Barcelona with Hemingway to try to do research for the film *The Sun Also Rises* but had developed a case of cold feet when he realized they were using real bullets and he couldn't yell, "Cut!" But someone had told me he had helped Hemingway run guns from Crete to the Loyalists, so I kissed him, and he put his arm around me, and we all trooped into the long, narrow living room. We sat down at one end on a big white curved sofa and were served enormous goblets of champagne and brandy.

Errol yelled at some invisible person over his head, "Thread up and start."

Yvonne stood up and said, "Could you wait a couple of minutes for the ladies to use the ladies' room?" The redhead and I took the hint, and we traipsed into the gold and crystal bathroom. While she was answering the call of nature, Yvonne turned both faucets on full force and whispered in my ear, "Which one do you like the most, Gable or Flynn?"

"Do I have a choice?"

Yvonne said she thought Errol really liked me, so she would sacrifice herself and take Gable. But she advised me not to show my brains too much. "I've noticed at Hollywood parties, the handsome leading men like to talk to the intelligent women writers, but they go home with the dumb blonde starlets." I got her message. But I wasn't sure if I wanted to play by those rules.

When we got back, Flynn was sitting on the right side of the ten-foot sofa and pulled me down next to him. Gable was to my left, Yvonne sat next to him, the handsome agent was far left and the redhead proceeded to sit on his lap.

As the lights went out and the MGM lion roared on the screen, I suddenly realized I really was sitting between CLARK GABLE and ERROL FLYNN! Mr. Flynn handed me my goblet, and I gulped the champagne. As he put his arm around me, all I could think was, this must be some sex fantasy I'm having at the Loew's Pitkin movie theater in Brownsville. I stared at the screen with complete concentration without the slightest idea what the picture was. Mr. Flynn took my empty goblet.

I never knew a man who smelled as wonderfully as he did. I don't know if it was the cologne or his soap or maybe it was a combination of both and especially his own outdoorsy smell. I almost swooned like a heroine in a Victorian novel.

When we got about an hour into the film, something shiny caught my eye. Mr. Flynn must have pressed a button because a twelve-foot sliding panel had slid open, and there on a raised platform was a huge bed covered with cream-colored satin sheets and pillows, the top sheet turned back, ready. As I gazed in stunned fascination, I saw that around the bed there were plants, books, scripts, telephones, a small wet bar, and on the other side were an icebox, a radio and a phonograph. On the ceiling above the bed was a huge mirror, and as I watched, the mirror slid away, and I could see the stars and the moon through a flowering magnolia tree.

I looked at the other people in the room, but their eyes were riveted to the screen except for Gable, who was kissing Yvonne's neck. Mr. Flynn just held my hand a bit tighter. I noticed he had rather large hands, quite calloused for an actor. He whispered some sweet nothing in my ear, and all I could think of to answer was: "I wonder what the poor people are doing."

He burst into laughter and the panel slid back in place. Dammit! Maybe I had dreamed it all. There wasn't much light from the movie, so how could I tell the sheets were cream-colored?

The movie ended, and the other two couples got up and started to leave. I think I tried to, but Flynn's arm kept me in my seat. Maybe I wasn't trying too hard. As everyone began to disappear, he said to Yvonne, "I'll see that Shelley calls home."

"Remember she has to be at work six-thirty Monday morning." What the hell was she talking about? This was only 11 P.M. Friday night!

In those days, when the film industry considered a scene censorable, the camera would pan to such things as the fireplace, or waves pounding on a beach, or fireworks exploding.

So . . . cut to:

A fire roaring in a fireplace,
Waves pounding a beach,
Fireworks exploding,
Tchaikovsky's 1812 Overture, complete with cannons.

Monday morning I did not get to the studio. That was the one and only time in my memory that I missed a morning's work. Flynn and I arrived at the studio in my little red Pontiac in time for lunch, I clutching his first edition of Fitzgerald's *The Great Gatsby*. I was worried about knowing my lines for the afternoon's work, and Errol was slightly concerned about the very physical stunt he had to do.

He made me go into the executive commissary, although I was terrified. Everyone was staring at us. His secretary had obviously phoned the Production departments of our respective films and notified them to find something else to shoot Monday morning. I felt I had committed the cardinal sin by being late, but since UI was trying to make a multiple picture deal with Mr. Flynn, it wanted him to be happy with the properties Universal had to offer, and no one seemed mad at me.

Late Friday night I had managed a quick phone call to my mother and had told her that on impulse I had gone out to Malibu to spend the weekend at John and Joan Houseman's house. I knew they had an unlisted number. Did she believe me? I wonder.

During the next month or so I got to know Errol Flynn quite well. His two small daughters were living with him; he was separated from their mother and had won temporary custody. On weekends I would take them for pony rides in La Cienega Kiddie Park, or we all would drive out to the beach to any isolated picnic area that we could find. Errol had a special quality that made it necessary for him to isolate himself from the public. Women between fifteen and seventy-five went bananas if they saw him. I fully understood their compulsive madness.

He told me all about his childhood in Australia, his fruitless efforts to get on the British stage, his stevedore days and his marriage failures. He was very literate and somehow had acquired a very good British public school education. But he was cynical about all things that most people hold valuable, and he had no ideals or aspirations of any kind, and he would gently make fun of mine. I realize now that his living-for-the-moment philosophy was a powerful self-destructive force that he could not or would not do anything about.

I loved it mostly when we went sailing. Back then it was a sport reserved for the rich, and I had never done it before. He had a sailing boat berthed in San Pedro, and he took me out with the children several times. Even a couple of times without the children. In those days there was no smog in California. One summer night we sailed to Catalina, and the reflection of the stars was so bright on the water, and the Pacific was so dark blue and calm, that I felt that I was actually sailing through heaven with stars all around me.

The columnists were calling my house constantly, and for once I wouldn't speak to them. And my father and mother weren't speaking to me again.

I started to do fittings for The Great Gatsby, and thank God it was in black and white because if it had been in color, I would have had to be replaced. I had a wonderful golden tan from sailing, and tans can't be photographed in Technicolor; they drive the color cameramen crazy because they can't balance the color with the skin tint of the other actors. But the makeup man just covered me with light pancake, and the black-and-white wardrobe tests looked sensational, as did my figure suddenly sans powder puffs. One day during the tests I had on a black satin dress with a white fox fur; my waist was small, and my legs looked very sexy. Skinny, flat-chested Shirley Schrift had finally disappeared.

Errol thought I was very childish because I wouldn't move in with him. He couldn't understand a girl my age still living with her mother and father. He kept reminding me that I'd been married and divorced. Were they still pretending I was a virgin? There was no way to explain to this pleasure-loving, rich, intelligent Australian the American middle-class morality of my family. I didn't even try.

Out of the blue one day, Errol informed me I shouldn't have signed an exclusive contract with Universal since its aim was to make commercial product, not distinguished film. "But maybe I can help you fix that," he announced. "In two weeks I'm giving a party in your honor."

"But, Errol, you never go out in public, not to premieres, parties, nothing! You hate them!"

"Well, I think it's time I gave a big party for the entire Hollywood press, including what foreign press is here, and you get Orry-Kelly to design a beautiful dress for you, and I'll get Clark Gable to be your escort. Then I'll get jealous, have a make-believe fight with him, and the press will have a field day."

"Are you sure this is such a good idea?"

"Baby, as long as they spell your name right, and it appears in every newspaper in the world, it's a great idea."

Orry-Kelly designed me a beautiful strapless gold lamé dress, and we had a terrible fight because he insisted I wear plain gold pumps. He said the dress was sexy enough. He also wouldn't let me wear my sables but made me a beautiful pale green chiffon stole and had Marvin Hime lend me some real diamond earrings. "The dress and your figure are sexy enough. Don't you dare go to this party looking like a Christmas tree. You have beautiful shoulders and breasts, and I designed the dress for them."

Orry charged this dress to *Take One False Step*, the film I was to do with William Powell after I finished *Gatsby*. Spitz & Goetz were a little confused about why Mr. Kelly was making a dress for me three months before the picture was to go, but Orry was such a temperamental and famous designer that they didn't dare question him.

The night of the big party arrived. There was a knock on my door, and when my mother opened it, there stood Clark Gable. She said nothing, not even "Come in." I'll try to explain. A few years ago I did a film for Paul Mazursky called *Next Stop Greenwich Village* in which I based my character on my mother. I say to my son going to Hollywood, "If you ever actually meet Clark Gable, tell him I've loved him all my life and I've seen every picture he's ever done." I had no trouble making that one of the most poignant moments in the film because the memory of my mother looking at Clark Gable in the flesh on the stoop is implanted in my mind forever.

Gable put the pale green chiffon scarf around my shoulders and pinned a green orchid to my gold beaded bag. He said, "Good evening," to my stunned family and as he ushered me to the door, I can't be sure, but I almost thought my mother breathed in my ear, "*Don't* be careful." There was a huge navy blue Rolls-Royce waiting for us, and the entire population of Peyton Hall watched as "The King" helped me into the car and we drove away.

We went to Romanoff's first and had champagne cocktails at the bar. I was shaking so I couldn't eat any of the free hors d'oeuvres. I asked Mr. Gable what we were waiting for and why we just didn't go up to Errol's house. He asked if he was boring me.

"No, you paralyze me. I'm sure that if we wait too long, the Rolls is going to turn into a pumpkin and the gold lamé dress will disappear and I'll be left in front of the Loew's Pitkin in rags." He pinched my fanny, and I yelled, "Ouch!"

"Shelley, that feeling of unreality is an occupational hazard. Every time they say, 'Cut,' and it's the last take of a movie, I feel I'll never be hired for another one, and I'll be back tomorrow doing extra work again." I gazed at him with disbelief. "Honest," he said, "even me. All actors feel they're not entitled to happiness and all that money, that some evil god will take it away from us when we do get it. And please call me Clark."

I told Mr. Clark that I had always felt I was alone in this insecurity, and it made me feel better to know that the most successful actor in films had the same fears.

We got back in the Rolls; it was now late enough for us to make an entrance, and we drove up to Errol's house. As we walked in, you would have thought it was the opening of the Potsdam Conference. There seemed to be thousands of photographers and hundreds of reporters, including Louella, Hedda and some of the foreign press I knew by sight. Every top star, producer, agent and studio head seemed to be there. They all were a little confused as to why Errol was giving me, a relatively new actress, this party. But since he gave so few parties or even appeared in public, they all came.

Errol was wearing a white silk Hamlet-type shirt with a dark red cummerbund and black pants. Only he could come to his party without a tuxedo. He welcomed us and acted as though Gable were really my date. Kenny Carter, one of the heads of UI's Publicity Department, brought me a glass of champagne and whispered in my ear, "Stay calm, no matter what happens." What the hell did that mean? I was already blinded from the flashbulbs, but that remark made me even more nervous.

There was a striped green and white tent over the whole pool area and many round tables, which accommodated about ten people each. The waiters and waitresses all were dressed in Hawaiian costumes. I later read it was a Hawaiian luau. There were three musicians floating on a raft in the pool, along with many rare, fragrant flowers. There were twinkling lights of different colors all over the place and many candles.

Gable asked me to dance, and I was a little annoyed because Errol was so busy playing host. But the feeling disappeared when Gable held me very close. I mean close, and we started to do a sort of Hawaiian rumba. I'd never learned this dance, but somehow his thighs guided mine. He kissed and whispered in my ear; then Errol patted him on the shoulder and cut in. Gable looked very annoyed but gave me up, and I danced with Errol.

"You having a good time, baby?" he asked. I nodded. Then he said, "Keep calm no matter what happens." Now, what the hell. . . .

Gable cut in again, and he and Errol had a few heated words. I began to feel the whole thing was silly. Even Harrison Carroll, another famous grandmotherly-type columnist of that day, wouldn't believe that the two most desirable men in Hollywood would fight over me. They would realize it was a silly hoax. I began to whisper this to Gable, but he just smiled and said, "Well, enjoy yourself while you can . . . and keep calm no matter what happens."

I had been dancing for about half an hour when we heard sirens approaching. Someone must have left the iron gates open because two vast police cars and three motorcycle policemen with gold helmets almost drove into the pool. Two huge policemen got out of the car while everyone stood with mouths agape, and one of them came over to me. He informed me of my rights under the laws of the United States and the State of California and arrested and handcuffed me to himself and put me into one of the big police cars. Kenny Carter jumped in the front.

I was too dazed to do anything. As the bulbs were flashing, I noticed Gable trying to hit one of the policemen, the raft with the musicians in the pool overturned, and I could hear Mr. Goetz saying, "Shelley, I'll call Jerry Giesler, and don't you dare say a word till he gets there." A candle turned over, and a paper tablecloth caught fire as we drove away, and I felt as if I'd left Errol's house in flames and disaster.

I couldn't imagine what they were arresting me for. I vaguely figured it had something to do with my father's fire or the strike I had caused at Woolworth's so many years ago. Hollywood was very antiunion just then. I began to cry. Kenny Carter was giving me Kleenex and trying to explain something to me. I wouldn't listen. All I knew was that I was handcuffed to this Gestapo agent next to me.

Finally, we drove up in front of the Hollywood Canteen, and Kenny managed to scream through my sobs, "Don't you remember? You promised to entertain tonight at the policemen's benefit for the USO. After you do some songs from *Oklahoma!*, they'll take you back to the party."

I stared at everyone. The policemen and Kenny Carter were laughing, and I wanted to kill them all. As far as I was concerned, I had indeed turned into a pumpkin. But I remembered everybody had told me to keep calm, so as soon as the Gestapo agent removed the handcuffs, I fixed my face and went into the Hollywood Canteen where all the armed forces present cheered my gold lamé dress.

I sang "All 'er Nothin'," and when I sang "I Cain't Say No," the policemen had to hold back the soldiers. Just for spite, I sang "Union Label" too. In between numbers I asked Kenny to phone Errol and tell him what had happened, but he told me that everything had been taken care of. After about an hour and a half of singing and joking with the soldiers, sailors and marines, the same policemen, who had now shrunk considerably, drove Kenny and me back up to Errol's house.

The policemen seemed to think it was a wonderful practical joke and told me that Errol and Gable had played many jokes on them. I asked Kenny if everyone had been in cahoots over this. He tried to look innocent but failed miserably. When we arrived, the pool area was in a shambles, and all the press had left; they had dashed to their city rooms to try to find out what precinct I'd been taken to and what exactly the charge was. Of course, they couldn't find out any of these things. Both Gable and Flynn were quite drunk now and laughing happily. I was quietly enraged. My beautiful dream of being honored at an important Hollywood party had turned into a nightmare. Flynn tried to say, "Darling, as long as they spell your name right," but I stuffed a mango into his open mouth and got Kenny Carter to take me home.

The next morning there were indeed big headlines in every newspaper, and I was famous—or infamous. The name Shelley Winters was suddenly a household word. When I opened the door, there were six scripts on my doorstep. I brought them in and tried to read them, but Shirley Schrift was so angry and outraged that she had forgotten how to read and I put them all in the incinerator. I doubt to this day if that publicity stunt helped my career. Maybe it did in a way, but it certainly hurt my confidence in my own ability. The executives at UI kept reassuring me that the "party" had been a tremendous publicity break, and now everybody at the studio was treating me as if I were a superstar. Lana Turner, Ava Gardner, Rita Hayworth and especially Elizabeth Taylor were getting this kind of flaming romantic press coverage, but something deep inside me kept saying, "Wrong, wrong, WRONG." I silenced that voice and decided I should go along with the image the studio was building up about me. I have always thought of this time, when I was searching for my public image, as my struggle between the Myth and the *Mensch*.

CHAPTER 17

Robert Ryan, who occasionally attended performances at the Actors Lab, came one evening with his wife to see an extraordinary production of *The Evils of Tobacco* as performed by Lee Cobb. Cobb's technique, discipline, characterization and deep Method work left me exhilarated, proud to be an actress and very depressed at the Blonde Bombshell turn my career was taking.

Robert Ryan told me about a group that Charles Laughton was forming to work on Shakespeare, speech and the discipline and history of the theater. He asked me if I would like to meet Mr. Laughton and audition for the group. Excited after Lee Cobb's great performance, I said, "You mean tonight? After the show?" Robert laughed and suggested Sunday afternoon out at Charles Laughton's house.

I had been hanging around the Writers' Building at Paramount and had gotten to know Christopher Isherwood, Lion Feuchtwanger and John Farrow, who had written several books on the lives of the Popes. I questioned them all closely, hoping to fool Mr. Laughton into thinking I was an intellectual and therefore worthy of being trained by him. They told me to see as many of Laughton's pictures as I could and to be myself and tell him the truth about myself, especially my aspirations and feelings of inadequacy.

That Saturday afternoon there was a celebrity baseball game for a charity, and Marilyn Monroe and I were batgirls. I was so busy reading *King Lear* in the dugout that I got hit on the head with a ball. While putting ice on my head, Marilyn noticed the book, and even she thought it was strange for me to be reading *King Lear* aloud to myself during a ball game while being photographed by all the movie magazines. I explained to her what I was doing the next day, and she asked if she could come with me, saying she thought Laughton was the "sexiest man she'd ever seen." I told her that if I got accepted into the group, in a week or so I would introduce her to Laughton.

When Sunday came, I dressed as I thought a serious young actress would. I got to Laughton's house on top of a cliff in Santa Monica fifteen minutes early, so I sat in my car and waited. Elsa Lanchester came out to put something in the garbage can and did a double take. "Shelley, for God's sake, my husband likes to look at pretty girls. Put on some makeup, and take off those silly glasses and that damn babushka." I quickly did just that, and she brought me inside.

Sitting with Mr. Laughton around a luncheon table were Peter Ustinov; his then wife, Suzanne Cloutier, a beautiful French Canadian actress; Paulette Goddard; the Robert Ryans; and CHARLIE CHAPLIN. All over the walls of the dining room and living room were gorgeous paintings of fat naked ladies. I later found out that this was a priceless Renoir collection, which made me feel *good.*

Everyone treated me with kindness and respect, and unlike Errol's buddies, they seemed to have great respect for the "Art of the Cinema." I had never heard that expression before. They talked about the cultural power television could have on the masses. I never opened my mouth; now I knew I was finally on Mount Olympus!

Apropos of the Bloody Marys they were drinking, Laughton quoted a line of Shakespeare's: "O Sleep, that sometimes shuts up sorrow's eye,/Steal me awhile from mine own company. . . ." I knew immediately that Shakespeare was an insomniac, too, because to my knowledge no one had ever articulated the exact longing and need for sleep in that piercing way. Laughton noticed that my eyes filled up, and he began to ask me such kind questions that I forgot he was a famous actor who had performed in the Comédie Française and on the British stage and whom I'd seen in films since I was a child. He suddenly became like my Zayda, brought back to earth with a British accent; he even had the same twinkling blue eyes.

We moved to the den, and thank God, about twenty or more relatively unknown young actors and actresses arrived. For the next four hours Mr. Laughton talked about the priceless gift Shakespeare had given to all posterity. He explained to the whole class, and that included Chaplin and Paulette Goddard, that if we did the workshop, we would have to work every night since we all had daytime jobs, and for this kind of intense ensemble work one needed uninterrupted continuity.

Of the thirty people there, the only one who raised an objection was Paulette, who was covered with jewelry. Since it was Sunday, it was rubies. She protested about Saturday and Sunday nights, and Laughton explained that we all had to do it for a period of six months, or he couldn't be sure of the results, and he didn't want to waste his time. Paulette said she'd try, but I got the definite feeling that when she ran out of sets of jewels—diamonds, sapphires, emeralds, pearls and opals—she wouldn't come anymore. And that's what happened; she lasted twenty-one nights.

Several years later, I played Crystal in Clare Boothe Luce's *The Women*, with Helen Hayes, Mary Astor, Ruth Hussey, Paulette Goddard and many other female stars. The production was memorable because it was NBC's first color broadcast . . . and because, during the three weeks of rehearsal, Paulette never wore the same jewels twice.

Laughton told us to call him Charles and then explained that I must come right from the studio and spend an hour with Margaret Prendergast McLane, who had written a textbook called *Good American Speech*. Her husband had worked with the professor who had invented the science of phonetics that G. B. Shaw wrote about in *Pygmalion*, which later became *My Fair Lady*. Laughton said that if I worked with her every day for a year, I would be able to do any role in the English-speaking theater or films. I gratefully agreed, knowing that he was paying for all this. I told him I had once played Ariel in *The Tempest* in Detroit at Wayne University (then it was Wayne University—no "State"), and he smiled, saying that we would probably do it again sometime. Charlie Chaplin offered to give classes in pantomime.

There is no present or award I've received in my whole life comparable to that which was given to me that afternoon. Driving back from Santa Monica, I was calm. I suddenly liked and valued *me*, and with new self-esteem I began to plan my life. When I got home, I kissed my mother and father, and they knew things were different. They didn't know why, and I couldn't quite explain it to them. When we went to bed that night, I told Blanche about my day. She looked at me with great relief and said, "I've always been afraid for you. You're impetuous, and you don't value yourself enough. Especially your achievements. I feel something different and important has happened to you tonight, and I think I'm relieved of the burden of worrying about your safety in this crazy show business town of mixed-up values."

I stuck pretty close to my resolution for the next few years, but alas, so many of my intellectual resolutions are built of sand, and too often with very little pressure I will collapse and play the Hollywood Publicity Game as required.

The next six months were indeed my own personal "double life." By day I was UI's Blonde Bombshell, and by night I was a serious intelligent actress, studying Shakespeare, speech and acting technique and learning from Anne Revere and her husband how best to fulfill the writer's intent. My night life was sheer joy. The classes continued nightly, including Saturdays and Sundays. Then, because his house was slipping down the cliff, Laughton moved the group to a theater on La Cienega Boulevard, and after class we used to go to a lovely cocktail lounge and restaurant across the street. Laughton, and sometimes Chaplin, would tell us stories about the English theater and music halls until 2:00 A.M.

I began shooting *The Great Gatsby* at Paramount, and every night I rushed over to attend Laughton's class. Christmas Eve arrived, and I made my annual pilgrimage to deliver my presents to Hedda Hopper and Louella Parsons—boy, did they ever get loot!—then went back to Paramount to see what was happening on *The Great Gatsby* set. In those days, the studios gave enormous Christmas parties, on the huge sound stages, and each department had its own, with Christmas trees and booze and bonuses and presents.

The party on the *Gatsby* set was sort of dull. I joined Betty Field and Alan Ladd for one drink, then made for the Writers' Building which always had wild and woolly parties. They were serving martinis made of real Russian vodka which someone had brought back from Moscow, and different kinds of herring with red and green onions, in keeping with the Christmas spirit. By midnight all the dignified producers and writers were dancing on the desks. The directors had already passed out. I guess they started earlier.

There's a little green park in front of the Writers' Building, and I found myself drinking a large vodka out of a fifteenth-century goblet, courtesy of the Prop Department, and dancing with William Holden. I didn't know if he knew my name but I knew his. Cornel Wilde, in cape and costume, did a perfect jump from a second-story window and yelled, "Bill, we're out of ice." Holden took my hand and made for his dressing room across the street to get ice. Bing Crosby was in his dressing room next door—with Joan Caulfield—also looking for ice.

I don't exactly remember how it happened, but situations developed in such a way that we forgot about the importance of the ice. So cut only to:

Waves pounding on a beach,
Trees swaying in a storm . . .

But Mr. Holden was quite drunk that Christmas Eve and passed out.

About 4 A.M. I woke with a terrible headache and wondered what they put in vodka in Moscow. I stumbled around and realized that what looked like Mr. Holden's car was out in front of his dressing room with lots of toys in the back seat. I made some black coffee in the kitchen, but no matter how I tried, I couldn't wake Bill Holden up. There was a sink with a long spray hose next to his makeup table, so when the coffee was ready I got the water as cold as possible and sprayed him. He woke up, ready to kill me. I shoved the black coffee at him and said, "Mr. Holden, don't you have children at home? It's four A.M. Christmas morning."

He looked around groggily and gulped down the coffee. He took a very hot and then very cold shower and insisted I join him. After three more cups of black coffee, when he looked like he could drive, I helped him put his clothes on and he did the same for me. We almost got sidetracked but I wouldn't allow it. I kept thinking of those poor children waiting for their presents. As Holden drove away in the dawn, he shouted back, "By the way, what's your name?"

And for some strange reason I answered, "Sonia Epstein."

When I finished *The Great Gatsby* at Paramount, I immediately started *Take One False Step* at Universal. In this film I played a gorgeous blonde who almost wrecks William Powell's life. A few weeks later I got a note from the assistant director that Mr. Goetz wanted to see me on my lunch hour. That was when I usually slept so I rather resented the summons, but I showed up half asleep in my gold lamé dress.

Mr. Goetz informed me that the cameraman was complaining that I had rings under my eyes that even makeup and special lighting could not completely wipe out. "I know how it is when you're young and every love affair seems so important, but you've just got to get some sleep. We've got lots of money invested in you, and we're building your career."

I explained that I was studying Shakespeare with Charles Laughton every night in order to train myself to become a better actress. There was a long pause while he stared at me in disbelief. Finally, he said, "We don't do much Shakespeare out here at the Valley lot, so you sleep at night, you hear me?"

I nodded my assent, then proceeded to ignore his command. But I didn't go to the cocktail lounge when the class ended at 11:00 P.M. anymore, and Gale taught me how to set my hair with rubber rollers so I didn't have to come in until 7:00. My lovely makeup man, Jack Kevan, got so he could put my makeup on in thirty minutes while I napped, and with careful planning and eating a large lunch and no dinner, I managed to get about seven hours' sleep every twenty-four hours and a lot more on weekends. The rings under my eyes more or less disappeared.

The only excuse Laughton would permit for missing a class was when one had to go on location or when I would fly to New York between films to attend the Actors' Studio and see ten shows in four days. Don't ask me how I did this, but I did. After *Take One False Step* I finally had a week off, and UI sent me to New York to do publicity for *Larceny*. I stayed at the Gotham Hotel and did an interview with Leonard Lyons, and Earl Wilson conducted a famous one with me while I was taking a shower because I was hurrying to go to the theater.

I had managed to get one ticket for the back row for the second night of *South Pacific*; the reviews of the opening had been fantastic, and Ezio Pinza and Mary Martin were extraordinary performers.

That night when I got in the hotel elevator, dressed in Universal's finery, there stood Burt Lancaster. We were nodding acquaintances from the studio commissary, and his star dressing-room bungalow was next to mine. He was charming and funny and, oh, God, so handsome! And he was, I think, one of the most gracefully athletic men I've ever seen. Just watching him walk was almost a physical pleasure.

Burt casually mentioned that he had two tickets, fifth row center, for that night's performance of *South Pacific*, and he had no one to go with. I showed him my rotten ticket, so he asked me if I would go with him, and I gladly accepted. As I got into his limousine, I reminded myself this beautiful man was very married, but I quickly brushed the thought from my mind. After all, I was only going to the theater with a fellow actor from UI.

When we got to the box office, Burt gave my ticket to a fan who asked for our autographs. As we went into the theater, the crowd parted like the Red Sea, and the flashbulbs flashed. I was a little uneasy about the newspaper photographs and the resulting publicity. When we got to our seats, I asked Burt about it, and he repeated those famous words: "Yes, but my wife and I are not getting along and are discussing a separation." I quickly asked him if his kids were having orthodontia work done, and he looked at me strangely. He answered that the older one was four and had to have operations on his foot, and the younger one was· about two.

The overture had started, and for the next three hours we really spent an enchanted evening. Each number got such an ovation that it had to be done twice because the audience wouldn't let the show go on. When Bloody Mary sang the words, "Most people live on a lonely island," both Burt and I were weeping. I knew why *I* was weeping, but he seemed so strong. I couldn't imagine what could make him relate to that song so deeply. He was rich, famous and at the beginning of what promised to be a great career. He was married and had children and a beautiful home in Bel-Air. How could that song evoke such sadness in him?

When they sang "Some Enchanted Evening," Burt took my hand and whispered, "Do you remember meeting me at a party at Mickey Knox's house about six months ago?" Mickey Knox was a young Actors Lab actor under contract to Hal Wallis. I said I just remembered the party, but he knew I was lying in my teeth.

This romantically powerful show went on till about midnight, and until this day, when I listen to the record of *South Pacific*, the happiness and the memories of that great performance overwhelm me. When the show ended and they took their curtain calls, I thought Pinza was going to break Mary Martin's ribs as he hugged and kissed her. The audience was throwing flowers and scarves on the stage. The reviews were all in from opening night, and the actors knew they had one of the biggest hits in the history of the theater (and a show which also made a searing statement about the war in the Pacific and racial prejudice).

I cheered so wildy that I began to get hoarse, and after about the fifteenth curtain call Burt picked me up and carried me out of the theater as if I were a feather. There was a gold carriage out front with a white horse and a driver with a diamond jacket and a satin top hat. Or so it seemed. We drove up Fifth Avenue and through Central Park. Burt and I were so high from the great show we could hardly talk; vocal communication wasn't necessary anyway.

He took me to Le Pavillon for supper, which consisted mostly of champagne and caviar. We were shown to the number one booth, I with my white mink jacket—borrowed from Fuhrman's—casually draped over my bare shoulders and he with his wild red hair and strong, young, virile face. We gazed into each other's eyes. I guess we threw off such an aura of success, desire and beauty that everyone who was anyone in the restaurant came up to talk to us, wanting to be included.

Norman Mailer sat down with us and began talking to Burt about buying his great war novel, *The Naked and the Dead*, for a film. I couldn't figure out what I could play in that book, so I kept

trying to change the subject. Finally, when Burt got up to call the
Gotham for our messages, Norman said, "Gee, thanks, Shelley.
Here I am making a quarter-of-a-million-dollar sale on my book,
and you keep trying to sit on Lancaster's lap."

I knew he was kidding, but I got very dignified and explained to
him that Burt and I had just seen a great show, and it was a very
romantic evening, and he was lousing it up. When Burt came back
from the phone, he suggested that he and Norman meet for lunch
at "21" the next day. That was okay with me because I had an
interview with *The New York Times* at the hotel, after which I had
a ticket to see José Ferrer in *The Silver Whistle*. Mailer kissed my
cheek as he got up to leave and whispered, "You're on a fast track,
kid."

Burt and I sat and talked for hours and told each other about our
similar backgrounds. He had come from a poor Irish family very
much like mine, but he had reached stardom almost overnight in a
play by Arthur Laurents called *Home of the Brave*. Mark Hellinger
had seen it and signed him, and he became a film star with his first
picture, *The Killers*. He had that special magnetism in real life and
on the screen that made people line up at the box office and women
in the lobbies of the hotels walk into poles and doors.

When we finally started back to the Gotham on that night in
early spring, New York was silent; even the lights in the windows
on Fifth Avenue were out. New York was empty, a silent magnificent set built solely for us. We skipped and sang and ran along the
middle of an empty Fifth Avenue like kids, our voices echoing back
at us. When we got to the hotel, the doorman was asleep, and we
had to pound on the revolving door for him to let us in.

Burt got off at my floor, and as we walked to my door, I realized
I'd forogtten to get my key at the desk. I said a feeble good-night,
and he put his hand out for my key. I giggled, and he realized too
that I'd forgotten to get it. "I'm one flight up and my key's in my
pocket," he whispered. "RCA has given me a collection of great
opera records. Would you like to hear some of them?" At least he
hadn't said "my etchings."

He put his arm around my bare shoulder, and as we walked down
the hall to the stairwell and up the stairs to his penthouse, I babbled,
"You know, Burt, we're just going to listen to the records, and then
I'm going to go down and get my key. After all, you're married, and
I have a girlfriend who has had a very unhappy love affair with a
married man. . . ." I kept rattling on like that, and I didn't know
how to stop. Burt agreed with everything I said, and then somehow

we were in his beautiful blue and white suite, and there really was a portable phonograph in it.

Burt opened the windows, and the then-beautiful aroma of New York in the spring filled the room, and I could see all the lights from the rich people's apartments on Park Avenue. He filled two snifters with a wonderful old brandy, and while he was putting on the records, I drank mine quickly. He drank his, filled them again and asked me if I wanted to use the bathroom. But I wasn't about to go into his bedroom, and that was the only way to get to his bathroom. So we danced and sang to the records of *South Pacific*. I don't know quite how it happened, but all I remember is being on a blue and white bedspread on a thick white rug on the living-room floor and Burt didn't have any clothes on and he was gorgeous and I didn't have any clothes on and I felt gorgeous and now Gigli was singing "O Paradiso" on the phonograph.

Cut to:

A galloping army with banners,
Meteors flashing in a spangled sky, and
The top of the world.

The next morning I awakened with the sun streaming on my face. Burt was awake and looking at me. "Good morning, Miss Winters. Would you like to have breakfast?"

I realized I was famished and answered, "Yes, Mr. Lancaster. I want everything on the menu."

I dashed through Burt's bedroom to the bathroom that I'd avoided the night before. As I showered and brushed my teeth with his toothbrush, I felt glowing and happy, but when I came out of the bathroom, wearing his large robe, I noticed a picture of two young children on the nightstand. Everything collapsed. I sat down and studied the picture. They were beautiful babies, and guilt rose like bile in my throat. What the hell did I think I was doing? He was a family man, and I resolved to get out of there as soon as possible and never see him again.

When I went back into the living room, Burt was wearing the bedspread, and a huge breakfast had arrived. And so had the key to my room, which was on the table next to my orange juice. When Burt went to the bathroom, I got into my cocktail dress, gulped down some orange juice and was out the door when he caught me. "Aren't you going to eat my expensive breakfast?" he asked. I tried to squirm out of it by saying that I had an interview with *The New*

York Times. "But it's only ten o'clock," he said. I stood in the hall-way, undecided, torn between my hunger and my guilt. "I'll tell you what," Burt suggested. "I'll give you your girdle and stockings if you give me my robe."

I suddenly realized he didn't have any clothes on. I scurried back in, closed and locked the door, found his robe and gave it to him. He rescued my girdle and stockings from inside the phonograph, where he'd obviously hidden them. We both started to laugh, and as we ate, he quietly told me how much he loved his children.

"Perhaps it's my fault that our marriage is having problems because I'm so busy building my career." Maybe it was the usual married man's line, but he was so quiet and sad about telling me that I believed him. Or maybe I wanted to.

Any girl or woman who allows herself to become seriously involved with a man who is married is taking a step toward pain and guilt. Never mind the usual clichés of always being alone on weekends and holidays; if you have any imagination and know how much children need their father, every moment you spend with him is something you are taking away from them.

Despite the immediate powerful chemistry that was between us as well as the love and friendship, some wise part of myself knew that Burt would never abandon his children while they were young and needed him. Although I silenced that voice at the time, events and much anguish proved it right. But on that lovely spring morning I put all voices and doubts behind me and gloried in the fact that my Mr. Right had arrived. Burt talked a mile a minute. He was bright and knowledgeable and funny and fascinating.

He asked me how long I was staying in New York, and I told him that I was staying for the Actors' Studio session on Tuesday morning and that I'd be taking a late-afternoon plane back to California. He gave me a kiss and said he would try to get tickets for a good show that night, and we would have supper again. I happily agreed. When he gave me my white mink jacket, I noticed that Gigli's "O Paradiso" record was wrapped in it.

I finished my interview with *The Times* and quickly put on an afternoon dress and hat and gloves; in those days people didn't go to the theater unless they were properly dressed, and I wish that custom would return. I threw my sables over my shoulder and went out to grab a cab. There was none. It had begun to rain, and there's a custom in New York that just before matinees or evening performances, when it rains all the cabs go hide somewhere. So I began to hoof it to the theater. I had a rather tight skirt on, and I was walking as fast as I could.

There were two beautiful little girls walking with their mother near me, and when I started to run, they began to run. One was a toddler holding the hand of her sister, who was about five, and to this day I can remember exactly what they were wearing. When we got to Sixth Avenue, their mother screamed, "Stop," which they did. But I crossed Sixth Avenue, at the same time looking in my purse for my theater ticket.

All of a sudden I was hit by a car, was thrown at least six feet and landed on my back on the asphalt. For a second or two I lay there dazed. Then I got up and started brushing myself off, looking for my purse and sables and one of my shoes. My white gloves were dirty, and I started to cry. A little fat lady started to help me and whispered, "Dumbbell, lay down. You fell on your back. It's a limousine, don't be an idiot. I was a witness. Lay down!"

All I wanted to do was get away and get to the theater. Luckily the car had braked when it hit me, but the chauffeur was white with fear. He seemed to know who I was, and he was apologizing all over the place. "Miss Winters, you ran right in front of my car."

A small crowd and a policeman appeared, and the mother of the two little children handed me a handkerchief and sat me down on the curb. The children were crying bitterly, too. I looked at the handkerchief in a dazed fashion, and one lisped, "Your nose! Your nose is bleeding!" Somebody brought water and ice, and I put some in the handkerchief and held it on my nose and hoped that the bump had improved the shape. I kept saying, "I'm sorry . . . I'm sorry . . . I have to go to the theater . . . leave me alone."

An ambulance from Roosevelt Hospital arrived, and I refused to get in it. The young doctor who examined me briefly said that he didn't think anything serious had happened but that he couldn't really tell unless I was X-rayed. I agreed, saying, "Okay, I'll come to the hospital tomorrow; I have to go to the theater now." The little fat lady was practically screaming with rage, and she kept repeating, how could I be so stupid. Somehow she'd found out it was J. J. Shubert's car, and as I rushed into the Stage Door Delicatessen to clean myself up, all I could hear was her loud voice: "Well, I guess she really is a dumb blonde." I stayed in the ladies' room until I'd cleaned myself up, fixed my face and the crowd had dispersed. Then I hobbled to the theater and sat through the matinee of *The Silver Whistle* in agony.

The theater doorman got me a cab, and when I returned to the hotel, Burt was standing in the lobby, talking to Norman Mailer. They took one look and rushed me to an orthopedic specialist, who X-rayed everything and said that I would have to wear a brace on my back and that I would be in pain for a few days and that I really should go to the hospital. I refused, knowing that Universal would never let me go to New York alone again.

Burt carried me back to my room, had a board put under my mattress and made me swallow some of the antipain pills the doctor had given me. I couldn't eat anything, but Burt kept pouring tea and lots of sugar down me. He wouldn't take no for an answer. I realized later that was the treatment for shock. I hurt everywhere. He massaged me gently and was so kind as he kept trying to distract me with funny stories. He bought me flowers and dolls and stuffed animals and took care of me until the Sunday night he had to leave. For some reason he seemed to think my accident was his fault because he'd let me out alone.

Saturday J. J. Shubert's lawyer showed up and insisted on having all the medical bills and asked me to sign a release. He wanted the X rays, and I made him promise that J. J. Shubert wouldn't fire the chauffeur. He promised, and I signed the release. The lawyer then beamed and told me that J.J. remembered me from when I was a kid running around New York and wanted to make sure that I had the best medical attention available and that I would see a specialist in California. He gave me the name of one, and I gladly agreed to it. I wondered if that little fat lady who had witnessed the accident had scared them.

Burt ushered him out, and I said, "Burt, could I please have a tuna fish salad sandwich and a double chocolate milk shake?" About an hour later he gave me the milk shake in a beautiful silver goblet from Tiffany (which I still have). I smiled at him and wondered why the shake tasted like hemlock.

Tuesday morning I went to the Actors' Studio in Burt's rented limousine, which he had left for me until I went to La Guardia Airport. My suitcases were packed and in the trunk. Those were the days of propeller planes which left New York at 5:00 P.M. and arrived in L.A. at about 6:00 or 7:00 the next morning.

Lee Strasberg, whose private classes I also attended at the Malin Studios when I could, was moderating that day at the Actors' Studio. A young actor by the name of James Dean was doing an exercise called a Private Moment, which is an activity you do at home when no one else is around, and in it must be the germ of something you need for a scene you're working on. For me in those days it was dancing around the house and fantasizing while listening to records.

The Actors' Studio had by now bought an old Greek church on West Forty-fourth Street near Tenth Avenue. I sat down stiffly and carefully in my observer's seat on the side in the front row, almost behind a pole. Jimmy Dean came in wearing an immense old overcoat over a white T-shirt and from the way he moved we knew he was very alone in an imaginary crowd. Then he stepped to stage right, where he shrugged off the coat, and took out a switchblade. Leaning on the pole next to me, he began to weep. I looked at Strasberg, who was watching Jimmy in an intellectual and dispassionate manner. Jimmy began playing with the unopened knife. He was smiling, but the tears were flowing down his face. I was terrified for him and kept looking at Strasberg, hoping he would stop the exercise. I thought I noticed a thin line of blood on Jimmy's wrist which Strasberg could not see from where he was sitting. I automatically reached out and grabbed Jimmy's hand. We struggled for the knife, and he started laughing.

For the next few minutes I didn't know if I was in a Method Exercise or in Real Life. As we struggled, I noticed a white scar on Jimmy's right wrist, and when I grabbed his other hand, I saw that his left wrist also had a white scar on it. He was quite strong for such a slight boy, and all I could think of to say was: "Stop, Jimmy! I've got a back brace on. I've been in an automobile accident!"

Instantly the Private Moment exercise became an improvisation. His attention changed like an infant's, and he forgot the knife and let me take it. He carefully sat me down on a bench in front of the class and then began a serious improvisatory discussion about *my accident*. I found myself weeping, too, and the sum total of the scene became: Why had the chocolate milk shake in the goblet tasted like hemlock; why had *I* tried to commit suicide? I told Jimmy what had happened but didn't mention any names. He put his arm around me and kissed me consolingly, his wrist bleeding slightly on my sables. Then, pulling on his coat, he turned to Lee and said, "Okay, that's it," as if the whole thing had been a rehearsed scene.

Lee asked Jimmy what he was working for, and although he was rather inarticulate, he managed to explain that he was trying to fight his feelings of alienation because he felt everybody else wasn't real. When Lee asked me what I was working for, I didn't want to tell him I'd interrupted a scene; after all, I was still an observer. I made up some cockamamie exercise off the top of my head about a movie starlet's attempt to interfere with fate. To this day I don't know whether Strasberg believed either one of us. In retrospect, I think he was teaching us how to use anything that happens accidentally onstage that isn't planned. From this comes the famous Method expression "Use it."

At the break I was so shaken I went downstairs to have a cup of coffee. Jimmy followed me. There's a terrible Chinese proverb that if you save someone's life, then you're responsible for him for the rest of his existence. I don't believe it, but Jimmy immediately attached himself to me. He tried to clean the blood off my sables with hot coffee, and I got some iodine from the first-aid kit and put a Band-Aid on the very little cut on his wrist.

I decided I felt too shaken up to stay for the second scene, and as I went out to my waiting limousine, Jimmy followed me like a puppy. He was very impressed with the limousine but wouldn't show it, and he got right in with me, clutching an old airline bag. "Shelley," he said, "I'm very hungry." We had time, so I had the car stop at Downey's and bought him a huge breakfast. I didn't want him to feel self-conscious, so I had one, too. He also had three double Irish coffees.

For the next few hours I kept trying to get rid of him, but he obviously had no place to go. He wanted to drive out to the airport with me, so I let him. He told me that he had some place to stay in the Village, and I said he could use the limousine to take him there afterward.

His existence seemed so pointless and haphazard, and no matter how I questioned him, I couldn't get a straight answer. He was obviously very beautiful and a gifted actor, but he didn't seem to want anything. In some weird way he reminded me of Peter Pan, but without the joy, as if he had sprung from never-never land and would disappear back into it. What I didn't realize was that I was with a forerunner of the Beat Generation. He seemed to be clinging to me in some emotional way, but I didn't understand it. Besides, I was so mixed up myself I couldn't have done anything about it if I had.

When we got to La Guardia, I wouldn't let him get out of the car because I was sure he would manage by hook or crook to get on the plane to California with me. I gave him my phone number in L.A. and put $20 in his breast pocket. He smiled as if he were doing me a favor by taking it. I somehow felt he was. I told him to go to the YMCA, and when he drove away, he was smiling, but there were tears in his eyes.

When I entered the terminal, I felt terribly guilty, as if I had failed his whole generation. He wasn't much younger than I, but he looked absolutely defenseless. I thanked God for the tough Brooklyn neighborhood I had been raised in because it had made me strong. I guess that's what it does if it doesn't kill you.

CHAPTER 18

My father was waiting for me at L.A. Airport and was really concerned about my automobile accident. My various escapades in New York had made the papers and were on the radio. He was very quiet as he drove me over Sepulveda Boulevard to our house and talked to me in a tone of voice that I'd never heard before. He said stupid things like: "Shirley, any man who is unfaithful to his wife will do exactly the same to you."

I smart-assed answered, "And where's that written? In the Talmud?"

He surprised me with "As a matter of fact, yes."

"Listen, Dad, I'm a grown-up woman; I've been married and divorced; I'm an intelligent movie star. Stop dictating to me how I should run my life."

"You're a dumb snotnose. I can't believe a daughter of mine could be so dumb. You're putting your life and everything you've worked for in danger. And you could at least take out a life insurance policy for your mother and me if you're going to go around throwing yourself in front of automobiles."

I refused to answer. When I got home, nobody was talking to me. I took off my back brace and slept for a few hours. When I awoke, the script of *East of Java* was waiting for me, and Blanche told me that Kenny Carter had called ten times, as had every other columnist in Hollywood.

I took the script out to the pool—the New York doctor had told me that swimming would be good for my back. I was trying to get myself in a comfortable position on a chaise longue when my father came out and went clear down to the other end of the pool and began to play his eternal gin rummy game with Lou Irwin, Bob Hope's agent. My mother came out, sat on the other side of the pool and started to play Mah-Jongg with her three cronies. Blanche came out and bravely sat sort of near me. It was a beautiful day, and everyone else was chatting and swimming. I was trying to concentrate and read the inane script when I suddenly realized the pool had gotten very quiet.

I looked up, and there was Burt Lancaster walking toward me, carrying a small boy with red-blonde hair. I could either say hello or drown myself. Burt sat down near me on the edge of the pool. The little boy, who was named Jim after Burt's brother, had a bandage on one foot, but he was so longing to jump in the pool and tried to squirm out of his father's arms. Burt finally calmed him down and introduced him to me. Jimmy solemnly shook my hand. Blanche, sensing my embarrassment—I think I was pretending I barely knew Burt—came over and introduced herself.

Burt asked me if I had a good trip. I nodded. He asked if my back still hurt. I nodded.

"Was it an interesting session at the Actors' Studio?"

I nodded.

"Did you think of me?"

I nodded.

"You want to see my new film at UI tomorrow afternoon?"

I nodded.

"Daddy, hasn't Shelley Winters learned to talk yet?" Jimmy asked.

Burt tried to introduce himself to my mother, but she was too busy blowing her nose. Blanche took him over to my father to introduce him, and my father never looked up from his cards. The lifeguard came over and informed us that children under eight were not allowed at the pool. Burt got the message, picked up Jimmy and left. I jumped in the pool and learned to cry underwater. I stayed under so long the lifeguard came in to get me. I told him to mind his own business, and I swam around the pool for a couple of hours. I didn't want to go back into the apartment because I was sure my parents were sitting *shiva*. (When a member of an Orthodox Jewish family dies, everyone sits on a wooden box, shoeless, puts ashes on his forehead and turns all mirrors to the wall.)

That night I went over to Moki Vidor's apartment, and she slept in my apartment; my parents had *nothing* to say to me. When I got dressed in the morning to go to the studio, everyone had disappeared. I drove to Universal and found Burt sitting on the steps of his dressing room, waiting for me. He got in my car, kissed me and said, "Jesus, and I thought the Irish were bad. Didn't you explain anything to them?" I told him that they still lived in another century and only Blanche sort of understood. Burt thought about it for a while and said, "Baby, you've just got to move out of there."

He wasn't saying exactly the right things, but the specter of Louella Parsons was hanging over both of us, so I agreed. Apartments were still very hard to get, but he told me not to worry—in a couple of days he would find us one. I didn't know exactly what the "us" meant, but by that time I was so dazzled by this beautiful man that I didn't ask him.

That night we stayed in my dressing room. He went home about 3:00 A.M. I called Blanche to tell her I wasn't coming home *ever*. She said that the family had had a powwow, and my father and mother felt that if I wanted to flout their beliefs in this fashion, it would be best if I got my own apartment. I didn't feel anything, or maybe I was so angry I couldn't feel anything. I could, however, understand my father's attitude, but how could my wonderful mother not understand my loneliness and need? Besides, Burt wouldn't have brought his child over to meet them if I were just a casual romance. I didn't understand then that they were using their trump card to try to save me from the the anguish and heartbreak that could result from this dangerous relationship. But I was of the age that G. B. Shaw refers to as consumed by "the fires that proliferate the world," and I wouldn't see or hear or listen to anything except my own desires and need.

The week I was sleeping at the studio (which, incidentally, was against the insurance rules) was the happiest Burt and I ever knew in a relationship that lasted a couple of years or more. The whole thing was so traumatic that it's now a little blurred. Burt finally found me a penthouse apartment, complete with leopard couch, at the Villa Italia, which had the added advantage of being close to Schwab's. It also had an underground garage that you could drive into, get right into the elevator and go up to any floor you wanted to without being seen in the lobby. This anonymous feature of the building seemed a contradiction in our relationship and annoyed me; I always parked my car in the garage, then walked around the corner and reentered the building through the front lobby.

To be fair to Burt, I think he really did try to get some sort of legal separation or divorce, but I believe his wife was ambivalent about it, to say the least, because of their small children. I'm sure she loved him, and everything I ever heard about her made me know that she was a patient wife and a wonderful mother. Some years later I learned myself that being married to a movie star is an almost untenable position for any intelligent, self-respecting woman. But in those days I wouldn't allow myself to hear about Burt's wife and was careful never to meet her. With this magical thinking, in a way, for me she didn't exist. So why, during this period (before TM—Transcendental Meditation), did I develop such a bad case of insomnia?

The day I moved out of Peyton Hall only Blanche helped me pack. My parents had disappeared. It was a terrible jolt. We'd never really been separated since I was born; even when I was married to Paul, my clothes were in their home and their home was my home. I know young people now get out of the nest as soon as possible, but for me it was as if my family had abandoned me.

As I drove over to my newly furnished apartment with somebody's pickup truck following with my suitcases and books, I swear that if my father had come after me and said, "Shirley, come home. You belong with us and not in some strange sexy apartment with a leopard couch," I would have turned around and gone home. But he didn't come after me. As I took my possessions up in that miserable elevator, I felt as though I were crossing over the river Styx.

Burt had bought me a Capehart record player, and the apartment was full of flowers. There was a fancy dressing room, and a uniformed maid appeared to hang up all my clothes, first putting them in special bags. The refrigerator was full of food, and the bar was stocked with wine and champagne and all kinds of booze. So I had a shot of whiskey, put *South Pacific* on the Capehart and looked out the window over the city, telling myself I felt free and happy.

Burt took me out for an early dinner because he had to get home before eight or he'd turn into a pumpkin. He was with Norman Mailer, who had just arrived in Hollywood with his beautiful wife, Bea, and rented a lovely home in the hills. Obviously Burt had brought Norman along to sit with me when he left. We went to a great Mexican restaurant, and after three margaritas I didn't care much about anything.

I told Norman all about *East of Java*—later called *South Sea Sinner*—keeping the conversation away from *The Naked and the Dead*. I sang several songs I had in it and explained that the picture had the same phony, crappy dialogue, and all that was required of me was to pose around on banisters and pianos and look sexy. Come to think of it, the piano was easier to act with than the young Liberace because it was his first film, and he was so frightened he never took his eyes off the keys. I was down to 118 pounds, and Orry-Kelly designed twenty sensational costumes for me. The director, Lucky Humberstone, would sometimes have me change costumes in the middle of a scene for any ridiculous reason, just to get them all in. I sometimes felt like part of the scenery.

After Burt left the restaurant, Norman ordered coffee and asked me why I was so depressed. I didn't really know him too well, but I had read *The Naked and the Dead* three times, and he had compassionate blue eyes, so I put my head on his shoulder and said, "Norman, I don't know which is worse, my professional or private life. In both cases I'm not on the first team."

Norman said, "I just saw a rough cut of *The Great Gatsby*, and your performance is outstanding. Paramount is doing *An American Tragedy* next year, so why don't you try to get the part of the factory girl?"

I was all ears. *The Great Gatsby* was another sexpot part, but it was a fine film. I felt I could play that factory girl in *An American Tragedy* better than anyone else, but George Stevens was a very tough director, and with all that Blonde Bombshell publicity, I knew he would never even let me test for it. Norman told me not to be so sure and then started to question me about what I knew about Theodore Dreiser's work, specifically *An American Tragedy*.

We went back to my apartment, and for three hours the young, handsome Norman Mailer talked to me about the inner workings of that girl's soul and mind and what Dreiser wanted the reader to feel about the whole American syndrome of success at any price. Norman knew so much about Dreiser that I got the feeling he had been his protégé, figuratively and perhaps literally.

The next day I started my campaign for the role that every young actress in Hollywood wanted. Neither Mr. Feldman nor Mr. Blum could get George Stevens to consider me or even meet me. His answer was that I was wonderful in *A Double Life* but was completely wrong for this plain, meek little factory girl. I wouldn't take no for an answer. I read *An American Tragedy* again. When Burt used to come over to my apartment at 5:00 A.M., no doubt telling his wife he was running around the UCLA track, he would find himself running around my apartment, looking for me, because I would be hiding in any obscure place I could find to read the book. Finally, he said, "I give up. I'll see you after you make the test."

"What makes you sure I'll get a test?"

"When an irresistible force meets an immovable object, my money's on the irresistible force. You."

That made me feel much better. He also told me he thought Greg Bautzer, whom I knew slightly, was George Stevens's lawyer.

The next thing I did was call Bautzer and promise him anything, including Arpège, if he could get Stevens just to talk to me. Later I gave Bautzer a beautiful famous Impressionist watercolor I got in Paris.

Bautzer called me back twenty minutes later to tell me that Stevens had seen hundreds of girls for the role. Even though he was scraping the bottom of the barrel, he wouldn't let me come to his offices at the studio. He would, however, meet me at five-thirty in the lobby of the Hollywood Athletic Club.

Thank goodness I had a day off from *South Sea Sinner*. I rushed out to the Firestone Tire factory and looked at all the girls on the assembly line. Then I dashed back to Peyton Hall and borrowed a checkered dirndl of Blanche's, a plain cotton blouse with a jabot and a fingertip-length loose gray coat. I rushed back to my apartment, dyed my hair brown, took the polish off my nails, combed my hair flat with sad little curls on the end below my ears, with two bobby pins on the side, and washed my face clean of makeup. Then I made myself a sandwich and put it in a brown paper bag.

I got to the Hollywood Athletic Club at five o'clock. No one recognized me, and if anyone did look at me, he must have thought I was one of the maids waiting for a lift. Holding my paper bag, I sat sort of crumpled up in a chair on the far side of the lobby.

George Stevens, a big beautiful bear of a man, came in exactly at five-thirty, looked around the lobby, sat down and started to look at a *Life* magazine. Every few minutes or so he would look at his watch. I didn't move. I sat there with my feet, in my white bobby socks and Blanche's old brown and white shoes, nailed to the floor, clutching the brown paper bag and staring into space, no doubt looking as frightened as I felt.

Finally, Stevens got up to leave. I almost moved, but luckily his head swiveled around, and he stared at me with one of his tough, yet kindly, piercing looks that I came to know and love. Slowly he walked over to me, touched the little bobby pins on the side of my head and said the words that changed my life: "Shelley, if I test you for this role and you get it, will you let me photograph you like this?"

"Mr. Stevens, if I get this role, you can photograph me any way you want to."

I had seen every picture that Stevens had ever made, and I knew the thrust of his films was always "man's inhumanity to man." The chance of working with this great director made me tremble with hope—hope for my work, hope for my life. He told me that as soon as I finished at Universal, he would test me for *An American Tragedy*.

He was the greatest director I've ever worked for. He made me understand that acting, especially film acting, is not *emotion*, but *thinking*. He had been a famous cameraman since the Keystone Kops days, and he showed me how the camera photographs your thoughts and sometimes your soul. I think I came to love him more than any man in my life. Truly, he treasured and cared for the thing that I trust most—my talent. Through my association with George Stevens I came to know that no matter what I said or did, the functioning of that talent was the most important thing to me. That was my real priority. I often didn't want it that way, but I had no choice. That was the way it was and is. The experience of testing for *An American Tragedy* and getting the role and the day-by-day working with George Stevens changed my decisions for the rest of my life. Perhaps it wasn't immediately apparent to me, but his values about our world and any role that reflects our world have stayed with me. Six months later he tested me.

During the period that I researched and rehearsed, did the test, then waited for the results I was invited to a party at Ira Gershwin's house. I wanted to go very badly but had no one to take me. In fact, my social life and friends were drifting away because I was working so hard during the day, and studying with Laughton at night, and seeing Burt in dressing rooms when I could, and on weekends staring at the telephone, hoping he could get away for an hour. How can girls be so stupid? But they are sometimes, and I was. I kept wanting to believe, and maybe it was true, that his marriage had emotionally ended and he was just trying to straighten out all the details so that his children and wife would be uprooted as little as possible by his departure.

I really abandoned Shirley Schrift's values and certainly any religious training I had. I wouldn't go to Passover dinners and certainly would never go to Temple with my family on Rosh Hashonah and Yom Kippur. In fact, I got into the habit of unconsciously closing my eyes whenever I'd pass a Temple. Not too good for my driving, but better for my conscience.

Finally, in desperation I called Kenny Carter at UI and told him I had no one to take me to Ira Gershwin's house, and I wanted very much to meet all the famous MGM musical people who would be there. Kenny told me that he knew a very nice young man who had just gotten out of the Navy and Sam Goldwyn was

If this picture looks slightly schizophrenic, it's how I often felt amid the demands of the dream factory.

A Johnny Engstead classic. Gee, I wish I looked like this.

Blanche at Lake Tahoe during the filming of *A Place in the Sun*

il McGary, my talented and
urageous hairdresser who gave me
e Shelley look"

ABOVE: The finest actor I ever worked with—and somehow the loneliest—Montgomery Clift

LEFT: My famous phone call when I threaten Monty and tell him he must marry me

LEFT: A poignant moment in *A Place in the Sun* that George Stevens improvised on the set . . . I think

BELOW LEFT: Testing in my sister Blanche's clothes

BELOW RIGHT: George Stevens —the finest director and kindest man I was ever privileged to work with

Margaret Pendergast-McLean, Charles Laughton's speech teacher, whom I spent many loving hours with

Ivan Goff, Ben Roberts, and Liam O'Brien, young writers (and intellectuals). I'd meet them at The Players Restaurant every night and study the lines of my Universal programmers.

Frenchie. The studio was giving me what would later be called the Blonde Bombshell buildup. The open-mouth smile I later gave to Marilyn—and she did it better.

At the Beverly Hills Tennis Club with John Garfield. I was later to do his last film with him, *He Ran All the Way*.

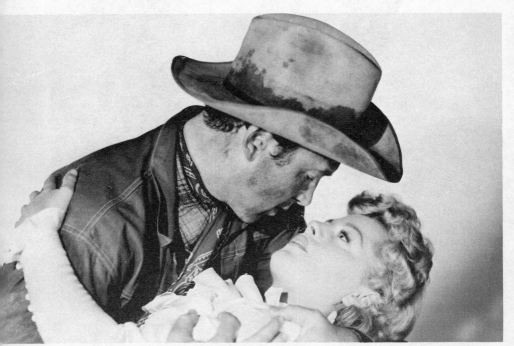

With Jimmy Stewart in *Winchester 73*. Doing love scenes with Jimmy was very difficult because we both had good *left sides*.

ABOVE: *Meet Danny Wilson.*
Sinatra was an enigma—a joy
to work with, but he terrified me
off the set.

RIGHT: Wasn't I wise to do *any*
film at MGM when Elizabeth
Taylor was acting with my
handsome young husband?

LEFT: Wouldn't you know when we got off the plane in Tel-Aviv, Farley Granger was advertised in huge letters which neither of us could understand?

BELOW LEFT: One of our happy publicity beach parties. When the photographers left we would both cry.

BELOW RIGHT: My favorite photo of Farfel from *Roseanna McCoy*

ABOVE: The dress I bought for $500 at Christian Dior—and felt guilty about ever after

LEFT: With Olivia de Havilland, one of my favorite actresses and people. And not just because she took the seven-year-contract "issue" to the Supreme Court—and won for all of us, including baseball players.

RIGHT: At last, legal marriage in Juarez.

BELOW: One of the famous premieres with Louella Parsons. I believe I had just introduced Janet Leigh and Tony Curtis.

LEFT: Vittorio and I on the lawn of our new home, newly married, when he could hardly speak English. If only we could have kept it that way.

BELOW: The minister at the Little Church Around the Corner said, "Even for actors, you must have your previous divorce papers."

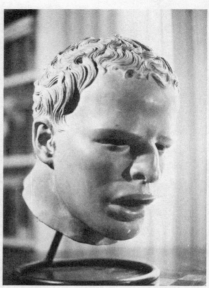

Marlon playing Mark Antony. I visited him on the set during my lonely pregnancy, and he presented me with a terra cotta statue of his head, which filled out my collection.

Jerry Paris rolling me out to a premiere while Vittorio was *Hamlet*-ing in Italy.

ABOVE: A real surprise baby shower. My mother Rose did the catering at Dawn Addams' apartment. Connie Dowling and Pier Angeli help count the presents—enough for several babies.

My one and only nightclub act—
at the Flamingo in Las Vegas.
I wanted them to stop the
gambling while I performed.

Vittorio visiting me on the
set of one of my
innumerable Westerns. He
had made some comment
about my spaghetti the
night before.

building him up to superstar status. He said he was very nice but rather shy, and if I didn't mind a blind date, he would have him pick me up and take me to the party. I readily agreed. After I hung up, I realized I had forgotten to ask Kenny his name. But it didn't really matter; I figured whoever knocked on my door at seven-thirty on Saturday night would obviously be the right fellow.

At seven-thirty sharp the doorbell rang. I opened the door, and in walked one of the handsomest young men I'd ever seen. He was stuttering with shyness and trying to be sophisticated and blasé. He had bought me a corsage of gardenias, and the first thing he did was drop it, and when we both bent down to retrieve it, we hit our heads together. We've been hitting our heads together ever since.

Farley Granger and I became inseparable friends, sometimes lovers, certainly as close as brother and sister—and always there when we needed each other. We now live in the same building in New York, two floors apart. He prefers the theater now, and he does movies and TV only when he has to. He is just as handsome as he was then, except that his beautiful black curly hair is now pepper and salt, and he is more disciplined about food and exercise than I am. It's strange how our friendship has lasted through husbands and wives and fiancés and lovers and children growing up and long and short separations. Once we were talking about something, then for some reason didn't see each other for about five years, and the next time we met we just continued the same conversation. There is almost nothing I can't tell him, and I think he feels the same way about me.

That night, all dressed up, we went to Ira Gershwin's house in the fancy part of Beverly Hills. I was stunned by the array of talent that was present. George Gershwin had been dead a decade but obviously his friends still loved to come to his brother's house. Present were Oscar Levant, Kay Thompson, Judy Garland, Andy Williams of the Williams Brothers, Saul Chaplin, his wife, Ethel, and their very young daughter, Judy, who is now Mrs. Hal Prince, Gene Kelly and his then wife, Betsy Blair, Fred Astaire and his wife and many others. Farley and I were so nervous and felt so unaccomplished that we immediately hid behind a huge plant. Mrs. Ira Gershwin wouldn't allow that and made us feel welcome and was kindness itself.

Farley went to get us some food from the buffet, and a very nice skinny young man with huge, thick horn-rimmed glasses sat down next to me. I talked to him for five minutes before I realized he was Robert Walker. He seemed lonely, and like the idiot I was, I said something like: "Is Jennifer at the buffet?"

"I don't think so, unless David Selznick's with her."

I didn't know what to make of that. When Farley came back and reclaimed his seat, Bob went to the buffet and Farley explained to me that Jennifer and Bob were divorced and he thought she was going to marry David Selznick, and since he was so powerful, most of the Walkers' friends had drifted Jennifer-ward. I thought that over for a minute. "Don't they have twin boys?"

"Yes, and I believe Bob has custody of them." I lost my appetite. Was I doing this to two other young children?

After some great numbers by Kay Thompson, accompanied by the Williams Brothers including Andy, Oscar Levant sat down at the piano and played "Slaughter on Tenth Avenue." I was entranced. Every now and then he made a very funny but cutting remark about somebody present. I mean, really cutting. He was obviously a very tortured man who sprayed his self-loathing on anyone within range. I didn't think he knew me or anything about me, but I was very quiet. Although I was watching his hands playing so brilliantly, I couldn't help noticing that now and then he was glancing at me. I was trying not to listen to his caustic remarks after every musical phrase or so but couldn't help hearing some very vicious remark about young Judy Garland, that she could probably do the musical version of *Tugboat Annie* if she continued growing sideways. She got up and ran out onto the side porch.

Then he started to play "Embraceable You" and said, "I'm dedicating this to Shelley Wintertime." When he sang "In your arms I find love so delectable, dear, I'm afraid it isn't quite respectable, dear," he called out, "Come on, Shelley, tell us. Does Burt Lancaster ever come down off his trapeze?" I quickly got up and joined Judy on the porch.

We sat there crying for the next hour. Farley and Bob Walker kept bringing us cold washrags, Coca-Colas and brandy, while we indulged ourselves in an orgy of hysterics. I wasn't sure what Judy was crying about, but I was humiliated and felt like The Scarlet Woman. Everybody was there—creative directors whom I respected; my old friends from New York, Gene Kelly and Betsy Blair, Betty Comden, Adolph Green and Judy Holliday—most of them respectable married people. I just couldn't stop crying. Here I was already married and divorced and having an affair with a married man.

Farley and Bob got our wraps and two boxes of Kleenex, and we sneaked out the porch door. Farley put me in his car and started to drive me home. I was crying so bitterly he must have known there was some truth to Levant's vicious remark. He took me to a drive-in. (Why have so many of the important moments of my life taken place in drive-ins?) When the carhop brought us the trays and glasses of ice-cold water, Farley threw his ice water in my face and said, "If you cry anymore, I'm going to slap you." I stared at him, stunned. So did the carhop. She got us a bunch of paper napkins, and he tried to dry me off. He then ordered two double hamburgers with everything and four cups of coffee. The carhop fled with the order.

He lit two cigarettes just like Paul Henreid, and gave me one. "Now listen, Shell. Everyone has to do what they have to do in this life. Everybody uses everybody else, and you just do your best not to hurt anyone. Don't make everything such a big deal. Not every love affair has to be for always. I'm sure you're not the first extramarital fling in Burt's life, and I bet his wife grits her teeth and waits. Just enjoy it, and it will help you grow. This is really a small town; I've been an actor here since I was fourteen, and if they ain't got what to gossip about, they'll make it up. The only thing that really matters is what you do up there on that screen, and you know that's really all you care about."

By the time he brought me to my door, he had me laughing, and for some reason my shame and fear of being ostracized from respectable society had vanished. I wanted to invite him in, but Burt sometimes came to my apartment early Sunday mornings for breakfast, and I still had some ridiculous sense of faithfulness to him, although that evening had somehow made me know deep in my heart that he most probably would never divorce his wife. I wasn't really sure if I wanted him to. I finally faced the fact that I didn't want to sit on Burt Lancaster's sets while he acted. If he wanted to give up his career and sit on my sets while I acted, that was another story.

CHAPTER 19

I did the test for *An American Tragedy* with Montgomery Clift one month after finishing *South Sea Sinner* (which had taken all of six weeks). We did the famous rowboat scene. In the script Monty's name was George. Why Stevens had given the boy his own name always puzzled me; in the book it was Clyde. Stevens had given me the script the night before and told me not to study it too much. He told me to visit as many factories as I could, watch the girls who worked on the assembly lines, and to ride on buses in East Los Angeles and Boyle Heights to watch girls under twenty who were exhausted from some kind of mindless occupation. I did this for two weeks before the test.

George Stevens had a very unusual way of working. He would discuss the scene, but not the lines, and would photograph the second or third rehearsal so the scene had an almost improvisatory quality. Monty was such a joy to work with that I felt as if I already knew him very well. Stevens would print the first take, then spend the next three hours minutely rehearsing the scene, then film it again. He explained to me that in this way he often got actors' unplanned reactions that were spontaneous and human and often exactly right. And often when actors overintellectualize or plan their reactions, they aren't as good. Then, later on, he would rehearse for hours to get exactly what he needed for the scene. But his direction was so kind and quiet that you knew that you were in the hands of a master and that you always inadvertently did exactly what he wanted you to do. I came away from the test knowing that this man had photographed my soul and that if I got the part, it would be the greatest picture I would ever be in. Time has proved me right so far.

While I waited for George Stevens's decision, because no one but George cast his movies, I had to put the whole thing out of my mind because I couldn't bear not getting it. During the week I waited, I saw only Farley and my sister, and we would take long rides up the coast to Santa Barbara. And when I worked in Charles Laughton's class at night, I could hardly speak, much less recite the beautiful lines of Shakespeare. Laughton knew I had done the test, and one evening after I had stuttered through "If mmmusic be the fffood of love, pppplay on . . ." he took me for a drink across the street from our little theater and said, "I know you're going through a very anxious time, but you must believe in yourself. If you're going to have a long career, and I think you will, you will have up periods and down periods, periods of wonderful roles and periods of no roles or bad ones. An actor, just like a pianist, must use his instrument, and you must believe in the inevitability of your artistic growth and recognition." God, how I loved that man!

The very next morning George Stevens called and told me that Paramount was in negotiation with Universal, and as far as he was concerned, the role of the factory girl in *An American Tragedy* was mine.

I went into my living room, held Theodore Dreiser's great book close to my heart and looked out of my window over Hollywood, then quickly got dressed, took the book and drove over to Peyton Hall, to the surprise of my family. I asked my pop and mom to forgive me and told them what had happened about *An American Tragedy*. My mom's eyes filled with tears, and my pop said, "Now you can call yourself an *artiste*. By the way, what did Stevens mean, Paramount's negotiating with Universal?"

"Dad, don't you dare do anything."

He ignored me and called Bill Goetz. In three sentences he settled the matter with: "Mr. Goetz, I advised my daughter to sign that seven-year contract with you. Now I understand George Stevens wants her to play the role of the factory girl in Theodore Dreiser's great classic, *An American Tragedy*. Mr. Goetz, I'm a long-time union man, so I don't care what that contract says, if you make any problems with Paramount, I will personally see to it that Shelley *never* works for you again." With that he hung up.

My agent called five minutes later and informed me that Universal had lent me to Paramount where I was to report immediately to get the script and have costume and wardrobe fittings. We were to leave for location in ten days and be at Lake Tahoe for two months. The picture would take *six months* to shoot.

When my mother heard two months at Lake Tahoe, she looked at Blanche, who answered before my mother could ask. "All right, all right. I've got a vacation coming. As long as she doesn't have any *visitors* up there, I'll stay with her."

The three of them looked at me. "How could I have any visitors?" I answered innocently. "This is the most important role of my life. All I want to do is concentrate on it."

That night Burt surprised me by coming over at eight o'clock. I had made dinner for Farley, and he was telling me about Hitchcock's direction of *Strangers on a Train*, which he and Bob Walker were in. He had brought a bottle of champagne to drink to my good luck and success. When Burt walked in, both he and Farley looked upset. I didn't know whether they knew each other. Burt, of course, had seen us listed as an "item" in the movie magazines and columns but chose to believe it was a platonic relationship. I chose not to tell him whether it was or wasn't. He said quietly to Farley, "Listen, kid, would you do me a favor? Go ride around the block for a while. I want to talk to Shelley."

And Farley did it—right in the middle of his dinner—I guess because he didn't know if I was still in love with Burt or not. I didn't know either. As soon as Farley left, Burt grabbed me and kissed me, and I knew instantly I was still mad about him, but I protested his treatment of Farley. He told me he'd been calling for several days at UI, at my apartment and at my home, and Blanche and my mother had hung up on him twice.

I explained to him about the test and getting the part in *A Place in the Sun*, which *An American Tragedy* was now called. At the time I thought they changed the title because it was downbeat; later I came to realize that the House Un-American Activities Committee had begun to sniff around Hollywood, and Paramount was unrealistically hoping that nobody would notice that Theodore Dreiser, who had been a left-winger, had written the novel upon which the film was based. Burt congratulated me on having gotten this film and on having George Stevens to direct me. He lay down on my leopard couch, and I quickly turned on the lights, then realizing how exhausted and strained he looked. I locked the door and put Gigli's "O Paradiso" on the record player, turned the lights off and we made love. He halfheartedly tried to talk to me about lawyers and alimony and child custody, but I shushed him.

He asked if he could come up to Lake Tahoe, and I told him that I'd promised Blanche, who was going with me, that I would not let him come up there because the location would be crawling with reporters. I knew he was caught in an unsolvable situation, but I couldn't try to force him to leave his children and wife and then be able to live with myself. He asked if he could see me the next morning at five, and I made a feeble joke like: "Are you afraid Farley's still going to be here?" He told me that wasn't the reason, and I kissed him and told him, of course, I would be home, and he could come over anytime.

When he left, I watched myself take Farley's champagne and sit in the middle of the living room and carefully drink all of it and a quart bottle of Burt's brandy as well. In the middle of this, Farley knocked on the door. I didn't answer. I didn't want to talk to anyone. The record player was still playing. Farley had come back with Arthur Laurents, a friend of his who had written *Home of the Brave*, which Burt had starred in on Broadway. I guess Farley thought they would have a lot to talk about. But they had met Burt in the garage as he was leaving. When I didn't answer the door, Farley kicked the lock in.

I began laughing and crying hysterically. Arthur stuck a spoon down my throat, and I threw up all over the bathroom: the dinner, the champagne, the liquor, my lousy double life. In fact, I could not stop throwing up for a couple of hours until they got rhubarb and soda and ginger ale and calmed my stomach. Farley was berating himself for having left me alone with Burt and was ready to go find him and beat him up, but Arthur was older and wiser and knew that just one incident does not an hysteric make. When I was more or less relaxed, he dialed a famous L.A. psychiatrist's number, and I made an appointment with him. I'll always be grateful to Arthur for introducing me to a source of help that saved my career and possibly my life.

I took a shower and got into my flannel pajamas. Farley and Arthur were reluctant to let me go to sleep and began to give me lots of coffee. When Burt arrived at five o'clock the next morning, they both were still there: I in my flannel pajamas and they, exhausted, in their shirt sleeves. Over my objections they told him what had happened, and Burt was truly frightened. I could not explain what had made me do that. In all honesty, it had something to do with the film script I was studying. The hopeless situation of the poor pregnant girl I was about to play and my own real hopeless relationship with Burt had somehow combined into a moment of inexplicable drunken aberration.

The next day, after seventeen hours of sleep, I found Blanche cleaning up my apartment. She had taken a leave of absence from Cedars of Lebanon Hospital and went with me to Stevens's office to talk about the total meanings of Dreiser's work. I had been carefully briefed by Norman Mailer that what Dreiser was really saying was when economic pressures are intolerable, ethics, morals and family love disappear. The mother in *A Place in the Sun* was played by Anne Revere, who evoked the stoicism of a Grant Wood classic. When she questions her son about the pregnant girl's drowning, the boy denies having drowned her. Then she asks, "Son, did you try to help her?" He can't answer; the golden opportunity to live up there in the sun with the rich people has paralyzed his moral values.

Stevens had had a great deal of trouble with my wardrobe for the role, and while I was talking to him, he kept looking at Blanche. For a minute I was afraid he was going to give *her* the part. "Blanche," he said suddenly, "your clothes look exactly right for Shelley's wardrobe. Can Paramount buy that dress and coat?"

My overly honest sister said, "Of course. They cost twenty-one dollars new." So most of the clothes I wore in *A Place in the Sun* were Blanche's.

Farley and Bob Walker began to film *Strangers on a Train* for Hitchcock. Burt went on location for a cockamamie picture called *Kiss the Blood off My Hands* with Joan Fontaine, and Blanche and I left for Lake Tahoe to do *A Place in the Sun*. All these titles seemed appropriately symbolic. During that period I was a very symbolic thinker; I hope I've changed.

Thank goodness we had a comfortable, warm cabin at Lake Tahoe. In the film it was supposed to be Labor Day, but some mornings the crew would have to hose the snow off the trees before we could do a scene, it was so cold. I was very nervous for professional and personal reasons; I couldn't eat and was the thinnest I had been since I was fourteen. The only time I was really relaxed was when I was working with George Stevens. Both Elizabeth Taylor and I fell madly in love with him. When we would see the rushes at night in the projection tent, we would each sit on opposite sides of him, so close he would be scared to move for fear of touching one of his sexy starlets. Stevens would print several takes of each scene and then explain to us why one was better than the other. The whole experience was a joy.

Lake Tahoe was bottomless, so Monty and I made a solemn pact that our stunt people could do the doubling of the boat turning over in the real lake. We would do the close-ups in the tank at Paramount. After all, he was the big star, so I ceased worrying about it.

Stevens talked to us about our roles all the time, and we relaxed only at dinner or when he would show funny movies on weekends. The scriptwriters, Michael Wilson, Ivan Moffat and Harry Brown, were always on the set. They were brilliant, funny and handsome young men. But no one ever fooled around during the shooting of a Stevens film, from the craft serviceman who made the coffee to the head gaffer and the great cameraman, William Mellor. Everyone was quiet and concentrating. Nobody had to yell, "Silence," on George Stevens's sets. You proudly knew that you were involved in the creation of something timeless and extraordinary, and you instinctively wanted to watch all the creative processes and never interfere with them.

One of Stevens's tricks was to have us rehearse a scene with the dialogue, and then, when the assistant yelled, "Roll 'em," Stevens would tell us to do the scene without talking. IT WORKED. George Stevens felt that films deteriorated after the invention of sound, that up to that point film had spoken in an international language, and the purpose of film was to communicate universal ideas and humanity's common experience. The invention of sound, he felt, had limited rather than expanded the scope of film. I'm not so sure he was wrong.

I did a remarkable scene that wasn't in the script and that he created on the spot. I'm about five months pregnant, alone and sick. He had me walk to a mailbox, open it and look inside. There is no letter, just a newspaper with a picture of Monty and the beautiful and rich Elizabeth Taylor motorboating. Stevens made that scene so real for me that I actually got sick, and I think it's one of the most powerful moments in the film.

For some weird reason, the gifted Monty always had a famous woman drama coach with him. Can you imagine having a coach when you were being directed by George Stevens? But I guess Monty was insecure at that stage in his career and needed someone with him. She was his coach, nutritionist, friend and perhaps lover. And although she was on that film for the whole six months, Stevens never acknowledged her existence. He never said good morning to her or looked at her. Sometimes she would accidentally get her hand in front of the camera as she gave instructions to Monty, of course, ruining the take. George would just quietly tell the assistant director to put her more to the side and do another take. I tried to argue with Monty about this lady, but since I had Blanche—although she always watched from way behind the camera and was helping the location nurse—and Elizabeth Taylor had her mother—who kept running around, complaining that because George Stevens had made Elizabeth go in that cold lake in a bathing suit, she would never be able to have children; to my knowledge, for the next twenty years Elizabeth never stopped having children—I guess Monty was entitled to his coach, although she did some strange things.

I worked for George Stevens in two other films, *The Diary of Anne Frank*, for which I won an Oscar for my portrayal of Mrs. Van Daan, and *The Greatest Story Ever Told*. Each of those films was a wonderful creative experience. But *A Place in the Sun* was in a class by itself.

One day I was sitting in the one warm dressing room with Elizabeth, who was about seventeen then and had been an MGM baby and had gone to the MGM Little Red Schoolhouse along with Judy Garland, Debbie Reynolds and Mickey Rooney. I was writing a letter to Burt, and I asked Elizabeth for the date. She answered that she didn't know. I noticed the *Hollywood Reporter* on a chair next to her and asked her to look. She did and said, "It's no good, it's yesterday's *Reporter!*" So much for MGM's Little Red Schoolhouse! I guess Elizabeth went to the Richard Burton University because when I met her again in later years she had acquired a very good British public school education and was much wiser, if sadder.

Another time Elizabeth showed me how to use an eyelash curler. She had such long eyelashes she had to curl them up and away from her eyes. Since Stevens wasn't letting me use any makeup at all, she told me it would open my eyes, and after all, that was what the camera photographs. She must have known what she was talking about because she had been making pictures since she was about three.

So one day, when I was sitting on a rock behind a redwood tree, busily curling my eyelashes with a little steel curler, almost taking my eye out in the process, all of a sudden George Stevens came sneaking around the redwood and pounced on me. In a stern voice he reminded me what I had promised at the Hollywood Athletic Club, and I quickly agreed to keep my promise but plaintively asked Mr. Stevens if Elizabeth had to look so gorgeous. I was kidding, but I wasn't. I mean, with that beautiful black, curly hair, enormous violet eyes, tiny waist and gorgeous bosom. . . . Besides that, she kept driving an enormous white convertible Cadillac throughout the picture.

George got that funny bear look on his face and said, "This picture is in black and white, Shelley, and you're going to get nominated for Best Actress. I'll see that Paramount gets you a white convertible Cadillac wholesale." He was right on all counts, and I have driven a series of white convertible Cadillacs ever since, to make up for my feelings of deprivation and Elizabeth Taylor's beauty in that film.

When we came to the famous boat scene, Blanche and I went out to the lake at seven in the morning. Blanche became almost as hysterical as Mrs. Taylor, informing the assistants that although I was a good swimmer, Lake Tahoe was freezing in August and this was the beginning of November. They paid no attention, and the wardrobe and makeup ladies proceeded to rub grease all over my body and put some kind of rubber suit on me under my costume. Then Blanche and I were taken out to the camera raft.

The rowboat we were to use was wired with photographically invisible wires which would pull the oars away and turn over the boat. Monty was already in the boat, looking down at his feet with his hand over his face. There was an ambulance on the shore, lifeguards on the raft with oxygen respirators, three cameras and lights.

Stevens said, "Now, Shelley, you're a good swimmer. When the boat turns over, I want you to come up the first time and yell, 'Help me, George, help me.' Then go down, come up the second time and yell, 'Oh, God, George, help me.' Go down and come up again and just sort of gurgle and yell, and when you go down the third time, swim over here out of camera range." I looked at him as if he were out of his mind but got in the little wired rowboat with Monty. Blanche looked as if she were ready to kill Stevens. I must have had a strange look on my face, too, because George said, "What's the matter, Shelley?"

I gave the silent Monty a dirty look, then told the truth. "Mr. Stevens," I said, "I'm afraid. It's a bottomless lake, and one of the oars could hit me on the head. Monty and I agreed *not* to do this stunt, but to let the doubles do it. They're trained to do this sort of thing. I mean, this is only the middle of the picture. Suppose we drown? You won't be able to finish the movie."

Without a word, George Stevens, complete with boots, fleece-lined coat and Stetson, jumped off the camera raft, swam around the raft, then climbed back on. With blue and trembling lips he said to me, "Never mind the dialogue, Shelley. We'll dub it in later."

So we did the stunt, and it came off beautifully. I guess the grease on my body kept me warm because I did exactly what Mr. Stevens asked me to, even to the dialogue, drowning very artistically, then swimming out of camera range. The danger was worth it. When I got back on the raft, George Stevens hugged me and said, "As Fanny Brice used to say about Esther Williams, 'Wet she's a star.'" It's true, in every film where I've either drowned or had to swim, such as *The Night of the Hunter* and *The Poseidon Adventure*, I have had a great personal success.

As the location shooting progressed, we all became a close-knit family. I was aware that Monty was developing a terrific crush on Elizabeth, but I think she felt about him the way I did about Farley.

She loved being with him; he was fun and intelligent, and she had great respect for his talent. But she had been a working, sheltered child. Even then she was longing for the bright lights and the glamorous figures of the celebrity world. While we were on location, she got engaged to a famous All-American football player. Now that I think about it, she got engaged to two famous football players. After all, we were on location for three months.

Monty realized that she was going through emotional growing pains and was just beginning to realize the power of her beauty and he was very patient with her. But since he was a withdrawn boy to begin with, the effect of her whirlwind romances made him withdraw even more. Sometimes he would drive me around the mountains in the little Ford jalopy that we used in the picture, and he would talk about other things. But he would make a special hesitant sound in his throat and had a dark look in his beautiful black eyes when he spoke about Elizabeth. It was a dead giveaway to the depths of his feelings for her. She would tease him and flirt with any attractive man within range of those violet eyes, but I think she was too young to realize how much she was hurting him.

I have often wondered how different their lives would have been if Elizabeth had been mature enough and Monty free enough to make this friendship flower into something more important. Elizabeth married Nicky Hilton right after the film was finished. She was longing to have her own home and get away from her parents. It never occurred to her that she was making a lot of money and could get her own house or apartment as soon as she was eighteen. Instead, she thought she had to have a husband and a huge wedding. Well, the publicity was great and the photographs were lovely, even if the marriage didn't work.

When we got back to Los Angeles and continued shooting at Paramount, Burt was doing a publicity tour, and I was very glad of it. As much as I longed to see and be with him, I knew his presence would be destructive to my concentration on the picture.

Marlon Brando was shooting his first film with Stanley Kramer called *The Men*, about World War II paraplegics, at a small studio near Paramount. Sometimes Marlon would visit our set in his wheelchair, and sometimes Monty and I would go over to his. Marlon seemed strangely impervious to Elizabeth's beauty. Since every other man on the set was falling all over her, it was very obvious how they avoided each other. Someday I'll have to find out why.

Monty and I were doing the date sequence in the film in which he, a young shop foreman in the bathing suit factory, and I, a girl on the assembly line, have a secret date since it is against company rules. It's raining; drunks insult us; Monty's car won't start; my pretty little J. C. Penney dress gets wet and dirty and torn. Stevens shot this sad, disastrous date carefully, treating it all with humor and pathos. It took a couple of weeks to shoot.

When we get to the culmination of that evening, as we hide on my little porch because it's raining so hard, I whisper to him, "Gee, I wish I could ask you in, but my landlady is very strict." We stand there on the damp, rainy porch, and Monty kisses me longingly, with all the loneliness and need of this ostracized young boy. I then turn on my little old-fashioned Philco radio on the windowsill. It is too loud, and Monty quickly runs inside the room, turns it down and whispers out the window to me, "Gee, I wish I could ask you in, but my landlady is very strict."

The rehearsal went beautifully. When we took the break to have our makeup and wardrobe checked, I noticed his coach talking to Monty very intently. Then, when we started to shoot the scene, Monty was very passive and not doing the scene at all the way we had rehearsed it. I stopped and looked at Mr. Stevens. I thought he would yell at Monty. Instead, he said, "Shelley, why did you stop? I'm the director here. For the rest of your life remember that only the director says, 'Cut.'"

"But, Mr. Stevens," I stuttered, "Monty's not doing it the way we rehearsed it."

"Never mind," he said. "Let's do it again, and don't stop."

We did the scene, and again Monty was passive and alienated and not at all expressing his desire and need for me. I was almost crying with exasperation, but I finished the scene. I couldn't understand what had happened. Stevens walked up to Monty slowly and said, "Monty, is that the way you want to play this scene?"

Monty, with all his naïve innocence, replied, "Well, my coach thinks it's better like this."

Stevens said, "Oh, I see." He didn't argue with Monty. Instead, he went over and talked to the sound man and the head electrician. I was whispering to Monty, trying to tell him that it didn't feel right and that Stevens had directed it differently, but he just looked confused and unhappy about it.

His lady coach kept whispering to Monty in Russian or French or something, "That's good, Montgomery. Exactly right. Don't change anything."

Stevens didn't argue with any of us. We did the scene again, and

he printed the take, then went on to the next shot. I was really
crying with vexation now because I knew it was all wrong.

When we went to the rushes the next night, all we saw on the
screen were Monty's eyes, lit up (with the rest of his face in
shadow), my face lit up and his hands lit up, holding my naked
shoulders tightly. The sound man had turned up the sound so
that Monty's breathing sounded very heavy. Stevens wouldn't argue;
he just fixed the technical things so that he got the qualities of
loneliness, need and passion that he wanted for the scene. I was
stunned when I saw those rushes.

The next time I saw Norman Mailer I told him what had happened. He laughed and said, "No one's going to fool around with
an old fox like Stevens. All that lady was doing was changing
Theodore Dreiser's story, which is about two working-class youngsters who come together out of loneliness and their terrible need
for each other. She was changing Monty's need for you, which in
effect makes *you* seduce *him*, and would change the story to—A
poor girl who seduces a potentially rich boy, then tries to make
him marry her. So he kills her." I blinked. I hadn't thought that one
scene could change a whole story. But Norman was right. Stevens
had defeated this attempt, but I hadn't even understood what was
going on. From then on I tried to remember how each scene can
affect the totality of a film.

Before I knew it, it was Christmas Eve again, and I wondered
why, although Universal was my home studio, I always seemed to
spend Christmas Eve at Paramount. Farley was in New York. Burt
was in Aspen or Mexico for the holidays with his family, and I
was alone as usual. The same Christmas parties were going on, and
as I looked for a place to park near the Writers' Building, I saw
William Holden standing in the doorway of his dressing room—
WAITING FOR ME? We hadn't seen or spoken to each other all year.
How did he know I would be there?

As Bill ushered me into his dressing room, I thanked whatever
gods may be that I didn't have my drab factory-girl outfit on, but
was dressed in a glamorous get-up and my now brown hair was
curled and tied on top of my head with a red and green ribbon. It
wasn't even dark yet, but there was a beautiful dinner set out on
the coffee table, champagne waiting in a cooler, and flowers all
over the dressing room. I stared at Bill in amazement. He kissed
me and said, "I've been waiting for you all year. I knew you were
working on the lot, but I wanted to surprise you, Sonia."

"I'd love to have dinner with you, Bill, but I've made other emotional commitments this past year."

"I'm sure, but can't you at least open your present?" On one of the dinner plates was a long thin package tied with Marvin Hime Christmas wrapping. (Marvin Hime—"jeweler to the stars"—I still love to play in his store.)

Could any woman in the world resist? I opened the package. It was a real diamond wrist watch. A diamond band on the right, a diamond band on the left, and a Hamilton watch nestled in a square of beautiful diamonds in the middle. I went into shock. "What's this for?"

"The left band of diamonds is for last year, the right band of diamonds is for this year, and the watch is for—"

So cut to:

> A fireplace warming a cold room,
> Waves pounding an empty beach,
> Fireworks happily exploding,
> Trees swaying gracefully in a lonely storm.

This strange relationship with Bill Holden went on in this manner for the seven years of my seven-year UI contract. I only missed two Christmases when I was married. Sometime during that seven-year period, Bill and I filmed *Executive Suite* together. We met formally for the "first time" on the set at MGM, and always treated each other like the casual acquaintances we weren't.

I must say our brief love affairs which lasted from 4 P.M. to 4 A.M. Christmas Eves had more fun and happiness than many other relationships in my life that contained commitment, responsibility, deep love, concern, fights and anguish. I never told anyone about it, hugging it close as my own personal Christmas secret.

A couple of years ago, I was on the *Merv Griffin Show* and William Holden, by then long divorced, was also a guest, doing publicity for *Network*. He began to relate how he loved to play Father Christmas. I kept trying to interrupt him, knowing my family and friends and 30 million other people were watching. Merv, who is very quick, realized there was some hitherto untold Hollywood story hovering around his microphone. I managed to shut Holden up by maneuvering the conversation back to the making of *Network*, *Sunset Boulevard*, his African safaris, anything. But Merv kept trying to bring the subject back to Christmas. Holden was giggling like a little boy. After the show I told him I'd meet him Christmas Eve, same time, same place, with a diamond-studded hammer.

CHAPTER 20

Happy new decade. The year 1950 arrived, and I was a Movie Star. No doubt about it. But I began to realize that I was a good actress only when I had a very good director, so I kept working with Laughton and the Actors Lab, hoping no one besides myself would notice that fact. On weekends I did publicity with Farley for the movie magazines and the columnists. We went to parties, premieres and especially openings at the Coconut Grove. There were very definite rules on those occasions. You must always look beautiful and gloriously happy, and you must be photographed only with someone more important than yourself, like people who had won Oscars. I wasn't too good at that because I was always trying to get my struggling actor friends from Laughton's group into the publicity shots. In those days young stars, male and female, were all virgins until married, and if divorced, they returned magically to that condition.

One Sunday Farley and I did a famous radio show live with Louella Parsons. She not only kept dropping her pages but was a poor reader at her soberest. She would pause for a breath in the oddest places, distorting the sense of her questions into high comedy. I'm sure that's why the whole country listened every week. Farley and I barely got through the program, we were in such pain from our suppressed laughter.

UI's and Paramount's publicity men caught on quickly that I was a good interviewee and would brief me with nonsensical Blonde Bombshell repartee such as:

REPORTER: Miss Winters, we hear you have an appointment to see Darryl Zanuck about a big role in an important film.

SHELLEY: Yes, but I have so many appointments that my secretary has to remind me of them each morning. [The only secretary I had was a pre-Depression "antique" I was refinishing.]

REPORTER: Miss Winters, we hear that Mr. Zanuck chases beautiful young girls around his desk and tears off their dresses.

SHELLEY: Really? Okay. So I'll wear an old dress.

288

These silly zingers gave me the training that made me a much-desired guest when the TV talk shows began, starting with Steve Allen and Jack Paar, until today with Johnny Carson and Merv Griffin. The weird thing about these shows is that the TV audience often feels as though you're actually in their living room. All over the world I've had people call out, "Hey, Shelley!" They kiss me; we chat and have drinks while I frantically try to remember which branch of my family they belong to. Eventually I realize they are just continuing the conversation they had with me in their living room during a talk show. Once, when I was very depressed about my lack of public dignity, Charlie Chaplin bolstered my ego to the skies when he reminded me that no one ever called him Mr. Chaplin. His name was Charlie or Charlot everywhere.

Meanwhile, back at the RKO ranch, one midnight I was very tired, and my feet hurt after Monty and I had been shooting a walking scene since twilight. We had a little rest while they lit the next shot, in which Monty and I turn a corner and walk down another street. During the pause I put on my own shoes because Blanche's were a size smaller than mine. What a relief! Then Monty and I continued this wonderful walking scene which was about five minutes long.

The next day we all went to the rushes at Paramount. And I mean *all*. Everybody in all departments wanted to see Stevens's work before he edited it. The scene started with Monty and me walking in the long shot, and then we turn the corner. A gasp of horror went up in the crowded projection room, which was usually so silent. In the new angle after Monty and I turned the corner, my shoes had magically changed from brown and white to black. I shriveled in my seat.

The rushes lasted another twenty minutes, and then the lights went on. I wanted to hide under my seat. After a pause, the assistant director asked Mr. Stevens when he should schedule the retake of that scene, which would entail taking the whole company back out to the RKO ranch. Stevens got that bear look on his lovely face, glared at the assistant director and said, "If they are watching her feet, I might as well go home. We are not redoing the scene."

He was right. That picture has been shown continuously all over the world for thirty years, and no one has ever noticed that I changed my shoes in the middle of the scene. So don't tell anybody.

During the shooting I began to see Monty go into strange depressions, wander off into some dark corner of the stage and sit staring into space. I assumed he was working on his character, but even then, when he was so handsome, talented and young and his career was zooming, I would feel an inexplicable fear for him.

Ivan Moffat, who was British and witty and George Stevens's right-hand man all through the picture, knew just about everything connected with *An American Tragedy*: how Dreiser had been a reporter on the actual case in upstate New York in 1911, about the play that Patrick Kearney had adapted from Dreiser's novel and about the early production in the late twenties that Eisenstein had written and directed with Sylvia Sidney playing my role and with a talented young actor named Phillips Holmes, who later committed suicide. Ivan also mentioned that out of guilt and religious conviction, the real boy had purposely helped the district attorney convict him. I was very annoyed and upset with this information and with Ivan, who was usually so positive, bright and intelligent.

He made up for this unwittingly scary information one morning when I arrived on the set not knowing what they were going to shoot. Ivan came in with six yellow pages in his hand and gave them to George Stevens. George invited me to sit down, and I began trembling. I knew it was another scene for me. The set was the office of a country doctor. George read the yellow pages, then said, "Shelley, this is a scene from the book that I was going to leave out of the film. It's rather censorable, but I think if we handle it delicately, it will illuminate the factory girl's terrible plight." He handed me the yellow pages. "Now get dressed, and remember that this girl hasn't slept all night. We'll rehearse the scene once, then shoot it."

As the hairdresser combed my hair neatly, I memorized the scene. It was almost an exact copy of the famous scene in the book in which the girl asks the doctor to help her. I had no trouble memorizing it. I had lived it twice.

The doctor was played by Ian Wolfe, a wonderful character actor who was kindness itself, very easy and quiet to work with. The set was still as death. George blocked and rehearsed the scene once, and the only thing he said to me was: "Remember, Shelley, you need help from this doctor, but you're afraid to tell him exactly what you want. He is your last hope."

When he called, "Action!" I was already crying. I twisted my white handkerchief into a shredded ball. The scene was nine minutes long. A full camera load. Boy, did I ever act!

When it was over, George said, "Cut and print." I felt I had equaled Bernhardt *and* Duse. I'd cried through the whole scene. In fact, I couldn't stop crying. George took me aside and said quietly,

"All right, get yourself under control, and we'll talk about the scene." I gave him a look of sheer hatred since *I* thought I'd been marvelous. He smiled and said, "We're going to print that take, and we'll look at it. Now, Shelley, let's talk about it a little. What are you in this office for?"

Of course, I had to answer, "To try to get the doctor to help me."

"If a young girl began to weep in front of a country doctor like that, what would he do?"

And I had to answer, "Well, I guess he'd get frightened and ask me to leave."

George patted my cheek. He knew what a toll my honesty had cost me. "All right, let's do the scene again. This time try to be very matter-of-fact with the doctor, so that you won't frighten him. If you start to cry, stop yourself any way you can. Look out the window. Play with your handkerchief, fix your coat, touch the things on his desk—anything. Just don't cry."

Of course, when we saw the two takes the next day, the one in which I had followed his exact direction was remarkable, even if I say so myself. One heard the agony in the girl's voice and saw the doctor being careful and frightened of her. In only one place did I get a little out of control, and that was when the doctor said, "Have you got any money?" I shook my head. He hesitated. "Well, you will make a very healthy mother."

Every time I've seen that scene in a theater, every man in the audience groans and every woman weeps. George had taught me another lifelong acting lesson: don't indulge yourself—make the audience weep.

One Sunday, just when Burt was getting ready to leave my apartment, the doorbell rang. It was Farley. We were going to the Sportsman's Lodge out in the Valley, where you caught your own trout from a stream and it was broiled for you. For a minute Burt looked like a kid who wanted to go with us, but I reminded him he was an acrobat, not a fisherman, and if he didn't get home for dinner in eleven minutes, the movie star would turn into a frog. He left hurriedly with a very suspicious look in his eye.

Farley and I had to study our next day's work, so we took our scripts to the outdoor patio of the Sportsman's Lodge and cued each other as we drank a glass of wine. I had a very long scene the next day with Monty, his birthday scene where I've made him a cake and bought ice cream and he's very late because he's been with the beautiful rich girl, and he's slowly being accepted by her family. Out of anger and fear, I tell him abruptly, "George, we are in trouble. I think I'm pregnant." It was one of the most important scenes in the film, and Farley carefully cued me in the lines, and the pauses.

I think he was working on a scene from *Strangers on a Train.* Alfred Hitchcock was very exact about every if, and, and but, so I drilled Farley thoroughly. By the time we went to catch our trout tourists were following us and saying loudly, "Aren't they darling together?" . . . "I wonder what picture they're doing?" . . . "I bet it's something sweet." . . . "Do you think they'll get married?" Maybe they thought we were deaf.

The maître d' showed us to a secluded corner, and we had salad with our fresh-caught trout, and Farley wouldn't let me have dessert. It was getting late, and I had to get up at six-thirty, so Farley paid the check quickly and we left. He would never let me split the check with him, so I invited him over to eat at my house as much as I could.

When we stopped at a light somewhere on Ventura Boulevard, he said suddenly, "Look, there's your god."

I saw a steel gray foreign car drive out of a motel. It was George Stevens's car, and he was with a sexy blonde who worked in Casting at UI. I couldn't believe my eyes! Farley stayed behind the car, but I don't think George saw me. I was stricken. It was as if I had seen my father or President Roosevelt or my Zayda in a comparable situation. I mean, such men didn't *do* things like that! I became hysterical. Farley kept trying to explain to me that George Stevens was a normal human being, and just because people were geniuses didn't mean they weren't allowed to have sex lives. But I would have none of it. The idea of George Stevens sleeping with anybody, I mean anybody, especially *not me*, was more than I could stand.

As soon as he got me to my apartment, I became *really* ill. I threw up nonstop all night. Farley got a doctor through UI to come to the house at about 3:00 A.M., and he gave me a shot of atropine. The doctor questioned Farley about seafood poisoning, but Farley replied that we both had eaten the same trout. I guess in those days I could win any psychosomatic contest around.

Farley had to go to work at eight, so Blanche came over to relieve him. I couldn't go to work; I could barely crawl. I was really green. At ten the phone rang. It was Monty. He whispered to Blanche—because he was on the stage—that Stevens thought I was malingering and had a double for me with my dress and a wig on, and he was shooting over her back and would dub in my dialogue later. Blanche got a pot of ice, some lemons and some more atropine and somehow got me to the studio.

Stevens took one look at my green face and said, "You look really great for this scene. That's exactly how this poor girl should look. If I had known you could get green on request, I would have done the picture in Technicolor." I didn't laugh. I just looked at him with tears in my eyes.

The makeup people fixed me up as best they could for the scene. They didn't have to work too hard, I looked so bedraggled. George Stevens, Jr., who was then only about sixteen, came into my dressing room to bring me some more iced ginger ale for my queasy stomach. When I saw him, I started to cry, "Oh, Georgie, you know what our father did?"

He said, "What do you mean, 'our father'? Like 'who art in heaven'?" Blanche quickly shut me up and got me out on the set, and Monty and I did the scene.

Some years later George Stevens married that blonde girl for some unaccountable reason. How could he have done this when he could have had me or Elizabeth Taylor? Just because she was a lovely, calm, intelligent lady who loved him? But, oh, so selfish!

And if you ever see *A Place in the Sun*, watch for the scene in which I tell Monty I'm pregnant, and you'll see that the beginning of it is on my back. And if you look closely, you'll see that it isn't even *my* back.

Meanwhile, my life had developed a slightly schizophrenic quality; I was the poor simple factory girl all day at Paramount, and I was the "other woman *femme fatale*" at night and on my days off at UI. If I have given the impression that my relationship with Burt was all Back Street agony, it was. Not because of Burt, who was as thoughtful as his complicated life situation allowed him to be. But I guess there was some wheat among the chaff. It was lousy Shirley Schrift's ethical middle-of-the-night appearances that caused my sleeplessness.

Burt and I were young and full of fun, like the time we went with Hugh Griffith to the downstairs Players Nightclub and the maître d' insisted they wear ties, which had to be rented. Burt and Hugh carefully put the ties on and then just as carefully took off their pants since there was no rule about that.

Burt was wearing very sexy underwear, but Hugh's looked like an English antique. At least their shirttails covered most of them. Of course, I had to take off my skirt. I had on black net stockings and a period pink satin chemise left over from some Western, so

I didn't look too bad. Then we sat down elegantly and ordered a sumptuous dinner with appropriate wines.

We three calmly ate dinner, with the rest of the diners silently staring. Burt insisted on doing a rumba with me. Thank God Universal's publicity man got there before the police. In those days the major studios had great influence with the cops. Hugh was falling down drunk, and while Burt and I were dancing, an ambulance arrived, and they took him away, protesting, on a stretcher. Burt and I indignantly got dressed, to the applause of the rest of the diners, and although he cheerfully paid about $100 for the dinner, Burt insisted on his $2 deposit back for the damn ties.

Burt had a twelve-foot trapeze rig set up in the backyard of his dressing room and decided I should get exercise by learning to become an aerialist. For a couple of weeks while Monty and Elizabeth were doing their scenes, Burt and I used to practice on the trapeze, and I loved it. I got to the point where Burt, swinging by his legs, would throw me and I could do a half somersault and Nick Cravat, his partner, would catch me. Not bad for a klutz. Of course, they were strong and did most of the work, but I flew through the air with the greatest of ease.

One afternoon Spitz & Goetz were showing some of the New York brass around the studio. They heard the commotion and came down the alley between the dressing rooms and stood there staring, aghast.

At the time Burt and I both were in the middle of million-dollar films and had about five unreleased pictures between us. But I was busy showing off to the brass how Burt and I could do a circus picture, hoping they would do one with us.

In a quiet, small voice Mr. Goetz said, "Shelley, come down. I want to introduce you to your New York bosses."

Burt lowered me to the ground, and I pulled my dirty gray sweat suit together and wiped my face. Goetz took me firmly by the wrist and started to curse Burt, me, Nick, Mark Hellinger, our agents and our unmarried mothers and fathers. Were we such idiots that we didn't realize we were putting millions of dollars in jeopardy?

With that, Burt and Nick proceeded to do triple somersaults and pretended to fall off the high bars. "Burt," I yelled, "they're not young men. They might have heart attacks. Cut it out!" The upshot of this whole thing was they took away Burt's trapeze. They also took out extra insurance on both of us.

Burt also had a dressing room at Paramount where he was under contract to Hal Wallis too, so our dressing-room fridges were always filled with wonderful things to eat from a gourmet shop where he had a charge account. Whenever I had night shooting at Paramount, we always had lunch together. Delicious food, rare wines and "Thou/beside me singing in the Wilderness." Once, while watching my rushes, Stevens said to me with a twinkle, "Shelley, I don't know why your work is so different before and after lunch. I mean, in the morning you're okay, but after lunch your skin and eyes are glowing. You're calm, and nothing that happens on the set upsets you." All I could answer was that I preferred working in the afternoon because I was basically a New York actress and therefore a night person. What a lie!

One evening, when Burt had night shooting, he called the Paramount operator and left a message that "Mr. Richards" (his code name) had called and would like to have dinner with me. My code name was "Miss Gitsey" because Burt said I had gitsey legs, which means "knock-kneed" in carny talk.

I was through rather early so I picked up some huge cooked shrimps, cocktail sauce and vodka at his gourmet shop and went to his dressing room, to which I had a key. I got myself showered and perfumed and put on a transparent sexy *shmatte*.

That night he was quite late getting to our little den of iniquity, and the sirloin steaks he had sent from the commissary were cold when his film broke for dinner. I couldn't get irritated with him because he was working so hard. But I had an important scene to do the next day on *A Place in the Sun*, which was making me very nervous, and I wanted to get to sleep early. I mean in *my* bed, in *my* apartment.

We had our lovely, if slightly cold, dinner and some special French wine. Burt was on a sort of talking jag, explaining to me at great length the self-destructive drift the studios were taking in relation to the political witch-hunt of that time. I ate my dinner quickly, one eye on my watch. It was nearly ten, and Burt had not been called back to the set yet. Right in the middle of one of his erudite discourses, I interrupted in an appealing little voice. "Burt, I have to get up awfully early. Could you please give me a pamphlet and make love to me fast so I can go home?"

The shock of my meek request sent him into peals of laughter. Tears were rolling down his cheeks, he was laughing so hard. But he understood how important *A Place in the Sun* was to me.

So cut to:

A hurried Fourth of July fireworks display.

When I got home at about eleven, I was happily exhausted and slept very quickly.

One day on the set we all received telegrams from Mr. and Mrs. Norman Mailer inviting us to a big bash at their home high in the Hollywood Hills. I suggested that Monty take Elizabeth. Of course, I couldn't go with Burt, and Farley was on location. So Marlon, who had been invited and wanted to meet Charlie Chaplin, agreed to take me. I informed him firmly that he had to wear a suit, a shirt and a tie and that I would *not* pick him up at his grandmother's house in Silver Lake. He had to take a cab to the Villa Italia, pick me up like a gentleman, and then I would drive us up to Norman's house. We had to get there early because I promised Norman's wife, Bea, to help her with the party.

Marlon was outraged and treated me like a friend who had betrayed him. He insisted he didn't have a suit, and he didn't know the geography of Hollywood yet, so how could he tell the cabdriver where my apartment was?

I also informed him that if he wanted to go to the party, he could not go in his wheelchair, which he used all the time so he wouldn't slip out of his role in *The Men*. We argued about this by phone for several days, but he finally capitulated with dire threats.

The night of the party arrived, and it had been raining for two days. I was all done up and waiting at seven o'clock. I still had my little red Pontiac, although it was practically falling apart. However, keeping Stevens's promise, Paramount had ordered a new 1950 white convertible Cadillac, which I was getting through the Purchasing Department. Would you believe $2,400? All extras included.

As I waited for Marlon, Elizabeth called me, and we compared what we were wearing. Cocktail-length strapless dresses, hers white, mine black. It was so cold and rainy we decided to wear our new blonde sheared beaver coats, which we had recently got wholesale from Fuhrman's because we'd bought two. They were exactly alike—mine one size larger—and we loved them. With some foreboding I told Elizabeth that when Monty arrived, they should go to the party, and if Marlon hadn't arrived by eight, I would come by myself.

At eight-ten there was a knock on my door, and there stood Marlon in his agent Jay Kanter's suit. I think Jay Kanter was then about five-five and a very slim 125 pounds. The sleeves of the jacket came just below Marlon's elbows, and although he managed to zip up the pants, they barely came to his calf, just touching his black motorcycle boots. But he had on a starched white shirt and a blue tie and was proudly carrying a bunch of soggy wild flowers that he had picked in his grandmother's yard. He had one of them in his buttonhole.

I couldn't believe it. I wanted to protest—after all, I had my Movie Star outfit on—but Marlon looked so proud of himself. He was very clean, and his hair was combed neatly and slicked down, and after all, he had done exactly what I had asked him to do.

He explained that he was late because the cab had gone to Crescent Drive in Beverly Hills instead of Crescent Heights in Hollywood. It had cost him $12, and he'd almost gotten into a fight with the cabdriver because he didn't have any money left for a tip.

"Marlon, you only went out with twelve dollars?"

He looked surprised. After all, we were going to eat free at the party. We had some apple cider and celery juice, then went down and got in my Pontiac. By then it was eight forty-five and raining cats and dogs and bunny rabbits. I gave Marlon the written directions and a flashlight, then began the drive up into the Hollywood Hills. Either Marlon couldn't read, or the directions were all wrong because it took us an hour to find the place and then only because I saw an enormous cliff jammed with parked cars. Norman had not thought to get a car valet service. We were the last to arrive, and I was afraid of tackling the steep driveway, so we parked below the cliff. I didn't have an umbrella, so we got soaked, running up the hill through the parked cars to the front door.

I don't know whether Norman, who was more than bright, had gotten all these people together as research for some weird political book or as a black comedy practical joke, but the group he had collected consisted of political, artistic, social and moral enemies. All Hollywood was there—actors, directors, producers, writers and other local intelligentsia. Charlie Chaplin and Cecil B. de Mille were glaring at each other, as was everyone else, reading from left to right. As the Mailers greeted us, I asked Norman what the hell he'd done. "Well," he answered innocently, "we just got the *Players' Directory*, the Screen Directors and Producers Guild book and the *Writers' Almanac* and sent wires to all the people we thought might be interested in meeting the author of *The Naked and the Dead*."

Elizabeth was arguing with Benny Thau, an executive producer at Metro, and Victor McLaglen was asking Monty why such a talented young actor wanted to work in a Commie picture. The ordinarily silent Monty looked at him with his immobile stare and said, "Mr. McLaglen, now I understand why you were so good in *The Informer*." They were immediately separated.

Marlon went behind the bar and would talk only to the bartender. The bartender's wife, Norman, Bea and I began to set up television tables for dinner. Bea had catered the party herself and had made a fancy bouillabaisse and paella and filled the Sparklett's five-gallon water bottle with sangria. Then Marlon pretended to be one of the help and, complete with napkin draped over his arm, handed out paper plates and cups. He looked so odd in that kiddie suit that most of the people there thought he *was* one of the help. Monty and Elizabeth were rolling on the floor with laughter. We were the only people having a good time. Everyone else was beginning to have deadly serious political disagreements. Suddenly Marlon grabbed a raincoat, Elizabeth's blonde fur coat and my arm. "Let's go have some Chinese food. This party is making me nervous."

As we got to the door, Norman stopped us. "Marlon, you can't leave. No one has met you yet, and we're just beginning to serve dinner."

In a loud voice Marlon said, "Norman, what the fuck are you doing here? You're not a screenwriter. Why aren't you on a farm in Vermont writing your next novel? What kind of shit is this?" With that he dragged me out the door, and we ran through the teeming rain. It was difficult getting back to my car because Mickey Knox, who was also a friend of Norman's, had arrived after us and had to leave his car halfway up the hill, blocking the driveway. We both were soaking wet by the time I managed to get the car started. I was so angry I silently drove Marlon back to his grandmother's house in Silver Lake. He was furious, too. "Jesus Christ," he said, "Jay loaned me his suit, and I've ruined it. I've done all the things you wanted me to, and I'm starving, and my grandmother doesn't have anything in the icebox." I told him he had behaved like a boor and insulted everyone. "But I told the truth, didn't I?" he asked. "He is a great writer, isn't he? What the hell is he doing on a Hollywood hill hobnobbing with celebrities?"

I complained but took him all the way out to his grandmother's house. He reminded me that I had told him not to come out to Hollywood without relatives, which in a way he hadn't. I gave him a good-night kiss which turned into a sort of wrestling match that stopped when his grandmother put on the porch light. Gently he asked me if I thought I would be able to get home all right. Even though I assured him I would, he told me he would call in half an hour to make sure.

I drove slowly up Sunset Boulevard, and it was about 3:00 A.M. when I got back to my apartment. The phone was ringing, and I got out of Elizabeth's wet fur coat before I answered it. It was Hal Wallis, Burt's and Mickey Knox's boss at Paramount. It seemed Marlon had taken Mickey's raincoat when he left—I didn't remember Marlon having had one when he arrived—and Mickey's car keys were in the coat pocket, and Mickey's car was blocking all the other cars. The Automobile Club couldn't budge the old clunker, and Norman's guests by now were dangerous physical enemies.

I explained to the furious Mr. Wallis that the keys to Mickey's car were probably in the pocket of Mickey's raincoat, which was at Marlon's grandmother's house in Silver Lake. A police captain got on the phone and asked for Marlon's address. I didn't know it exactly, but I described the house and street.

Marlon's grandmother almost had a heart attack when two police cars arrived at 4:00 A.M., sirens going full blast, to retrieve Mickey Knox's raincoat. For some strange reason, this was the last Hollywood party I was invited to for a long time.

A few weeks later I had to go to Universal for my semiannual gallery sitting. I always hated to do portrait sittings except when John Engstead did them. I'm very much of a "moving" picture actress, and it's agony for me to have to sit perfectly still. Thank goodness they have Nikons now. Because my hair was brownish for *A Place in the Sun*, Universal's famous still photographer was driving both himself and me crazy trying to make me look like a blonde glamor queen. I decided to ask Mr. Stevens to tell UI that I couldn't do anything there until I was finished with his film, even though it was taking nine months, because they were making me schizophrenic; on Tuesday I was a simple plain factory girl, and on Wednesday we had spent the entire day from seven to seven trying to make me look like a sexpot. I think I only made the "pot" part in that sitting.

As I drove home over Laurel Canyon, I realized I hadn't even broken for lunch or read the *Hollywood Reporter*, as I did religiously every day. So I stopped at Schwab's and picked up a *Reporter*. While I was waiting for a prescription to be filled, I glanced through Mike Connolly's column, and there it was, in big bold print. Burt Lancaster's wife, Norma, was expecting their third child.

Leon Schwab seemed a little reluctant to give me my medicine; I'd gotten a prescription from the studio doctor for Seconal. I don't know what showed on my face, but Leon suggested he give me one pill and I get the rest the next day. I asked him how he'd like to cancel my account with Schwab's. Legally it was my medicine, wasn't it? With a remark both insulting and troubled, he gave it to me, first going into the back room to type something on the label and, years later I suspected, to substitute the Seconal with placebo. I still hate these psychic Hollywood pharmacists.

I left my car in the parking lot and walked across Sunset Boulevard to Victor's. It was noted for its inexpensive good food and drinks and its very dark bar. I sat at the bar alone, something I never did, and ordered a triple gin martini. The bartender looked at me with the same look as Leon Schwab. "You want to make something out of it?" I asked softly.

He said, "Shelley, I just work here. But I'm a good listener." I told him I had a very expensive psychiatrist I paid to do that. "Okay, but before I give you the drink, why don't you give me that bottle of Seconals you're holding?" I told him to shut up and give me my drink, but I put the pills in the pocket of Elizabeth's blonde sheared beaver coat, which I still had neglected to exchange for mine.

In the space of about fifteen minutes I downed two triple martinis, and soon I no longer felt anything. Then I lit a match and looked at Mike Connolly's column again; maybe I had read it wrong. I had read it right. The bartender kept shoving hors d'oeuvres in front of me. I was finishing the dregs of my second triple and was not even getting drunk, I thought.

A familiar voice close to me said, "Hey, Shell, you want to go to a party in the Hollywood Hills?" Through a glass darkly I saw Marlon sitting next to me and said, "Hi," then realized the only place I wanted to go was to the ladies' room. I left the drinks, hors d'oeuvres, my purse and the *Reporter* on the bar, hung Elizabeth's coat on the floor and excused myself. When I got to the john, I turned on the faucets full force and then watched myself in the mirror, weeping full force. I knew it was the end of my make-believe life with Burt. I heard a pounding on the door. I ignored it. I started to wash my makeup-streaked face, and when I could see, I realized Marlon was in the ladies' room, looking at me with Leon Schwab's funny look. He gave me a paper towel to wipe my face, then said, "That Mike Connolly never gets anything straight. Don't jump to conclusions."

I started to weep again, with such violence that Marlon had to hold me up. I managed to blubber through my tears, "I know in my heart it's true. That bastard is fucking his wife."

Marlon took me back to the bar. The *Reporter* had disappeared, and the bartender gave me back my purse and coat, *sans* the imitation Seconals, I later discovered. The maître d' appeared and said, "Mr. Brando, your table's ready." I didn't want anything to eat, but Marlon wouldn't listen and half carried me to the booth. Victor's was full of young working actors and actresses, not stars. They obviously knew who Brando and I were, but throughout the next miserable hour not one of them came near us or even seemed to notice the condition I was in or what followed.

Marlon ordered two complete dinners, which were a real buy, but all I remember is that the onion soup got very salty. I refused to eat anything unless I could have something alcoholic, so he ordered spritzers. I guess I sobered up because he managed to tell me some funny stories about the paraplegics from the Birmingham General Hospital he was working with, and the practical jokes they played on him. There was a purpose to his stories, and somewhere around the salad course I got it. Here he was telling me about boys without arms and legs managing to live and laugh about their troubles, while I was wallowing in self-pity. All because a married movie star I had foolishly gotten involved with had behaved exactly as most married men behave. What the hell did I really have to cry about? Here I was a pretty, young, soon-to-be-rich girl with a family who loved me and with the most priceless gift of this world: health. When it finally sank in, Marlon whispered a line from *As You Like It*: "Men have died from time to time and worms have eaten them, but not for love."

I knew he was making gentle fun of me, but I slapped him. After all, it was *my* heartbreak. He returned the slap with a kiss, which got so passionate that the maître d' interrupted us with the suggestion that perhaps we didn't want the entrée after all, and if we wanted to go home, he wouldn't charge us for it.

That's exactly what we did, on Marlon's motorcycle. He left it at a gas station across the street from the Villa Italia because the fuel pump needed repairing. We walked through the lousy garage and took the elevator up to my apartment. While I took a long cold shower, Marlon lit every candle he could find, putting them in Coca-Cola bottles, glasses and ashtrays. He also lit little pyramids of incense, which I had never seen before; they smelled of orange and sandalwood and were quite sexy. And with what could only be precognizance, he put *The Pines of Rome* on the Capehart.

I saw that he had collected all the pictures of Burt from the bedroom, dressing room, dinette and kitchen—about fifteen in all—and had piled them on the coffee table in front of my leopard couch. "What do you want to do with these?" he asked.

With only a small twinge I said, "The incinerator is just down the hall."

"Are you sure?"

I held my breath but managed to say, "Yes, I'm sure."

Marlon, who, incidentally, was nude, picked up all the pictures, walked down the hall and did as I'd told him. An elderly woman opened her door as he passed, then slammed it. I think the whole floor, which consisted of six apartments, heard the clatter and bang of the fifteen pictures in their glass and silver frames going down the incinerator. As Marlon walked back to my apartment, several doors opened. I quickly took off my robe and greeted him in the hall with a kiss. The doors shut.

Marlon had two bottles of wine in the pockets of his jacket, and in a little while my heart wasn't breaking anymore. In fact, I felt rather free and happy. We were drinking the delicious wine out of big brandy snifters, and I don't know whether it was the company or the wine, but suddenly all I felt was relief.

Rejection must be a powerful aphrodisiac because we made love all night. Nonstop. Somewhere around 5:00 A.M. we both were in an exhausted sleep in my bed when someone began pounding on the door. I knew it was Burt. Marlon awoke, and I put my finger over his lips as a sign for him to be silent. There was a long hallway from my living room to my bedroom, and I knew that Burt would think I had taken sleeping pills and didn't hear him. He most probably would go down and phone me from the gas station's public phone. Or at least I hoped he would. Soon I heard the elevator door slam, and I knew that was what he had done.

I told Marlon to hurry and get all his clothes together and go up on the roof because I didn't know whether Burt would come back up the elevator or run up the stairs. After all, he was an athlete, and if the elevator took too long, he just might do that. Marlon was rather reluctant to run from anybody, but I hurriedly convinced him he was exhausted since he hadn't had much sleep, and it was a combination of Man Mountain Dean and Joe Louis who had been pounding on my door. Unwillingly he got his clothes together and did as I begged him to.

The phone rang, and it was Burt calling from the phone booth, as I expected. I pretended to be drugged and said that I didn't want to see him. I certainly didn't want him to find another man in my apartment at 5:00 A.M. As Marlon left, he made many obscene gestures to whomever I was talking to on the phone, but I heard him go up on the roof as the stairway was next to my bedroom wall.

Burt was very insistent on the phone and worried about me. He guessed I had read the Item in the *Reporter*, and so he would come back up no matter what I said. I figured that after he came into my apartment, Marlon could safely go down the elevator, get his motorcycle and go home. It seems funny now, but then it was terrifying. No matter how intelligent men are, something very primitive and brutal happens when their territory is invaded. And I didn't want anybody hurt, especially me, because of this sexually therapeutic night.

Burt came up on the slow elevator, and I quickly straightened the apartment up as much as I could and then threw on a flannel nightgown. He charged in with a frightened look on his face, to find me calm and sleepy. But then he began to look around the apartment in a strange manner. I had gotten rid of most of the candles and the incense, and I didn't care if he noticed that his pictures had disappeared. He didn't.

When he wandered into my bedroom, I saw one of Marlon's sneakers next to my bed and kicked it under the bed just in time. I started to draw the drapes to shut out the sunrise, and looking down, I saw Marlon limping down to Santa Monica Boulevard, I guess to take the streetcar to his studio. I couldn't understand why he didn't take his motorcycle; later I realized it was because the gas station was closed and the attendant had his keys. I closed the drapes.

There was nothing Burt could point to as an example of my unfaithfulness, but knowing that the best defense is an attack, when I got him back into the living room, I said, "You've been fucking your wife all along, haven't you?"

"I guess so," he mumbled.

"What do you mean, 'I guess so'?" I demanded. "Is your third child an immaculate conception?"

Whether it was the tension of the past twenty-four hours or the final realization that my relationship with Burt was over, I began to laugh and cry at the same time. Burt tried to calm me down, but I couldn't stop. My life had taken on the quality of a nightmare. I'd been running back and forth between Paramount and Universal, trying to be a factory girl *and* a sex goddess. Seeing Farley in public and Burt in private, endangering my career and my life with these shenanigans. Dieting constantly and taking sleeping pills because I was so hungry I couldn't sleep. If this was movie stardom, I'd take vanilla.

I held myself together until we came to my last scene in *A Place in the Sun* in which I phone Monty from the bus station and threaten him. He then leaves the rich people's house where they are celebrating his engagement to Elizabeth.

But before that scene they were doing the end of the picture, which was the prison and execution sequence. I don't know if it was because of that time I visited Sing Sing as a child, but I went to Paramount only once while they shot that sequence, even though I admired Anne Revere, who played Monty's mother. I've seen *A Place in the Sun* completely through only twice; I always close my eyes after I drown. One time was when Stevens allowed me to see a rough cut in a projection room at Paramount. He was showing it to Mrs. Theodore Dreiser, Charlie Chaplin and Henry Ginsberg, who was then head of the studio.

The film upset me so deeply I became quite irrational. I turned on my beloved George Stevens and screamed, "Don't you ever talk to me again as long as I live." Then I ran to my car. The Paramount guard wouldn't let me drive and took me home to my parents' house.

The film had made me so irrationally angry because I felt so helpless before the injustices of our society. It didn't seem like a movie to me; it was too real. My sister got me to a doctor from Cedars, who immediately put me in the hospital for three days. My psychiatrist came to see me every day to try to make me understand that the best way for me to fight the injustices I couldn't bear would be with my craft and my art. As, for instance, with *A Place in the Sun*, when an audience was moved by the way I played this young victim of the American success syndrome. The film would be of great help to the forces in the United States that even then were fighting for the equality of women, and against the death penalty and the insidious belief creeping into the mainstream of American life that existence has no value unless you find your Place in the Sun of Success and Money.

CHAPTER 21

One midnight Burt managed to sneak up the back stairs of Cedars. He bribed a floor nurse and visited me, bearing a huge box of roses and $3,000 in cash. I told him to keep the roses, but I kept the $3,000. My severance pay, I guess. Ever since, whenever I've worked with Burt or seen him in film capitals all over the world (and I'm sure he is now a multimillionaire) he gets a pseudoferocious look on his face and asks about the $3,000 he "loaned" me. "What three thousand dollars?" I always reply. And who was the guy in the apartment *that* night? "Nobody," I reply innocently. Now he knows.

With his great insight, George Stevens understood how seeing the tragic life of the little girl I had portrayed had sent me into irrational terror. I assume he didn't know about my personal Double Life.

When *A Place in the Sun* was finished, I made a flying trip to New York with Monty and watched some wonderful acting. The growth and development of the young actors who had worked continuously at the Actors' Studio since its inception stunned me. It confirmed my resolve that when my contract was up in 1955, I would somehow go back and live in New York and learn to become an actress. Even Monty's reassurance that I would be nominated for Best Actress and maybe even win the coveted Oscar couldn't change my mind. I knew I owed this performance to George Stevens's wonderful direction.

I was glad I had kept my little apartment and began to get over my depression and enjoy New York, rediscovering that there was a whole other world out there besides Hollywood. I was then notified by Universal to report back to costar in *The Raging Tide* with Richard Conte and Joan Caulfield. The script was the usual "good girl gone bad," the same story, different costumes, but it took place on a ship in San Francisco Harbor. Howard Duff and other UI contractees were also in it.

The only good thing about it was that my part took only five weeks to shoot. Going from *A Place in the Sun* to *The Raging Tide* was really going from the sublime to the ridiculous. But I held my breath, collected my salary and prayed to God that I would soon meet Mr. Right, get married and have a baby. They couldn't put me on suspension for *that* and add the time to the seven-year contract.

Once in a while in that cockamamie picture I would try to use the Method work I was learning in New York, but Richard Conte would go off into peals of laughter. He finally explained to me that these pictures were made for a fourteen-year-old mentality, and if I tried to drag in any reality, it would just confuse the audience. Like the tradition in westerns where the good guys wear the white hats and the bad guys wear the black hats, if I tried to get any depth into these Blonde Bombshells I was playing, the audience would stop looking at my blonde curls and boobs and start thinking about me as a real person. They might get confused and even ask for their money back.

One morning, while delaying reporting for my eternal fittings, I was having breakfast at Schwab's. Marilyn came in, looking blonde and skinny and gorgeous, lugging her usual large book and followed, of course, by Sidney Skolsky. She was back under contract to Twentieth but was waiting in line behind Betty Grable and Alice Faye for some kind of decent part. I took her out to the parking lot and showed her my new white convertible Cadillac. She was getting a great deal of publicity by now. I told her that next time a studio wanted to borrow her from Twentieth, her agent could damn well get her some extras. Sometime later, when she did a Jack Benny radio show, she insisted on getting a black convertible Cadillac—what 10 percent her agent got, I don't know. Probably a hubcap.

As Marilyn and I walked back to Schwab's, she thanked me and asked if I still lived with my sister and my family. I told her I was looking for another apartment. A wistful look came over her face, and as we sat back down with Sidney, I said, "Marilyn, if I find a reasonable apartment with two bedrooms and two bathrooms, you want to share it with me?" Her face lit up so that I was again ashamed of my past year's preoccupation with myself and realized that I'd forgotten my grandfather's dictum: "If I am only for myself, what am I?"

Sidney said he knew about an apartment on Holloway Drive which was up three flights of outdoor steps. There was a huge empty lot next to it which was almost like a park. (It's still there.) He told us the apartment had a balcony view of the city, two bedrooms, two baths, a large living room, a small dining room and a kitchen. The only hitch was that it was unfurnished, and all the furniture Marilyn had was a white piano her mother had left in storage. "What the hell," I said, "let's look at it. I've acquired quite a bit of furniture, and all you'll have to buy is a bed, and you can ask the studio Prop Department to loan you a dressing table. We'll go to the secondhand places on Western Avenue and get whatever else we need." Marilyn looked like a kid who had just found out that Santa Claus was real.

The apartment was very nice and was only $227 a month—rent-controlled—but I had to slip the manager $300 to get it. He was a little doubtful about giving this choice apartment to two blonde actresses, so my father came over and signed and guaranteed the lease.

Marilyn borrowed $1,000—from Twentieth's Credit Union—and we had a marvelous time buying unpainted bookcases, a dining-room set and two unmatching armchairs for the living room. The apartment was now furnished in "early relative." Marilyn wanted the smaller bedroom—she felt more secure in small places—and when I got back from a week's location in San Francisco's *Raging Tide*, the apartment was all fixed up and cute.

Marilyn and I hated Sundays and holidays, and every Sunday morning we would earnestly play classical records on my Capehart and read the accompanying literature. In those days the 78 rpm classical records came three in a box with little booklets telling you about the composers, with tips on musical appreciation. Since we both were hell-bent on culture, we spent a couple of hours every Sunday morning listening to it. At 12:01 promptly we would put on Frank Sinatra or Nat King Cole.

One Sunday we were playing the records and looking at our pictures in the *Academy Players' Directory*, the book in which film actors must list their current credits, their most attractive photographs and their agents' names so that producers can contact them. I looked at the photos of all the *single* leading men and said, "I wonder why we put ourselves through this agony called LOVE."

Marilyn, who was also recovering from an unhappy love affair, said, "Wouldn't it be nice to be like men and just get notches in your belt and sleep with the most attractive men and not get emotionally involved?"

I thought about that and said, "Why not? Anyway, I think the double standard ended with the Second World War. There is no earthly reason why we shouldn't just concentrate on our careers and sleep with whoever is attractive to us, like men do." *We two girls were obviously never afraid of flying.*

She said, "What a wonderful idea. Let's get pencil and paper and go through the *Directory* and make lists. Should we just stick to actors and directors?"

"No," I said. "Any man in politics, music, science or literature who appeals to us can be put on our lists. Okay? A new Hollywood game!"

She thought it over. "But aren't most of them dead? I mean the ones in literature and music."

"Of course not. There's Ernest Hemingway, Irwin Shaw, Clifford Odets, Thornton Wilder—"

"He's an actor, isn't he?"

"No," I answered, not too sure. "I think he's a famous writer like Eugene O'Neill."

"Should we include Europeans, Chinese and Russians?"

I was a little doubtful about the Russians, and I knew China had built a wall. "I think that would be a little difficult. But let's include anybody we like. Presidents, generals, explorers, animal trainers, industrialists."

We decided to take an hour and not show each other our lists until we finished; then we would exchange them. My list consisted mostly of handsome actors I had fantasized about when I was an adolescent, headed by Clark Gable, Jeff Chandler, Ralph Richardson, Jean Gabin, Laurence Olivier, John Garfield, Clifford Odets, Irwin Shaw, Peter Finch, James Mason, Michael Redgrave, Cary Grant, Chet Huntley and Eric Sevareid. I threw in Ralph Bunche and Albert Schweitzer for dignity.

When I read Marilyn's choices, I dropped the huge *Players' Directory*. She had listed Zero Mostel, Eli Wallach, Charles Boyer, Jean Renoir, Lee Strasberg, Nick Ray, John Huston, Elia Kazan, Harry Belafonte, Yves Montand, Charles Bickford—who, I had heard, untruthfully, did not like girls; she said, "I can try, can't I?, those are the rules"—Ernest Hemingway, Charles Laughton, Clifford Odets, Dean Jagger, Arthur Miller and Albert Einstein.

"Marilyn, there's no way you can sleep with Albert Einstein. He's the most famous scientist of this century, and besides, he's an old man."

"That has nothing to do with it. I hear he's very healthy."

I don't know how many of her choices she achieved, but after her death when many of her possessions were sent to Lee Strasberg's apartment, there on Marilyn's mother's white baby grand I saw a large framed photograph of Albert Einstein. On it was written "To Marilyn, with respect and love and thanks, Albert Einstein."

I took Marilyn with me a couple of times to Laughton's group, which I was attending religiously. Her whispery voice would become completely inaudible, and she seemed to shrivel up. After the second time I realized it was such agony for her that I resolved not to invite her again unless she asked me and I really felt she could handle it. That night she did what every woman recognizes as an act of despair, she cut off her beautiful long, blonde hair. The next morning, when I looked at her, she said, "Do you think a hairdresser at Twentieth will fix it like yours?"

I said, "Sure, honey," but in my heart I felt that Darryl Zanuck would scalp her. She already had famous posters and pictures all over the world, especially with the armed forces, with her shoulder-length platinum hair flowing in the wind. She was obviously trying to fix on the outside of her head what my psychiatrist was trying to help me fix on the inside of mine.

When I had been fitting costumes for *The Raging Tide*, the studio had rented a beautiful natural wild mink coat for me. It had enough minks in it for two coats and was a wonderfully blonde color. The rental on it was $500 a week for five weeks. When I got back to L.A., Marilyn insisted on taking me over to Fuhrman's and in her meek whisper explained to Mrs. Fuhrman that the practice at Twentieth was that when a studio rented a coat for more than two weeks, if the actress who wore it wanted it, the furrier deducted the rental cost from the purchase price. Mrs. Fuhrman almost fainted, but Marilyn whispered that if she sold it to me this way, we both would wear it to all our premieres and parties and tell all the movie magazines where we'd got the coat, and it would be great publicity for her business.

Mrs. Fuhrman thought it a little odd that I paid the balance for the coat in cash—it was Burt's $3,000. That's how I got my first mink coat, and it was the most beautiful one I ever had. If you see pictures of Marilyn or me around 1950 in a mink coat, you'll know it's the same one. Huge turned-back cuffs, a stand-up collar and ankle length. I still have this coat; only now the minks are a little tired, and it lines a black cloth coat, which is the warmest one I have.

When my father found out about this purchase, even though he thought it was another bonus from my agent, Mr. Blum, he had a small fit. "Two fur coats, a new apartment and a Cadillac all in one year!" (I kept the diamond wristwatch in a vault.)

One evening Laughton announced that he was going to do *Galileo*, by a German playwright, and we all would be in it. The play took place in the 1600s and was about the famous Italian physicist and astronomer who proved the earth moved around the sun and was not the center of the universe. And as in history, the church forced him to deny this knowledge and recant. After a run-through for the group, Laughton asked me my opinion of the play. I told him I thought it was wonderful, but the ending was too "downbeat and they should change it." This work does not sound like dramatic material, but in the hands of Bertolt Brecht, it was devastating and the first play I ever saw that got to my emotions through my intellect, although I didn't understand that at the time.

Immediately after *The Raging Tide*, Universal shoved me into a film called *Winchester 73*. It had a good director, Tony Mann, and I costarred with Jimmy Stewart. But the real star of that film was the goddamn Winchester rifle. I had a terrible fight with Spitz & Goetz and my agent because they wouldn't let me play the small part of the seventeenth-century nun in *Galileo*. I had to do *Winchester* or take a suspension, and then I couldn't work anywhere anyway. Laughton assured me that if the play went to New York, I would be in it. I wasn't; Universal wouldn't let me do it.

So whenever possible, I would dash from Universal, not even stopping to take off my long blonde wig, and sit in the third or fourth row at the Coronet Theater and watch the rehearsals. Joe Losey, the director, was very nice to me and never objected to my sitting there, but I began to feel that my long platinum hair was distracting the actors, so I moved to the back.

One day I noticed a little man, who seemed to need a shave and who was wearing greenish coveralls, hovering around the back of the theater, picking up pieces of paper and putting them in the trash basket. I assumed he was the janitor and asked him for a program, which he went and got for me. He had a heavy German accent, and I asked him if he was a refugee. He said he was. We sat together and watched the rehearsal. He didn't seem to understand English too well and the rehearsals often put him to sleep.

He always looked lonely and hungry, so one Friday afternoon I invited him home for the Sabbath meal—my mother still made glorious chicken soup—and to meet my father and mother, who also spoke German. The little man gratefully accepted and enjoyed my parents so much I left him there playing pinochle with my father. For several months after that, he was there every Friday night.

The next few times I went to rehearsals Joe Losey, John Houseman and Charles Laughton seemed quite upset—they wanted rewrites and were having trouble as the playwright seemed to have disappeared. In all innocence I just sat there and watched what went on and wondered myself where this irresponsible playwright had gone.

Plummer Park is about ten blocks from where my parents lived, and senior citizens still go there on lovely days to play pinochle, klaberjass, chess and boccie. By that time my father was so busy taking care of my career and finances that he had retired, so every morning he and the German refugee janitor would walk to Plummer Park and talk endlessly about their experiences as young men. Pop had never told anybody about his troubles with the New York judicial system and the racketeering in the men's garment union in both New York and Los Angeles. But in German he was able to tell this little man all about it; for some reason, in that language he could reveal his agonies.

When my daughter graduated from Harvard recently, she and I and her father, Vittorio Gassman, saw Al Pacino do *Arturo Ui*, another of Bertolt Brecht's great plays. It was about gangsters in the Chicago unions and the characterizations were parallel to Hitler and his henchmen. Vittorio, who is very familiar with Brecht's work, told me that probably while the playwright was playing klaberjass with my father, he was no doubt confirming his research on this the most American of his plays.

But I didn't discover Bertolt Brecht's identity until after my father's death, when I was living in New York with my mother and very young daughter and went to see *Brecht on Brecht* in an Off-Broadway theater in Greenwich Village. When the curtain went up, to the right of the stage, hanging from the top of the set, was an enormous picture of my father's pinochle partner. I said to my companion, "What the hell is that picture of my father's friend doing up there?"

He turned to me in amazement. "That's Bertolt Brecht." I started to give him an argument, but the people around shushed me. As the play progressed, I began to remember where and under what circumstances I had met this little man. After the play, which was another extraordinary work, I went home in a daze and took out a huge book of Brecht's plays. My mother had awakened and was making us tea. I asked her if she remembered the little German janitor who was a friend of Daddy's in about 1950. "Oh, yes, Mr. Brechstein. Did you know, Shelley, after everything Hitler did, that man went back to Germany. Maybe he went to look for his family."

"Mother," I said, showing her the book, "that man's name was Bertolt Brecht, and he wrote all these plays. He's famous all over the world."

With a pitying look my mother said, "Shelley, don't be silly. He was a costume jeweler."

"Mom, why do you think that?"

"Well, once Daddy asked him what he did in the old country, and he told us he made jewels for poor people." I didn't argue.

In a few months Mr. Stevens sent a print of the completed *A Place in the Sun* over to the UI brass for them to screen in their projection room. I sat in the back with my agent and watched it till the character I played drowns, then I closed my eyes. Now I could be more dispassionate about the film, and I finally allowed myself to be proud and happy that I was part of such a great film. But coming out of the projection room, Mr. Goetz looked very disgruntled and said, "IF I HAD KNOWN STEVENS WAS GOING TO HAVE YOU LOOK LIKE THAT, I WOULDN'T HAVE LET YOU DO THE PICTURE."

My agent just held my hand tightly and whispered, "Don't say anything. I bet you win the Oscar next year."

The next morning I sent George Stevens a small peach tree in full bloom. I had read somewhere that after the flood this was the first thing Noah saw on dry land.

I met Laurence Olivier at one of Ralph Blum's parties. He and his wife, Vivien Leigh, were having one of their periodic separations, both geographic and emotional. He seemed to like me and find me amusing and pretty, and of course, I found him brilliant, charming, an extraordinary talent and, in fact, godlike in every respect. While he was talking to me, he noticed that I kept getting blue in the face and would have to take deep breaths. It was because I was so in awe of him and felt the atmosphere around him was so rarefied that I was literally holding my breath, forgetting to breathe. He inquired if I was studying breath control with Laughton. I nodded.

He didn't have a car, so I offered to give him a lift to the Beverly Hills Hotel. On the way he asked if we could stop at my apartment for a drink. I froze but acquiesced. I mean, he *was* Laurence Olivier. I had seen his *Hamlet* maybe six times and wept at *Wuthering Heights* endlessly. I brought this glorious creature to my apartment, sat him on the straightest chair on my little balcony and gave him a light scotch and soda; I had a Coke. While we looked at the Hollywood lights, he talked about the British technique of acting and the training those lucky British actors get at the Liverpool Rep and all the government-subsidized theaters in England. I turned from breathless blue to green with envy.

When I deplored my speech problems, he told me he'd been a poor boy from the North Country and had had a terrible regional accent—which he had obviously overcome—but I was truly overcome. I was also a big fan of his wife's and I guess I had had enough relationships with married men, so about midnight I called him a cab. Maybe he wanted one anyway.

Marilyn came in, and I introduced them quickly as his cab was honking down below; then she and I stood on the balcony and watched him drive away. "Are you crazy?" she said. "He's on your list."

"I know, but it would be like sleeping with Adlai Stevenson."

"Oh, boy, and you think *I* have problems about sex!"

I worked on that problem, and years later, when Adlai Stevenson was U.S. Ambassador to the United Nations, I was his hostess at an official dinner in the Waldorf Towers . . . problem solved.

Back when I was making *South Sea Sinner* at UI, I got to know Robert Walker rather well. He was doing a film on the lot with Ava Gardner, and we used to meet in the commissary for lunch a couple of times a week.

In my opinion Bob was a consummate actor and had that same extraordinary quality that Spencer Tracy had: his eyes were truly a mirror of his soul. He never needed words to let you know what he was thinking or feeling. I saw *The Clock*, the film he did with Judy Garland, at least ten times. Watching him was a profound lesson in film acting. He had a special sense of humor that would make the audience laugh immediately after his most poignant moments. He never took himself or his problems seriously. It was a very difficult period of his life; when he was working on that film, he was exhausted at night, so between reading stories to his two young sons and learning his lines, he would manage to get five or six hours' sleep.

During this period I believe he was avoiding MGM, his home studio, and used to hang around my set sometimes because he was lonely and had nowhere to go. He used to tease me gently about my Blonde Bombshell image. I casually mentioned once that I liked clowns and stuffed animals, and so, whenever he came over to my dressing room, he would bring one; his fans all over the country knew about his divorce and sent him thousands of toys for his sons. My stage dressing room began to look like a toy shop.

Sam Goldwyn's policy was to make millions by lending out his name players, so Farley was away doing research for a new Hitchcock movie. I was always free in the evenings now, and Bob took me all over Southern California to strange out-of-the-way places I didn't even know existed. Somewhere in L.A. there is a Japanese garden teahouse that you can get to only by climbing a mountain. We also went to what surely must have been the first commune somewhere down the beach toward Laguna, where lots of kids, married and unmarried, lived in Quonset huts. None of them worked, and they caught giant California crabs and made their own wine. Bob also drove me up to see the Saroyan country, and once we even met Saroyan himself.

We went to little theater plays, operas and concerts. Up to then I hadn't known there was so much culture in and around L.A. He even knew the rich producers and directors who had wonderful art collections and would con them into letting us spend an afternoon looking at their collections. We went to Edward G. Robinson's house once and found Mr. and Mrs. Robinson in the middle of a terrible fight. But Bob and I just drifted among their priceless collection and ignored them, as they did us.

That summer, when we both finished our pictures, Bob converted a tennis court in the Malibu Colony into an open-air theater where he did several plays, directing some and acting in others. I was in *Hello Out There* with him and was stage manager on another.

Once we drove up to Big Sur, and he talked of buying a house and raising his children up there. I never raised any objections to these daydreams because he was so obviously trying to put his life together again.

My parents liked Bob very much, but he could never sit still very long. In fact, his right foot and left hand twitched almost continuously. Blanche kept saying, "That young man is not well. He should stop forcing himself from picture to picture and go to the Menninger Clinic or someplace like that." I told her to stick to obstetrics. He was a quiet, gentle, lovely young man. One morning about six-thirty, when I was in Makeup, getting ready for one of the endless portrait sittings, I got a phone call from his sons' nurse, Emily. She told me that Bob was dead.

He had always been a heavy drinker but never showed it. He was working on a new film and couldn't get to sleep, so had called the local Malibu doctor to give him a shot of Demerol. He had probably not told the doctor how much liquor he had consumed, and I guess the combination was too much for his frail body.

The studio brass immediately called me in and told me to pack

my bags as I was to go on a tour of twenty major cities with *South
Sea Sinner*, of which I, unfortunately, was the star. In each city I
would do a show with Liberace, his brother, George, would conduct
the orchestras, and Jerry Paris—a dear friend and fellow actor at
the Actors Lab who is now a prominent television director—would
be the comedian and MC. Bobby True and his trio would go with
us, and Kenny Carter would be the publicity director of the tour
and take care of everything.

We would visit each city when the picture opened, visit the Universal film exchanges, have a cocktail party with the local jour-
nalists, do some radio and television interviews and perform our
little vaudeville act after each showing of the film on its opening
day, and Liberace and I would sign autographs. It didn't sound too
tough, but when you multiply it by twenty cities it's quite a chore.

They were going to let me stay in St. Louis for three days because my mother would fly there to meet me, and the city was going
to have a Shelley Winters Day on the stage of the Ambassador
Theater—the same theater where my uncle Joe Winter had conducted the orchestra and where he had held me in his arms while
I saw Al Jolson and the first talking picture, *The Jazz Singer*. The
whole trip seemed worth it for the chance to see my St. Louis family again and perform on the stage where I had toddled around
in back of the screen, trying to find the people who were talking.

As I performed "live" in all those American cities, I was still
amazed at the dream-come-true quality of my life, that all those
beautiful make-believe people I had watched up there on the silver
screen were now a real part of my professional and personal life.

When we finally arrived in St. Louis, it was one of the high points
of my and my relatives' lives. The mayor presented me with a key
to the city, and we had a small parade from the hotel to the theater.
My mother rode with me in an open car, and although it was a hot
St. Louis spring day, she wore the mink coat I had bought her for
Christmas. We passed Famous-Barr, the biggest department store
in St. Louis, where my mother and aunts had worked. And a banner was stretched across the street saying, "Welcome home Shelley
Winter." (To this day, never mind the *s*.)

After the show at the Ambassador, all my Winter relatives gave
me a big dinner at the Chase Roof nightclub. All my new little
nieces and nephews were with us; my Uncle Joe must have been
there in spirit. I never again was to see my mother as happy as she
was that night. In a way that party was really for her. *She* sat in
the spotlight and later on she got up on the nightclub floor and sang

"The Indian Love Call" better than Jeanette MacDonald ever thought of singing it. All my struggles and unhappiness, the bit parts and the conniving, the lying to casting agents, the terrible disappointments, the study and the work, everything paid off the night I sat and watched my mother singing on that nightclub floor on the Chase Roof in her hometown.

CHAPTER 22

Whoever the powers are who run the Motion Picture Producers Association, they are obviously very shortsighted and slightly bananas. I believe every other major industry in America has very highly paid and well-trained experts to research and advise it on the direction its companies should take. Not only did the major studios allow their best directors, actors, writers and, in some cases, important producers to be blacklisted and fired without discussion or denial, but they failed to judge the effect it would have on their box office and therefore on their own survival. During this period most of them were also pretending that television would go away. With their usual backbones they were kowtowing to the exhibitors.

There is no reason in the world why that huge beautiful MGM studio, with its acres of back lots, an enormous Wardrobe Department, Music Department, editing rooms, film vaults and sound stages, couldn't have been turned into, say, CBS. And Twentieth perhaps into NBC. And Columbia perhaps into ABC. Only Lew Wasserman was bold, farsighted and powerful enough to dissolve the biggest agency in Hollywood, the Music Corporation of America—which had then been my agency for a number of years after Mr. Blum died—and then MCA became the major television producer at Universal, which makes zillions every year because it still owns and controls most of the hours of television, besides running a very successful film company.

Whenever I have to go to Metro or Columbia and see those empty studios with their crumbling stages, my heart breaks. A couple of years ago I did a television show on one of the stages at Columbia. Two of the stages have been sold as indoor tennis courts, and the once busy studio that produced such great films as *The More the Merrier, It Happened One Night* and *Mr. Smith Goes to Washington* stands empty and forlorn. I felt that Harry Cohn must surely be churning in his grave.

I often secretly wish we had some of those tough pioneer bastards, like Cohn and Louis B. Mayer, among us again. They lived and breathed film. They worked sixteen hours a day and cared about and treasured the quality of their work. Although they did "program" pictures, they also made many attempts to create and nurture an appetite in the American people for great music, ballet, art and literature. Sometimes the attempts failed and were even silly, like *Chopin, Symphony* and *Rhapsody in Blue*. But they did make films such as *The Good Earth, The Agony and the Ecstasy, The Moon and Sixpence, Lust for Life, Fantasia, A Midsummer Night's Dream, Romeo and Juliet* and *Les Misérables*.

Although I have worked on television a great deal, it always seems to me that when something good is done, it's in spite of the working hours and conditions. In my experience, no one has ever set out to make a bad film; the creators always hope it will be an artistic sleeper, even with low-budget films. I'm not so sure with television—they need quantity. Not necessarily quality.

It was during that period that the structure of the large studios was undermined, although the effects weren't realized for a decade, when, in a panic, they sold off their real estate and film libraries, instead of renting them for ninety-nine years. During that turbulent period Paramount sold its huge library of wonderfully written and skillfully made films to television for $48 million, which, compared to the air hours they are used for, are worth easily hundreds of millions. The studio brass should have only rented them, but they were desperate to keep their jobs by showing some kind of quick profit to the stockholders. To this day, when I sit in a theater and see the Paramount logo and under it the words "This is a Gulf & Western Company," I want to throw oil on the screen. All my poor beloved studios are now just part of huge conglomerates. And when I see some of their films, I'm sure they're just used for tax write-offs. When I see the automobile companies in my beloved Detroit slowly putting themselves out of business by refusing to convert to electric cars, I remember how during the Second World War they quickly converted to tanks, and I remember how in the early fifties I watched the film industry almost destroy itself with the same shortsightedness.

I returned from St. Louis and found myself sailing quickly from the *South Sea Sinner* tour into the Universal port to film *Meet Danny Wilson*, which was a comedy-drama-sort-of-musical with Frank Sinatra playing a crooner. This epic was written by Frank's buddy Don Maguire and also starred Alex Nicol, a lovely guy from the Actors' Studio. I had four production numbers to do with Mr. Sinatra and only four days in which to learn them. The costumes were already made on my wardrobe dummy—which is exactly how I felt. Why did I have to start this film in such a hurry? The best information I could get was that Mr. Sinatra's career was at its lowest ebb, and he urgently needed the $25,000 Universal was paying him for the film. My information may have been erroneous, but that was the studio scuttlebutt.

Alex Nicol played his best friend, and Frank's girlfriend—played by me—was in love with that friend. But at the final fade it all ended happily, and the crooner went on to bigger and better things. So much for the plot. But on the positive side, we had a wonderful cameraman, who was making me look like Lana Turner —although my father still couldn't see it—and my clothes and hats and furs were gorgeous.

This forgettable picture began shooting in chaos and ended in disaster. Frank Sinatra was in the process of divorcing Nancy to marry Ava Gardner—I think he thought that's what he wanted. His children were quite young, and there were always psychiatrists and priests and his kids visiting him on the set or in the commissary.

The only good part of the picture was Sinatra's wonderful singing. During the prerecording he did a version of "One for My Baby" that neither he nor anyone else has ever equaled. Everyone in Hollywood knew of his struggles "to divorce or not to divorce," and the columnists as well as the industry were giving him a very bad time. Everyone in the studio regaled me with tales of his temper tantrums and his kindness; consequently, I was really scared of him and had the feeling I was about to make a film with Dr. Jekyll *and* Mr. Hyde.

Our relationship started out just great. The first day of rehearsal he sent me a note suggesting that we rehearse in his dressing room. I sent him one back—suspecting the worst or the best—that this was *my* studio, and we would rehearse on the stage, as arranged by the Casting Department. It wasn't that I didn't find him attractive. He was. And glamorous and certainly an exciting and gifted performer. I too had sat in the orchestra at the Paramount Theater when I was a teenager and screamed every time he opened his mouth. But he was married to Nancy, whom I knew and liked from various charity committees, and there were the children. I was determined to keep my association with Mr. Sinatra as professional as possible. In retrospect, I suspect he wanted the same thing.

He arrived on the stage fifteen minutes late, looking as though he were ready to chew me up and spit out the pieces. We started to rehearse. His work was rather improvisatory, and he was such an old hand at musicals that he could almost rehearse a number once and then shoot it. I still didn't know my left foot from my right, and the realization I was singing with Frank Sinatra klutzed me up worse. So my leading man and I started the film snarling at each other, and it went downhill from there. Sometimes the children would come to the commissary, and I would join them. A priest from the Catholic Family Counseling Service would sometimes be with them. The priest was a very nice man, but the afternoons he visited Frank on the set we all might as well have gone home. Frank was truly impossible and so disturbed that he couldn't hear anything that anyone said to him, including the other actors, the crew and the director, Joe Pevney. Also, Frank was losing about a pound a week, which made me look heavier in the rushes.

Late one afternoon we three had a long funny scene in a convertible. When the director finally yelled, "Cut!" Sinatra got out of the car and said, "That was great, right?"

The little man who ran the back-projection machine came up to the director and said, "It was out of sync," which means that the back-projection machine was not locked with the camera and all you would see on the screen was us pretending to drive a car and behind us a blank screen instead of the city streets.

Frank, in a rage, turned to the little man. "Okay, but was the acting good?"

The little man stuttered, "Yes . . . I mean . . ."

Sinatra, not understanding the technical problems involved, announced, "That's all that counts," and strode off to his dressing room and refused to do the scene again. We never did get that scene and had to repeat the dialogue somewhere else in the film.

I must say, to Frank's credit, that no matter how many arguments we had, he never would let them dub my voice. He knew that when I was finally secure with a song, I sounded pretty good. He even taught me tricks about mouthing back to your own voice in close-ups. But we had so many "artistic" differences that the rest of the cast, the director, the crew and the front-office brass all threw up their hands in despair.

We finally came to night shooting, which is usually filmed toward the end of the picture schedule so they won't lose money on a turnaround in hours. It was shot at Burbank Airport, where Frank is taking me to a plane and I finally get up the courage to tell him that I'm in love with his best friend, Alex Nicol. I can't remember what started our vicious argument, but the mildest things we called each other were "bowlegged bitch of a Brooklyn blonde" and "skinny, no-talent, stupid Hoboken bastard." I mean, really high-class stuff like that. Our language was so bad that all the tourists watching the shooting disappeared like magic. Joe Pevney, trying to lighten the atmosphere, said he was making a great mistake not photographing our personal arguments between takes.

At about three in the morning Frank flew into a terrible rage at me, and despite my gorgeous hat and white gloves and beautiful elegant navy dress and stone martens, I screamed like a fishwife and I think I slugged him. For a second I thought Frank's makeup man/bodyguard—who I suspected carried a gun—was going to shoot me. Contrary to other Italians I have known since, he didn't hit me back—I guess I was lucky—he just slammed into his limousine and roared away. Maybe he went home and hit Ava Gardner.

When I got back to my apartment, I calmly picked up the telephone, got the Western Union operator and sent one of my now-famous telegrams. It was all about "human rights, artistic integrity, the Four Freedoms, the inherent respect one artist must have for another, and I was going to tell my father." The telegram went on for about three pages, and I told the operator to send it to Sinatra, with copies to Spitz & Goetz, Sinatra's agent, my agent, Jerry Giesler, the UI board of directors in New York, President Harry Truman and the United Nations Human Rights Commission.

When I was through, the Western Union operator said, "Miss Winters, listen. It's four A.M. Why don't you sleep on this, and if you still feel the same way in the morning, I'll send it at the night letter rate."

"Send it now!" I shouted.

The next morning Herb Brenner, my agent, called me. He was newly with MCA, a big important agency, and Lew Wasserman was his boss, and I guess I was his first important client. In a tremulous voice he informed me that the UI brass wished to meet us in the head office at 9:00 A.M., if not sooner. Mr. Frank Sinatra and his agent would be there, too. I refused to go unless they spoke to us separately. I wanted to be in Mr. Frank Sinatra's presence only when I had to act with him, and I wasn't even sure I wanted to do that anymore.

Herb picked me up in half an hour, looking more frightened than I was. I was still angry. He tried to use his lawyer's logic on me, but after a couple of blocks I yelled, "Herb, I don't care if I'm never allowed to act in anything, anywhere, anytime. Nobody can insult me like that." When we got to Leo Spitz's office, it was crowded with Joe Pevney, Edward Muhl, chief of production, Rufus LeMaire, head of casting, Kenny Carter and for some odd reason, Frankie Van, who ran the UI gym and was the referee for the fights at the American Legion Stadium. We all sat down, and the trembling secretary served coffee.

Mr. Leo Spitz, an elderly and wise man and the financial wizard of UI, did not try to argue with me. What he said was: "Shelley, I know you don't believe it now, 'But this too will pass.' From all the rumors we hear, you're going to be nominated Best Actress for *A Place in the Sun.* If we keep your publicity as dignified as possible—given your explosive personality—there's a good chance the Academy members will vote your performance, and you will get the Oscar. Most of the newspapers owe us favors, and we can keep all this nonsense out of the press. You are at the top of your career. Every studio is sending scripts to us for you and offering one hundred thousand dollars minimum for you.

"Mr. Sinatra is going through a terrible and troubled period of his life and career. He's going against all his religious training and has periods when he loses his voice, and it terrifies him. And he is not famous as an actor but a singer. You speak about humanity in that document you sent me last night, Shelley. Perhaps you should examine your own humanity and realize the terrible trouble that young man is in. That's no excuse for him behaving so outrageously, but you're both liberals, and maybe with your ideals of brotherhood you can bring yourself to understand the reasons that are making him behave the way he did."

I meekly got up from my seat and asked Mr. Goetz what time the call was. He told me they were cutting out a sequence or two and were going to shoot the final scene in the New York hospital where I'm ill in bed and Frank and Alex fly in from California. Frank was going to tell me he's forgiven me, and then Alex and I openly declare our love for each other.

Mr. Goetz told me to get made up, and we would start shooting at twelve-thirty, "having had lunch." I don't know what Mr. Spitz told Sinatra, but we both were ready on the set at twelve-thirty, I in my hospital gown with the hastily learned lines under the blanket. Joe Pevney delicately rehearsed the scene, and everything went beautifully until Sinatra's last line, which was something sweet like: "I'll have a cup of coffee and leave you two lovebirds alone." The scene and the picture fade out on Sinatra's sad but funny grin.

We rehearsed the scene just great. Then we started to shoot. When he got to his last line, he said, "I'll go have a cup of Jack

Daniel's, or I'm gonna pull that blonde broad's hair out by its black roots." Before the camera could fade, I grabbed a convenient bedpan and threw it. It connected. The brouhaha that followed was worse than the previous night's. Frank's friend Don, who had written the script, insisted that he wanted the picture to end with that line.

"Not with this blonde you don't," I said, and stormed off the set.

For the next two days the picture was shut down. Herb Brenner came over and told me that since they had no end for the picture, UI would have to release it this way—instead of saying "The End," it would have a frame that read, "Miss Winters and Mr. Sinatra do not speak to each other, so this is the end." I stayed home for those two days with the phone shut off. Marilyn came home from Twentieth one evening with an urgent message from Nancy Sinatra please to phone her. When I returned Nancy's call, she was in tears. "Shelley, Frank doesn't get the twenty-five thousand dollars for the picture. The bank might foreclose the mortgage on the house. My children are going to be out in the street. Please finish the picture, or they won't give me the twenty-five thousand dollars."

I said, "Okay, Nancy."

I informed the studio that Frank Sinatra could say any damn thing he wanted to, and I reported to the set at 9:00 A.M. I got in my hospital bed again but said to Sinatra before we started the rehearsal, "You can say any damn thing you want. But you just might want to make another picture again sometime, and the audience is going to think you're tacky and tasteless."

Pevney hurriedly decided not to rehearse. He just said, "Roll 'em. Action." And at the end of the scene at the final fade-out the perverse Frank Sinatra said, "I'll go have a cup of coffee and leave you two lovebirds alone." And he winked into the camera.

I wonder what his version of this story is. But I'm almost sure mine is the truthful, unbiased one.

That season Frank had a weekly television show, and at the end of each show, instead of ending it like Jimmy Durante, who said, "Good night, Mrs. Calabash, wherever you are," Sinatra would say, as if he were cursing, "I leave you with two words . . . SHELLEY WINTERS." He did this until Jerry Giesler sent notices to William Paley, CBS and Sinatra's lawyer that he must "cease and desist," or we would sue them all for millions. After weeks of threats Sinatra finally stopped, but probably because he didn't want to give me all that free publicity. Ah, well, the fires of youth.

I never have real good fights with anyone anymore. And during the last decade or so Frank Sinatra always invites me to his openings at Caesar's Palace, and I always go. And he is indeed Boss, one of the great entertainers of our time.

While I was shooting *Meet Danny Wilson*, I got a call from Jerry Wald, who was the nominal head of RKO, which Howard Hughes now owned. The studio had been dormant for nearly a decade and was now beginning to revive. Hughes was having Wald go into the production of half-hour movies for television, secretly, because the exhibitors, who owned the theaters, were fighting tooth and nail and threatening boycotts if the studios cooperated with TV.

Jerry, whom I knew from the Beverly Hills Tennis Club, asked me if I would like to do a comedy with Farley. It was called *Behave Yourself* and was about a young married couple who get into very strange adventures with all the gangsters west of the Mississippi because of a dog that follows the husband home one night and that the wife thinks is her anniversary present. But the adorable dog has been trained by gangsters to carry drugs and money.

Mr. Wald wanted me to come to RKO and have a meeting with him about it. I told him I would love to but I was working from six to six, so I asked if he could please have the script delivered to Schwab's and I would pick it up on my way home, read it and talk with him on Sunday. But Mr. Wald kept insisting that I should come to RKO on my lunch hour or at night. I explained again that it was impossible because of the mercurial nature of *Danny Wilson*. After about fifteen minutes of this pointless discussion he said he would call my agent and discuss it with him. This really made me mad because I wanted to work with Farley, and I hoped to keep the money from this picture, having just done two or five for UI.

I've always had a theory that all the phones and offices in the studios were bugged. I've had several proofs of this, and what happened next was one of them. The next day Mr. Wald's secretary called and asked me to phone her when I'd finished work, and Mr. Jerry Wald himself would meet me at Schwab's drugstore with the script. Not understanding, I said, "Please, that isn't necessary, just send the script there. He's the head of the studio, and I don't want him meeting me in a drugstore."

She repeated in a strange voice, "No, Mr. Wald will meet you at Schwab's drugstore with the script when you finish shooting." Then she hung up.

That evening I drove to Schwab's in my new white convertible Cadillac, and there was Mr. Jerry Wald, head of RKO, chief of production, and possibly now my former friend. I joined him at the counter and said quickly, "Jerry, I left my car double-parked. Please, let's go to the Players or the Marquis or anywhere. This is embarrassing me."

He said, "What the fuck do you think it's doing to me?" He was white with anger, and rightly so. I couldn't understand what had happened that he had personally delivered a script to me at Schwab's. He said, "Why the hell didn't you tell me you knew Howard Hughes?" I replied that I hardly did, that once during the war I had dinner with him at a New Year's Eve party at Sam Spiegel's. Wald looked at me suspiciously. "That's all?" I swore on my brand-new Cadillac's life. He laughed and relaxed. Then he told me what had happened. He was awakened at home at 5:00 A.M. by a phone call from Howard Hughes, who said, "Jerry, when Shelley Winters finishes work this evening, take the script of *Behave Yourself* to her at Schwab's drugstore."

Sleepily Jerry had replied, "Well, Mr. Hughes, I'll send it to her agent, and we'll meet Sunday and discuss it."

Hughes then said, "Jerry, when Shelley finishes work this evening, take the script of *Behave Yourself* to Schwab's drugstore and give it to her."

Jerry said, "Mr. Hughes, I'm busy looking at rushes at that time. I'll have a messenger take it over and leave it for her, and she can pick it up on her way home."

Mr. Howard Hughes then said, "Mr. Wald, if you wish to keep your job, *you* take the script over to Schwab's drugstore, and when Shelley finishes work, *you* will personally give it to her. You understand?" And he hung up.

I was almost crying with embarrassment. Jerry Wald was really a very nice man, and here he was offering me a lovely comedy and the chance to work with my dear friend Farley, and I had unwittingly caused him terrible humiliation. All I could say was: "Jerry, I'm so sorry. I'm going to call up Howard Hughes and tell him he's a son of a bitch."

Wald laughed and put his arm around me. "He already knows that. Besides, I spent my early years as a producer working for Jack Warner. He can give Hughes lessons."

We both laughed, and he ordered us hamburgers and egg creams, and over them he explained to me that there was only one hitch about the film. George Beck, who had written the script,

insisted on directing it. (To my knowledge it was the first and
last picture he ever directed.) But it was a wonderful script, and
Jerry told me he would try to make it one of my free loan-out
films, so I could keep the money. (But UI wanted $100,000 from
Hughes and got it.)

The gangsters would be played by Sheldon Leonard, Marc
Lawrence, Elisha Cook, Jr., and all the other recognizable gangster
types in Hollywood. They had a little dog who was almost human
—in fact, that dog stole the film. Jerry's eyes twinkled as he told
me they were arranging to borrow Farley from Sam Goldwyn; he
knew the movie magazines and gossip columnists would have a
picnic with us working together in the same film.

By the time the *Meet Danny Wilson* peace treaty was ratified
Behave Yourself had started without me. Farley and I had been
blocking and rehearsing every scene at night and weekends, and
we had even shown several of them at a sort of Actors' Studio West
that Arthur Kennedy, Tony Quinn and I had started at the Women's
Club on Highland Avenue. Neither Farley nor I had done this
kind of zany comedy before, and we ran all over Los Angeles and
its environs, looking at old Cary Grant-Katharine Hepburn and
Jean Arthur-Joel McCrea pictures. We also rehearsed with the cute
little dog, whose IQ must have been about 140 and who could
have put Benji to shame. By the time the film started all the director, George Beck, had to do was say, "Action," and, "Cut," and
we shot so quickly that the Production Department always had to
schedule more work than it planned to do. The scared young
writer/director was so delighted with our work that he let us put
in all kinds of shtiks and bits of business, and as the film
progressed, Jerry Wald, George Beck and, I assume, Howard
Hughes found the film a delight.

One day Marvin Hime came on the set with his leather case full
of jewels, and Farley bought me a huge cocktail ring with lots of
diamonds in it. He had been on location that Christmas and had
forgotten my present. It looked a little garish to me, and I wasn't
quite sure what a cocktail ring represented. I assumed it was a sort
of "friendship" ring. He also bought me a miniature silver gray
poodle from the animal trainer, which I adored. Never being a
girl to turn down diamonds, I thanked Farley prettily for the
ring and the dog and wore them both everywhere. We were constantly doing publicity interviews, and the Hollywood Press Corps
chose to believe it was an engagement ring, no matter how much
we kept insisting it was a *friendship* ring. We got tired of wasting

our breath and said the hell with it, let them print what they want, as long as they spell our names right.

One day they were shooting a long scene with the gangsters and the dog, so Farley and I had a leisurely, delicious lunch at Lucey's. The headwaiter brought me a phone and whispered with terror, "It's for you, Miss Winters. Mr. Sam Goldwyn." I didn't know Mr. Goldwyn except casually when I had worked on his lot years before in *Knickerbocker Holiday* and Connie had introduced us. But from the beginning of our phone conversation I realized that he knew me. He seemed to be rather concerned about the possibility of Farley's getting married. In those days—in fact, now, too—executive producers feel it's better for the careers of young leading men if they remain single. I guess they feel that then every girl in the country can fantasize about herself being *his* bride. But in those days, much more so than now, producers loved to manipulate their stars' private lives.

Farley listened on the same phone while Mr. Goldwyn told me that he admired my work and felt that all the publicity Farley and I were getting in the movie magazines was very important for our careers. Then he floored me with this statement and sent Farley under the table with suppressed laughter. "Shelley," he said, "if you and Farley get married, I'll give you a big present. But if you and Farley *don't* get married, I will give you an even bigger present." All I could think of was to thank him on both counts and tell him that we had no plans whatsoever for getting married, and I wasn't so sure we were even engaged. We were just sort of engaged to be engaged. "Well, darlink," he said, "keep me posted," and hung up.

Farley and I were still laughing when we got back to the set at about two-thirty. They were doing the close-up of the dog, and Johnny Meyers, Howard Hughes's only visible contact, was waiting for us. Hughes had reached that period in his life when he was mostly invisible. He still talked on the phone, but Johnny Meyers supervised his artistic holdings and reported back to him. Johnny told us that Mr. Hughes was very pleased with the rushes and especially so about how thin and beautiful I looked. I thanked Johnny and told him that my wardrobe was beautiful. I think that was the first time Edith Head had dressed me, and my clothes were chic and flattering and expensive. I mean, I was playing your average suburban housewife!

Johnny told me that Mr. Hughes wanted me to keep my wardrobe, including the mink jacket, as soon as they had a final cut of the picture and that Farley could keep his expensive suits, too. I told Johnny to thank Mr. Hughes; then I said jokingly, "The assistant director tells me we are going to finish two days ahead of schedule. Won't that save RKO a lot of money?" Johnny nodded. "Well, I just read that TWA circles the globe now. I have never been to Europe, and Farley's been there only once for a couple of weeks. Wouldn't it be great if he and I continued our 'engagement to be engaged' in New York, London, Paris, Rome, Athens, Cairo, Ceylon, Hong Kong, Tokyo, Manila, Hawaii and back to Los Angeles?"

Farley was again on the floor laughing, but Johnny seemed to take the suggestion seriously. "Would you two really like to take a trip like that and do publicity for the film?"

Farley stood up quickly and shouted, "You bet we would!"

Johnny said, "It sounds like good publicity for both TWA and RKO. I'll talk to Mr. Hughes about it."

I continued shooting the rest of the day in a sort of daze. I was strictly an all-American girl and was even nervous the one time I drove through Canada, so why had I jokingly suggested going around the world? Sure enough, the next day Johnny Meyers arrived on the set with two thick first-class TWA tickets divided into many sections, going east from L.A., around the world and back to L.A., with stopovers in any city or country that TWA serviced. So when *Behave Yourself* finished, we spent a couple of days getting our passports, visas and vaccinations and buying hot and cold clothes.

I finally got around to really packing, and one day the phone rang, and Marilyn answered it. With a dazed look she said, "It's Howard Hughes and he wants to talk to you."

I took the phone and said, "Hello, Mr. Hughes."

"Don't you call me Hugh anymore, Shelley, now that you're a big star?" I laughed and thanked him for the lovely film, the clothes and the wonderful TWA trip around the world. Then he said in a very serious voice, "Shelley, you and Farley are getting wonderful press. But just because I gave you this trip does not mean you really have to get married. It's a great publicity stunt for the picture, and you'll get a great deal of romantic coverage. The foreign film market is getting very important. But you've already had one divorce in your young life, so don't you marry anybody unless you're absolutely sure you want to spend the rest of your life with him. That's a hard decision for an actress to make. Men have a habit of believing that their wives should live where they are, and actresses usually go where their pictures are being shot. I've seen *Behave Yourself* and *A Place in the Sun,* and you are a very gifted actress and comedienne."

I thanked him, and he hung up. I felt somewhat sad. He sounded so alone. Marilyn whispered, "Shelley, you didn't even have him on your list. Why?"

I said something odd, even for me. "Because I like him and he really likes and respects me. I wish I could be his friend."

Marilyn thought about that, then said, "You could do that only if you were a recluse. They're saying around Twentieth that he's seeing a new girl, Jean Peters. They meet on the top of Lookout Mountain at midnight once a week." I looked at her sharply, but she just stared back innocently.

The "engaged to be engaged" couple was finally ready. Our families saw us off, and I was flashing my diamond cocktail ring, diamond wristwatch and mink coat and carrying my sable stole. Who knows, maybe it would be freezing in Europe, even though it was June. I have never been able to travel light, even though I've traveled hundreds of thousands of air miles and done pictures all over the world. But on that trip I had only six large suitcases and one slightly smaller one filled with makeup and Schwab's complete line of pharmaceutical goods in case I got anything or drank the local water.

After we had posed for innumerable photos against the TWA logo, Farley and I collapsed in our seats. The stewardess brought us a bottle of champagne, and Farley asked me why I looked so frightened. I had to tell him the truth. I wasn't afraid of flying—I had flown to and from New York many times—but I guess I had been traumatized by the stories I had heard about Europe: the pogroms, the escape via steerage and the recent holocaust. Farfel —that's what I called him when we were alone—put his arms around me. "Don't be silly. There's an enormous, beautiful and ancient culture in Europe, the Middle East and the Orient that we must get to know. Once you're there you'll love it, and everyone will love you, Shell."

When we arrived in New York, we were met by John Springer, a young publicist RKO was sending along to make sure Farley and I behaved ourselves. The entire New York Press Corps was there, as were white orchids for me and a white carnation for Farley, as well as a beautiful white limousine and a four-motorcycle police escort with white helmets. While we were being interviewed and photographed by TV and the press, I managed, panic-stricken, to ask Farley if John was taking us directly to a church to get married. "Don't be silly," he reassured me. "We have to take this trip around the world first."

The limousine and the motorcycle escort whisked us to the front entrance of the Plaza. I tried to argue with John that we had planned to stay at my little apartment hotel, while Farley kept muttering under his breath, "I don't like the Plaza. It's too big."

John gave us a disgusted look and said, "Christ, don't you two know how to act like movie stars? Besides, RKO is paying for it."

There were a lot of fans in front of the hotel screaming for our autographs. It was all happening too fast. John swept us past the desk, as he had already registered us, followed by six bellboys with our luggage and keys. The elevator whisked us up to a top-floor suite which gave lip service to the morals of the time by having two bedrooms with an enormous living room between. It contained a bar with an icebox and baskets of flowers from Howard Hughes, Jerry Wald, Universal, RKO and Paramount. There were bottles of every kind of booze imaginable on the bar from Sam Goldwyn and champagne in an ice bucket from the Plaza management. On the cocktail table there was a huge tray of cheese, crackers and cookies under an orange cellophane wrapping from the Theatre Guild. And even though Judy Garland was singing "I love New York in June, how about you?" on a phonograph, the whole thing somehow reminded me of an Irish wake. I was exhausted from the flight, nervous about all the publicity we had to do, my arm was hurting from my vaccination and I really didn't want to go to Europe. Farley looked at me and said, "Gee, we never have to go out. Everything's here. We can stay here until we have to catch the Sunday plane to London." I responded with a scared laugh. He kissed me and said, "Come on, as soon as we get all the suitcases in the right bedrooms [the bellhops had mixed them up hopelessly], we'll walk down Fifth Avenue and spend money. I know shopping is your favorite occupation next to eating."

I told him I had a terrible headache. "Please, Farfel, if I don't take a shower and a nap, I'll be good for nothing tonight." We had a press conference at cocktail time, tickets for a hit show and dinner at Sardi's with Leonard Lyons and Earl Wilson. The rest of our time was free.

He took our week's publicity schedule out of my hand and said, "Okay, you do that. I'll visit some of my New York pals. I'll be back at four, and we'll get dressed and paint the town." When he left, I locked the doors, put the chains on and took a very hot, then cold shower. Afterward I put on a flannel nightgown, opened my pharmaceutical suitcase and took two strong headache pills. I sat on the bed and looked out at the beautiful view over Central Park. The last time I had seen it I had been with Burt.

Two tears rolled down my cheeks. I knew I had three months of vacation and fun in front of me. Had I become so habituated to work, practically sixteen hours a day, that the idea of having fun terrified me? True, I was going to a psychiatrist, but I couldn't be that crazy! Nevertheless, I got into bed with my heating pad clutched to my chest. Even though it was quite a warm June day, I was very cold. I finally dozed off, wondering why I felt so frightened and lonely. I had returned to my beloved New York a movie star knocking down two grand a week. My agent was waiting with many good scripts for me, and I was with a handsome friend, a wonderful boy, who loved me dearly. Why was I in despair?

I pulled Shelley—the Movie Star—Winters together and plunged into a whirlwind week of interviews, with Farley being questioned by columnists and serious magazine writers about Hitchcock's method of work, and me about George Stevens.

Farley dragged me through the Metropolitan and Modern Art and Frick museums for three days! When I complained that my feet hurt, he told me to buy some comfortable shoes. I got myself some very unattractive flat ones with gum soles and tried again. I saw so many pictures that all the centuries and schools of great art blurred. Farley didn't notice. He kept eagerly promising me the Tate Gallery in London, the Louvre in Paris, the Prado in Madrid and the treasures of the Vatican and Florence with a thousand of Michelangelo's glories. I absolutely refused to go to the Prado in Spain. Franco was very much in power then, and the memory of all my amputee friends who had been in the Abraham Lincoln Brigade was still very much in my heart. I didn't want to spend five cents to keep the Franco government in power; it could get its tourists somewhere else. I used Sam Goldwyn's phrase and said, "When it comes to Spain, include me out."

I didn't realize it then, but Farley was preparing me for an enormous culture shock. He had been to Europe for a short time and had been to Japan in the Navy, so he understood that America was a very young country, and for actors it was very important to be acquainted with all the cultures and art mankind had produced.

One of the unexpected bonuses of visiting museums was that John and the press would disappear. We knew John meant well and was making sure we were on the front pages almost every day, but sometimes we didn't want to be Movie Stars. We just wanted to wander around Greenwich Village and listen to earnest young performers sing protest songs in coffee bars. That was the beginning of the Beat Generation, and its poetry, music and literature were powerful and fascinating. Farley and I were followed everywhere, and although the fans were nice kids, I longed for some privacy. There was no way of disguising ourselves in New York, especially if I opened my mouth. I told Farley that when we got to Paris, I wanted to stay in an unfashionable hotel; I wanted us to be alone the first time he showed me Paris. He agreed with me.

As the day of our departure approached, I began to get more irritable. Besides, my clothes were getting too tight. We were having wonderful breakfasts at the Plaza, huge lunches at "21" and suppers at the chicest restaurants. We also squeezed in five plays.

When we arrived back at our hotel suite after the Saturday matinee, we found the entire Actors' Studio there, busily calling room service. During one of my flying visits, I had promised them a posh party. They were taking me up on it. There were about fifty kids in the suite, and most of them ordered steak, some two steaks. When I apologized to John for this imposition, he told me that Mr. Hughes himself had okayed it. All the future great actors in the cinema were there to help us celebrate the Betrothal. I think the crowd included Maureen Stapleton, Geraldine Page, Eli Wallach, Anne Jackson and Jimmy Dean, among others.

Our TWA clipper was to leave Sunday night at nine; that meant we had to be at the airport at seven. The plane would stop in Gander, Shannon and then Gatwick Airport near London. John had arranged our engagement party for four that afternoon in the Palm Court of the Plaza, and the three of us would leave for the airport directly from the party.

By this time both Farley and I were a little dazed by this official engagement. But the party was so frenzied, with so many photographers, that nobody listened to our doubts and uncertainties about spending the rest of our lives together. All I do remember of the party is that my eyes were blinded from the flashbulbs and that at one point I went to the ladies' room to take off my tight girdle because it was killing me and put it in a paper bag I found. When I came out, I hid the bag under a potted palm in the Palm Court. Finally, it was time to go, and with a superhuman effort Farley managed to get us away from the crowd and into the limousine.

The chauffeur was getting nervous about making it to the airport on time. Suddenly I remembered my expensive girdle and whispered to Farley what I had done. We both rushed back to the Palm Court to find it, the captain and waiters trying to help us, though they didn't know quite what they were looking for, and we *couldn't* tell them. Finally, Farley found it, stuffed it into his coat pocket and we dashed back to the car. Thank God John had arranged for a motorcycle escort to take us back to the airport. Still, the transatlantic clipper had to be delayed five minutes for us. Hughes must have told them to hold it while the press photographed us against the TWA plane.

During the trip Farley and I calmly discussed whether we really were ready to marry, settle down and have a family. In fact, somewhere over the Atlantic we both made lists of the pros and cons of marriage. I think the cons outweighed the pros. But the flight was so long in those days we had to do something.

After dinner and lots of wine Farley and John promptly went to sleep, but I was too restless. I kept looking at the stars and the moon and the sea below me and thought about my father and grandparents leaving the Old World for the New. And the months it had taken them in the steerage of the old ships, and how terrible it must have been to leave their home and friends forever. Going to a new country and a strange language. But my father had firmly believed the streets of America were paved with gold. They hadn't been for him, but in a way they had been for his daughter.

BOOK THREE

My Spaghetti Years

CHAPTER 23

Arriving at Gatwick Airport, we were met by more photographers than had greeted us in New York. London was still experiencing rationing, but it was emerging from its postwar doldrums, and here we were, two of the first American film stars to descend from their TWA chariot, sent especially to give them gossip and fun with their morning newspapers and "cuppa char."

We were also met by two dear friends of Farley's whom he had met during his first trip abroad. They were Peter and Mary Noble, and they have been my close friends ever since. Whenever I go to London, I stay with them in their house on Abbey Road, and when they come to America, they stay with me. Then Mary was a struggling young actress, and Peter an equally struggling young journalist, and he sometimes did bits and pieces for the BBC television and radio. He looked like a younger handsome Alan Ladd, and she was quite dark and exotic. Years later, when I did Nabokov's *Lolita*, Kubrick picked her to play Peter Sellers's mysterious lady friend.

Over the years their special contribution to my life has been that they never take themselves or their worth very seriously, contrary to my New York and Hollywood chums. Every morning they wake up they insist this is a day to have fun and enjoy the beautiful world, their lovely garden and their gorgeous daughters. They have never been much interested in money, but they have managed to go practically all over the world on those cheap British "all in" trips, and often they've dragged me with them. And the only real vacations I've ever taken and had rest and fun have been with the Nobles.

While John arranged our schedule, Farley and I had a few days to ourselves—a whirlwind of Westminster Abbey, the Tower, the silver vaults, the Tate Museum and Fleet Street. With my lifelong fear of unfamiliar places, I suddenly announced to Farley that if it wasn't for the bombed-out areas, the City looked just like Wall Street in New York. Farley could only glare hopelessly at me.

John Gielgud, who knew Farley (and who, I hoped, did not remember me from the elevator incident), gave us *another* engagement cocktail party in his beautiful town house, and all the stars of the British theater and films came and congratulated Farley and wished me luck. (I felt they should have done it the other way around.) It was so crowded I recognized only Olivier and his wife, Vivien Leigh, and Ralph Richardson. *Strangers on a Train* and *A Place in the Sun* had just been released in England, and everyone was bestowing dignified compliments on us.

Very early the next morning the porter got me a small American car with an automatic gearshift, and for once the steering wheel was on the American side. I woke Farley, and we sneaked out of the hotel, leaving a sweet letter for John who would have to cope with canceling interviews with three of the most important London newspapers.

Farley was very sleepy after a late night in Soho, so I let him sleep off his hangover in the back seat. I spread the map out on the seat next to me and drove carefully to Stratford-upon-Avon. There weren't many cars on the road, but the drivers coming toward me were very friendly and kept waving. I waved back, making the Churchill V for Victory sign. Farley slept soundly till we got to a little village just before Stratford. When he woke, I asked him how he was feeling, my eyes on the road, and he began to shout, "Pull over, for God's sake! Pull over on the grass!" I thought he'd had an attack of appendicitis, he was so frantic. When we got out of the car, he was the color of chalk. As I began to feel his stomach, he said quietly, "Have you driven like this all the way from London?"

"Of course, and very well, too."

"I don't believe it," he muttered.

Very irritated, I answered, "I drove very well. We're almost to Stratford-upon-Avon, and British drivers are very friendly. They all waved at me."

"They were trying to wave you over to the other side of the road, dopey. In England they drive on the *left* side of the road."

Then I got frightened, but I defended myself. "Well, it's your fault. You should have come back to the hotel at a decent hour last night and slept, and then I wouldn't have had to drive."

Farley, whose mother was a Christian Scientist, just said, "You are the living proof of the power of positive thinking." He took over the wheel and drove us the rest of the way on the left side which was the right side.

We registered at a quaint inn and then collected our tickets for that night's performance of *Hamlet* with Richard Burton. I know Vittorio Gassman, Laurence Olivier and Albert Finney may disagree with my opinion, but I must say now that Richard Burton's

Hamlet then, when he was so young and his talent was so powerful and mercurial, was the greatest I have ever seen. I felt that Burton was talking to me personally as he posed Hamlet's great questions of life and death and gave his instructions to the actors and spoke his great soliloquies about the purpose or purposelessness of life. At last I understood the feelings that paralyzed Hamlet, and when Hamlet died, both Farley and I wept like children watching *Bambi*.

We had expected to be in awe of the techniques and training of British actors, but we were stunned by Richard Burton's beautiful yet realistic performance. We went backstage feeling like gauche Americans, but we had to tell him how extraordinary we thought he was. He was taking off his makeup with the help of his sweet Welsh wife, Sybil, and he grinned like a kid when we heaped praise on him. They had seen Farley and me in the "flicks," and he seemed to have great respect for our opinions. On impulse Farley invited them to dinner, and they immediately accepted. Sybil told me that Richard had signed a ten-month contract with Stratford, and all the actors in the troupe got paid the same amount, whether they played leads or not. Nine pounds a week—about the equivalent of $30!

They guided us to a great Stratford restaurant which had lovely English roast beef—meat was still rationed except in tourist restaurants—and Yorkshire pudding with all the trimmings. Farley and Richard polished off a quart of Irish whiskey, and Sybil and I a bottle of French wine. We sat in that restaurant until about two in the morning while Richard and Sybil taught us haunting Welsh ballads the melodies and lyrics of which I remember to this day.

Farley and I rushed back to the hotel and slept until it was time to see *Henry V*. As before, Burton was a delight and one of the funniest and cleverest actors I'd seen. His scene with the French Queen was so good that even though it was in French, I felt as if I understood every word.

After dining again at the same restaurant, we all drove back to London together, with several bottles of ale. We drunkenly vowed eternal friendship and exchanged addresses because Richard said he was sure he would be going to Hollywood in a couple of years. I felt sad that this gifted young actor, who had fought his way up from the Welsh mines, needed money so badly that he had to turn his back on the wonderful British theater and go to Hollywood to make money so he and Sybil could afford to have children.

The Festival of Britain, which was a sort of English World's Fair, was about to open, and the BBC got Peter Noble to talk to us about doing its first live television interview from Festival Hall, which was part of the Festival complex. Farley hated these new TV talk shows and could never think of the right answers until after the program was over. John insisted that it would be great publicity, and I nagged him until he agreed.

Meanwhile, we saw all the wonderful British theaters. I remember seeing a play with Ralph Richardson. Then, as now, I believe he is the best actor in the English-speaking theater. Not too long ago I did a so-so film, *Who Slew Auntie Roo?*, in London. It was a sort of rehash of the Hansel and Gretel story, but I had the honor of acting in several scenes with Ralph Richardson. Like most British actors, he pooh-poohs his talent and technique, but he is indeed a master. The only thing that drove me crazy was that although he is in his seventies, he drives to and from work on a motorcycle. When I tried to remonstrate with him about this, he laughed and told me that it used only a thimbleful of petrol, and he had never been one to live out of Britain to save taxes. "I must live in a corner of this blessed earth, this realm, this England." When he did the great Pinter play *No Man's Land* with John Gielgud, I sat spellbound, watching those ostensibly old men hold the audience enthralled. I think we shall never see the like again.

Charles Laughton was also on the British stage that season for the first time in many years. Performing with him was a young actor by the name of Albert Finney, who, Laughton assured me, was a genius. I had never heard him use that word about anyone except Charlie Chaplin. The years have proved Laughton right about Finney, but somehow I have never felt he lived up to his great theater potential; neither Richard Burton and Brando.

Back in London, the shit had hit the fan and the entire British press seemed to be gunning for us. John's head was bloody but unbowed as he kept explaining that we were impetuous romantic kids and had not meant to insult Fleet Street. We had just wanted to see the great theater at Stratford. But the Fourth Estate wasn't buying. (It took me a couple of years to get back on the good side of David Lewin and Roderick Mann, not to mention our dear friend Peter Noble.) Sam Goldwyn wanted John Springer back in New York.

I was very angry about what was being written about our wayward sense of responsibility, and called the American Consul. He told me politely that he thought it would be a good idea if Farley and I left for Paris and continued the publicity for *Behave Yourself* on a more positive note. So John, Farley and I slipped out of

London the next morning and TWA'd it over the Channel to Paris.

For some reason French customs opened all my suitcases. I can't imagine what they thought I was trying to smuggle into their country. The officer inspected my pharmaceutical suitcase, then looked up at the strange American transporting so many medical and feminine supplies, American colognes, toilet paper and cosmetics. "But, Mademoiselle Wintaires," he cried, "we invented all these things in France."

I said, "Okay. On my way out I'll buy another suitcase and fill that one up, too." He saluted and closed all my suitcases for me.

We were met by John's French RKO counterpart, who changed our money and got us a suitcase full of francs. So Farley bought a little convertible Renault, which was enormously expensive and which he then kept full of Blue Bell dancers from the Lido who weren't that attractive with their clothes on.

The modest St. James Hotel, where I had insisted we stay, was near the Place de la Concorde. The very first time Farley and I walked down the Champs-Élysées to the Arc de Triomphe, it was a golden summery day. Cities all have their own special colors; London is a silver blue-gray, Paris is the color of yellow autumn leaves, Rome is siena and Jerusalem is the most beautiful color of all, a sort of shimmering pinkish gold, as if all the treasures inside the churches, temples and mosques had spilled out over the buildings. And one of the most thrilling sights in the world is a Roman dawn with streaks of sunlight radiating from the dome of St. Peter's. Either God or Michelangelo figured it out and built it there to catch the rays of the sun at dawn and sunset.

That day, my first day in Paris, when the language, the statues and the beauty of the city assailed my senses dulled from the gimcracky California architecture, I was depressed by the realization of the millions of things I had not as yet experienced. I have always felt, and still feel, that the French are snobs; the only problem is that they certainly have *what* to be snobbish about. Can you imagine building a Museum of Men's Minds? Can you imagine developing a whole school of art in which the artists broke away from thousands of years of photographic painting to paint light and what it did to objects?

I gazed around the beautiful boulevards at all the elegantly dressed people sitting under yellow and white striped awnings, enjoying leisurely lunches and the art of conversation. I saw the signs that said *Liberté*, *Égalité* and *Fraternité* and remembered that too was what our country had been founded on. It was all too much for me and too sudden. When Farley asked me what I thought of the Champs-Élysées, for some perverse reason I looked him right in the eye and said, "Oh, it's just like the Grand Concourse, that wide street in the Bronx." He slugged me gently, understanding my culture shock and my attempts to find a common denominator in my limited frame of reference to absorb all these new things coming at me.

By the time we got to the Étoile my feet hurt. Farley said we would walk as far as Fouquet's, just another couple of long French blocks, and have lunch there. When we finally arrived we found Stella Adler in one of the chicest and slimmest of black dresses, a feathered hat, pearls and white gloves. As well as six of the handsomest young Frenchmen I'd ever seen. She immediately asked us to join them, and as I collapsed in a chair, I looked around. Although I had on a rather expensive Saks Fifth Avenue summer dress, compared to the chic Frenchwomen in the restaurant, I looked like somebody's maid. They all obviously spent their mornings at their hairdressers. Even the seams of their stockings were exactly straight, and they wore immaculate handmade lizard shoes—I guess their feet never hurt. I'm convinced that European feet are narrower than American feet, and Frenchwomen don't believe in hips, so they never develop any. Certainly not the upper classes.

Stella asked me what I thought of Paris, and Farley quickly stuck a peach in my mouth. Stella proceeded to order lunch for us, and I just have to mention the dessert—the greatest little wild strawberries ever, with something called *crème fraiche*. The wine was cold and white and strong. I knew right then and there that if we stayed in Paris very long, I wouldn't be able to go back to work at Universal; I'd have to get a job as the fat lady in a circus.

Stella asked where we were staying, and when Farley told her, she made a face. "Children, you must live like the celebrities you are." She pointed to a big billboard across the boulevard heralding the arrival of *La Tragédie américaine*, and my name was billed first. The billboard for *Strangers on a Train* was down the block. Stella said we must stay at the Plaza-Athenée or the Georges V, and I told her I really wanted to see Paris, not just do publicity all the time. She laughed and said, "Tomorrow I'll take you both to the flea market, the Left Bank, Christian Dior, Montmartre and Notre Dame. And I can get you a special rate at the Georges Cinq, and you must move there in a few days." When I told her it didn't matter because Howard Hughes was paying for everything, she said, "Shelley, I suspect you of reverse snobbery." She gave me a shrewd look and said, "I hear Howard Hughes is a bit of an eccentric and hides in out-of-the-way places and drives old green Fords. But you were born of poor people, so you must learn how to enjoy money. It's one of the first things a cultivated person must learn to do."

She was so outrageous and elegant I laughed and said, "Stella, you be my teacher. I'm willing to learn."

The prospect of all these additional activities exhausted me, so Farley took me back to the hotel, then went to the Lido to collect his Blue Bell show girls.

At eight the next morning Stella took us to the flea market, where I didn't buy any antiques but *really* caught fleas. I hobbled through Notre Dame, up the Eiffel and around the Louvre, and we finally arrived for lunch at Deux Magots, where Juliette Greco was singing among the tables, and everyone knew Stella. Many hot political arguments were in progress, and I could have killed myself that I hadn't paid attention in my French class at high school.

Stella had seats for the Christian Dior showing at three. Naturally, Farley wanted to see Montmartre, so Stella and I went alone. As we walked up the Champs-Élysées to the salon, Stella asked about "the engagement," and I told her I didn't think Farley really wanted to settle down yet.

At the Christian Dior showroom we sat on little gold chairs while the line was modeled by the skinniest, most beautiful girls I've ever seen. There was a strange attractive blonde woman sitting across the showroom whose secretary was writing down the number of every dress that went by. In the meager French I had by now acquired from a phrase book, I haltingly asked our saleslady who the woman was. "Eva Perón," she hissed. I stared so openly that Stella finally jabbed me in the ribs.

One dress caught my eye. It had a black velvet top, a square décolletage and a black satin and gold striped skirt. I asked Stella how much it was, and she rapidly computed the francs into dollars. It was $600. I just about fainted. Then $600 was comparable to about $3,000 now, and it was only a cocktail dress. But Stella insisted that I stay after the show and try the dress on, and perhaps she could get Christian Dior to make one for me at a discount, just to get me into the habit of buying French couturier dresses so that I would popularize them in America. Trembling, I stayed with her after the show, and a model came out in the dress to show it to me again. Eva Perón was talking in Spanish, which Stella understood. She told me that Eva Perón had bought every dress in the show, in every color that Dior was willing to make it in. I said something like: "I wonder if she knows that she's spending money made from the blood of her people."

Our chic saleslady, who up to that moment had not spoken or understood English, smiled and said in faultless English, "But, madame, isn't all money made of the people's blood, more or less?" I guiltily tried on the dress in front of my Marxist saleslady, and Stella got the price reduced to $500. I bought it in a moment of sheer insanity. They took my measurements and said I must have two more fittings while they made a canvas pattern and heavy silk lining, and the whole thing would be sewn by hand.

I wore that dress only about three times, and then it hung in my closet for years. I could never enjoy wearing it, although it looked lovely on me. I still keep thinking of the little French *modistes* sewing their eyes out with the millions of little stitches and coughing their lungs out like Mimi in *La Bohème*.

Farley and I were spending so much money—on cars, couturier clothes, paintings and perfumes—that one morning we decided we'd better end our French connection and get out of Paris while we still had some traveler's checks left. I had had my fill of European Cultural Activities and wanted to go home to L.A. But Farley insisted we go to Rome at least, so we packed hurriedly and dashed to Orly Airport, where we found that the next TWA flight was leaving for Rome.

When we arrived at Ciampino Airport, there were zillions of photographers waiting for us. How did they know we were on that airplane when we hadn't even known we were going to take it? But they posed us prettily up against the TWA signs, and I prayed that Howard Hughes saw all the photos. We drove into Rome in caravan, we in one cab, our increasing luggage in another, the *paparazzi* close behind, and finally arrived at the Excelsior Hotel.

If I had loved Paris, I adored Rome. It even seemed familiar, as if I had been there before. It was the middle of the tourist season, and we had no reservations, but when the manager arrived, he quickly found us two lovely rooms with an adjoining balcony. I took a hot bath in an even larger bathtub than the one in Paris. While I was bathing, a beautiful Roman bellhop brought in two large bouquets of flowers and a box of candy from the Roman UI and RKO offices. Although he kept bowing and saying, "*Scusi, scusi,*" and I kept burying myself in the soapy water and covering myself with a very small washcloth, he didn't leave. He just kept bowing and saying, "*Scusi.*" How had he gotten in? I'd locked the door. For a minute I was afraid he was going to scrub my back or get in the tub with me. I finally screamed, *"Farley!"* and Farley dashed across the balcony, and since he spoke some Italian, he tipped and dismissed this Italian peeping Tom. To my righteous indignation he just answered, "Oh, that's an Old Roman Custom." For the next ten days I was to hear that explanation for the most outlandish things I'd ever experienced.

Farley wanted to start right in on the museums and ruins, but my feet had had enough culture for a while, and all I wanted to do was sit on the Via Veneto and indulge in the favorite Italian sport: STARING. In those days the Via Veneto was the headquarters of *la dolce vita*, although the film hadn't been made yet. Farley seemed to know everyone. The *paparazzi* were really insatiable, following and photographing us constantly.

The next day Farley and I decided to disguise ourselves and separate and try to do some shopping. I walked down the Via Sistina, which curves down to the Spanish Steps, below which are the beautiful expensive shops on the Via Condotti. On the way I passed a little shop which was obviously newly opened. It had a sign in the window, ANNA, and one beautifully made dress. Inside I saw a young girl, a small boy and a sewing machine. I went in.

On a table there were many copies of international fashion magazines. The young girl said good morning in Neapolitan, which surprisingly I understood, I guess because of my childhood friend Lucy and all her Neapolitan brothers. Anna spoke a little English, and later I got the feeling that her little boy's father had been an American soldier.

I understood almost everything as Anna showed me that she was a talented dressmaker and needed the work very badly because it had taken all her capital to open this little shop. She explained to me that all I had to do was pick out a dress from any of the fashion magazines, go to a fabric shop with her to pick out the fabric, and she would make me an exact copy for the lira equivalent of about $15. I looked through the magazines and picked out six dresses and told her I had to pay a minimum of $25 each.

Anna locked the shop, took me by the hand, and we walked a few blocks to one of the loveliest fabric shops I had ever been in. Her little boy came along, importantly carrying the magazines. We sat on a bench in the corner, and she showed me swatches, carefully cutting a piece from those I liked. She then proceeded to give one of the most dramatic performances I've ever witnessed. For the next two hours she harangued the manager of the shop. I had obviously chosen the most expensive wools, silks and velvets, but Anna disparaged them and threw them around the shop. I just sat there, sure we all were going to be arrested, including her little boy, who had joined his mother and was kicking the stuff around. Later I was to find out that this was the normal bargaining procedure for Italian dressmakers. When the shop closed at one, we had everything Anna needed for my six outfits, the finest and most luxurious fabrics, all for less than $100. Somehow I now felt better about the $500 I'd spent on the Christian Dior dress. I didn't care if the dresses came out well or not.

During the next week Farley took me all over Rome, to the Appian Way and to the beach at Ostia, where we ate wonderful little black mussels steamed in garlic butter which popped open like peanuts, revealing the succulent insides. They were the most delicious shellfish I've ever eaten.

I couldn't understand Farley's preoccupation with the ruins. They all looked the same to me, and I couldn't understand why they were supposed to be romantic.

A week later Anna phoned, and I went back to the little shop on the Via Sistina to try on the dresses. They were expertly cut and carefully basted together and fitted as beautifully as anything that had ever been designed for me in Hollywood. I couldn't compliment Anna enough. I insisted on giving her another $200, which she really didn't want to take, and I told her to make herself a dress. Then she showed me a rack of dresses in back of the shop which were being readied for other customers. I told her to take her time finishing mine, and if I couldn't come back for a final fitting, Universal's representative would pick them up and ship them to me in Hollywood. She kissed me and said I had brought her luck, and I gave her an autographed picture for her window.

Farley was quite late getting back from a luncheon appointment with Luchino Visconti discussing *Senso*, a film Visconti was planning. I walked up the Via Veneto to the old Roman wall facing the Villa Borghese. I decided to turn right and walked a block or so, and there in front of me, draped from a building, was the white flag of Israel with the blue Star of David in its center. And there on the building, written in Hebrew, Italian and English, was a plaque that said "Embassy of the State of Israel." I stood there, and with my Zayda to the left of me and my Bubba to the right, we marched in.

A girl at the desk said, "*Shalom*," I said, "*Shalom*," back at her and then realized she had almost said my name in Hebrew, which is Shalomet. When I asked her why she had done that, she explained that *shalom* meant "hello," "good-bye," but especially "peace."

I answered, "But that's sort of my name."

She said, "Oh, in that case you're here to get a visa to go to Israel."

"Certainly, and Farley Granger wants one, too. Do we need any special papers?"

Back at the hotel, Farfel, darling and agreeable as ever, said, "I always knew you were going to change our grand tour into a religious pilgrimage, but I'm not having any part of that. I'll just go along for the ruins. They're older in the Holy Land."

The TWA plane headed for Israel, packed with Hassidim, young boys going to Israel to make their Bar Mitzvahs, nuns and priests on pilgrimages, very old Jewish men and women going to Israel to die, Arab holy men, refugees from Eastern Europe making their escape to the homeland, Jews from all over the world going for their *aliyah*, and American businessmen with their eyes on the new expanding market in the Middle East. As we approached Tel Aviv, the sun was setting, and suddenly I heard strange chanting. We were in the front of the plane, and when I looked back, I saw all the religious Jewish men and boys facing the front of the plane toward the Holy Land, Israel, their prayer shawls over their heads, weeping, singing and praying.

I was suddenly overcome with the knowledge that like every other Jewish person on that plane, I was returning after the centuries of the Diaspora. When we landed and I put my foot on Israeli soil, Shelley Winters, Movie Star, knelt and kissed the earth of Israel.

CHAPTER 24

Farley and I had a rather difficult time separating ourselves, my jewel cases and furs, from the pilgrims with their boxes of rosaries, crates of chickens—one of which had broken open—and a baby who got lost walking from the airplane to Passport Control. When our suitcases arrived, the customs officers went through them with a fine-tooth comb. Farley and I were beginning to feel like spies from the Universal film *A Sword in the Desert*. While we waited patiently, a gentleman by the name of Jacob Ben-Ari, who had been the technical adviser on that film and whom I had met at UI while they were shooting, spotted us and came rushing over. He was on some diplomatic mission and was leaving for Geneva in a few minutes. He was very angry that Farley and I had not been greeted in an official manner, but we explained that we had hardly known we were coming ourselves. He said something in angry Hebrew to the customs officials, and they quickly shut our suitcases, brushed off our clothes with whisk brooms, apologized and handed us a very cold orange drink that tasted as though it had been made from orange lollipops. We appreciated the gesture as it had been a hot, dusty journey from the airplane to the customs shed.

Mr. Ben-Ari made a couple of phone calls, then told us to wait there, and Azarria Rappaport, a young journalist who had been an actor, and his girlfriend would pick us up in a few minutes and take us to the Katy Dunn Hotel, which was the only hotel in Tel Aviv at that time. They would act as our guides wherever we wanted to go in Israel. Then Mr. Ben-Ari left reluctantly as his plane was about to take off.

About twenty-five minutes later a handsome young man and a beautiful sabra girl showed up, speaking a sort of English, and in in a few minutes we realized they were the Israeli equivalent of Peter and Mary Noble. They drove us along a rough, dusty road into Tel Aviv, apologizing all the way for everything, until Farley reminded them that we knew that the state was only two years old and they were straining all their economic capacities to absorb the hundreds of thousands of displaced persons from the refugee camps in Europe and emigrants from the Arab countries. They were not prepared for tourists, we knew, and we had not come to live in luxury. Both kids gave us big grins and told us how happy they were to have us there. We were the first American movie stars to come to Israel as tourists.

The windows of the car were closed tightly against the dust, but I was enchanted with everything. Farley kept noticing the eternal Roman ruins; the ancient Roman aqueducts were still being used to irrigate the fields, and the Israelis had built thousands of similar ones to irrigate the barren deserts. Enormous fields of little trees had been planted, and it was quite a sight to see. Hundreds of men, women and children were working in the fields, manually and with small tractors and carts with oxen.

Suddenly I realized I was not experiencing the sense of panic and fear I had had in almost every new country we'd visited, even though there was a realistic reason to be frightened. There were still sporadic battles with the Arabs, and the British still had not evacuated completely. But I wasn't fearful and didn't want Israel to be anything other than what it was, the State of Israel, the long-dreamed-of homeland of so many of my ancestors who had roamed the world.

When we arrived at the Katy Dunn Hotel, I found it was like one of the Borscht Circuit *kochalayns*, with an enormous serve-yourself dining room. Everyone there spoke Russian as well as a little Hebrew; now and then I could hear a few scraps of Yiddish, so I knew I was in the right country.

For the next few days Azarria and Ruthie, his fiancée, drove us all over Israel as well as to beautiful Jerusalem, where we stood in front of the weird Mandelbaum Gate, where people could come from Jordan into Israel but could not go the other way. The Arabs had begun their campaign of refusing to recognize the existence of the tiny State of Israel, and they repeatedly propagandized their resolve to push it into the sea. When I look at the map of that area of the world, I wonder how the United Nations stood for this policy for so many years. The enormous unpopulated Arab territory covers more than a continent, while Israel is not much bigger than Rhode Island.

I kept looking at the young people walking up and down the avenues with their arms around each other on this warm spring night, and if I hadn't known better, I would have thought I was in a town in Iowa. I'm not exactly sure what I had expected, but most of the kids looked like farmers from our Middle West. Most of the young people spoke Hebrew by then, but you would hear couples speaking Russian, German, Yugoslav, Polish, Czech, Hungarian,

Lithuanian and Arabic. Nearly everyone was trilingual at least. It was a very happy evening, and the only jarring thing was that since everyone had summery short-sleeved clothes on, every now and then I would see an inner arm with a number tattooed on it. When I went to bed that night, the last thought I had before I fell asleep was: Why had it taken Hitler and all those tattooed arms to force the world to bring Israel back into existence?

The next afternoon we all got into Azarria's little car—the government was supplying the gasoline—and drove about an hour and a half to someplace way out in the Negev. There, in a natural amphitheater with thousands of other people, we listened to the glorious Israeli Symphony Orchestra with Isaac Stern and watched the extraordinary Tel Aviv Ballet Company reenact in modern dance some of Israel's ancient history. Azarria had brought a blanket from the car for us to sit on because the night had gotten quite cold.

As the evening progressed, I became friendly with a woman sitting next to me who was a teacher from South Africa. She was a member of a kibbutz about five miles up the road, and she told me how happy she was teaching the young Israeli children English and math and how at last she had become proficient in Hebrew. All her life in South Africa, although she'd lived in comparative luxury, she had felt herself "a stranger in a strange land" with the ever-present apartheid. As the orchestra started to play the *Hatikva*, she casually asked me if I wouldn't like the experience of living on her kibbutz for two or three days and seeing her children. It would take us two hours to walk there. I informed Azarria and Farley that that was what I was going to do. Farley protested, saying, "But we have tickets for *Detective Story* in Haifa. We have to see the Roman ruins in Caesarea. How can you, who are scared of everything, wander off into the desert with a strange woman you don't even know?" But Azarria understood. There was no way for me to explain to Farley that she wasn't a stranger but in some way was almost a sister.

I told Farley I would meet him back in Tel Aviv in two or three days, and when the program was over, I set off into the desert with my new friend. When we arrived at the kibbutz, there were still a few people playing chess in the social hall, and they welcomed me in Hebrew, Yiddish and broken English. They gave me a very nice simple room, bottled mineral water, oranges, grapes and cheese, then told me they would call me at seven.

The next morning I woke, happy and full of energy, to find a young handsome Israeli boy with an automatic rifle over his shoulder, sitting on my doorstep. He shook my hand many times and with gestures and a kiss on the cheek managed to convey that he'd seen me in the movies but that I was prettier in person. I quickly got into jeans while he sat on the steps, singing beautiful Hebrew songs. When I was ready, he was singing one that Mr. Manischewitz had taught us in junior high school. It went: "*Annoo banoo atsalivnon delaheba naught baa. . . .*" I helped him finish the song in my high school Brooklyn Hebrew, and he was overjoyed at my knowing it. I had never known exactly what the words meant, but later the South African teacher explained that it was a pioneer song about building the State of Israel.

After I'd had a very substantial breakfast, my young Israeli farmer-soldier showed me everything: the orange groves, experimental tangerine groves, the chicken farms with all the chickens running wildly away from the roosters, the nesting barns, the young children gathering eggs that were fertilized and the egg-candling Quonset huts. A lot of work seemed to be getting done, but there was no assembly-line atmosphere. I gathered that all Israelis are individualists, and each one does his job in his own way or he won't do it.

We visited the infants' nursery, and the nurse in charge let me give a bottle of milk to a very small two-year-old whose parents had been killed while working in the fields. Although the baby was too young to understand what had happened, she wasn't eating very well and wasn't growing. I sat under a tree with this beautiful little baby in my arms, and for whatever reason I began to cry. The baby seemed to want to console me and played with my hair and drank her milk quickly. The nurse thought we should try some oatmeal, which the child hadn't been eating, and I got them to mash some banana in it. I played and laughed with the baby, and she ate most of it.

Until that moment I had never felt such love for any human being as I did for that child. I tried to convince the South African teacher that they should allow me to adopt her and take her back to California with me since she was a poor orphan and I was making a lot of money. At great length the teacher explained to me that the baby was an Israeli sabra, and it was against the laws of the kibbutz and the country to give her away. She shyly suggested that perhaps the solution was for me to come and work on the kibbutz and have my own children. She was pretty sure I'd have no trouble finding a husband as there were twice as many men as women there.

At about three o'clock a general alarm sounded, and everyone raced back to the social hall. The Arabs were strafing the fields, but we didn't know if it was a real attack or if the Arabs were bored that day and just practicing. With precision the Israelis got the 500 men, women and children into the concrete building, and for the next half hour we all lay under the tables on the floor while sharp-shooters returned the fire. At that time it was such a common occurrence that they didn't even phone the Army in Tel Aviv for help. As we had walked around the orange groves that morning, I had noticed the romantic-looking Arabs in white flowing robes up in the hills, and it was a shock to realize they had machine guns at the ready under them. When the strafing stopped, everyone went back to work.

That night everyone did Israeli square dances, and I saw the children playing with their mothers and fathers, kissing them and being given sweets, and parents helping with homework. My South African teacher explained that every child called every adult mama and papa in Hebrew, and every adult considered every child his child.

I went back to my bungalow and cried bitterly for about an hour, then stopped and began to have a conversation with myself. What was I doing with my life? I didn't really want to be a movie star; I wanted to be a fine actress, a responsible citizen and a mother. How had my life taken this crazy path away from what I wanted? I wanted my career, but I also equally needed a home and family. Why had I allowed myself to become engaged to Farley, who had not the slightest intention of settling down and having a family or even having a permanent home? (In later years Farley got engaged to Janice Rule, but when they sent out the wedding invitations, he suddenly decided he had to go see Thailand first. That was the end of the engagement. Only recently Farley did finally take his furniture out of storage, where it had been for twenty years.) But that night in the kibbutz I finally knew that no matter what I accomplished in my career, if I didn't have a family and a home, all the rest would be ashes.

The next morning I realized that although everyone was going out of his way to show me everything and be extra nice to me, they all had very definite jobs to do, and I was a distraction. Since no one was driving to Tel Aviv, I assured my South African teacher friend that I knew how to hitchhike, and at lunchtime she took me down to the main road. Tel Aviv was only about two hours away, but I promised I would phone her as soon as I got back to the Katy Dunn. I stood there alone in the broiling sun for half an hour before an elderly couple driving an old truck loaded with garden vegetables gave me a lift. I managed to squeeze into the cab with them. They were obviously immigrants and spoke only German and Hebrew. I guess I looked so strange that they didn't even try Yiddish on me. After about an hour of silent driving, the man said to his wife in Yiddish, "What is this pretty blonde *shiksa* wandering around the desert for? Maybe she's an Arab or a British spy."

I quickly explained in my Brooklyn Yiddish and my Zayda's German that I was a famous *actrissa* from Hollywood, doing tourism in Israel. They looked shocked. When they dropped me at the Katy Dunn, the woman managed to say to me in three languages, "It doesn't look nice for a good Jewish girl to run all over the world alone. You should settle here already. You'll find a handsome husband, he'll make a good living and you'll raise some beautiful Israeli children." Oh, why didn't I listen to her? We kissed each other good-bye, and they gave me some fresh vegetables.

Farley had left me a rather complicated note that he was off to Beersheba with the Rappaports for a special lunch and that he'd received a cable and we had to go back to Paris in two days to meet his agent and Sam Goldwyn, who wanted to have a long talk with him. So we would go back to Paris and have some more fun; he would have his conference and ship his Renault back to L.A. via the Panama Canal. Then we would fly to Ceylon, Hong Kong, Tokyo, Manila and Hawaii, then back to L.A.

We had one more day of tourism left, and I don't know how we did it, but we saw Jerusalem, Nazareth and King Solomon's Temple. Farley had a glorious time as we looked mostly at ruins. Jerusalem at dawn was indeed golden, and the sounds of church bells and Jewish prayers and Arab chanting filled the air. The sights and sounds of Jerusalem were such a profound mystical experience that I, who do not believe in mysticism, cannot even begin to describe it. We wandered around the famous sights, and I never opened my mouth. My companions began to think I was sick because usually I never shut up. In Nazareth, Farley, my sophisticated, atheistic, blasé friend, was also rather silent. He bought some kind of ancient coin for his mother, and I think secretly one for himself, too.

It was dusk when we got to the ruins of King Solomon's Temple, and we seemed to be the only people there. I remembered it from my Zayda's early stories about the wisdom of King Solomon, and I thought it was disappointingly small for the ruins of such a famous king's palace. As everyone was turning around to go back to the car, I leaned down and picked up a very, very small stone. I knew that in the years to come, if every tourist did that, pretty soon there wouldn't be any ruins left, but my spirit was sorely in need of Solomon's wisdom. There was a hazy sunset over the landscape, and I could hear the voices of Farley, Ruthie and Azarria from about 200 meters down the road, going back toward the car.

When I looked up, there was a man smiling at me. He was about twenty feet away and had on an old reddish brown robe; he had longish hair and was leaning on a staff. I thought he was the caretaker, so I guiltily dropped the stone. His smile became luminous. I figured that he spoke only Hebrew because he pointed to the stone and gestured for me to take it. I picked it up again and then, looking at his shining face, thanked him the only way I knew how to. Not with words, but with my eyes and thoughts. I had long known that actors communicate with each other this way, and as I looked at that lovely man, we somehow had the following conversation without any words. I told him I was troubled and confused and my life seemed a mess and that I wanted a baby and a home and a husband, but my life seemed to push me in the opposite direction from what I so deeply needed.

"Shalomet," he said, "be at peace. You will soon have what you want. Get off the plane at Rome. But remember, even life is not forever."

I thanked him and ran back to my companions and asked, "Azarria, is that man the caretaker of the temple?" We all looked back to where I had been standing, but there was no one there. But I still had the stone in my hand. His instructions were so explicit that I was suddenly happy and secure, and for no reason Ruthie kissed me and smilled.

We went back to Tel Aviv, and Farley took us all to dinner at an Arab tourist restaurant. We went to bed early as our plane was leaving the next morning. I packed in rather a strange way. I packed one overnight suitcase with the basic necessities and put everything else in the other six. When we got to the airport the next morning, I had quite a fight with the steward because I insisted on taking my large overnight suitcase into the cabin with me and would not check it through. As the plane took off, I said, "Farley, I know why I wanted this suitcase. If the plane stops in Rome, I have to pick up those dresses I ordered. Anna needs the money and one more fitting before she sends them to me."

Farley said patiently, "Shelley, this plane stops only in Athens, Geneva, then Paris."

"Well, if it *does* happen to stop in Rome, I'll get off and meet you in Paris the next night."

The plane we were on had never stopped in Rome before, but that morning it did. Why I don't know. Farley gave me an amazed good-bye kiss. I assured him I had a lot of lire left and got off the plane, lugging my suitcase. The Roman porters were a little confused because that flight had never stopped in Rome, and they scurried around and got the immigration officer away from his cappuccino to stamp my passport. I managed to get a taxi and with my meager Italian vocabulary made for the Excelsior Hotel, where I asked for my reservation with such assurance that they immediately found me a room.

As the bellboy took my suitcase up, I turned around and there was Frank Latimore, who had been a friend of mine when he had been under contract at Twentieth and I'd lived at Peyton Hall. We decided to have dinner together and go to the theater that evening. As I rode up in the Excelsior elevator, my feelings of euphoria increased, and I felt a strange subliminal happiness. My room number was 369 and faced the American Embassy, which for some reason was flying the American flag and the Italian flag next to each other that day. I found out later it was Rome's Liberation Day, the day they had kicked out the Nazi army, but riding to the theater that evening, I felt all the flags were hung out for me.

When we arrived, Frank had a box on the right side of the tiny, very elegant old theater. Plays in Rome start late because everyone wants to visit with each other for a while as they all have their own personal dramas going on. I looked down at the chic, chattering audience, fascinated. Frank pointed out Anna Magnani, sitting toward the front of the orchestra. I had met her once casually at Paramount. She was trying to catch my eye, and she was dressed in deep mourning for Rossellini, who was now living with Ingrid Bergman. She was all in black except for red patent leather shoes. She smiled and waved, then pointed to a box directly across the theater from where I was sitting. AND THERE HE WAS. Looking at me. I looked back. The houselights went down, and the play started. We still looked at each other across the darkened theater. He was somehow familiar, perhaps my adolescent Prince Charming come to life. Tall, intelligent-looking, black curly hair and impeccably groomed. I realized I'd seen a photo of him. Yes, he was the tall Italian actor who had played the villain in *Bitter Rice*. His photo that Connie had shown me seemed familiar even then.

Our staring at each other must have become obvious because as soon as the act was over, Frank informed me, "Shelley, he's a famous Italian *stage* actor. He played Stanley Kowalski last year in the Italian version of *A Streetcar Named Desire*. He does not speak a word of English, and he does movies only when he has to, for the money. He doesn't like anything American, especially American girls, and he's the most Italian of Italian men. I know he's handsome, but don't forget you're engaged to Farley."

Before I had time to answer, the door of our box opened, and there stood Signor Vittorio Gassman with another gentleman. Frank was obliged to present us to each other. Vittorio must have said, "How do you do?" in Italian, but he was quite pale and stuttered, which later I came to know was not his style. As he kissed my hand, I did understand him to say, "*Lei e una grande artiste. Ho visto* Un Posto nel Sole." I gathered that he had seen *A Place in the Sun* and was complimenting me on my performance. I had seen *Bitter Rice* in New York and tried to do the same, but Frank had to help me out. Both he and his uninvited friend joined us in our box for the rest of the play. The friend, a young progressive director by the name of Luigi Squarzina, spoke a little English.

Vittorio sent for champagne at the next interval, and with the translating of Luigi and Frank, we managed to discuss our mutual friends, Connie Dowling and Luchino Visconti. I told him I had seen the rehearsals of *Streetcar* in New York, and he was very interested in my impressions of the play, Tennessee Williams and the Actors' Studio Method of work (we are still fighting about that), but conversation was difficult, even with two translators. After the interval the play continued. I think it was rather old-fashioned, in both concept and acting, but I'll never know. Under the program Vittorio held my hand, and we both kept peeking at each other. He is not a person who reveals much of himself with his eyes, but that night he was very open, and despite the veneer of self-confidence and leading-man attitude, I could detect a dark uncertainty, which he covered with a vulnerable superiority complex. His reserve and special humor reminded me very much of Monty Clift.

After the play, as Frank searched for a taxi, Vittorio offered us a lift in his *Topolino* (Mickey Mouse). I don't quite know how it happened, but Frank was dropped off first, and then Luigi, and I was driving around Rome with a strange, very handsome young man who spoke no English, and I spoke no Italian he could understand.

He proceeded to show me Rome by moonlight: the Campidoglio,

which even in those days was bathed in romantic lighting, the Roman Forum and then up to the top of the Aventine Hill, which was lit only by the enormous moon. We couldn't communicate with words, and it was rather cold, so he gave me his jacket and kissed me. In the dark his profile looked like Mark Antony's, and for no reason I remembered the word for hot, which is *caldo*. He then took me to the glorious Piazza Navona, where we strolled past three of the most beautiful fountain statues I'd ever seen. He kept repeating, "Bernini, Bernini." We sat at a midnight café and had luscious ice cream, which I assumed was called bernini. He didn't stop kissing me, but all the strolling couples were so busy necking, no one noticed. There's nothing quite as delicious as berninis and kisses. At one point I didn't know who was eating which ice cream. I guess that's what they mean by chocolate-covered kisses.

Fortunately I could say "Albergo Excelsior" in Italian. He parked his car around the corner, and we walked into the lobby. Rome was a very strict Catholic city in those days, so I was embarrassed and surprised when the concierge handed my room key to Vittorio. I tried to say, "I don't sleep with anybody on the first date," but my Italian wasn't up to it. We went up in the gold elevator to Room 369.

That night I finally understood the passionate beauty of Italy which has lasted through all the centuries and that wherever you may wander, all roads lead to Rome. And you can't pan to anything because it hasn't been invented in pictures or words.

CHAPTER 25

When I awoke next morning, my room was full of yellow roses. A note, which the maid translated for me, said, "Dearest, I leave my heart here with you and the roses until tonight, Yours, Vittorio."

For the next three months some mysterious osmosis took place. I stopped being an actress and became just a happy woman. Anna had me try on the dresses until she and her son and I got tired of fitting them, and I kept telling Farley, when he called from Paris, that they weren't ready yet. After about a week he called late one night and said, "Shelley, I have a feeling those dresses are never going to be ready. Right?"

I said, "Yes, Farfel, darling, I think so."

Pause. "Well, be careful. And try to look before you leap, and remember I'm just a telephone call away if you need me." I wept as I thanked him. I wanted to send his ring back to him, and he said, "No, have one of those jewelers on the Via Condotti change it into a pin in the shape of a question mark, and when you wear it, think of me."

The next morning my six other suitcases arrived from Paris, and at Vittorio's insistence I moved into his apartment. I who had hardly ever spent a whole night with a man! His apartment had all marble floors, a small dining room that opened into a somewhat larger living room, a large bedroom and a strange kitchen with a stove but no refrigerator. There was also a tiny bedroom for his maid, Lisa, who had come from Naples when Vittorio was born and is *still* taking care of him. Lisa spoke only Neapolitan, but she never understood anything I said in any language, even gestures.

Vittorio had me meet his mother, who was a beautiful and dignified woman, his lovely young sister, Maria, her husband, Guido, and their two small daughters, Francesca and Giovanna. Vittorio had been separated for several years from his wife, who was now living with a successful young film director. They all were trying very hard to get some kind of divorce, which was practically impossible because at the time the church and state in Italy were one, and the Vatican refused to recognize divorce. Now there is civil marriage, but then no such thing existed. It caused great hardship, especially to the children.

I have never really liked living with another person, male or female, unless I have my own room, preferably my own apartment. I'm a sometime insomniac, and I eat, read and wander around at very strange hours during the night. But whatever chemistry existed between Vittorio and me, I loved living with him, sleeping with him in the same bed, and I slept soundly. In fact, I used to be so tired from keeping up with his hectic Roman schedule that I had very real trouble staying awake after midnight.

Vittorio was doing some film about dance hall girls, and I sat on the set like a meek little Italian wife and got him Cinzano and sandwiches, lit his cigarettes, helped with his wardobe and helped him memorize his lines. Quite a feat, since I could neither speak nor read Italian. I went to work with him every day and sometimes every night when he had all-night shooting. (Those dance hall girls were just too pretty.) I learned some Romana dialect and would bring him a hot meal from a nearby *trattoria*. Low-budget Italian films never stopped for lunch or dinner in those days; they worked eighteen hours a day, and the crews and actors got sandwiches or pasta on the run. But not this *amante*. I would bring pots and dishes, a tray, napkins and silver and glasses from our apartment, and after he had worked four or five hours, I would go to the nearest good restaurant and say the magic words "*Per* Vittorio Gassman." He was, and is, the matinee idol of Rome and was beginning to be a popular screen star, so they would fill my tray with wonderful home-cooked specialties, and during a scene he wasn't in, we would sit in his romantic, crummy little dressing room and eat very well and drink fruity homemade wine. When he continued shooting after our midnight dinners, I would curl up in his caravan under my huge mink coat and nap. He would wake me with kisses, and we would drive home through Michelangelo's Roman dawn.

We both were very happy, and it's the only time I can remember that neither Vittorio nor I minded the *paparazzi*. We used to pose until they ran out of film, buy them drinks and tease them. They finally got so bored with our happiness they left us alone.

In this book I have described several love affairs I indulged in during my adolescence and youth. But there are really no words to describe the complete mental, physical and spiritual affinity Vittorio and I had for each other. He hardly spoke English, and I spoke hardly any Italian, yet we seemed to find ways of revealing to each other our innermost thoughts and needs. In Italian, the word *amante* means "lover" and *amico* means "friend." To me, *amante* is composed of both these words. With mutual humor we laughed for hours over our linguistic mistakes, and we were quick to sense anything that displeased the other. I have often sincerely wished that Vittorio and I had never learned to communicate with words because during this time we were forced to discourse with much more primitive and revealing sides of ourselves. Of course, many funny misunderstandings occurred, but more often sensitive exchanges would happen between us. Sometimes it made me feel as if the love affairs I'd had before were just exercises I had indulged in for good reviews. Of course, they didn't seem so at the time, but I did not have this frame of reference to compare them with.

The magic of the Roman spring was all around me. The Italian word for "spring" is *primavera*, and the words for "first truth" are *prima verità*. These Italian words are firmly confused in my mind. In fact, some years later, despite Vittorio's many explanations, I wrote a play called *Albergo Primavera*, with the total assurance that it meant *The Green Hotel of the First Truth*. Well, nobody at the Actors' Studio knew the difference either.

Vittorio's apartment had a balcony covered with plants and flowers, as was the apartment itself. I became practically an English gardener, taking care of all these lovely plants, even mashing up vitamins and putting them into the water. Vittorio's maid, Lisa, by now knew I was *pazza* ("crazy") and expressed to his mother concern for any children we might have. In her opinion, one of the most insane things I'd done was to insist that Vittorio buy a small refrigerator. Lisa believed that anybody in his right mind knew that electricity destroyed food. It was a constant battle between us, I connecting the refrigerator and she disconnecting it. She would yell at me in Neapolitan, "You must buy food fresh every morning from the shops and consume it within eight hours. Otherwise, it is dangerous." I tried to convince her that this was what the refrigerator was for, but she just kicked it every time she went past this dangerous American invention. Nothing I could say could convince her that food was safe in the refrigerator. What I didn't understand was that shopping and her Sunday morning church were her only social life.

One evening Vittorio and I had a date for cocktails with his lawyer, then dinner at Luchino Visconti's house, where we were going to see his unreleased picture *La Terra Trema*, the first important film to be made about Sicily. Before we left that evening, as a gesture of reconciliation I gave Lisa 1,000 lire—almost $2 in those days—and explained with gestures that we wouldn't be home until very late, and perhaps she would like to see one of Vittorio's films, which was playing at the corner cinema. Then I went out to Vittorio's new little silver gray Fiat and carefully got me and my sables into it.

In about five minutes Vittorio came barreling out of the apartment, furious. So furious he could almost speak English. He demanded to know why I had kicked Lisa out of the house. Just as angrily I replied in my broken Italian that I had given her money to go see his new film at the neighborhood cinema since we would not be home until late.

"But suppose I came home unexpectedly and needed a glass of milk?"

I stared at him unbelievingly. "Well, you would open the refrigerator and get yourself a glass of milk. Or if you had been hit by a car, I would get it for you."

His answer almost floored me. "Shelley, do not meddle with things you do not understand. If *I* had to get myself a glass of milk, Lisa would cry for a year. She goes to church only when she knows I'm sleeping. You do not understand her Neapolitan mentality. Her whole life is My Welfare." That glimpse into the difference between our cultures should have given me a hint! I went back in the house, apologized to the tearful Lisa and took back my 1,000 lire. That made her cry harder.

When I got back in the car, I was very angry and realized that this was our first serious fight. He drove fast, even for an Italian, and suddenly, when we came to a huge *piazza* where all the cars had to go in a huge one-way circle, he stopped the car right in the middle, took me in his arms and gave me a big kiss. I began to cry harder than Lisa. There was no way, with my limited Italian, that I could explain to him that I was only trying to do her a favor and did not want her to have to sit alone in the house all evening.

While we were kissing and I was blubbering, a tall, handsome *carabiniere* in a beautiful white and gold uniform knocked on Vittorio's window. All the cars next to us had stopped to watch our romantic reconciliation. They were even throwing in obscene suggestions. This, of course, blocked the whole traffic system in the *piazza*. The traffic policeman and Vittorio proceeded to have a very dramatic argument. I thought the least that would happen was that we would have to appear in court, though I hoped not that night. It ended up with Vittorio giving the policeman the 1,000-lire note that was still in my hand and the policeman giving me his handkerchief.

As we went on to our destination, I asked Vittorio what had

happened. He explained that he had committed a 3,000-lire offense, but for romantic and financial reasons the policeman had settled for Lisa's 1,000 lire after he heard the whole story. In the coming years I was to learn that most government business in Italy is conducted in this fashion. A woman who cries can get almost anything from a government official, especially if she has a baby. If the baby cries, they pay *her*.

Vittorio was to start another picture almost immediately, and although I was a pretty good driver in California, I refused to learn to drive in Rome, where they were forever playing "chicken." So, whenever Vittorio had a script conference or fitting at the studio, or I wanted to go shopping or walk around Rome alone, either his mother, sister or sister-in-law would accompany me. For the first couple of months I thought they all were just being very nice and making sure I didn't get lost. But after a while I began to realize that they accompanied me because at that time no respectable Italian woman was seen in the streets alone. One day I managed to escape and went to Anna's famous fabric store and bought a lot of beautiful dark green striped satin to make drapes for Vittorio's dining room, living room and bedroom since all these rooms had only heavy rolled wooden blinds that kept out the light and dirt but weren't very attractive. Anna Moda made the drapes for me, and I had the *portiere* hang them.

It became a major family crisis. Lisa had hysterics. Vittorio's mother kept questioning me about exactly how much money the material had cost, and Guido explained that things like that were done only after a family conference. Vittorio kept explaining to them that I was an American, after all, and his sister, Maria, kept insisting that it was high time the Napoleonic Code was rescinded. What the hell all this had to do with my green drapes I didn't understand. The drapes had cost less than $100 for three rooms, and it was my money! Maybe they were superstitious about the color green. I never did find out the answer to that one; it remains a family secret that no one will discuss with me. They just look pained when the subject of "Shelley's green drapes" comes up. But they damn well stayed up there when I lived in our first apartment.

In the midst of all this turmoil Vittorio and I went to see a wonderful new film of Vittorio de Sica's called *Umberto D.* Magnani was at the showing with Palmiro Togliatti, who was then head of the Italian Communist Party. Rossellini was there with a very pregnant Ingrid Bergman and many of the new foreign producers who in later years became the nucleus of the new "Hollywood on the Tiber." After this remarkable and sensitive film, Vittorio and I, and De Sica and his *amante*, went to dinner and dancing at a very posh club. Most directors and well-to-do men in Rome at that time seemed to have two families: a legal one they supported and saw on Sundays and an illegal one they also supported, loved and lived with.

The evening was very exhilarating and romantic, and while Vittorio and I were dancing to the strains of "Scalinatella" (a Neapolitan song meaning "Little Steps/That Lead Up to My Love"), Vittorio began to discuss our marriage. He didn't ask me if I wanted to marry him; he explained at great length why he couldn't marry me yet. For an Italian it was almost impossible to get a divorce, but he would try. For $10,000 a judge in Genoa could get him an annulment, and we could perhaps be legally married in Italy, or we could be married in Mexico and by some hocus-pocus the marriage could perhaps be registered in the Vatican. There were other cockamamie things you could do in Switzerland or the Azores or Andorra. . . . Before he could continue, I quietly reminded him that I was an American citizen and a resident of California, and I wasn't sure if his previous marriage had any validity in *my* country, and if it did, he could get a divorce there. If we really were considering this—I had begun to tremble—I first had to ask the American consul and my father.

His English was improving, but his whole speech had been singularly unromantic. Besides, over his shoulder I could see De Sica nuzzling and kissing his beautiful mistress by whom he already had two gorgeous babies and with whom he was to live for the rest of his life. Vittorio noticed where my eyes were and said, "Shelley, we love each other, but I don't think your parents would like the idea of us living together in Italy and having children while unmarried." About that I had to agree.

The next day he bought me a lovely antique engagement ring with two claws holding two beautiful, tasteful diamonds. Then started a series of divorce attempts by Vittorio and his separated wife and marriage attempts by Vittorio and me that lasted for two years and took place in almost every country in the world.

During this idyllic spring a rather terrifying thing happened. In the middle of the night, when Vittorio was working on his serious new war film, I awoke and heard a dog howling outside. I rushed to the window, raised the wooden blinds and, hiding behind my green drapes, tried to see the insane dog outside. Then with cold fear I became aware that there was no dog. The terrifying sound was coming from Vittorio. He was sitting up in bed, his eyes wide open, howling in this almost inhumane manner. Lisa rushed in and motioned for me to be silent. She cradled him in her arms, and he began slowly to come out of his nightmare. His skin had taken on a green tinge, and he was bathed in sweat as he looked around the room in sheer terror. He started to walk around the apartment, but Lisa and I guided him away from the front door. I still didn't know if he was awake or asleep. When we got to the kitchen, Lisa started to warm some milk for him, and the opening and closing of the refrigerator door seemed to awaken him more fully. Then they both laughed about it, and although they were talking in Italian, I understood that he was a sleepwalker but had almost grown out of it in his middle twenties. After he drank the hot milk, we all went back to bed. Vittorio went right to sleep, but I stared into the darkness and wondered how much I really knew about this man I was so much in love with and to whom I planned to join my life. And whose children I wanted.

To this day Vittorio has never told me very much about his wartime experiences. He jokes about his mother's having gotten him out of the Fascist Army by driving his colonel crazy with letters.

His war film had a relatively short schedule, thank goodness, and he was also getting more money for it than he'd ever got before. So, after he finished it, he decided that he should show me some of Italy. We would drive in his new Fiat and visit the judge "with connections" in Genoa and start the legal process by which he could perhaps get an annulment. Also, Vittorio had been born in Genoa, and we could visit his mother's family, who lived there.

We left early the next morning, and for the next hour or so he recited to me—and I tried to memorize—beautiful little Romana poems, and I reveled in his reciting of Dante's *Inferno*. It was late July, and by fall I could almost read Dante's adventures in the underworld but still could not speak everyday Italian. But I understood Dante's cantos, and I could recite a wonderful poem about a little town with its own little star and another one in Romana dialect about the funerals in Rome, which told how the rich were buried with pomp in the morning, the middle class during the traffic in the afternoon, and the poor people were thrown out with the garbage at night.

I was stunned by the beauty of Florence, and Vittorio kept laughing at my naïve American reaction to this ancient Italian city I had hardly heard of; no one in Hollywood had talked about

Florence, Italy. Vittorio decided that since we didn't have much time we would only go to meet "David" at the Galleria dell'Accademia. I couldn't understand what he was making such a production about. It was getting late, and we could see it another time. But when we finally got there and paid the few lire to get in, as I walked toward this Eighth Wonder of the World, I was sure I could see the blood flowing in the veins under the marble skin. I stared at it, almost in idolatry. I walked around it slowly and then stared at it some more. Vittorio finally said, "No, Shelley! No matter how hard I work, I can never buy it for you." I was close to tears. The genius of that sculpture affects one physically. I took Vittorio's hand, and we left quickly. If I couldn't have it, I didn't want to look at it anymore at that time. After all, America had helped Italy so much during and after the war, the least they could do was give us "David." Vittorio laughed and teased me for the next fifty kilometers. I was silent. I finally said, "If I ever have any daughters, I won't let them see 'David' until they're grown up and married. All men are a disappointment after him." That deflated Vittorio's ego. But he understands the reaction to my first glimpse of "glory."

When we got to Portofino, we registered at a *pensione* overlooking the sea. I had the traditional cigar-band wedding ring on, or they wouldn't have given us a room together. The proprietor was very suspicious when, as required, we gave him our passports. Vittorio, in very rapid Italian, doubletalked a fancy story that it took longer to change names on American passports for newly married brides who had not been in the Army. The proprietor believed him, or maybe it was the extra 1,000 lire that did it.

In our simple room with a view of the sea there was only one thing wrong. Was it ever cold! I closed all the windows, put on my flannel pajamas and a couple of heavy sweaters and turned on my Italian heating pad. But Vittorio slept in the nude under a single sheet—I had all the blankets anyway. As soon as I got to sleep, Vittorio opened the windows. I have sinus trouble, then and now. Rome is damp, but Portofino is practically in the ocean, so we had a restful romantic night, with him opening the windows and me waiting until *he* was sound asleep, then closing them and burying my head under the pillow and my heating pad. To this day Vittorio swears that he was never sure whether it was always me he was making love to or if I had slipped in another girl because most of that time in Italy I had my head covered with the pillow and the heating pad.

The next morning, when we collected the Fiat, the garage owner was talking excitedly on the phone. Vittorio whispered to me that this man was the head of the Communist Party in the area and was talking to Togliatti, planning a strike in a Fiat factory. As he talked, his two little daughters in communion dresses came in with their mother to be kissed and given new rosaries. It was a Sunday, and obviously everyone in Portofino was going to church except this garage owner. We paid him and drove away. I asked Vittorio how it was possible for an official of the Communist Party to have his daughters confirmed. Vittorio gave me a pitying look and said, "That's Italian Communism."

"But," I argued, "this man has to be an atheist if he is a big-shot Communist."

"Perhaps in the USSR," Vittorio explained, "but I think in Italy there is no contradiction between true Marxism and Catholicism. After all, Catholicism is based on the teachings of Jesus, the lack of possessions and sharing the fruits of your labor, and you are your brother's keeper and must not allow him to suffer."

In Genoa we stayed at a lovely apartment that obviously belonged to a rich relative who was away on vacation. His housekeeper couldn't do enough for us, and Vittorio showed me the port of Genoa and the theaters he had played in during the war, many of which were leveled by the Allied bombs. I casually mentioned that perhaps my ex-husband, Paul, might have done some of this damage when his squadron was flying from England to Africa. Vittorio pinched my cheek real hard in the Italian manner and said, "Well, at least he didn't drop a bomb with my name on it."

The next day we had an enormous lunch with the "important judge," who also happened to be one of the Vatican's *avvocati* ("lawyers") in its Genovese branch. We hoped that he could get Vittorio's annulment through the back door of the Vatican. During this twelve-course lunch Vittorio handed his man an envelope stuffed with $10,000. This was the first installment to legalize my name as Signora Gassman. If successful, the whole thing was going to cost about $30,000. I found the whole operation suspect. The man ate too much and spoke English too well, even with a slight German accent. But Vittorio felt it was worth the chance as he said his ex-wife desired this annulment profoundly "because she has to live and work in Italy." This remark cheered me considerably because I interpreted it to mean that he didn't have to, and wasn't planning to, work in Italy.

That afternoon Vittorio's brother-in-law, Guido, called to tell him that an important producer wanted to talk to him about a film called *Big Deal on Madonna Street* with a wonderful director, Mario Monicelli, and that my mother and Universal were phoning frantically from California. Vittorio and I looked at each other hopelessly, but we knew this was an actor's life, so we sped down the direct inland route, nonstop to Rome.

I immediately called California, and my mother spoke to me— my father wouldn't. She told me that Universal's lawyers were preparing to institute a suit for half a million dollars against me if I didn't report to the studio within ten days. They had two films waiting for me and were very angry with my "international shenanigans." Blanche, on the other extension, had to say, "Shelley, call your psychiatrist immediately. I think you're identifying with Ingrid Bergman and Roberto Rossellini." I told my mother I would be home within ten days and hung up.

Vittorio would not allow me to leave Rome, no matter what Universal did, without attending the opera. Fortunately the La Scala company of Milan had a short season in Rome at that time, and we heard Maria Callas, who weighed about 200 pounds then and had the most powerful voice and incredible vocal range I've ever heard, sing in *Andrea Chénier*. When we saw her in *Tosca*, I cried so hard that Vittorio had to remove me from the theater. We also saw *Aida*, complete with one small elephant and a huge baritone.

The only thing about the Rome opera house that troubled me was that way up, approximately 300 feet above the stage, there is a quote of Mussolini's engraved in marble. It bothered me throughout the performances. I asked Vittorio why it hadn't been taken down after the war. He said it was so inaccessible it was very expensive to take down. I replied, "They damn well got it up there, they can damn well take it down."

His sanguine answer was: "Are you sure they want to?"

But I became a Puccini and Verdi fan for the rest of my life. That night over dinner Vittorio and I actually came to blows. He insisted that Mozart, Bach, Beethoven and Brahms were greater composers than the Italians I had just heard. We ended up calling each other dreadful names, the mildest of which was: "You simplistic, sentimental American." And I told him he was a "callous Germanic snob who had crept into Italy by accident." We almost didn't make up after this artistic fight. But when we went to bed in the middle of the night, he took the heating pad and pillow off my head and said in some language, "I think we have such violent artistic disagreements because we care for one another so much, and that's why it's so important to impose our opinions on each other."

Vittorio had planned to accompany me back to California, but the script of *Big Deal on Madonna Street* was a magnificent comedy, and he was going to be paid a great deal of money. He would join me in Hollywood as soon as it was finished. Somehow my world and plans were falling to pieces around me. I don't know if Universal could have won a financial battle in court against me, but I called Jerry Giesler, and he advised me to come back as perhaps it would be better for Vittorio to get a divorce in Mexico and for us to get married in California.

We had just enough time in Rome to attend my friend Dawn Addams's *Life* cover wedding to Prince Vittorio Massimo, which made her a princess. I went with Vittorio to the American consulate to get his tourist visa and had a very strange afternoon there with the consul. He asked Vittorio questions like: "Were you ever in the Fascist Party?"

Vittorio, whose English wasn't so good, answered, "Only when I was a little boy. They wouldn't let me go to school otherwise." Then they asked him if he was a Communist, and he answered quickly, "No, no. Not yet." I kicked him under the table and explained to the consul about his lack of English; what I didn't explain was his peculiar Italian sense of humor. Then he asked Vittorio if he wanted an early number for U.S. immigration. He looked confused. I think he thought the consul meant a U.S. Social Security number which you needed in order to work in the United States. I was hoping he'd do that from then on.

The consul couldn't get it through his head—and for that matter neither could I—that Vittorio didn't want to become an American citizen. I had thought that was the purpose of our visit to the consul. Finally, he suggested that the Italian interpreter and Vittorio go into the other room and he would talk to me. For the next fifteen minutes he regaled me with horror stories about Italians who had married poor unsuspecting American girls just to become American citizens and then divorced them as soon as they had their citizenship papers. All I could think of was to answer hopefully, "Do you think you can get Vittorio to become an American citizen?"

The Italian interpreter wasn't having any better luck with Vittorio in Italian. So what the consul finally did was just give Vittorio a tourist visa, and if he worked in America or we got married there, he could apply to Immigration in California for the appropriate papers. The consul whispered to me as we left, "If you're pregnant, be sure to have the baby in America. And don't let the Italian Embassy give you a passport for the baby." I didn't know whether to smack his face or thank him.

After this long afternoon of misunderstanding we finally were mailed a year's tourist visa for Vittorio, and unbeknownst to him, I went to TWA and changed my first-class ticket for Greece, India, Hong Kong, Manila, Hawaii, etc., to two round-trip tourist tickets, Rome–New York–Los Angeles. It wasn't exactly kosher, but the TWA clerk was Italian, and his eyes twinkled as he gave me one ticket for Shelley Winters and one for Vittorio Gassman, with even some TWA script left over. He then said these priceless words, "Well, Miss Winters, you don't have the husband-to-be you started out with, but you now have the best Italy has to offer, and I think your marriage will do wonders for Italian tourism."

CHAPTER 26

Vittorio waved me off at Ciampino Airport with my Italian Berlitz records and books, a great classic Italian novel, *I Promessi Sposi*, in large print and three dozen yellow roses in my arms. "With tears in my eyes and distraction in my aspect."

When we got to Shannon, there was a cable from Vittorio which said, "Why don't you write, you rat? *Io molto triste. Tuo fidanzato* ["I am very sad. Your fiancé"], Vittorio." When I got back on the plane, I didn't know whether to laugh or cry. So I did both and started a twelve-page letter to him, which I finished by the time I got to California two days later. Only when Vittorio received it, he was faced with the terrible discovery that no one could read my handwriting in any language. What was I doing while they were teaching the Palmer Method back there in Brooklyn?

When I got to New York, I went to my apartment and called Vittorio. After three minutes of "I love you" in several languages, I hung up and went right to sleep.

Next morning, Connie was at the Studio, on West Forty-fourth Street, between Ninth and Tenth avenues. It was a wonderful place for actors to experiment and work. Afterward Connie and I walked up to the local greasy spoon and had a "dangerous" lunch while I told her all about Vittorio. She told me she was living in a small apartment on the East Side, but she seemed quite lonely and lost. After a lot of discussion, I finally convinced her to come back to Los Angeles, where her family were waiting for her, and to try to resume her Hollywood career. It took her about three hours to pack all her belongings, and close her apartment. I changed my first-class ticket to two tourist, and that's how we movie stars returned to the Land of Make-Believe. Connie's smile, the twinkle in her eye and her lovely wit began to return the closer we got to sunny California. She even began to plan a wedding in her garden for Vittorio and me if he could get his annulment firmly annulled.

When we arrived at the L.A. Airport, there was Connie's family welcoming her with open arms and my family waiting with clenched fists. But we all kissed each other, and Connie drove to Hollywood with her family, and I drove in my father's old Dodge (not my brand-new Cadillac) to Holloway Drive. After about fifteen minutes of driving carefully at thirty-five miles an hour, my mother said, "He *has* to be Catholic."

I said, "Mother, there are a lot of Jewish people in Italy."

My father, with his mine of misinformation, said, "Have you forgotten so soon? The Fascists and Nazis killed them all."

In a quiet rage I turned on them all, including Blanche and her new husband, George Boroff, and said, "I love you all very much, but if you cannot accept my future husband, Vittorio Gassman, I will understand how you feel, and we need not ever see each other again." Silence for the rest of the trip. When we got there, the janitor was taking Marilyn's stuff down the steps. She was moving to a ritzy apartment on Doheny. Then the janitor carried my ten suitcases into the apartment. Marilyn kissed me and whispered in my ear, "Shell, I know you're in love, but remember they're your only family. And they'll always be there for you."

I kept myself from crying as I walked up the long steps. When the family gathered together in the living room, they stared at me. My father just said, "Mr. Edward Muhl, head of production at Universal, wants you to report to his office at ten tomorrow morning. If you'll allow me, I suggest you bring your agent along."

I then proceeded to plead my case and my love for Vittorio and his for me, with as much eloquence as Clarence Darrow must have had at the famous Scopes trial. I told them what a serious and great theater actor Vittorio was and how middle-class and thrifty his mother, sister and sister-in-law were. How well they had taken care of me in Rome and how concerned they were to protect my reputation and career. I also told them that Vittorio's grandfather had been Jewish and had had to convert to Catholicism in order to get a license to practice medicine, and I thought that there was a similar situation among his German relatives in Baden-Baden. After all, his father's name was Gassmann.

I don't know exactly what they believed or didn't believe, but they knew that since my divorce from Paul my personal life had been lonely and chaotic. Now I was ready to ditch everything to be with this Italian stranger I loved so much. I had never before actually put my career in such jeopardy, and they got the message that for my future happiness I was prepared to give up my professional life, my family and all I possessed. I went into the bathroom and took a shower (I'd gotten very adept at crying underwater) so they could have a conference.

When I came back, my mother put her arms around me and said, "Shelley, if you love him so much, he must be a good man, what-

ever his religion is. After all, there is only one God, and we believe
only He understands the human heart." George got his dog, Nafke,
out of the car, and we all had a little lunch celebration. I had
brought everyone presents from Israel, Rome, Paris and London,
and they had fun opening them.

As soon as they all left, I telephoned Vittorio, about 2:00 A.M. his
time, and told him that my family were eagerly looking forward
to meeting him. He told me the picture had started, but it was
going so slowly that he was planning to murder Mario Monicelli,
the director. He reminded me to study my Italian a lot, and he
was forgetting his English *momentino.* Conversing in person in two
languages had been difficult enough, but on the telephone it was
almost impossible. We finally secured the services of a romantic
bilingual Italian operator. These phone conversations managed to
cost Vittorio and me $1,000 each before he arrived in Hollywood.

The days dragged, and we both were very lonely. He would send
me long, beautiful, poetic letters written on his set, but since they
were mostly in Italian, it took me a long time to read them with
my English-Italian dictionary, and he could hardly read mine with
any dictionary.

Herb Brenner, who was now a very important agent at MCA,
drove me out to Mr. Muhl's office. I perversely wore old tight
slacks, an old blouse, sandals and a kerchief on my hair. *Sans*
makeup. I was really very angry at Universal for making me come
home without Vittorio. Mr. Muhl was sitting with the head of the
Legal Department of Universal and took a long look at me, from
head to toe. "Miss Winters, this studio is a business, and we have
a program of pictures we must release every year if we are to stay
in business. You may not appreciate that, but we do. We have
paid you a great deal of money, and we have also invested a great
deal of money in you. And now you are destroying our investment.
You may not have noticed it, but Ingrid Bergman's career is finished
in the United States and perhaps throughout the world. Are you
ready to have that happen to you?"

I was torn between my fear and anger. Herb Brenner said, "Mr.
Muhl, Miss Winters is reporting for work. As of this moment. Aren't
you, Miss Winters?"

"Yes," Miss Winters answered.

"Well, in that case, Shelley," Eddie Muhl said, "we had been
planning to star you in a movie called *Untamed Frontier* in two
weeks. But perhaps you would like to get back in shape for a

couple of weeks first. So you will report to Frankie Van's gym every morning at eight, and we are paying your nice stand-in to supervise your diet and act as your secretary [your keeper, he meant]. All your traveling has obviously tired you out. She will also see to it that you get your proper rest."

The meeting ended on a note of sweetness and light, and he gave me the script to yet another forgettable film. When I got outside the studio gate, I hit Herb Brenner over the head with *Untamed Frontier*. The next two weeks were boredom personified, relieved only by Italian lessons at Berlitz and Vittorio's letters and phone calls. I noticed in the *Reporter* one day that they were shooting *A Streetcar Named Desire* at Warner Brothers. I convinced my stand-in keeper that they had very good diet lunches at the Warner commissary, so after our morning horseback riding lesson, exercises, steambath and massage at Frankie's gym, we both put on our eyelashes and high heels and went over to Warner's for lunch. And to visit Kazan and Marlon on the *Streetcar* set.

When we got to the set, it was as still as death. Gadge was directing Vivien Leigh, using his whispering method. I left my stand-in watchdog to watch and looked around the stage for Marlon, noticing the head of Warner's Publicity Department escorting some newspapermen, who stood well back from the lighted set and watched quietly. Marlon was beginning to talk to the press only occasionally.

I found Marlon in his stage dressing room, a fancy twelve-by-twelve structure on wheels. He invited me in for some apple cider and celery, and we began a whispered conversation on how the film was going and how it compared with the stage version that he had stayed in for two years. "Christ," he teased me, "you've been a wheel this year. How did you manage to go to Italy engaged to one guy and come back engaged to another?"

I laughed and punched him in his torn T-shirt. "I've been reading your press, and you're hiding from the press so hard all they do is write about you." He asked me who this Vittorio Gassman was, and with my face aglow I told him that he had played in the Italian version of *Streetcar* directed by Luchino Visconti, he spoke five languages and was brilliant and he was a famous theater star as well as beginning to be a famous film star. But most of all, he was beautiful inside and out, and funny, and I loved being with him, and I was at last ready to settle down and have his children and just do good pictures occasionally.

While I was reciting this rapturous litany, my pal Marlon suddenly locked the door of his dressing room, then began to shake it and pound the walls and whispered that I must scream and yell while he uttered guttural cries of passion. Since the dressing room was on wheels, we were careening around that large silent sound stage. When I refused to yell loud enough for him, he whispered, "You're not helping my image enough. For God's sake, you studied voice projection. Use it!"

Laughingly I had to oblige. In about five minutes Kazan was breaking down the door. By the time the lock broke and the door finally flew open, Marlon had mussed me up enough to make our improvisation look like the real thing. The entire cast and crew, visitors, executives and the press were staring at us from behind Kazan. I hurriedly assured Gadge that Marlon had been playing a practical joke, but that lousy Marlon pretended that the pseudorape had been real. Our press audience was confused at whose version to believe. I rushed back to the safety of Universal.

That night I got a Professor Pasinetti, a friend of Vittorio's who taught Italian at UCLA, to come to my house. I got Vittorio on the phone, and Pasinetti told him in pure Italian about Marlon's idea of a practical joke, in case the AP and the Roman press had picked up the silly story. I think Vittorio believed me, but for the next few years he was very dignified and aloofly Roman whenever we met Marlon.

After three weeks of Frankie Van's efforts and my 1,000-calorie-a-day diet and my nine hours of sleep at night, I began again to look like UI's sexpot. We started *Untamed Frontier* on Halloween, which seemed appropriate. Elsa Lanchester was my sidekick and was dressed in very bizarre outfits. Joel McCrea was the heroic sheriff. I think I was a good girl gone bad. No, in this one I was a bad girl gone good, who came back to this untamed frontier town with dozens of outrageously sexy costumes to find her father's killer. Joseph Cotten was in the film, too, but neither he nor I nor the director was ever quite sure what his role was. But he looked great and lolled gracefully around front porches and had long speeches in which he tried to imbue in me "the honest frontier spirit."

The holiday season had always been an especially lonely time for me, so a few days before Thanksgiving, on the spur of the moment, I sent a cable to Vittorio in my Berlitz Italian: "I miss you. Send me a kiss for Thanksgiving."

His answer was a dozen yellow roses and a cable that said, in English, "I'm bringing it myself [meaning the kiss]. Can I have Thanksgiving dinner with your family? All my love, Vittorio."

The next week moved like lightning because I knew the confrontation between my father's prejudice against anything from the old country—especially a Catholic man—and the reality of Vittorio's admittance into the family circle was imminent. Vittorio's plane from New York got into L.A. quite late in the evening, so I was able to meet him. When I got to the airport, the airport policeman let me park in a No Parking zone while I strolled in my mink jacket, Capri pants and blue chiffon blouse to the gate to wait an hour until the plane finally arrived.

Vittorio was the first one off the plane. When he held me in his arms, all my fears vanished. I knew that whatever the future obstacles were, we would somehow survive them.

We walked out to my car, and Vittorio stared at it unbelievingly. I had forgotten how small Italian cars were in comparison to ours. Vittorio managed to say, "Why didn't you tell me you had a white tank? Is it war surplus?" I asked him if he would like to drive, and he looked at me as if I had suggested some dangerous stunt. He managed to convey to me that after I had given him some lessons, he would try. But only in daylight.

When the porter brought his luggage, I noticed, to my joy, that Vittorio had brought four big suitcases, which meant to me that he planned to stay a long time. After we put the luggage in the trunk, he said wistfully, "I could have brought my Fiat. It would have fitted in the trunk, too."

When at last he carried all his suitcases up the little steps to my balcony apartment, he said in Italian, "I understand now why we first discussed our marriage to the tune of 'Scalinatella' ["Little Steps"]." We stood on my balcony, and Hollywood did its best to look beautiful and twinkled all its lights.

While I was unpacking for him, I heard him turn on the television in the living room. I had an enormous "Madman Muntz" set in those days, with about a twenty-eight-inch screen. The "culture" of television had not yet arrived in Italy, and Vittorio was obviously anxious to look at it. When I came into the living room, he was staring at the set in a daze. Oral Roberts was staring out of the set right at him, saying, "Send in a dollar for your own personal Jesus Christ." Vittorio quickly turned the set off. "Shelley, I don't think I can live in this country." I just laughed and kissed him.

Vittorio took my family—my parents, Blanche and George, and my Uncle Al and Aunt Helen from St. Louis—to dinner at Chasen's. I don't know how Vittorio managed it, but he won my parents over completely. He was obviously a well-educated, serious man who loved me very much. He had survived the Nazi horrors and told my parents a little of the agonies he and his mother (who had been hidden in the Vatican) had lived through because of their Jewish blood.

We socialized with people Vittorio knew in Italy so he could sometimes speak Italian. Connie gave us a party, inviting Fernando Rey, Professor Pasinetti, Maria and Pier Angeli, Claude Dauphin, Richard Basehart and his wife, Valentina Cortesa, and other members of the foreign Hollywood contingent who adored Connie and could speak French and Italian. Vittorio spoke French well enough to act in it; his aptitude for languages has always amazed me. He had a very good time.

I showed him around MGM, and he was awed at its enormousness. Most Roman studios have one or two stages: Cinecittà, the largest, has perhaps ten. He was entranced by MGM's back lot, even as I had been, and had seen all the famous thirties historical pictures that had been filmed there.

Salka Viertel gave us an afternoon engagement brunch, serving her famous Viennese chocolate cake to Aldous Huxley, Christopher Isherwood, Lillian Hellman, the Housemans, Charlie Chaplin, Oona O'Neill, Iris Tree—the poetess whose son was Ivan Moffat—Lion Feuchtwanger and Thomas Mann. This was sort of the end of the Hollywood intellectual era, but we didn't know it yet. Vittorio was elegant, switching languages as easily as most of the other guests, and all the women present were smitten with his Latin good looks. I must say he was quite impressed by my intellectual friends. At one point Iris Tree took me over to a corner and said quietly, but with great sincerity, "Shelley, at your age it's wonderful and almost necessary to have an Italian lover. Like good wine, they don't travel well. But, darling, you mustn't marry them." I thought she was just being bitchy and jealous, and I ignored her worldly, unasked-for advice.

During that winter Vittorio was continuously getting contract offers from all the major studios. He didn't have, and didn't want, an agent. He didn't even answer their phone calls, filling me with dismay.

Jerry Giesler was trying to find a way for Vittorio to get a divorce in America that would be recognized in Italy, so that when we were married, it would allow us to work sometimes in Italy as Signor and Signora Gassman.

We attended a very elegant benefit for Boys Town of Italy. Since Vittorio was a Roman and, of course, Catholic, we were seated at the "Professional Catholics' Table" with Irene Dunne, Loretta Young and their husbands, Maureen O'Sullivan and her husband, John Farrow—who was now a prince of the church because of his books on the lives of the Popes—Bing Crosby and several other prominent Catholic producers and directors.

The sumptuous dinner progressed, with several different kinds of wines, and Vittorio and I had had two martinis each during the preceding cocktail party. One of the elegant first ladies of Hollywood turned to him and said, "Mr. Gassman, it must be wonderful to live in Rome. Do you get to see the Holy Father often?" Vittorio's English had either disappeared, or he was angry at having to sit through this long, dull banquet, or his outrageous sense of humor surfaced. "Of course, we sleep together every Wednesday."

Everyone at the table froze. I thought John Farrow was going to pick up a knife and ritually sacrifice him. Vittorio was smiling pleasantly, plainly waiting for his laugh. I jumped in and explained that when I had been trying to learn a simple Italian vocabulary in Italy, Vittorio had teased me by teaching me vulgar words for everyday usage. So I had been doing the same to him in English, and he thought that "to sleep" meant "to visit." I don't think there was a person at that table who believed me because Vittorio and I might as well have been invisible for the rest of that evening.

Vittorio liked my little apartment, but he seemed to feel we should buy a duplex apartment. I tried to find out why he wanted this kind of home, but all I understood was: "We only need a living room, dining room, kitchen and three bedrooms. Two for the babies and the nurse. Your mother and father can live upstairs. Why do you want a house where we have to pay servants all year if we are not here?"

"Why won't we be here?"

"They are beginning to make films all over the world, especially in Italy. And I have my own theater group subsidized by the Italian government."

We started house hunting furiously, but the day came when I had to go on location in Nevada for *Untamed Frontier*. Vittorio was so tired from a year of theater work and four films nonstop he gladly trailed along to be with me, to see Nevada and especially to see the American Indians. While we were on location, he received some important letters of agreement from his ex-wife, and I believe he obtained some sort of Nevada divorce for $50. We had some kind of ceremony performed by an evangelist who spoke so rapidly that neither Vittorio nor I knew if he baptized or married us. He then sent all these papers to our judge with connections in Genoa with another $10,000. No wonder he wanted to buy a simple duplex!

Connie's boyfriend Ivan Tors, a Hungarian writer and producer (whom she soon married and by whom she had three gorgeous sons), offered Vittorio the leading role in a film called *The Glass Wall*, which was to be filmed the following May. It was about a Hungarian who escapes from Budapest and stows away on a freighter to the United States. He manages to swim ashore in New York, and after hiding throughout the city, he seeks political asylum at the United Nations. In the empty Security Council chamber at night, he passionately addresses the empty delegates' seats, with the names of each country in front of them, and pleads on behalf of all the displaced persons whose homelands had been usurped in the outrageous dividing up of Europe. This low-budget artistic picture was to be shot mostly in New York, with a couple of scenes in Hollywood. There was a small part for a girl in it, but of course, Universal wouldn't let me do it.

While I was finishing *Untamed Frontier* in Hollywood, Vittorio went with me to the studio every day and took care of me the way I had of him when he had been shooting in Italy. Our love was young and new, and twenty-four hours a day weren't quite enough to be with each other.

I finished my movie around Christmastime, and Vittorio and Valentina Cortesa decided to give a benefit recital at the Circle Theater, which my brother-in-law owned. Everyone who was anybody in Hollywood attended this cultural event and cheered lustily, although practically no one understood a word of what was being said, but Vittorio and Valentina had the kind of vocal training an American actor never gets. In fact, Vittorio can read a page of dialogue with one breath and recite effortlessly in three octaves.

In January Vittorio finally signed with an agent by the name of Paul Kohner, who quickly got him a seven-year nonexclusive contract at MGM, starting at $25,000 a picture for two pictures a year and ending after seven years at $250,000 a picture. When I talked about all that money in seven years, Vittorio just laughed. I didn't understand then that Italians will sign anything if it means immediate money and suits their purposes. But I was happy with the illusion that perhaps Vittorio intended to stay in America for the next seven years. (Vittorio eventually did fulfil his MGM commitments, but mostly in their Italian pictures.)

He was immediately assigned to some film at MGM, and I did a film, also at MGM, on loan-out from Universal, named *Letter to the President,* or maybe it was *My Man and I,* I'm not sure. I'm only sure Ricardo Montalban was in it. Vittorio and I enjoyed sharing a gorgeous dressing room in the star dressing-room building, which was very scandalous and forbidden by Louis B. Mayer. His actors must *rest* during their lunch hour. So we were ordered to eat in the commissary, where we met and talked to all the famous writers, producers and directors who at that time didn't know if they would be working there the next day because of the growing libelous blacklist.

One morning George Stevens called to tell me I had been nominated for Best Actress for *A Place in the Sun.* Since I wasn't an Academy member yet, I hadn't even known the nominating was going on; once you are nominated, you automatically become a member and see all the nominated pictures free. The little Academy theater was just a few blocks from Holloway Drive, so Vittorio and I spent the next two or three weeks seeing all the good movies free. He felt quite sincerely after seeing all the performances that I would certainly win the Best Actress Oscar. I thought so, too. Ronald Colman, who had won the Best Actor Oscar for *A Double Life,* called to congratulate me on my nomination.

When Oscar night arrived, I was a wreck. The Oscar presentations no longer took place at a small dinner at the Coconut Grove; for the past few years they had been at the enormous Pantages Theater. Orry-Kelly had made me a simple off-the-shoulder mauve chiffon gown—mauve was my lucky color from my *Rosalinda* days. Vittorio rented a limousine, as he was too nervous to drive, and he held my hand tightly as we got out of the car onto the red carpet in front of the theater. It seemed thousands of fans in the bleachers cheered us, but some of them called him Mr. Granger, which upset me considerably, but he just smiled. Army Archerd interviewed us on the radio while Greer Garson and Deborah Kerr were waiting next in line. In my confusion and anxiety, I introduced Greer Garson to Vittorio as Deborah Kerr and Deborah Kerr as Greer Garson. Vittorio did not know the difference anyway because after all, they both had red hair. They laughed good-naturedly, understanding, I hope, my glazed look and non compos mentis condition. Vittorio guided me to our seats, which were at the end of a row halfway down the center aisle, and he sat me down in readiness in the aisle seat.

The show seemed interminable, and I have almost no idea who was nominated in any of the other categories. When it came time for the Best Actress Oscar, Ronald Colman, who had won a couple of years before for *Double Life*, came out to present it. Naturally I knew I was in. After all, he was *my* Ronald Colman from my *Double Life*, and I knew the Academy was sentimental. When he opened the envelope, I'll swear to this day he said, "Shelley Winters."

I was almost to the steps leading up to the stage when Vittorio tackled me. As we lay on the floor of the aisle, I thought he'd gone insane. He whispered, "Shelley, it's Vivien Leigh."

"You're crazy! He said Shelley Winters."

Meanwhile, someone had come up from the side steps and was accepting the Oscar on Vivien Leigh's behalf. Vittorio and I managed to crawl back to our seats as inconspicuously as possible. Thank God there was no television broadcast then!

I felt nothing. I couldn't believe it. The rest of the evening I felt as if Ronald Colman had betrayed me. He could at least have said my name and swallowed the card if he were any kind of English gentleman. Vittorio made me go to the Academy's Governor's Ball afterward, but I don't remember anything about it. I just knew that that gold statue was not on MY table. But Vittorio kept saying, "*Coraggio*, smile. You are young. You will win many of them." On the way home in the limousine, he put his arm around me and said again, "You see? We cannot live in this country."

Vittorio was having English speech lessons, and I was studying Italian. There was a duplex apartment house on a choice corner in Beverly Hills for $40,000, on the wrong side of the railroad tracks from where the superstars lived, but it had a big living room with a fireplace, a dining room and three bedrooms. We bought it. I am writing from that living room right now.

On the way to New York for location shooting of *The Glass Wall*, we stopped in Juárez. I noticed Dino de Laurentiis, a friend of Vittorio's, on the plane and was surprised when he crossed into Mexico and came along for our wedding ceremony. After Vittorio got another divorce we were married in Spanish and exchanged our gold wedding rings yet again. I was beginning to feel one of two things, as if none of these annulments or marriages was for real, or that I was so married that nothing could ever blast us apart if we ever chose to do so.

When I had signed the Mexican marriage license, Vittorio gave me a black scarf and said, "Cover your hair. And this time when the clerk says, 'Silvana,' you say, '*Si*,' then sign this other marriage license 'Silvana Mangano.' Understand?" I had just signed my own wedding certificate "Shelley Winters, A.K.A. Shirley Schrift." I didn't want to sign another one, but Dino was so upset he forgot all his English, and Vittorio managed to explain to me that I had to stand in for Silvana, who was in Rome expecting a baby momentarily, and I would be marrying Dino only by proxy for her under her name. While we had been getting married, Dino had been getting his annulment from his wife in the other office.

So the official who had just married Vittorio and me married Dino and me and didn't even notice I was the same girl, or maybe he didn't care. Crazy foreigners, he must have thought. In Mexico in those days, marriage and divorce by proxy and even by mail were quite common. Jerry Giesler filed Vittorio's Mexican divorce in Rome, his Nevada divorce in L.A., his Mexican divorce and our marriage in Santa Monica, California. What Dino did was his problem!

Vittorio bought me a white orchid and a white carnation for himself. Dino, acting as photographer out of gratitude, took our picture. We all scurried back across the border, they pretending they were Italians from Brooklyn, and we had a huge Mexican wedding feast, and I drank two glasses of champagne, one for me and one for Silvana. When Dino phoned her in Rome to tell her they were married at last, she was having her first labor pains and wasn't too interested in anything else. One thing I'm sure of: Although I spent my wedding night in a berth on an airplane on the way to New York, there were only two of us in that berth, and the man in the berth was Vittorio.

CHAPTER 27

When we arrived in New York, we had a week's honeymoon before Vittorio had to start shooting *The Glass Wall*. He insisted we go to the St. Moritz Hotel on Central Park South, not the Meurice Hotel, where I had planned for us to stay. In twenty-four hours I had changed from Shelley Winters, independent career girl, to His Wife and had to conduct myself accordingly. I found it rather amusing and went along with it and was even a little flattered by his possessiveness.

I took him on the regulation tour of New York: the Statue of Liberty, the Empire State Building, the garment center, which fascinated him, and Columbus Circle. Looking up at the statue of Columbus, Vittorio said something in Italian under his breath, and I twisted his arm to make him translate. "*Bastardo*, couldn't you have stayed home and enjoyed the wonderful food and wine? You had to go and discover this melting pot that won't melt." Then I reminded him Columbus originally came from Genoa, where Vittorio had been born.

He enjoyed the Actors' Studio very much and seemed to agree with most of the Method ideas of Kazan and Strasberg. He, of course, had read all of Stanislavsky's books in Italian, and he had seen the Moscow Art Theater in Rome when it was on tour. I believe we saw Eli Wallach and Jimmy Dean do an improvisation on *All My Sons*, which somewhat confused Vittorio because no one could hear anything Jimmy said. But Lee commented that Jimmy's inaudibility wasn't important. That infuriated Vittorio, who was immersing himself in Shakespeare and the technical aspects of the theater. Many years later he admitted to me that a shrug of a hunched shoulder of Jimmy Dean's captured the imagination of all the kids of his generation from Japan to Timbuktu. It didn't matter if he mumbled. He could project his loneliness and despair with its covering coolness so eloquently that he became an international symbol, with only the three films he did before his death.

At the end of the session Lee Strasberg asked Vittorio if he understood the Method work. Vittorio's answer made me wish the floor would swallow me up. "Yes," he replied, "I appreciate this kind of inner use and examination and the necessity for it. But,

Vittorio visiting me during the shooting of *Saskatchewan* in Canada. J. Carrol Naish and Alan Ladd gave us a second-anniversary party.

ABOVE: Robert Mitchum listening to Marilyn's and my convoluted plans for controlling the studios, who thought they controlled us

LEFT: There was a method to her madness when Otto Preminger directed Marilyn Monroe in *River of No Return.* Here she is in my photo with her "Method" broken leg.

ABOVE: Marilyn using open-mouth smile as I help from the sidelines. Note: She is showing only one leg. The other is in a cast which I had carefully covered with the blanket.

Otto Preminger directing. He has never hired me for a film. I wonder why.

Executive Suite. With William Holden—and a lot of other stars, "thank God"

With my mother Rose and Vittoria

LEFT: My favorite fan photo for 20 years—another Engstead classic

On my way from Los Angeles to Genoa to rejoin Vittorio, I stopped for a Command Performance in London and met the Queen. I also stopped everywhere else I could think of.

Part of the infamous press conference Vittorio and I had in Italy, in which we attempted to explain how we happened to get married, never intending to live in the same country

Vittorio and Silvana Mangano dancing. He kept an eye on me watching from the sidelines.

Vittorio, Michael Rennie, and Silvana Mangano in a motorboat going to a gondola in Venice for a scene. Vittorio swam back from this one.

LIFE

THE NEW BOSSES OF FORD
BY ROBERT COUGHLAN

BIGTIME BASKETBALL GOES SOUTH—IN COLOR

SHELLEY WINTERS
IN 'THE WOMEN'

20 CENTS

FEBRUARY 28, 1955

Charles Laughton, whose class I was in for many years, directed Mitchum and me in *The Night of the Hunter*, a classic, I believe, and the only film Laughton directed, written by James Agee from the novel by Davis Grubb.

The New York premiere of *The Diary of Anne Frank*, with Martin
Luther King, Jr., Coretta King, and Julie and Harry Belafonte. Julie
was also my Venice roommate.

Otto Frank, Anne's father, talking with me during the shooting of her
Diary. I have recently seen him in Amsterdam, where I brought my Oscar
to the Anne Frank museum.

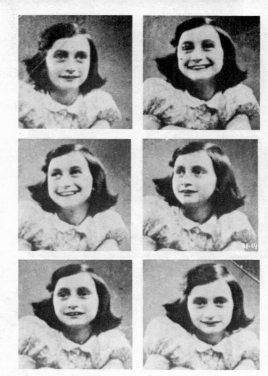

A bust of President John Kennedy I received from his brother Robert Kennedy after JFK's assassination, when I was helping Robert run for the Senate

BELOW: A scene from Stevens' film *The Diary of Anne Frank*, with Diane Baker, Richard Beymer, Gusti Huber, Millie Perkins, Joseph Schildkraut, and Lou Jacobi

Anne Frank, whose memory and words have inspired me all of my adult life

Getting to know Mrs. Eleanor Roosevelt while helping to form the Reform Democratic Committee of New York

JFK teasing me about my fear of the crowds in the Garment Center. (With Myrna Loy, Arthur Goldberg, and Governor Lehman)

With the President at the White House Press Photographers Ball, where I had the honor of being the Mistress of Ceremonies

Judy Garland introducing me as I attempt to imitate her at a New Year's Eve bash at the Actors Studio

Art Carney, Joanne Woodward, Paul Newman, me, Henry Fonda, Marlene Dietrich, and Henry Morgan listening to John F. Kennedy speak at a dinner for General Omar Bradley at the Waldorf during a JFK campaign

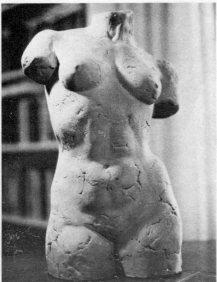

ABOVE: A scene from *A Patch of Blue*, for which I won my second Oscar. (With Elizabeth Hartman and Sidney Poitier)

A torso of me just before I had to gain 40 pounds for *The Poseidon Adventure*—which I'm still trying to take off

My daughter—who nicknamed herself Tory about the time we moved to New York

Peter Ustinov presenting my Oscar to me

RIGHT: *Harper*, with Paul Newman

With Lee Strasberg at an opening at the Actors Studio

OPPOSITE ABOVE: *Bloody Mama.* The four sons of Ma Barker who went on to bigger and better things—Robert Walden, Robert De Niro, Clint Kimbrough, and Don Straud

OPPOSITE BELOW: In a scene with Ralph Richardson from an English film, *Who Slew Auntie Roo?*

RIGHT: Since I began at Columbia as a minor and had to put half my salary in government bonds, it started a wonderful habit.

The smog-stricken palm tree in front of my house, high up in Beverly Hills

The Emmy for *The Number Is Two*, Chrysler Theater

The Foreign Press Award for *The Poseidon Adventure*

Italy's David of Donatello Award for *Borghese Piccolo Piccolo*

The Academy Award for *A Patch of Blue*. The other one (for *Anne Frank*) is at the Anne Frank museum.

Professor Strasberg, don't you think all these young actors would do it better if they had technical training, too, with their voices and bodies?" Strangely enough, Lee agreed with him, and I got Vittorio out of the building as soon as possible.

Ivan Tors and Vittorio had wardrobe fittings that afternoon, so Ivan suggested that Connie and I go to the United Nations Building as the Security Council was then in session. He and Vittorio would meet us there later as they wanted to look at the Security Council Hall after everyone left—they were going to spend two nights filming there when it was empty. *The Glass Wall* was the only film ever shot in the UN building; it has never allowed another one to be filmed there perhaps because of the political nature of *The Glass Wall*.

Connie and I sat in the visitors' section. She looked happier than I had seen her for years, and her wonderful and wicked wit had returned. Mrs. Roosevelt, who was then U.S. delegate to the UN, was sitting with Adlai Stevenson, listening to the translation phones. Toward the end of the session we were joined by Vittorio and Ivan. On the way out, Mrs. Roosevelt and Mr. Stevenson came over. I had met Stevenson briefly years before at an Independent Citizens Committee Rally for Henry Wallace in L.A. Marilyn Monroe and I had been ushers. I remember how shocked we had been backstage when we had seen Louis B. Mayer threatening Katharine Hepburn if she dared appear at this pinko rally. (She appeared on that stage anyway.) Mrs. Roosevelt and Mr. Stevenson congratulated me on my performance in *A Place in the Sun*. Mrs. Roosevelt seemed very familiar with Vittorio's work and his unceasing efforts to bring Italian literature and culture to the Italian people, especially the children. After they left, Vittorio behaved as if we both had just won Oscars. No one I had introduced him to until then, including all the Hollywood moguls and great film and stage stars, impressed him as much as Mrs. Roosevelt and Adlai Stevenson. He looked at me with new respect.

When we got back to the St. Moritz, he started going through my wardrobe, eliminating the sexy dresses he thought no longer appropriate for me to wear. It rather irritated me, although I guess it was complimentary in a way, and I said, "Vittorio, you're trying to make me be something I'm not."

He took me in his arms and said, "No, it is the other way around. You are trying to be something you really are not. When you started that silly seven-year contract at UI, they obviously convinced you that you must hide your intelligence and dress and behave like a blonde *bomba*. You're a thinking and serious woman and actress. You have greatly moved the public with your two best characterizations, and you have the respect of people like Mrs. Roosevelt and Mr. Stevenson. You must dress and behave like the dignified woman you are."

I thought it over and decided he was 90 percent right, but how could I explain to him that I had abandoned Shirley Schrift and her intellectual aspirations in that producer's office so long ago when I had changed my name? Had I really abandoned her feelings of responsibility to mankind and decided more or less to take care of Number One? To my knowledge, Vittorio wasn't involved in the crazy politics of Italy at that time; although many of his films were political satires, I think they were statements of the Italian directors. But I told him I appreciated his opinion of the real me, and I would try to live up to the image he had of his wife.

That night we skipped dinner and had martinis because of the dental work we were having done during our honeymoon. I don't know what brought it on, but Vittorio suddenly had an attack of Truth. He told me about his eight-year-old daughter, Poala, whom he loved very much and was sure I would, too, although she was a shy child. After I digested that startling bit of information, he told me that his ex-wife, Nora Ricci, who was living with this prominent Italian director, had recently had a child who was ill. This man could not, by Italian law, give the child his name. Vittorio explained this was the reason he was so anxious to get Nora's and his annulment recognized by the Vatican. Otherwise, she and her child's father could not get married in Italy.

Nora was a dedicated theater actress and Eleonora Duse's great-grandniece. She and Vittorio had married when they were going to dramatic school, and their careers had caused separations, terrible conflict and jealousies. They had been too young and too poor to handle the responsibility of a child during that troubled time, and I think he had a great deal of guilt about the whole situation.

Now I understood some of the agony in back of his eyes when he didn't know I was looking at him. I asked him why he hadn't told me all this before we had married. Didn't we have enough faith that I would understand and try to help him in any way I could?

"No, that was not the reason. You were so happy I didn't want to put my burdens on your shoulders."

I took his hand and said, "Vittorio, I don't care who or in what language people have married us and legally or illegally joined us together. As far as I am concerned, you are my husband for the rest of my life. I know we are in a difficult position. We come from different cultures and even think in different languages. We both love our professions, and where and how we work and live is still to be solved. But what I just said, I mean. Forever. I will always be connected to you in some way." Then Vittorio said to me the words I had just said to him. And despite all the judges and lawyers and officials, I finally felt for the first time that we were truly married.

I wanted Vittorio to watch a rehearsal of the famous Group Theatre, which was doing a revival of *Golden Boy* with most of the original company. We made our way into the darkened lobby of the beautiful old Yiddish Art Theater, where they were rehearsing, and sat in the back of the house. We watched Harold Clurman take the gifted members of the Group Theatre through a rehearsal of the second act, including the scene where Lorna Moon, I think played by Frances Farmer, tells the young prizefighter Joe Bonaparte, played by John Garfield, of her love for him and her terrible guilt because of her love and responsibility to his manager, played by Franchot Tone, because he had rescued her from a life of near prostitution. Joe tells her of his feelings of treachery toward his family, who have sacrificed for years to train him as a violinist, and now he is ruining his hands by becoming a fighter. The acting was so extraordinary, even at rehearsal, I was weeping. I was so deeply moved by this scene that in some strange way I identified with Lorna Moon's guilt. To whom? To make matters worse, Vittorio, who was also moved by this fine acting, whispered to himself, "*Mea culpa, mea culpa.*"

"What the hell does that mean?" I asked angrily. He grimaced a smile, and maybe because of our talking, Clurman suddenly called for a fifteen-minute coffee break. Vittorio whispered to me that he felt Clurman did not like observers at his rehearsals. So, as the actors were waiting for their coffee, I took Vittorio up to meet the company. They obviously wanted to meet him, and he they.

It was a very low-budget production, and they only had a wooden plank stretching over the orchestra pit from the aisle railing to the stage. We made our way carefully across the plank, and I introduced Vittorio to John Garfield, Frances Farmer, Stella Adler, Franchot Tone, Lee Cobb and the rest of the talented cast. In almost perfect English he told them how eagerly we were looking forward to seeing their production, or at least a preview, before he was finished filming in New York and had to return to California. I didn't say a word. The cast, all of whom I knew from the Actors Lab, looked at me rather strangely. Most of them knew about my previous marriage and "entanglements," and since Vittorio was obviously such a different kind of man, a domineering and cultured Italian intellectual, they seemed to find it highly amusing that the independent Shelley Winters was now going to be the subservient Italian wife.

Vittorio led me back across the plank, and I don't know whether it was nerves at introducing my new husband, the guilt that the play had awakened in me about his legal Italian child, or perhaps I was just klutzy, but suddenly I fell, at least ten feet into the orchestra pit. I lay there among the broken chairs and music stands and did not move. I wasn't unconscious. I was thinking. Was this like the time I had been hit "accidentally on purpose" by a car, or was I acting out the line from one of Ado Annie's songs, "I know I mustn't fall into the pit, but when I'm with a fella I forgit"? I didn't realize it yet, but like Freud, I don't believe too much in "accidents" unless people need to have them.

I insisted that Vittorio and I go back to the hotel, where he immediately called the hotel physician, who examined me carefully and said that by some miracle nothing was broken or too badly sprained, but I was badly bruised everywhere. The next day I hobbled over to the same orthopedic specialist as before, and this time he taped up my right ankle, refitted my back brace and taped my left ribs, which weren't cracked but bent. As was my spirit. He also gave me some pain pills and told me to stay in bed alone for at least a week. I abided by everything he said except the "alone" part. After all, it *was* my honeymoon!

The next night I insisted Vittorio go alone to see Laurence Olivier and Vivien Leigh in *Antony and Cleopatra*. He protested he didn't understand English well enough. "Quit the kidding," I said. "You know what the play's about." He admitted he'd done it in drama school. So he went alone to see the Oliviers, then brought me the program from the show and told me all about it. He adored Vivien Leigh—she was much better than she'd been in *Streetcar*, for which she had taken my Oscar. He grudgingly admitted that Olivier had a certain something. TALENT. Vittorio knew how really disappointed I was to have missed them, so he regaled me with funny stories about his rehearsing Shakespeare with Anna Magnani and an improvisatory Neapolitan theater company, who made up the words as they went along. He soon had me laughing so hard he had to retape my ribs. I must say it seemed a very Method way to rehearse Shakespeare. Then I cued him in his long speech for *The Glass Wall* in which he addresses the empty Security Council chamber, and something of Larry Olivier's style seemed to have crept into his delivery.

I told Connie about Vittorio's daughter, Poala, but she already knew of her existence and was surprised that I had not known about her. She also knew Nora Ricci and said she was a very nice woman, who would be glad now that Poala had the chance to visit America on holidays and learn English and have an American family. She was sure Nora was worried that Poala must be deeply affected by the abnormal conditions of her family life as both Nora and Vittorio were traveling constantly and she lived with grandmothers and other relatives a great deal of the time. My sweet friend made me feel better about everything, and I was so glad she had met Ivan and they cared for each other.

As Italian as Vittorio is, when we saw the rushes every night, I really believed he was Hungarian. He had copied Ivan Tors's Hungarian accent and gestures exactly. How he did this is a mystery to me. As I sat in the projection room and watched his impassioned plea for the freedom of the Hungarian people and all the enslaved Eastern European countries to the empty seats of the Security Council, his grasp of the technical problems of the scene amazed me. I was truly enthralled by his intellectual understanding and the hopeless and despairing quality he managed to get into this six-minute soliloquy that indicted all the member countries of the United Nations who had endorsed the principles of the Four Freedoms and yet abandoned all these peoples and did not insist on plebiscites. The Western countries were in the majority then and could have done so.

We finally finished the location shooting at midnight Friday, and he had to be back in L.A. to shoot at eight on Monday morning. We got in late Saturday night and slept all day Sunday. Vittorio felt he was familiar enough now with the language so that I didn't have to sit with him on the set.

About this time we were notified by the bank that our mortgage request had been accepted and our escrow would close in four weeks and we could move into our new duplex. I was very excited at finally owning my own home, but when I had a conference with my mother and father, they said they felt we should rent the upstairs apartment to strangers for at least a year as it wasn't a good idea for young married couples to be too close to their in-laws. Isn't it strange how much smarter your parents get as you get older? When I told Vittorio about their decision, he thought it was Freudian nonsense. His mother always had an apartment near him.

No comment. I remembered the case of the green drapes only too well.

While Vittorio was finishing *The Glass Wall,* he began to study *Amleto* (Hamlet) in earnest as he had to report to rehearsals in Rome in the fall. If I wasn't working in a picture, I would go to Italy with him, sit in his dressing room and study Italian. The prospect "thrilled" me.

I began decorating our new home inside and out. Vittorio finally finished *The Glass Wall,* then sat on the balcony at Holloway Drive and studied *Amleto* eight hours a day. His mother, Donna Luisa, had sent exact instructions on how to cook pasta, and he liked my broiled fish, chicken, lamb chops and steaks, so I refused to eat out anymore since it was too expensive as we were buying a new building and furnishing the lower apartment. The problem was that Vittorio really liked to have his large meal with wine in the middle of the day, from 1:00 P.M. to 3:00 P.M., then take a nap and/ or make love. Then back to work for a few hours. This is the Italian custom. At night he really liked to eat only an omelet and a salad.

The eating habits of Americans thoroughly confused him. He also never quite understood why American men made love at night after they had worked so hard all day and were somewhat drunk and exhausted. He felt that sex was a very important part of life and should be given its proper attention when people were rested and their energies were at their highest. That was something I found very difficult to adjust to. I felt that night was the most romantic time for lovemaking. We compromised. I got black shades and heavy drapes for the bedroom. Once I suggested that we should move the TV set into our bedroom when we moved, as they were beginning to show films, especially foreign ones, late at night. Vittorio's answer was a puzzled expression, and he said, "I think I don't understand your English. You want our guests to come into our bedroom with us?"

When moving day arrived, my sister and I, my mother and girl-friends carefully wrapped all my dishes, glasses and other break-ables in newspapers and packed them in large barrels the moving company had given us. Vittorio sat on the balcony and studied *Amleto.* It started to rain slightly, so he moved his chair into the living room and sat off the rug out of our way. The rest of us, plus the four moving men, busily packed books and moved furniture, lamps and bric-a-brac, etc. Vittorio studied *Amleto.* Finally, when everything was out of the Holloway Drive apartment, the moving man, who had already rolled up the rug, tapped him on the shoulder and said, "Mr. Gassman, I need your chair. It's the last thing." Vittorio smiled pleasantly, put the book under his arm, went down and got into the car.

I was ready to kill him. I came down to the car in a rage, threw his toothbrush at him and said, "You forgot something."

He did not understand my anger at all. He said these famous words: "But you are the wife; I am the husband. Moving is your business, and that's what we are paying the moving men for. I must learn these five acts of this immortal work of literature so that it becomes second nature to me. Why should I be occupied with such a silly thing as moving?" There was no way to explain it to him. His upbringing and frame of reference were the antitheses of mine. At the new apartment, after a terrible struggle, I got him to empty the garbage in an outdoor bin at the back of the garage the days the maid didn't come. She came four times a week. The first time I asked Vittorio to do this he looked as though I had deliberately insulted his soul. But he finally did it.

We had a lot of fun furnishing our new home. Vittorio loved to buy books and records, and I still have the armchairs we bought, re-covered a few times. He liked simple Early American furniture which seemed to fit in with the Spanish style of the building. He bought a big white leather armchair with a hassock, and I guess the colors of our house were brown, white and tan, except for the second bedroom, which he insisted on painting blue. By now he wanted a baby as much as I did, and my gynecologist, Dr. Krahulick, had advised me to keep track of when I ovulated and to keep trying.

That June Vittorio started a film for MGM called *Sombrero*, which would do location work in Mexico City and had lots of stars besides Vittorio. I think he did a dance with Cyd Charisse. I was still turning down cockamamie scripts that UI was sending me. Universal began to realize that I had a husband to support me now and didn't mind going on suspension, even though they were using the weapon of bad publicity about how temperamental I was. I was accepting Vittorio's philosophy of *Non mi frega niente!* So I was not surprised when I was sent a loan-out script from MGM called *Executive Suite*, which was to star Fredric March, Paul Douglas, June Allyson and also William Holden. It was a wonderful script and part, and all my scenes were with either Paul Douglas or Fredric March. I had one short one with William Holden, even the idea of which made me shake.

Why hadn't MGM signed me when it borrowed me from UI so

much? I think Universal was charging $150,000 a picture for me by then. It could have gotten me under an exclusive contract for much, much less. But that's the way the ball bounces in Hollywood.

I was happy to be working at MGM the same time Vittorio was. The only thing that made me nervous was that Robert Wise, the director, wanted a two-week rehearsal period before the film started. My clothes were being designed by Edith Head, and Sidney Guilaroff was doing my hair. In other words, I was getting the superstar treatment. At that time, I think Lana Turner was "acting up" or, in other words, asking for more money.

When I reported to the stage for the first day of rehearsal, Robert Wise introduced me to all the other actors as Mrs. Gassman. I loved him forever after that. We all sat down around a table to read the script. William Holden sat down next to me and treated me as if we had never met before, thank God. When we came to a scene in which neither of us was involved, he held up his script, covering his face, and said out of the side of his mouth, "Where were you last Christmas?"

I held up my script and said, "I am a married lady now."

"So?"

I couldn't immediately think of an answer to that one, but after the next scene I managed to whisper to him that I loved my husband very much and the days of my extracurricular activities were over. He sighed then and whispered back, "All right, but in case anything changes, I'll be there the next few Christmases anyway."

"Oh, shut up and go to Acapulco."

Fredric March was a delight to work with. He was able to do a very emotional scene with tears in his eyes and pinch my fanny at the same time. If I hadn't been so in love with Vittorio, I would have fallen in love with him. He was a great actor and had great humor in front of and behind the camera. Where has that breed of actor, like March and Ronald Colman, disappeared to? They loved and enjoyed their work and were proud to be actors.

CHAPTER 28

We were seeing a lot of Richard Basehart and his wife, Valentina Cortesa, who had a house in Beverly Hills on the right side of the tracks where the very rich stars lived. Richard was already a much esteemed and highly paid actor because of *The House on Telegraph Hill* and other fine films. Frank Latimore, who had introduced Vittorio to me, had also been in that film. Valentina was one of the first Italian actresses to come to America, and Twentieth was giving her a big buildup. She was a very beautiful and accomplished actress. Many evenings Vittorio and I, and Connie and Ivan, would go to their home. Valentina would cook, and they all would talk Italian and rest their brains. I got even and pretended to talk Hungarian to Ivan. Valentina had just discovered she was pregnant and was very happy about it but she seemed to miss Italy terribly.

An Italian director, Luchino Visconti, wanted Vittorio for an important Italian film, but Metro preempted his time and would not allow him to go to Italy because he had to do *Sombrero* for them. That evening he came home from work and broke up all the lamps. I said nothing. I knew how upset he was to miss such an important film. I just bought more lamps.

On July 1 Vittorio had to start filming on location in Mexico City. I couldn't go because I was shooting my film at MGM. That year July 4 was on a Saturday, and one of my new dental caps fell out on Friday evening. I also was ovulating—it was the exact time for me to get pregnant. I called my dentist, Dr. Feder, and although it was 6:00 A.M. Saturday, he came into his office and recemented the cap. Then I rushed to the airport with just a pocketbook containing a nightgown and a toothbrush and flew to Mexico City.

Vittorio met me at the airport and was very glad to see me, but he felt I would be exhausted when I had to start shooting at 8:00 A.M. Monday. I explained why this July 4 was different from any other July 4, according to the Catholic rhythm theory. He thought about it and said, "Even if it works, I don't think the Vatican will recognize our marriage."

"Never mind," I said, "I'm planning to spend a lot of time in bed this weekend."

The studio car took us to the Hotel Reforma, and I asked him how the picture was going. He was very depressed about it and felt it was an MGM goulash musical, and he couldn't imagine why they had an Italian actor play a Mexican *vaquero*. Obviously to the MGM Casting Department a Latin is a Latin.

I got up to Vittorio's air-conditioned suite. He had put yellow roses all over the place, and there were delicious little Mexican tacos and a large pitcher of ice cold margaritas. It was almost dusk, which in July lasts a long time in Mexico City. Vittorio also had mariachis playing romantic Mexican music outside our window.

So after two margaritas we put our hearts and souls into fulfilling Dr. Krahulick's instructions. We then napped and awakened at about nine. When Vittorio came out of the shower, he saw I hadn't moved. "Come on, get dressed. They have some marvelous restaurants here, and you'll love the Mexican food." I told him that I couldn't move. "Why, for God's sake?"

"I'm conceiving," I explained.

Vittorio muttered something in Italian which translated to "Nobody in Rome will ever believe this," and with a deep sigh finished dressing and went down to the bar to wait. At about eleven o'clock I felt it was safe to move, so I joined him, by which time he was quite drunk. His first words to me were: "Do you think it's a boy?" I assured him I thought so, knowing how important sons were to Italian men.

We then had a lovely and loving twenty-four hours in Mexico City, and Vittorio put me on the Sunday night plane which got me into L.A. at 6:00 A.M. Monday. Thank goodness the airport was near MGM. Ricardo Montalban was in the commissary at lunchtime, and when he asked why I had made such a fast trip to Mexico City, I explained. He didn't see anything illogical in my behavior. In fact, he said, "Everyone gets pregnant in Mexico City, even when they're not trying." That made me very happy. . . . Ricardo was Mexican and had to know what he was talking about.

Executive Suite ended in two weeks, but Vittorio was now on location somewhere in the wilds of Mexico. The living conditions were quite primitive, and all the cast and crew of *Sombrero* were getting sick. When he called me on the radio phone, we decided it would be better for me to stay in L.A. until he finished his film.

One lonely evening I got a phone call from Richard Boone, who was also between pictures and had been the moderator of the acting group we'd had some time ago at the Hollywood Women's Club. He floored me with the following: "Charles Laughton tells me you're working very hard on your speech, and you want to do something that Hollywood would never cast you for. So how would you like to play the frail Blanche DuBois in *A Streetcar Named Desire* with Dennis Weaver as Stanley Kowalski?" Pause.

Remembering Vittorio's enormous acting range and how he was constantly stretching to play different kinds of characters, I said, "Dick, I'd love to."

I immediately called George Boroff, my brother-in-law, and asked him if we could do the play at his theater, even though it had been done in New York a few years before. George produced only original works of new young playwrights; he did Norman Lear's first play and produced *The Girl on the Via Flaminia*, Alfred Hayes's first work, and Sholom Aleichem's *Once Upon a Tailor* which was the forerunner of *Fiddler on the Roof*. George had great respect for Richard Boone and Tennessee Williams, and after thinking it over, he decided that the production would certainly be "original" and different enough "in the round" to warrant an experimental production at the Circle Theater.

George also told me he thought my sister, Blanche, was expecting a baby. I was overjoyed for her and said it should only happen to me. "You and your husband fly around the world so much, when would you have the time?" I told him we were working on it.

Rehearsals started in an improvisatory and exploratory fashion. Stella Kowalski was played by Jeanne Nicol, the wife of Alex Nicol, the actor who had been in the Sinatra picture with me. The cast consisted of members of the New York Actors' Studio, and this was my first experience of ensemble acting. I had to wait three years to have another such experience in *A Hatful of Rain* on Broadway.

I found the part of Blanche DuBois extremely difficult, and it was very hard for me to find the southern frailty and "poetic escape from reality" that the character has throughout the play. The nearest I could come to it was to recall when as a child my life had been so full of terror that I created a fragile fantasy world, and for Blanche DuBois's love of the delicate and beautiful, I used my memories of my teacher, Viola Speer. I listened to innumerable southern accents on records, then remembered how I had spoken in St. Louis when I was a child. It all came back quite easily and wiped out all remnants of my New Yorkese; it was as if a language I'd known and had forgotten returned with a little practice.

Dick Boone took us carefully through the play, scene by scene, and my favorite was the one in the second act where the young boy comes in to deliver a telegram. For me he became an apparition of Blanche DuBois's lost youth, the child she had never had, and her young lover who had committed suicide.

As I rehearsed Tennessee Williams's beautiful words, I saw clearly that what I had done with *most* of my professional life up to that point was to MAKE MONEY. I had been lucky with two or three films when I had fine scripts and good directors, but the continuity of working correctly had so far eluded me.

When Vittorio returned from Mexico, he would sit and watch rehearsals and listen closely to Dick Boone, who had acquired somewhere the ability to help actors work deeply. So few directors are able to do this for you. They direct you in terms of the results they want and then tell you where to stand. Your character's inner life is your business, and some are even embarrassed when you try to discuss it with them.

The set George's scenic designer had devised for this "in the round" irregular 200-seat house was very imaginative. Dick Boone made the audience feel as if they too lived in the huge Louisiana tenement that the Kowalski apartment was in. The porch was up one of the aisles, the front stoop was by one of the exits, the window was the theater's skylight, the front door was a mere outline hung from the ceiling, and a little stairway went up the aisle. I don't know how George achieved the quick and special lighting he used in different sections of the little theater, so that when one small area was lit, the rest of the theater was in darkness.

Alex Nicol haunted the old record stores, and we had lovely sound effects of the real New Orleans streetcar named Desire and street hawkers of the quarter selling wax flowers.

Dennis Weaver's Kowalski was very different from Marlon's. Dennis is really an Iowa farmboy, and he played the role as an uneducated farmer shoved into the congested factory atmosphere of the emerging industrial South, fighting for the safety of his home and marriage. I don't think he had the special sexual electricity that Marlon generated, but he had his own kind so that one saw Tennessee's play more clearly. And what our production was about is that no matter how much we love someone who is kind and foolish and even poetic, their senseless unintentional machinations can destroy one as fully as a premeditating enemy can.

When we finally opened, after four weeks of eight-hour-a-day rehearsals, I got some of the best theater reviews I've ever had. So did Dennis and everyone else in the cast and especially Tennessee Williams's beautiful play.

The next week nausea started hitting me at different times during the day, but I thought it was the emotional efforts of the play and all the ice water masquerading as gin that I was drinking during the show. I told Vittorio I was going to take a test anyway. It was negative. What I didn't understand was that to Vittorio a test meant a written examination of some kind.

For the next month we did SRO business, sometimes with Vittorio pitching in as stage manager. The actors had to have a high degree of concentration to pretend the audience was invisible. A family feud resulted from my complete immersion in my role. At intermission my brother-in-law, George, would sell Coca-Colas at a stand out in the lobby, but he would open the soda bottles during my favorite scene—with the telegraph boy—at the end of the second act, "Young, young, young man," which was a quiet and poetic scene. For several nights I heard him opening those damn bottles with that peculiar hissing sound. After asking him repeatedly please to not do this until the end of the act, he continued to do so through the entire scene so the Cokes would be ready for the intermission. One night I made my exit into the lobby and with one sweep of my left arm sent about two dozen Coca-Cola bottles crashing to the floor and continued on to my dressing room without breaking my stride. I'm glad my sister wasn't there that night. George was so startled that he just stared at me, and the audience in that small theater went into shock. They had only heard the crash, they hadn't seen it, but during the intermission they saw all the broken glass. Intellectually they agreed with me, but when you do a thing like that, you lose your audience for the rest of the play. They are never exactly sure what you're liable to do next, and in such a small theater they're worried for their *own* safety.

The next morning I was so upset and nauseated I told Vittorio that I was going to take another test. His answer was: "Can I help you with it?" I said, "No, thanks," and went to the doctor.

This time my rabbit test was equivocal. The doctor said, "Don't get your hopes up. We'll try another one next month. And stay off your feet as much as possible." Just in case, his nurse gave me a form for Vittorio to fill out, to state his income and other financial facts concerning our family. This is the way, in those days and probably now as well, Beverly Hills doctors charge you. If your income is high, their fee is high, and I assume if it is low, they charge less. When Vittorio filled out the form, he lied at every question, and as I looked over his shoulder, I got the feeling he was on his way to becoming a millionaire. I asked him if he had a secret income in Italy that I didn't know about, and he gave me another puzzling answer: "No, but it is probably safer this way." And he signed the form with a flourish.

I tried to do the play as unemotionally as possible, and Vittorio was still shooting Sombrero, which he said was a hat that never would get finished or fit. It was a sweltering September, so during the day I stayed in the house, tried to stay cool, stared at the television and took cool showers.

One night during the performance a man in the audience got so involved in the play that when Dennis grabbed the scissors to cut up my finery, the man leaped up and tried to take the scissors away from him. The audience didn't know if this was part of the play or not. Dennis threw the man out into the lobby, where George poured cold water on him and brought him back to reality. We continued the play. This happens quite often in small circle theaters.

Years later I was watching Robert De Niro do a play I had written for him called One Night Stands of a Noisy Passenger. The small Actors Playhouse in Greenwich Village had a thrust stage, and during a very emotional scene with Diane Ladd (who is also a special friend and fine actress) a young man in the front row suddenly joined in the emotional dialogue that Diane and Bobby were having. Bobby immediately stopped acting, turned to the young man and said in threatening tones, "This is a theater. We're the actors. You're the audience. We talk, you listen. You want to stay here, those are the rules." The young man nodded, shut up, and the play continued.

Back at the Circle Theater, my Streetcar began to move very slowly. I was tired and feeling rather sick all the time and was constantly getting notes from Dick Boone. I told him it must be the heat and the exhausting nature of the role that were lowering my energy.

The next day I went to the lab at Dr. Krahulick's instructions and took yet another rabbit test. The next day his nurse called and said to come to his office. I rushed over. Going up in the elevator, I was so nervous that I practically pushed the cute young operator to hurry the elevator up to the nineteenth floor. She said, "Listen, push me enough, and I can make it go sideways." When I got off, I ran down the hall to Dr. K.'s office. The nurse just smiled and said nothing. When the doctor finally saw me, he informed me that my last test was positive! I kissed him and the nurse and a strange and very pregnant lady. Dr. K. said, "Don't kiss us, kiss Vittorio. He followed my instructions exactly." After examining me, he informed me that I was almost four months pregnant and that I must leave the play and stay off my feet as much as possible to avoid a miscarriage. He gave me a sheet of instructions and a diet list and told me I must keep my weight down if I wanted an easy delivery.

Going down in the elevator, I did a little tap dance, and the pretty elevator operator said, "Good news, huh?"

I sang, "Yes, I'm going to have a baby."

"That's *good* news?"

"Of course. It's my first one, and I'm planning five more." She laughed, and I kissed her.

Vittorio wasn't shooting that day and was studying *Amleto* as usual. I had stopped and bought *him* champagne and flowers. What I didn't know was that the elevator operator was a "stringer" for Hedda Hopper. When I entered the house with my good news and presents, Vittorio was slightly irritated. I got upset because I didn't want anything to spoil this glorious day. "I'll never understand this country," he explained. "*One*, Hedda Hopper just called and gave us permission to have a baby. *Two*, you have to take these tests and get good marks. *Three*, I have to make a lot of money. Why? In Italy we just fuck."

When I got through laughing, I explained what a rabbit test was and that the regulation form was just so the doctor could charge poor people less. I said I would straighten out his financial exaggerations with Dr. K.'s nice nurse, explaining that he had misunderstood. And I told him that the elevator girl had probably called Hedda Hopper before I'd had a chance to get home and tell him. He relaxed and began to kiss me, but I was nervous about letting our lovemaking go any further until I had checked the set of instructions Dr. K. had given me. I didn't want to say, "Stop, Vittorio, while I look at Dr. Krahulick's mimeographed sheet," so I started to make lunch instead. "Do you think it will be a boy?" he asked me again.

I patted my now suddenly bulging stomach and said. "We'll take whatever we get. And if it isn't a boy, we'll try again now that we know how."

When I told George I had to leave the play, we found out that not only were my sister and I pregnant, but Alex Nicol's wife, Dennis Weaver's wife and Dr. Feder's wife were all pregnant too. That must have been some Fourth of July!

Vittorio got a wire from an Italian producer telling him that he had a wonderful part in a film for him if he could squeeze it in before beginning his *Amleto* rehearsals. And he would pay him

$100,000 (not lire). When Vittorio read the script, he felt he had to accept the role. I immediately developed intense morning, afternoon and evening sickness. In fact, I was so nauseated the doctor had to give me calcium injections to counteract the nausea. George was rather put out when we all decided to close the play. It was doing S.R.O. business, but he understood that it was an act of God, which even Equity recognizes.

I wanted Vittorio to get to know Charles Laughton, who by now had built a pool next to his beautiful early Spanish hacienda in Hollywood. He had built the pool into a replica of an outdoor Roman bath. Vittorio and Oskar Werner and I and my big belly would sometimes go over to Laughton's house. While Laughton and I floated in the pool like whales, Oskar Werner and Vittorio would argue about in which language Shakespeare was best, and Laughton listened in stunned amazement. Werner insisted that Moissi, the famous German poet, had done such a great job that his translation was superior to the original. Vittorio almost drowned Oskar, insisting that some ancient Italian poet was far greater and had not only translated Shakespeare's immortal words but had improved on them. After cocktails, when we all dried off and dressed, Laughton recited Shakespeare's sonnets and put these young foreign upstarts to shame. They both knew just enough English to realize how silly their arguments had been.

In the middle of one night I was so nauseated I started vomiting in earnest. I yelled, "Vittorio, a pail! Quick!"

After running around the house for five minutes, Vittorio suddenly ran to my bed and said, "What's a pail?" I started to laugh so hard I didn't need the pail.

One day the nausea stopped, and I began to look, I think, quite lovely and relaxed. I had stopped bleaching my hair and let it grow back into its natural dark blonde. Vittorio took me to the most expensive maternity shop in Beverly Hills and bought me six outfits, most of them huge. When I protested, he said, "This is an Italian baby, and whatever Dr. K. says, you will probably gain a lot of weight before the nine months are up. And we can always use the clothes for other babies."

At that time there was a ground swell going on all over the country for Adlai Stevenson, as my liberal stomach swelled along with it. One night, as we were watching Stevenson making a speech on television, with Vittorio absolutely positive that the American people had to elect this wise man whose presidency would be so good for the whole world, I had a very strange sensation in my stomach. It was like a little flutter from the inside. Every woman who has had a baby knows what I mean. It's a miraculous sensation, this first feeling of life. I got very quiet and listened to it again with my inner ear and my hand on my stomach. And the reality of the other human being who was about to join us made me smile with wonder. Vittorio noticed my face and said, "I don't think Stevenson is that miraculous." I turned off the set, took his hand and put it on my stomach. He also listened and felt carefully, but his reaction was totally different from mine. He snatched his hand away quickly, and there was an expression of sheer terror on his face. It quite upset me. I used that moment with Ben Gazzara in *A Hatful of Rain.*

I began to take lessons in knitting and bought a beautiful white bassinet and started lining it with blue quilting and ruffles. Vittorio was arranging his *Amleto* schedule so he would be back April 1 in plenty of time for the birth of our baby. Both he and his family were a little put out because I refused to come to Italy and gestate there while he rehearsed. But I wanted to be close to my family and my doctor. And since Vittorio would be on the road quite a bit, and it was cold and damp in the north of Italy, where he'd be performing, all I would have been doing was sitting in cold hotel and dressing rooms. So I wrote to them, arguing that it was safer for me to lie still in California. I enclosed a letter from Dr. K. to prove it.

Vittorio had to leave for his film around Thanksgiving, which made his sojourn in America exactly one year. My, we had gotten a lot accomplished in that year. This Thanksgiving we had dinner at Chasen's again, and I tried not to weep into it.

We went to the airport alone the next day, although the doctor had told me not to drive. Vittorio had received from his mother about a thousand instructions, some of them old Italian folk customs, about what I was to do until his return in April. He passed them on to me while waiting for his plane. I waved him off with smiles and headed for the parking lot, then drove back slowly and alone to our sturdy Spanish duplex.

Vittorio's Italian lemon after-shave lotion seemed to permeate the entire apartment. His very neat side of the room, with all his books, notes and pencils in a glass, stared at me. My side of the big bedroom was pretty messy. I started straightening it up, and although it was a fairly mild day, I suddenly developed that familiar chill and turned the heat full up. Thank goodness the upstairs apartment was still empty, so that no one would roast up there. I could not get warm, despite woolen underwear, a flannel nightgown, sweaters and Vittorio's woolen bathrobe. When I phoned the doctor, he didn't understand it and suggested that perhaps it was some kind of psychosomatic reaction to Vittorio's departure. He told me to take some more vitamins and get a larger heating pad from Schwab's. I then completed my outfit with Vittorio's white wool tennis socks. This remained my uniform for a good part of my pregnacy.

Once in a while Connie, Farley, Dawn Addams, Nick Ray, Jimmy Dean, Jerry Paris or Marlon would drag me out of the house on a mild day to go to a movie or Barney's Beanery. I would wear my mink coat, sweaters and wool leotards. I began to have the nausea again and found that the only things I could eat and keep down were soft white Wonder bread, cheap bologna with yellow Gulden's mustard, pickles, milk and spaghetti. The doctor told me to eat what I could and gave me more vitamins.

Whether my loneliness gave out a special ESP or not, I don't know, but one night, when I was sitting in front of the TV and watching Milton Berle and crying, the doorbell rang. It was Connie and a small suitcase. I greeted them both with open arms and kissed and hugged her after she told me she planned to spend this difficult part of my pregnancy with me.

She soon had me laughing so much I turned off Milton Berle and was entertained by Connie Dowling's Irish wit. We curled up on the sofa, and she began to make lists of things we had to do for the next couple of months. On the top of her list was that we had to go visit Marlon on the set at Metro, where he was playing Mark Antony in *Julius Caesar*. *Two*, we had to have all my girlfriends give me a "surprise" baby shower at Dawn Addams's apartment so I would get lots of clothes for the baby. *Three*, I had to start wearing my beautiful maternity outfits and go to Romanoff's or the Polo Lounge at the Beverly Hills Hotel for cocktails to get out of my depression. I reminded her that I had to stay off my feet and that I could only drink milk. She said, "If necessary, we'll get a gorgeous antique wheelchair from Goldwyn's Prop Department and you'll drink milk. All you've got to do is put your eyelashes on and wear off-the-shoulder maternity dresses and jewelry. Listen, if anyone can make pregnancy fashionable, it's you. *Four*," she continued, "we'll go to concerts and operas, and talk with our intellectual writer friends so the baby will be smart and musical. *Five*, hang around the most beautiful men and women we know so that the baby will be beautiful. *Six*, we'll drive to the beach and breathe

the fresh Pacific Ocean air as much as possible. *Seven*, we have a lot of charge accounts so we'll go shopping every day."

Because of Connie, my Christmas and New Year's were less lonely and even rather fun. The day of my shower arrived. I was seven months pregnant and weighed 160 pounds. I had already gained 36 pounds, which was worrying the doctor considerably. But I was feeling much better and enjoying the Italian restaurants Connie was always getting us invited to. Dawn Addams was in town doing a film at Metro, and the shower was held at her little old-fashioned duplex on Third Street. It was a wonderful party, and the guest list included Debbie Reynolds, Susan Cabot, Peggy Maley, Pier Angeli, Marisa Pavan, Elsa Lanchester, and all the young female stars and starlets from UI. It surprised me that I had so many close girlfriends—that was the best present and made me feel warm and loved. The girls catered the lunch from Chasen's, and I ate two helpings of everything. I passed up the innocent-looking champagne punch that turned lethal about seven o'clock. I stuck to milk.

Farley came to take me home at six, along with the other girls' boyfriends, and by that time all the girls were drunk. Thank goodness my mother was busily making coffee and handing out her homemade strudel. There were a couple of photographers there from the news services, and they had their wives come over to join the merriment. Universal must have had a sudden attack of generosity because it sent me a very expensive English baby carriage that was built like a Jaguar. This carriage was used by me and all my girlfriends for many years. I got so many presents they filled the carriage and the playpen—when we could get Farley and Peggy out of it—and we got the presents home at midnight by putting down the top of my Cadillac and loading up all my Actors' Studio friends' cars. The party then continued at my house.

When Vittorio called "the little mother" from Italy to find out how the baby shower had gone, Jimmy Dean answered the phone. Vittorio was deafened by the racket of the party, and when Jimmy finally condescended to give me this transatlantic call, he yelled, "I'll call back tomorrow. Be careful, and don't ride on anybody's motorcycle," and hung up. Like my father, he hates long-distance calls.

The next day, Connie had an interview for a part in a film (which she got), and I went out to visit Marlon at MGM and I rested in his dressing room while he was shooting a scene. On his dressing table I saw a beautiful terra-cotta bust of Marlon's head with his

Mark Antony haircut. It was a little larger than life size and exactly the same proportions as Ronald Colman's. When Marlon came in after finishing his scene, he saw me looking longingly at the bust. "Since I was working and couldn't attend your baby shower, would you like to have my head?"

"I'd love to have it, Marlon."

"Okay," he said. "But remember, give it to the baby when it grows up." I never did remember; Marlon's and Ronald's heads look so good gracing each side of my fireplace.

I had been writing to Vittorio every other day, printing carefully in my crummy Italian, and he was sending me, in his stilted English, detailed descriptions of the progress of the *Amleto* rehearsals.

Connie began working on her film. She had a lot of night shooting and sometimes didn't get home till after midnight, so we decided that, instead of her waking me up in the middle of the night, it would be better if she went back home. She left reluctantly, leaving me with firm instructions to get out of the house and make Farley and Jerry Paris take me to lots of movies and parties.

Jerry was starting a film with Marlon—as soon as Marlon's hair grew long enough—called *The Wild One* at Columbia. It was about a motorcycle gang that took over a town. In January 1953 this film seemed like an improbable fantasy in our more or less well-ordered society. Jerry had a good part in it, and I was glad for him. Farley had to leave for location to do a picture about a psychotic who murders a priest. Another delight! When he left, life was indeed dreary because he used to keep my spirits up with jokes and remarks like: "Just think, in a few weeks there'll be two or more of you." I would call him at 4:00 A.M. when I wanted Wil Wright's chocolate almond ice-cream cones or corned beef sandwiches, and he would always bring me what I craved. This was only my nighttime eating.

Suddenly it seemed that most of my friends had disappeared, working on location, doing repertory theater or going to New York to do plays. Then I began to really swell up, I think with edema. It was a very cold February in California, and I would put the living-room sofa cushions in front of the fireplace, with the heat full on, and sleep in my "uniform." My house was so hot that when anyone came over, he would talk to me through my living-room window, open only about two inches.

On the night of February 11, my mother called to say Blanche had gone into labor, and they were at the Hollywood Presbyterian Hospital. I had seen my doctor that morning, and he seemed a little worried about my condition. My parents wanted me to stay quiet and they would phone me when Blanche had her baby. I wanted to be with Bappy at this most important moment, but in all honesty I felt so lousy and huge and I guess I missed Vittorio so much that I took a sleeping pill that the doctor had okayed, lay down next to the wall heater and went to sleep, more or less.

The next day my mother called to tell me that Blanche had had a beautiful little girl named Alice Lea Boroff early that morning. I was very happy for her and sent flowers. That night, the twelfth, my parents were exhausted and went home at about ten to sleep. I was restless and watched some picture with Merle Oberon on TV. As I got up from the sofa to adjust the set, I noticed that I was standing in a pool of water and felt strange inside. I wasn't very frightened yet because I didn't understand what was happening.

I called the doctor, and his exchange told me he was in the operating room and would call as soon as he could. I didn't want to wake my parents because they had been with Blanche for two days. Connie was in New York with Ivan, and all my other girlfriends had early work calls, so I decided to call Jerry Paris, who was doing night work on *The Wild One* at Columbia. The operator put me through to the set, and Marlon answered the phone as he had been about to make a call. In a few minutes I heard two motorcycles roar out front, and there were Jerry and Marlon in their black leather costumes with their big black motorcycles, prepared to take me to Cedars of Lebanon. I refused. Marlon asked how fast the pains were coming, and with great dignity I informed him they weren't coming at all. And I wasn't about to go to the hospital on a motorcycle. After all, my husband was a great Italian Shakespearean actor, and I had to have his baby with some dignity. So we called a cab, and Jerry rode with me, Marlon following on his motorcycle. The nurse at the emergency entrance looked a little confused and said, "Which one is the father?"

"Neither," I said. "The father's in Italy." So with great authority, I can assure you that having a premature baby without your husband present is scary, painful and the loneliest thing in the world.

CHAPTER 29

As the nurse undressed me and put me into a hospital gown, my eyes fell on a calendar on the dresser. I asked her what time it was. She said 1:00 A.M. I held my breath and then asked what day. She smiled brightly and said Friday, February 13, 1953. I was not about to have my baby on Friday the thirteenth! No matter what anybody said, I would have my baby on February 14, Valentine's Day, and then everything would be all right. Typical of my crazy magical thinking.

The next twenty-four hours became a struggle between me and the entire Obstetrical Department of Cedars of Lebanon Hospital. They were determined that my baby be born as quickly and safely as possible. I was determined to make it Valentine's Day—a lovely birthday. A sleepy Dr. K. showed up in a few minutes to have a heart-to-heart talk with me. "Shelley, I've been a gynecologist and obstetrician for forty years, and I have delivered thousands of babies. You're sitting there in bed with your legs straight and your ankles crossed. [I'd hoped he hadn't noticed.] That is not the way one gives birth. You have to help nature by spreading your legs, bending your knees, breathing deeply and pushing. We want to get this over with, don't we? I don't know about you, but I have an important golf game this afternoon." He was making jokes, but there was an underlying seriousness in what he was saying.

Still, I held fast to my superstitious safety device. "Dr. K., at midnight I will be glad to follow all your instructions to the letter, but I've decided to have my baby tomorrow." I looked him straight in the eye as I said it; if Harry Cohn backed off from my resolute stare, what chance did the gentle Dr. K. have?

After what seemed like three days, that damned minute hand of the huge clock on the wall in front of me finally joined the twelve. It was midnight again. Somebody Italian must have been around because I heard *spingere* ("PUSH"), and I did with more energy and devotion than I've ever done anything in my whole life. My pains were coming so fast it seemed just a few minutes before they took me into the delivery room, but it was an hour before they gave me the saddle block; in reality, they told me later, it was just another few minutes.

My daughter was born at one o'clock in the morning on February 14, Valentine's Day, 1953. She gave a hearty cry when they smacked her bottom, and I joined her with happy tears. When they put this beautiful little girl on my stomach, I looked at her in amazement, not understanding this great miracle. The first thing I said was: "Where did she come from?" Dr. K. answered, "Probably from God. With the help of you and your husband." It was love at first sight, the most important love of my life that has continued ever since. She charmed the doctor and me during her first five minutes of life. The premature baby specialist had her placed immediately in a new kind of incubator called an Isolette, and they wheeled us both out of the delivery room.

Vittorio was in the middle of a performance when I telephoned his theater in Milan. He dashed through a soliloquy and to the phone. I explained that I was in the hospital and that he had a beautiful baby daughter. Something must have been wrong with the connection because his answer was rather peculiar. I think he said, "No, no. Don't do it yet because I'm returning April third."

"Vittorio, *attenzione! Attenzione! La bambina è arrivata troppo presto* . . . you understand? She's here!"

With that, I heard the phone drop, and while I listened, I heard from a distance Vittorio announcing to the audience in his loudest tones, *"La mia bambina, Vittoria Gassman, è già arrivata questa mattina in California."* I don't think this was part of his *Amleto* script, but the sentimental family-oriented Italian audience screamed its approval and applauded. He rushed back to the phone and said, "Shelley, *bene?* Okay? Baby okay? *Bene?"* In his excitement he had forgotten his English.

I said, "Yes, darling. I guess she was in a hurry. But what was that name you announced from the stage just now?"

"Vittoria Gassman, of course. In Italy you can name a daughter only after a father and a son after the mother. And I want her to have my name. It also means Victory. And she needs it as she is obviously rushing to her *destino."*

Meekly, I said, "But, Vittorio, she arrived on St. Valentine's Day, which is a holiday here. And I wanted to name her after Valentina Cortesa."

"Don't be silly," he replied. "That is a stupid made-up holiday. San Valentino is not a very important saint. And Valentina Cortesa has enough babies named after her."

"Could I give her the middle name of Gina?" I asked hopefully.

"Why?" he asked loudly.

"Because it was my grandmother's name in St. Louis, and Gina Lollobrigida is also one of the most beautiful women I've ever seen."

"Okay," he said. "I give you and Vittoria a kiss. She will be beautiful anyway because she will look like you."

"Darling, are you very disappointed it isn't a boy?"

"Next year," he said. "And now I have to go back onstage and finish the play. I will see both your faces on April third." With that he hung up, and I informed my family and the nurse who surrounded my bed that my daughter's name was Vittoria Gina Gassman.

My mother said, "What a long name for such a little baby." I told her that when she grew up, if it was too long, she could use her middle name. My mother was pleased that the middle name was her mother's. My family didn't want to tire me, so they all left their presents and my mother whispered happily in my ear, "I've waited all these years, and now I have two grandchildren in three days."

I smiled sleepily and said, "Mom, you must be used to Hollywood double features by now. How is Blanche doing?" She assured me she was fine, and so was little Alice. For the next week my family wore a path between Hollywood Presbyterian and Cedars of Lebanon hospitals.

I was really amazed at the number of telegrams, cables and flowers I got from all over the world from relatives, co-workers and especially my darling fans. I was most touched by the latter and answered every one myself. I had to send most of the flowers to the children's ward because, together with Lucy Ball's flowers—she'd had Desi, Jr., in that room just before me—the nurses and the lab technicians couldn't get into my room, which had taken on the look of a botanical garden.

They didn't let me see my baby that day or night, but I thought it was because I wasn't feeling well. The next morning Dr. Rosen and the premature baby specialist came into my room, and when I questioned them about how soon I could see my little Vittoria again, they were very evasive. I began to be frightened. When my mother came, I made her go down to the nursery many times to see Vittoria, who had lost weight and was down to four pounds three ounces. I hadn't known it, but I had a lot of stitches somewhere down below, and I wasn't allowed out of bed for anything.

That night I was so restless and in pain they gave me a strong shot of morphine, and I fell asleep immediately. At three in the morning I came wide-awake, unable to catch my breath. I struggled out of bed and started crawling out of my room, turning left down the hallway toward the nursery. To this day I have no idea how I knew the nursery was to the left. I had on only a hospital gown, open at the back, so I was practically naked. I had crawled about 100 feet when my private night nurse came running after me. "Mrs. Gassman," she cried, "you're not allowed out of bed! You can't walk!"

With terrible anger and gasping for breath and words, I said, "I know I can't walk, you idiot, that's why I'm crawling. You go get a wheelchair or I'll kill you later." And I kept right on crawling. One hundred feet later she arrived with a wheelchair and a blanket, and I made her run with it and me all the way to the nursery.

When we got there, one nurse, all in green with a green mask, was attending what seemed to be a great many premature babies. And there was my little Vittoria in the only Isolette, and she had turned blue and was gasping for breath. I pounded on the window with all my strength. The nurse turned. I pointed frantically to Vittoria. She rushed to the Isolette, put an electric apparatus into Vittoria's mouth and suctioned the phlegm out of my baby's chest. I sat there and prayed.

After an eternity, Vittoria's color returned to sort of normal, and the nurse gave her a special little bottle containing penicillin and something that cuts phlegm in premature babies' lungs. My little baby wound her tiny hand around the nurse's thumb and eagerly sucked on the bottle. When she finished the two ounces, she sucked on one of her own toes.

I wouldn't move, despite the pleadings of my night nurse. By 6:00 A.M. two other nurses in operating-room gowns came in to relieve the nurse who had been in the nursery. She came out weeping. "Miss Winters, honest, I didn't realize how sick your baby was or I wouldn't have taken my eyes off her. There were so many new preemies in the nursery tonight, and I was on duty alone. The other nurse was sick." I looked at her stone-eyed. By then Dr. K. and Dr. Rosen, Chief of Pediatrics, were there, and I asked them to order round-the-clock nurses for Vittoria so there would be somebody watching her constantly until her weight got up to the necessary five pounds and I could take her home.

After ten days, when they had taken out my stitches, the doctor began making firm suggestions about my going home. I began to malinger because I didn't want to go home without my baby, and now I secretly trusted nobody in that hospital. So hoping to starve me out, the doctor put me on a low-calorie diet.

I received a phone call from Fred Zinnemann asking if I had read

From Here to Eternity and if I would like to play the part of the prostitute in the film. I was so preoccupied with my baby I was barely civil to him, and when he informed me that the filming was scheduled to start in Hawaii in six weeks, I hung up. Donna Reed played the role and won a well-deserved Oscar for her performance.

Finally, somewhere toward the middle of March, when I came back from a visit to the nursery, there was another expectant mother in *my* bed. My mother and Farley were there to drag me home. Before I left the hospital, they let me get all sterile, put on a rubber glove and feed my baby six ounces of milk in the Isolette. She laughed, held onto my thumb and sucked all the milk quickly, then burped and yawned and stretched. In fact, the entire performance was the greatest I've ever seen, including Olivier and Lunt and Fontanne.

After three weeks, Dr. Rosen told me that Vittoria had achieved the enormous weight of five pounds, so we brought her home. I had been interviewing baby nurses for two weeks, and I finally settled on a young Scottish woman who came highly recommended and had taken care of many delicate babies. What I hadn't realized was that she practically never let the parents come into the nursery. She became very possessive of the baby and didn't think that my mother or I were capable of handling this little creature or that we were clean enough. She also did something that drove my mother and me insane. She took the baby outside every morning, rain or shine. Bundled up, of course, but she stood outside for half an hour while I sat by the window and cried.

Finally, April 3 arrived. For some reason Vittorio's plane was diverted to San Diego, and I drove there, breaking all speed limits, and picked him up. I was back to my fighting weight and had gone out to UI that morning and gotten glamored up. But I had on a dignified suit and no eyelashes, and my own dark-blonde hair had a rather simple hairdo.

Vittorio looked very different when he got off the plane, tired and strained from doing the film in the day and rehearsing *Amleto* at night, and then playing this enormous role for all these months had obviously exhausted him. He played an Italian joke on me. He walked right past me. When I yelled, "Vittorio!" he turned quickly and said, "I was looking for a roly-poly platinum blonde. I didn't recognize you. Who is this elegant model? She can't be Signora Gassman." He gave me a bear hug and a kiss and was so tired he didn't say a word when I said, "I'll drive us home."

Although I had been sending him pictures of Vittoria, he couldn't wait to see her. He insisted on stopping at a toy store in Beverly Hills and bought her a huge brown toy bear that she still has. He also had many presents from his family and a diamond and sapphire pin for me that had belonged to his grandmother. It was so delicate and beautiful that I immediately put it on and almost never took it off for months. His idea of jewelry for his seven-week-old daughter was a Florentine gold horse, about three inches in width, with a diamond mane and tail and ruby eyes. He gave it to me, saying, "Here, you wear it until she's sixteen."

When we got home to our duplex, Vittorio left his suitcases in the car and rushed into the house. The Scottish nurse said, "Just a minute, Mr. Gassman, will you please wash your hands before you go into the nursery?" He went into the bathroom, and I followed, and he scrubbed his hands. When we had gotten engaged, his agent had given us an enormous quantity of "His" and "Hers" towels. Vittorio was so angry at the nurse who had prevented him from seeing his daughter for another five minutes, he was quietly cursing in Italian as he dried his hands on "His" towel. He looked at it and said, "Everything is so hygienic in this country I don't understand how you ever got pregnant."

With that, he burst into the nursery, where Vittoria was lying on the big bed, dressed in a new pink linen dress with pink socks and booties. He knelt over her, and they gazed at each other. She grabbed his tie with all the Italian germs on it. The nurse almost fainted. He began to talk to her in Italian immediately, and he kissed her on the mouth. The nurse left the room.

The baby was only seven weeks old, but I swear they began to play a game. Vittorio would cover her little legs with a thin silk blanket, and she would lie very still. Then he would pretend to look away and talk to me in English, and she would furiously kick the blanket off, laughing and chortling. Vittorio would then call her a bad girl or something in Italian, and they would do it all over again. This intellectual game, called Kick the Blanket Off, went on for hours.

The nurse came in to dress Vittoria and take her outside. I argued that the baby's father had just arrived from Italy, and this was the first he'd seen of her. Besides, it was foggy and quite chilly. She said, "I'm sorry, Mrs. Gassman, but the baby is *my* responsibility, and she must get some fresh air every day." She took the baby out and stood in the rain in the backyard, holding her.

I stayed there and cried and said, "Oh, Vittorio, she must know what she's doing, but the baby had congested lungs when she was born, and I'm so afraid she'll catch a cold." Vittorio walked out the back door, took our daughter out of the nurse's arms, said something to her which I couldn't hear through the glass pane and brought the baby inside.

The nurse came in as red as a beet and said with great Scottish dignity, "Mrs. Gassman, I am the most famous and valuable nurse in Beverly Hills, and I will not be spoken to in that way."

Vittorio said, "Good. Pack up your things, and get the hell out of here." With some sixth sense my mother, who was now in residence with my father in the upstairs apartment, came in the front door just then, gave the departing nurse a month's check and must have scared the hell out of her because she got out of the house in ten minutes. Vittorio then discussed with my mother whether she knew how to take care of such a small baby.

I got very angry and said, "Listen, it's my baby, and the doctor and his nurse have given me instructions. I'm not an idiot. I can take care of her. Well . . . that is, until we get another nurse." Vittorio said he'd phone his mother in Italy for her advice, and then we'd all take care of her.

The next week all the Beverly Hills agencies were sending us nurses. But Vittorio insisted they were all slightly insane and/or smoked like chimneys and/or got more money than the president of Italy. Perhaps because of our nervousness with her, Vittoria developed colic, a fearsome baby ailment, which meant her little tummy hurt very badly after she ate and she would scream the house down for hours. The second time it happened, Vittorio *hit me*, as if it were my fault. I told him if he ever did it again, I would stab him like a Sicilian wife. But I forgave him because we were really beside ourselves when the baby screamed like that.

It took Dr. Rosen about three days to diagnose the cause. The baby had developed an allergy to cow's milk and could keep only goat's milk down. She was now back down to 5 pounds. I was down to 115. Vittorio wasn't eating at all, and he was furious at me for not being able to nurse her. So, starting the next morning at four-thirty, when it was still dark, he would get up and drive way down La Cienega Boulevard to a special dairy that pasteurized goat's milk, and he would buy his daughter a fresh supply each morning. He did this for the next six months. The constant screaming ceased.

One Friday morning the doorbell rang, and who should be standing there but Emily, the nurse who had taken care of Bob Walker's twin baby boys? I pulled her into the house before she could get away, kissed her, locked the door and shoved the baby into her arms. In five minutes Vittoria was burping on her shoulder and calmly fell asleep. Emily put her in her crib, then herded us two hysterical parents into the living room. She lit a cigarette, annoying Vittorio, but my look warned him that if he said one word, he would be back on the plane to Italy, MGM contract or no.

Emily first explained to us that she had taken care of many premature babies, then told us that since this was our first baby, we were communicating our terror, mostly unwarranted, about her tiny size. She explained that babies, like animals, are very attuned to different tones of voice, and it was very important for us to be relaxed and happy around her if we wanted her to get over her colic. Vittorio took me to lunch at Romanoff's, where we both got drunk in relief, and he decided that Emily's miraculous appearance was the result of his mother's novena in Italy. Vittorio then asked for a phone to be brought to the table, and I listened while his agent screamed at him. Vittorio finally said, "I will tell you Monday morning. I think we've found a good nurse, and now I will be able to do the film." He told me then that MGM wanted him to do a film called *Rhapsody* with Elizabeth Taylor and John Agar. He overcasually informed me that he was getting $100,000 for the picture but that he had been delaying the starting date until Vittoria got over her colic. So MGM also was hoping that Emily worked out since its theaters were clamoring for another Elizabeth Taylor movie.

Not to be outdone, I called my agent and told him that I weighed 118, the baby was almost four months old and we had a good nurse at last. I asked him if there were any films around for me. Vittorio looked like thunder. He whispered, "Can't you stay home for at least six months and supervise the baby and make sure the house is run correctly? And perhaps we should think about having the next baby. You said if it was a girl, we would try for a boy." I made no response to that remark. My lonely pregnancy and terrifying delivery were still too fresh in my mind to contemplate having another baby so soon. But before I could try to explain it to him, the phone at our table rang. It was my agent with the offer of a picture called *The Sunday Punch* to be made at Metro. It wasn't exactly *A Place in the Sun*, but I had been absent from the screen for more than a year, and the idea of working at MGM while Vittorio was working there with gorgeous Elizabeth Taylor seemed a sensible idea.

When Vittorio asked me about this MGM film I was contemplating, I said I had, of course, to read the script first. But I overcasually told him that my salary was $100,000 too, and UI was being mean by keeping half. We suddenly realized we were practicing movie one-upmanship on each other, and broke up. Vittorio said, "Perhaps I should retire. I really am very exhausted from *Amleto*, and I could stay home and take care of the baby and cook and you can support the family." I wiped the ironic grin off his face with a kiss, and we both went into gales of laughter. All the patrons in the bar at Romanoff's broke up, too, having caught our infectious hysteria.

Conditions were idyllic at MGM. Dore Schary was now in charge of production at Metro—L. B. Mayer had disappeared into Oz or somewhere—and Schary didn't care what his stars did at lunch as long as their work in front of the camera was good. So Vittorio and I shared a dressing room again. His film had a long schedule; I believe *Rhapsody* took six or more months to shoot, and he had to take violin lessons to simulate playing a violin. He would practice eight or nine hours a day, fingering and bowing a silent violin while listening to the concertos he was required to play at different concerts in the film. Vittoria would lie in her playpen, listen to the record and watch him by the hour, the way I used to watch and listen to Uncle Joe in St. Louis. She was developing into a strong, chubby baby under Emily's expert care. One day Vittorio and I almost fainted when, as he was practicing, we suddenly noticed that she had turned herself over and, her chin resting in her little hand, leaned up on her elbow as she critically watched her father mimicking the superb violinist on the record.

On April 28, our first anniversary, Paul Kohner, Vittorio's agent, took us to dinner at the famous La Rue restaurant on the Strip. In the past year we'd flown thousands of miles, I'd done a play and two pictures, he'd done *Hamlet* and three pictures and we'd bought a home and squeezed in having a baby. "And my Roman friends said it wouldn't last a year," Vittorio said. A cold chill came over me.

Paul Kohner's beautiful wife, Lupita, who had been a famous Mexican actress, gave me some womanly advice about the best way for a Latin wife to be happy. "You must be very subtle with Latin men, Shelley. You are a very straightforward American woman, but you must not always let them know what you are thinking or directly what you want. Make it always seem as if it is his idea. Even struggle against the ideas you agree with, then make him feel you are only going along with his desires because you love and respect him." I knew the Kohners had a very happy marriage. Her husband adored her and his children and his home and would never even think of taking the shortest vacation unless his beloved wife could go along. I listened carefully to her advice but I didn't believe I could change my character that much, although her words stayed with me for a long time, especially every morning when I looked at our "His" and "Hers" towels.

My little prizefight picture was almost over by mid-June, but Vittorio's cultural epic went on until about October 1. He began to get tired again and at four o'clock forgot his English, so his director scheduled his scenes early in the morning and right after lunch as much as possible. I suspected it was because Vittorio wanted to come home and play with Vittorina.

Emily gave us a body blow when she told us she never stayed with a baby longer than six months because she became too attached to it and it was too painful to leave. Vittorio offered to double her salary, but she said, "No, I have no children of my own, and I just can't get that attached to someone else's baby. But I will make sure you have a good permanent nanny when I leave. In fact, I'm working on a lady whose children have grown up and wants a permanent home and likes to travel. When she finishes her present job she'll come and meet you." She was the beloved Kathy Mc-Caskill, who stayed with me until Vittoria was eight.

I finished *The Sunday Punch*, and my agent waited the usual twenty-four hours before giving me the next offer, which was really a stunner. The Las Vegas casinos were beginning to have beautiful theaters and were booking stars. The Flamingo, which was the newest and biggest, had offered me $30,000 a week for four weeks, after a try-out in San Diego. I consulted Vittorio. He thought it was a good idea but looked a little disappointed because he said if *Rhapsody* was ever finished, he had hoped we would fly to Italy and show Vittorina off to all his relatives. This was a surprise to me because I had thought he intended to spend the following year in America. After all, he had a contract for seven years with M G M and had served only one. We compromised. He would come to Vegas with me for two weeks, then fly to Italy for a short engagement of *Amleto*.

One evening he came home from the studio in a towering rage and broke up all my lamps. It seemed that during the shooting of *Rhapsody* he had to wear a special tuxedo with four arms; then a famous Italian violinist, Zino Francescatti or somebody, huddled behind him and played the violin for him. They did this for eight hours. Of course, the violinist was paid a great deal of money for this "stunt," but Vittorio felt it was so humiliating to this great Italian artist and himself that at five o'clock he refused to do it

anymore and came home. As he broke up the lamps, he yelled,
"That's enough, Shelley! Okay, enough! Pack up the baby, we're
going home!"

As I grabbed the screaming baby, I looked at him with amazement and whispered, "What are you talking about? We are home."

Pause. Even the baby became silent and stared at him. He looked
back at me and said, "Shelley, what are you talking about? Rome is
home."

Through the two years of engagement and marriage and baby we
had never once dared discuss this explosive issue. And now there it
was between us.

CHAPTER 30

Our lives continued as though nothing had happened. Vittorina, when we were playing with her out in the garden, would sometimes grab our thumbs and look questioningly back and forth at us. Vittorio would bury his head into her tiny stomach, make funny noises and say, "*Mia bellissima,*" and I would look at the purple trees blooming on my safe Beverly Hills street and wonder if it would ever be possible for me to live in the Old World that my grandparents had fled from because of the subtle and not-so-subtle anti-Semitism and the lack of opportunity for all except the privileged class.

After several weeks rehearsing my act, I opened in San Diego. There is nothing as lonely as a nightclub floor when you're out there all alone. Even though the orchestrations were fantastic, Ray Gilbert's numbers were wonderful and Vittorio came down to San Diego to do an exciting job of lighting the "Shelley Winters Act," it was still me out there all alone on that stage.

The act started with a full-size screening of a musical number from *South Sea Sinner*—very innovative in those days. As my image on the screen faded, I stepped through the paper screen, and there I was in the same pose and costume they had seen up there on the silver screen. The effect was as if I had stepped right out of the movie onto the stage, and the audience were obviously thrilled to see UI's sexpot come to life.

In one number I made my entrance with gold hair, gold lamé sexy gown covered in gold jewels, dragging a gold-colored mink around the stage as I sang, "Everybody asks me where I got my mink. . . . Where do you think? First I met a cloak and suiter. Never was a suitor cuter. My wardrobe got more ample with each sample. That's how I got my start. Then I met a famous flier. Goodness was that guy a liar. [Whisper] Howard Hughes. . . . He loved me like a brother. . . . [Wink] That's another. . . . That's how I got my start. . . ." Despite my lack of authority in the nightclub medium, the audience liked my wisecracking patter and songs. I got wonderful reviews in *Variety*, and by the time I had played two weeks in San Diego I was ready for the big time in Las Vegas.

Opening night, as I pranced near the edge of the stage, I slipped and fell three feet—into Howard Hughes's lap! He was sitting at a ringside table. He caught me, wiped me off and stood me back up on the stage. I went on with the act, but my confidence, not to mention my newly acquired authority, was destroyed.

Howard Hughes was then living in the penthouse at the Flamingo and must have heard I mentioned his name in my act, so he made one of his rare public appearances. Thank goodness the audience and he thought my slip was funny and intentional. When he came backstage afterward to congratulate me, I thanked him for the loan of his lap. As he was leaving my dressing room, Vittorio arrived to tell me that the stage had been sanded, and when he saw Hughes, he said, "I thought you two only met on New Year's Eves." Hughes smiled and kept going. Even he, with all his bodyguards, wasn't about to test an Italian husband's possessiveness.

Vittorio was able to stay with me for about a week, as they were doing added scenes for *Rhapsody* that he was not involved with, and my mother was coming on the train with Vittorina, who was almost a year old by now. The night they were to arrive at midnight, I was putting my makeup on for the first show when the phone rang in the spare bedroom. It was a vicious obscene caller. I slammed the phone down and stood there in terror. Then I called the operator and asked for the Las Vegas police. I discovered a startling fact—there is no police force on the Las Vegas Strip; each hotel has its own, and when you stay at a hotel, you're not allowed to call the Las Vegas municipal police.

In a few minutes a big guard from the Flamingo security force knocked at my door. When I shakily told him what had happened, he got the head operator on the phone, and luckily she had a record of the room the call had been made from; in those days they didn't have those lousy new phones where anybody can dial you direct from another room, day or night. The big guard and I walked to the room on the other side of the hotel. The guard asked me to stand aside, drew his gun, then pounded loudly on the door. The door opened, and what looked to me like a naked, hairy and drunken gangster started to swear at the guard. I was hiding around the corner. The guard put away his gun and politely asked the man please to "cool it" because some of the other guests were complaining and the owner of the hotel would get upset if the entertainers got so insulted they refused to go on. That's the strongest language this "policeman" dared use to this creep. The guy mumbled something about "fun" and slammed the door in our faces. The guard took me back to my room rather sheepishly. I stared at him with disbelief and could think of nothing to say.

My dinner show that night felt as if it was "under water." I was terrified and ready to pack my clothes between shows, meet the train with my mother and baby, not let them get off, but get on with them and keep going to Salt Lake City and fly back to Hollywood from there.

Fortunately Howard Hughes was again watching my dinner show and sent me a note to come out afterward and join his table for "nectar and ambrosia." When I did, I tearfully blurted out what had happened. That my mother and baby were arriving and I didn't know exactly who the men were who ran the Flamingo, but I was scared of what could happen to me if I ran out on my contract between shows. I was also terrified of having my baby spend one night in that room. Mr. Hughes took my hand and said, "Shelley, we are old friends. You can trust me. Nothing, and I mean nothing, will happen to your child or your mother or you while you are playing here at the Flamingo. I will personally guarantee it. So you just go ahead with your shows, and I will have your mother met and bring her and the baby up to the room as planned." What could I do?

After my second show I ran up to the suite and got there just as my mother and the baby arrived. The train had been an hour late. As my mother was unpacking, I opened the outside door of their bedroom and saw a man who looked like a caricature of an FBI man, complete with gun in holster under his arm, sitting in a chair in front of the room, and another one, standing up. "What are you doing here?" I yelled. They looked like scary Yale men.

One of them said quietly, "Miss Winters, Mr. Hughes wants us to stay with your mother and baby and you for as long as you are in Las Vegas." That's exactly what they did. Whether we went out to the pool or I took the baby for a walk in the stroller or my mother gambled in the casino—and went home with $1,000 more than she'd come with—or went to the restaurants or shops, there were always two large men following little Vittoria Gina Gassman wherever she went. They worked twelve-hour shifts. Toward the end of the three weeks I'd even trained one of them to change her diaper.

Toward the end of the run they offered to extend my engagement for another two weeks at $35,000 a week. This was a lot of money and would have been pure gravy, but I just didn't want to do it. I think the audiences liked me, and it is a medium I guess I should have pursued, but it didn't have that extraordinary sensation one receives from an attentive theater audience. Despite the lucrative returns, I felt like a shill, and so I never played another nightclub.

Before I left, I met Mr. Hughes in one of the little dark bars off the lobby, and he obviously knew I had refused to extend my engagement, even for all that money. I stuttered my thanks and also tried to explain to him what the real theater meant to me. I was flattered when he told me that he hadn't seen my *Streetcar*, but Johnny Meyers had and had told him I was very moving and effective in it. I glowed with his praise. He then said something like: "I also know that there is no industry that you can do only part time. I am beginning to realize that it is especially true of films."

"My God," I said, "*Behave Yourself* didn't lose that much money for you, did it?"

"No." He laughed. "But what I'm trying to tell you is that obviously your first love is the stage, as flying is mine. I think sometime, while you are still young, you should go back to New York to work and study in the theater. I'm sure your husband would prefer living in New York, too, since New York has so much more for people like you."

I agreed with him and said, "I hope when Vittorio and I are sure of a steady income, we will be able to live there a great deal of the time."

He smiled his sweet sad smile and said, "Well, maybe I can help you do that." That is exactly what happened. A year or so later, when I was free of my UI contract, RKO sent me a script called *The Treasure of Pancho Villa* and offered me $50,000 for six weeks' work in a pseudorevolutionary Mexican cowboy picture. I phoned Edmund Grainger, the producer, and said I would do it if I were paid $1,000 a month for four years. Howard Hughes called me back instantly and said, "Shelley, why do you want to do the picture for forty-eight thousand dollars when we've offered you fifty thousand?"

I replied, "So I can go to New York, as you suggested at the Flamingo, and I'll have an assured income for four years, and I can stop making dumb pictures for a while and concentrate on good theater, which doesn't pay as well."

Pause. Then the terrifying Howard Hughes said, "I like good theater, too, Shelley. And since you're so weak on math, you don't understand that we're making the interest on your money. We will pay you the one thousand dollars a month for five years." And that's exactly what he did.

When my nightclub engagement was over, my mother, I and Vittoria, and all the costumes and orchestrations, took the train back to Los Angeles. Vittorina and I waited eagerly for Vittorio's return from Italy. She was beginning to say words, and her first one was "Papa," and he wasn't even there; I suspected he had secretly drilled it into her head before he left!

Vittorio's flying trip to Europe somehow stretched out to a couple of months, and when he finally got back, he didn't seem to think it strange that he'd stayed away so long. I did.

One night we were invited to play poker at Michael Todd's house. He was living up in the Hollywood Hills with Evelyn Keyes. Elizabeth Taylor, looking her gorgeous self, was there with her husband, Michael Wilding; so were Debbie Reynolds and a very loving Eddie Fisher, who was on his way to becoming a TV star.

After dinner on the patio, a serious poker game started around a very professional-looking poker table. The game was too steep and fast for all us girls. Vittorio caught on quickly to the American rules and was doing pretty well, but Michael Wilding and Eddie Fisher were losing between $25,000 and $30,000 each. Mike Todd was the big winner. Debbie looked slightly distressed, but her friend Elizabeth was really upset. She hadn't worked much for a couple of years, having almost retired to a happy marriage and having babies, but Michael Wilding's career wasn't doing well then, particularly in the United States.

The game rushed on, and Mike Todd's stacks of chips grew higher and higher. Then, when the betting was at its most furious, I saw Todd glance at the distressed faces of his friends' wives, then accidentally on purpose upset the table. Cards and chips and money went flying, and consequently nobody owed anybody anything.

Vittorio was slightly annoyed. Then I saw Elizabeth's expression as she looked at Mike Todd and thought to myself: "I wonder if Evelyn knows Elizabeth is planning to marry him," as, of course, she did, embarking on one of the most colorful romances of jet set history.

I've always believed Mike Todd was the true love of Elizabeth's life. I knew her quite well during that time, and she was so happy and beautiful that it almost hurt your eyes to look at her. She studied and adopted Todd's religion and had his baby as soon as possible. He treated her and dressed her like a queen. I'll never forget the premiere of *Around the World in Eighty Days* at Madison Square Garden. She was radiant in a flowing skin-colored chiffon dress, and with her diamond crown and violet eyes, she looked like a creature from Mount Olympus as she was carried around the Madison Square Garden ring in a glittering chariot drawn by white horses. Not only did Mike Todd shower her with jewels, Rolls-Royces and floor-length sable coats, but that night he showered the 15,000 people at the Garden with bottles of expensive perfume, gold compacts and cigarette lighters.

Perhaps human beings aren't allowed to stay on Mount Olympus too long; maybe Fate demands a sacrifice for those who have that experience. After Mike Todd's death, I think Elizabeth unconsciously took her revenge on everyone and everything she could. However it was presented in the press, she had to go on living, working for her children and pursuing her very public career for herself. The uncaring way she behaved toward those who loved her during that period was not in character with the sweet Elizabeth I had known when we were both young and so eager for life, almost like she was "getting even" with her tragic fate at Todd's death.

For myself and Vittorio and our little baby, we were having a sweet but often angry and strangely nostalgic time. Vittorio seemed to love me as much as ever; certainly our sex life had increased, if that was possible. But I used to wake up in the middle of the night and find him staring at me. I think he had begun to see clearly now that his destiny and his talent were forcing him to nonstop performing, mostly in the theater, for the rest of his life.

UI sent me my final script under my seven-year contract. It was *Saskatchewan* with Alan Ladd, and it was to be shot in Canada. Vittorio read the script too and asked me if I really wanted to do this Canadian western. "Not really," I answered truthfully. "But it will finish my UI contract, and then I will be a free agent and able to do any good films or plays that are offered me."

We were in our bedroom at the time and had just gotten through playing with Vittorina, who was now taking her morning nap. Vittorio was in bed, wearing his slightly worn, but still very sexy, red satin pajamas. I was in a slip, putting on my makeup to go out to Universal for an important magazine interview. Like a few other very special moments in my life, I will remember this one forever.

Vittorio looked at me wistfully and said, "Wouldn't you rather get back in bed with me than go to that stupid interview?" I realized that he was looking at my "female calendar." I looked at it too and saw that this was one of the mornings of those sure forty-eight hours when I could conceive. My ambivalence paralyzed me. I stood there in my slip, holding my stocking and shoes in one hand, my nail polish in the other, my makeup finished and my hair in curlers. I even remember, so many years later, that I was bare-footed. Vittorio said, "I remember a famous Fourth of July when you flew all the way to Mexico City to practice conceiving. You were very good at it. And so was the result. *Carissima,* I'm right here. You don't have to fly anywhere."

I stood still for an eternity and looked at him. Was our marriage first on his list of priorities? Did he intend to stay with me even if I didn't want to live in Italy? Did I intend to stay with him if he didn't want to live in America? I had just gotten my figure back. Would he stay with me, or would I have another lonely pregnancy? I had come to another fork in the road of my life and desired with all my heart to take both paths. I loved this man more than anyone I had ever known and wanted another of his babies dearly. But all the experience and training in my life since obliterating Shirley Schrift added up to "Don't trust anyone but yourself."

I dropped the shoes and stockings and nail polish and started to get back in bed with him. But before he could touch me, I got out again and covered my pretty pink slip with a dress. "Vittorio, please," I babbled, "I have to get finished with my UI contract. They make me do junk. This picture will only be eight weeks, and then I'll join you in Italy." The side of me which wanted to be more sure of the marriage before having another baby had won. He lay back in bed, lit a cigarette and looked at me, and with my female instinct I knew in that second that everything but the shouting was over. It would be a long time before anything official happened, but I knew.

All the way to the garage, and as I took out the car and drove to Universal, something inside of me screamed, "Go back. Go back. Trust him. Get in bed with him. It'll work. He'll take care of you and your family. You'll have more beautiful children." But I couldn't. For the rest of my life I have pondered and perhaps re-gretted the decision of that moment. But as I have matured and gained experience and wisdom, I hope, I have come to know that at any given moment in life one has to do what one has to.

Things seemed to be the same on the surface. Vittorio was get-ting many other offers for films in the United States, but he turned them down because *Rhapsody* had taken so long. They would never give him a stop date, and he had to commence rehearsals with his Italian theater company, which by now numbered forty actors. *Amleto* had been a big success in its try-out, and he now wanted to redesign the scenery, recast Ophelia and Polonius and rerehearse it and two other plays his company was doing. So during the day he dubbed *Rhapsody*, played with Vittorina or, when she was napping, sat in the garden, getting a tan, studying and occasionally playing tennis with Fernando Lamas.

I had acquired a wonderful, funny black cleaning lady, Pauline, who would come only every other day. With pseudo "Uncle Tom" speech, she could cut Vittorio's artistic dignity to shreds, though it took him a few minutes to understand her Texas dialect. She would deliver not so subtle insults such as: "My, my, such a big, beautiful strong man, aren't we the peacock! All you are allowed to do is sit in the garden and study while poor Miss Winters has to go to work at the studio, clean the house when I'm not here, shop at that funny Eyetalian grocery store and cook those big Eyetalian meals you eat. You're just like one of my black husbands. I had to get rid of the last one. I have three cats now instead. They're less trouble." I often thought of her in the 1960s, when Harry and Julie Belafonte asked me to appear at a rally in Selma, Alabama, to help the civil rights cause of the deprived and terrorized southern black people. I found I no longer could retreat to my Shelley Winters position of "take care of Number One." I flew to Selma with Ralph Bunche and Martin Luther King and many prominent film stars. Harry Belafonte carefully briefed us not to go near any southern policemen because the National Guard had been called out and were compelled by law to protect us. But rejecting your life conditioning comes hard, and as I left the airport to walk across the street to a waiting bus, a jovial Alabama sheriff said, "Oh, Shelley Winters, my longtime favorite." And he took my arm, ostensibly to escort me to the waiting bus. In the process he almost wrenched my arm out of its socket. All I could think to do was point to a national guardsman and yell weakly, "Mr. Soldier!" He came over quickly with his bayoneted rifle, and the jovial sheriff held his hands up in the air innocently, looking bewildered.

When we got to the Catholic church where that night's rally was being organized, it was already dusk. It was discovered that Delta Airlines had accidentally (on purpose?) sent all the equipment for this huge civil rights rally to New Orleans. This did not deter us. The local black mortician made a platform of about fifty of his coffins. Carlo Muzzarello, a friend of Vittorio's who was in charge of the Italian television, gave us his microphones and speakers; the BBC agreed to share with him their filmed coverage of the rally with Italy.

We still had no lights, and the rally was expecting a quarter of a million poor black people, who were walking to Selma from all over the South. I called the local air base and asked to speak to the colonel in charge. In an imperious voice I said this was Miss Shelley Winters who had traveled all over the country helping his Commander in Chief, President Lyndon Johnson, get elected, and I knew President Johnson would be very upset if the United States Air Force didn't send us two of its antiaircraft searchlights for our rally. The southern colonel was so angry he almost came through the telephone at my throat, but he delivered the lights himself with this line: "Mizz Winters, your water boy's here."

We finally managed to get everything in place as tens of thousands of people poured into the area. The civil rights workers all wore luminous yellow jackets so we could see them in the crowd. Harry was master of ceremonies. Sammy Davis, Jr., who was married to May Britt at the time, arrived aboard a helicopter, opened the show with *"The Star-Spangled Banner"* and left immediately in his helicopter. Then followed one of the most thrilling evenings of my life. All of this country's star entertainers with any kind of heart or conscience were there and performed or spoke. I spoke about my difficulty filming *A Patch of Blue*, in which I had acted such a good southern bigot that I had won an Oscar for the performance. In this picture I had to hit one of my dear friends Sidney Poitier and use the word "nigger" repeatedly. The black audience at the rally seemed to find this uproarious, and the kids yelled back at me that was one of the *nice* names they were called in the South.

When we returned to the convent before boarding the bus, the nuns created an aisle by joining hands because there were many white southerners there to see the movie stars, and no one was exactly sure what would happen, despite the protection of the National Guard. But the nuns were secure in their faith that no one would harm them. That night we stayed in a black hotel after a wonderful meal of soul food. Peter Lawford, in a moment of naïveté, went for a walk in front of the hotel and was shot at. He scurried back inside.

I couldn't continue with the march to Montgomery because I was filming in New York. The next morning a blonde woman from Detroit who had taken care of us could not take me to the airport, so a young black college boy drove me to my plane. But the temper of Selma was such that he made me lie on the floor in the back of the car so no one would see a white woman and a black man together. When I got back to New York, the first thing I heard on television was that that young blonde Detroit woman who had taken care of us and who was the mother of two had been shot and killed. I mourned that brave young woman, and was glad again that I had had the courage to go to Selma and reclaim some of Shirley Schrift's ideals.

Some years later when I returned to the Deep South to film *Bloody Mama*, I found that for the poor black and white farm workers nothing had changed very much, despite the fact that for the rest of the country the standard of living had improved tremendously.

Robert Di Niro, Don Stroud, Robert Walden and Clint Kimbrough played my sons in the film. In the first scene two local children played the two Bobbys, supposedly at the ages of two and four. When the scene was over, I found that these two boys were actually five and eight. They were suffering from malnutrition and pellagra so they looked like infants. I made arrangements with the local sheriff for those little boys to get milk and cod liver oil regularly. I hope they got it.

In my first scene with my teenage sons in *Bloody Mama*, I had to give them a bath in an outdoor washtub. I have never been particularly good at filming nude or sexy scenes—in color you can always see me blush. Bobby Di Niro made it easy for me by pretending very realistically to be a baby; it seemed as if I was bathing an infant and not a grown man. I can't say the same for his film brothers—they kept teasing me and saying, "Use it!" I refused to bathe Don Stroud.

Bloody Mama was one of Robert Di Niro's first films and he played a boy who becomes a junkie in the course of the film. Bobby stayed in character twenty-four hours a day, losing forty pounds and getting scabs all over his body. Toward the end of the film when he OD's and the Barker family must bury him hurriedly, Bobby insisted on getting into the grave so the camera could record the dirt covering his face. In the scene I was hysterical with grief, and I didn't realize until he was almost completely covered that it was Bobby and not a dummy in this grave. I immediately stopped the scene and pulled him out, saying, "For Christ's sake, Bobby! Even Marlon has never pulled such a dangerous stupid trick in a movie. This is not real life, it's only a film."

His soft answer has puzzled me for years. "But Shelley, for actors, aren't the movies our only real life?"

Once I had a very powerful hunk of real life. Ethel and Bob Kennedy had been kind enough to invite me for a picnic lunch on the *Honey Fitz* yacht. I had come to know them while helping in

John Kennedy's presidential campaign, flying all over the country in a private plane with them and many other celebrities. That day on the *Honey Fitz* Ethel was relaxed and very funny and interested about the goings-on in Hollywood and New York. There were a lot of sailors all over the yacht standing at attention, looking as if they were having nervous breakdowns because all the Kennedy kids were running all over the yacht. It looked as if one, if not all, of them would fall overboard any minute, so I asked the casual Ethel if we shouldn't round up the youngsters since the hot corn and hamburgers were just about ready. Ethel smiled and said, "Okay, but stop worrying about them, Shelley. They have to learn to take care of each other, and they all know how to swim." Still, during lunch I kept one eye busy counting noses to make sure all the children were present.

Just as we got to the dessert, there was a radio call from President John Kennedy telling his brother Robert, the attorney general, that two young students in Alabama had been refused admission to the University of Alabama. The radio speakers must have been turned up because I could hear Robert Kennedy talking angrily to the President. Then I heard John Kennedy said, "Well, I guess it's time, isn't it, Bob?" And Robert said, "You're right, Jack." "Okay, let the chips fall all over the Senate floor," said President John Kennedy. "Is that an order, Mr. President? Can I federalize the Army?" And John Kennedy said, "That's an order, Mr. Attorney General."

It took me a minute to realize I had just heard the President of the United States order the U.S. Army to Alabama to implement the decision of the Supreme Court. The next day I watched that little girl—who is now a schoolteacher—escorted into that all-white school, as George Wallace tried to bar her way. I knew the barriers of a great injustice in our country were going to crumble, and I hoped it would be in my lifetime. But I knew, too, that order of John Kennedy's was the opening of the door for many educational opportunities and a good and better life for millions of black American citizens.

After that day on the *Honey Fitz*, when I watched Ethel casually handle her huge brood and her many guests as the hostess for the attorney general, I remembered the one and only time I gave a dinner party for Vittorio's friends. I think we had only six guests— Richard and Valentina Basehart, Fernando Lamas and his wife, Arlene Dahl, Professor Pasinetti and an Italian lady friend. The menu was very simple—steaks and salad and, of course, spaghetti. Vittorio's mother had taught me how to make a simple marinara sauce and Vittorio warned me that the spaghetti must be *al dente* (firm to the teeth) or the meal would be ruined. This menu sounds very easy to prepare, but I was going to the studio every day, practicing horseback riding while fording a river and getting fitted for a long blonde wig (why do heroines in westerns always have to have long blonde hair?) and having absolutely flat "period" shoes handmade because Alan Ladd was only about an inch taller in boots than I was barefooted. I also liked to have a little time to feed and play with my baby every day. And Pauline had to leave early because even back then she was afraid to go home to Watts on the bus after dark.

The evening went well until I plunged three pounds of imported spaghetti into the boiling salted water. Then I remembered to start the steaks for those who liked them well done, put on the peas that Pauline had shelled and prayed that everything would be ready together.

A few minutes later I was a little suspicious about the *al dente*-ness of the spaghetti, so I brought a few strands out on a fork and asked Vittorio to taste it. He was now quite drunk, having polished off a gallon of wine with his friends, and they all were yelling and laughing in rapid Italian, which I, of course, didn't understand. Vittorio tasted the spaghetti, then looked at me as if I had just crawled out from under a rock. "*Morbido, troppo morbido,*" he said. "Too soft. Can't you just follow simple directions on a package?"

I went back to the kitchen, took the steaks off the broiler, boiled up another three gallons of water and tried again. This time, when I brought out the spaghetti for Vittorio to test, he said, "*Al dente* means firm to the teeth, but not like nails."

I went back to the kitchen. I was so tired and mad that I didn't give a damn anymore. He was out there with his friends, having a wonderful time, knowing I was alone in the kitchen, exhausted from my day at the studio, and he made no attempt whatsoever to help me. I let the spaghetti cook for another three minutes, drained it and put it in a beautiful big bowl, then poured the sauce over it. I carried it out on a tray with the parmesan cheese. Before I could start serving, Vittorio, with an imperious gesture, ordered me to come to him first at the head of the table so he could taste the spaghetti. He did so, then said, "I don't believe it. She couldn't have done it wrong three times." The next thing he knew he was wearing the spaghetti, the sauce and the parmesan cheese.

I don't know what happened to my first formal dinner party after that because I was in the shower, crying. And since he had stubbornly bought a house with only one bathroom, he couldn't get in to remove his marinara clothes and take a shower. I suppose the guests finished the meal somehow and departed. When I finally came out two hours later, Vittorio was cleaned up. He'd gone upstairs to my parents' apartment to shower and was wearing one of my father's old bathrobes and slippers. He took me in his arms and laughed at the whole episode. "We must use that scene in a film someday. If you could have seen your face!"

"I'm glad you aren't angry," I replied. "Of course, I didn't want to humiliate you in front of your guests, but I was so tired and trying so hard."

I sat on his lap, and he said, "Well, I don't think you can run a house, even a little one like this, and be an actress at the same time."

"Maybe not," I replied. "When I'm preparing a film or shooting one, we'll have to get a full-time housekeeper."

"Where will she sleep?"

"Well, if she's pretty enough, she can sleep on the other side of you." (We had a king-size bed.) He seemed to take the suggestion seriously, so I added quickly, "We'll turn the breakfast room into another bedroom and add bathrooms in both apartments." With that, the baby woke up and started to scream. Vittorio, as usual, went in and picked her up. So we three all sat on the sofa, his arm around both of us, and silently and sadly watched some silly late-night movie.

CHAPTER 31

The next day, coming back from a fitting at UI, I stopped at Charles Laughton's house. I was in an emotional quandary. I felt I had to do *Saskatchewan* and finish my confining seven-year contract, but I didn't know if I could live with my decision if it meant a possible break with Vittorio. My lovely friend Laughton was in his pool, talking to James Agee, the screenwriter and novelist. They were discussing a new novel by Davis Grubb called *The Night of the Hunter*. Laughton told me that he himself would direct the film next year and I was to work on reclaiming my Missouri speech to play the lead opposite Robert Mitchum. "Charles," I wailed, "here you've had me improving my speech with Mrs. McLane for more than five years, getting rid of my bad speech habits, and now you want me to talk with that Missouri accent again."

Laughton replied, "In this life we never forget our bad habits, Shelley. They stay around somewhere and are easily recalled when we need them."

I hung around, hoping that the brilliant Mr. Agee would leave soon; I wanted to discuss my personal problems with Charles, who must have sensed this because he quickly uninvited Agee. He dried himself off, put on a huge terry-cloth blanket, and we had Camparis by the pool.

In the next few minutes I told Charles of my dilemma and anguish. When I finished, he thought for a few minutes. Then he told me something I didn't want to hear, but even as he said it, I knew it was true. "Vittorio is born to the theater," he said, "and before he dies, he will play all the great roles written in all languages. He must, of course, play them in Italian because that is the language he thinks in both consciously and unconsciously. It is the one nearest to his soul. You cannot translate the great ideas of men of literature into a second language when you act. You must learn and feel and communicate in your first language. Maybe some genius who has learned a second language when very young has been able to do it, but I doubt it. Words are our first impressions of how the world and its occupants are. How can you demand of Vittorio that he renounce his calling and become just another Hollywood tennis-playing movie star? No more than he can demand

444

of you, who are also an artist, that you try to learn to act in silly films in Italy and in his language, which is not your first language. And you don't even have the facility or ear for languages that your husband has. You both have a destiny that was decided for you long ago, and if either one of you submits or relinquishes his talents to our society's bourgeois idea of what a marriage should be, you will be killing some part of the other one." I thanked Charles for his wisdom, and when I kissed him on the cheek, I noticed his eyes were wet.

When I got home, I told Vittorio I had to leave for the Banff Springs Hotel in a week. I was overjoyed when he said he would join me there for a while; he knew it was very beautiful country, and he could use a rest in the brisk air of the Rockies, and perhaps if there was enough snow, he could even ski. (Oh, yes, he was good at that, too!) I was nervous about leaving Vittorina for two months, but my mother, my sister, Kathy and Pauline were all there to take care of this little baby, who, truth to tell, did much better when her tense parents were not around.

Banff is indeed one of the most beautiful spots in the world, and the hotel is huge, with rooms that are large, warm and immaculate. I had a living room which became the gambling den of the company as the weeks of the location dragged on. *Saskatchewan* was really a good western story, and Alan Ladd was a very good actor and fun to work with. I had known him from *The Great Gatsby*, although I hadn't had any scenes with him in that film.

At the time, Marilyn Monroe and Robert Mitchum were also in Banff, doing a film called *River of No Return*. Marilyn was playing something very foreign to her, a schoolteacher in the 1800s in the wilds of Canada. Mitchum was beginning to call it *The Picture of No Return* since they had been shooting for one month and were already twenty-eight days behind schedule. Otto Preminger was directing, and never having been known for his patience, he was terrorizing Marilyn into total immobility. The night of my arrival, I sat with Mitchum at the bar, and he asked sadly, "Do they talk about us in Hollywood? Do they know we're up here, or have they forgotten our existence? The phone communication is lousy after five, and we never get back from location until then."

The *Saskatchewan* location was an hour from the hotel, and Robert Douglas, a very dignified English actor, Hugh O'Brian and I started a nonstop gin rummy game. We became so obsessed with this three-way gin game for a penny a point that we stopped playing only while we were getting made up, acting or sleeping only six hours a night. I think gambling occupies your mind so much when you're troubled that it wipes out all other thinking processes. This game continued while we drove an hour to location, between scenes and all day long and while we drove back from location. Then we all would run to our rooms, take fast showers to get rid of the dirt from the location, drape ourselves in clean sheets, meet in my little living room, order steaks, salad and wine, and continue this frantic nonstop game. Soon we owed each other thousands of dollars.

Marilyn was troubled about the direction her life and career were taking. To cheer her up, I tried to teach her the game so we could make it a four-handed gin match. But every time she lost she started to cry, and I don't think it was about the money. She was terrified of not knowing her lines the next day, and she was convinced that Preminger hadn't wanted her in the picture—I think she was quite right there—and that he was secretly planning to do away with her while she was going over some rapids on a raft, then claiming it was an accident. These difficult stunts were usually done at the end of a picture by stunt people, but for some strange reason Preminger was doing them at the beginning and *not* with the stunt people.

Vittorio called one night to say he was finished with dubbing *Rhapsody* and Vittorina had given him permission to return to Italy. We had a testy discussion about his taking her with him. I absolutely refused, saying I would bring her. (I did. Six years later.) However, he was joining me in Banff and would stay ten days before he had to report for rehearsals with his Italian company.

He arrived at the location at noon a few days later. I was doing a crucial scene with Alan Ladd. I introduced him to Alan and his wife, Sue, a very nice lady who used to be an agent, then told him to sit down quickly in the director's chair. He didn't know why, but he did it. After the shooting I explained to him that he was too tall and I felt that Alan Ladd, whom I liked very much and wanted to get along with, had a terrible complex about his height.

At lunch, Vittorio and I walked around the lake with photographers trailing us. Vittorio had on an Italian blue knit sweater and looked very handsome against the Canadian sky; I, with my long blonde fall and off-the-shoulder western costume, looked pretty fetching myself. The photographers—Italian, Canadian and American—had a ball taking photos, black and white and color, all over the place with the beautiful scenery in the background. I think we did a great deal for Canadian tourism that day.

In the afternoon Alan Ladd and I had a crucial scene with Leo Carrillo, who was playing the villain. I was to sit on the front seat of a covered wagon, and Carrillo restrained me with his left arm while driving the mule team with his right hand. Of course, the gold he was stealing was hidden in the wagon. I wore a very heavy gray wool skirt with many petticoats, and he was to drag down my off-the-shoulder blouse to expose my bosom as much as the traffic would bear. The Indians were to shoot flaming arrows at us from the other side of the river, and the wagon was to catch fire. Alan Ladd, dressed in his red Mountie uniform, was to ride across the river and point his gun at Carrillo, who had to release me from the flaming wagon. Then Alan Ladd, the brave Mountie, was to sweep me onto the back of his large horse and, while I held him tightly around the waist, ride back to safety, thus saving me from a flaming death and/or fate worse than death.

We had lit and rehearsed this scene since 8:00 A.M. Now, after lunch, we were finally ready to shoot. Vittorio was fascinated by the logistics of the scene, the hundreds of Indians, the wagon and mules, and the villainous cowboys wired with little pellets that would burst into flame, making it look as though the Indians' flaming arrows had hit their mark. Raoul Walsh, who wore a patch over one eye, was on the other side of the river with two cameras, directing us with a bullhorn because we would dub in the dialogue later.

The scene started exactly as rehearsed. I struggled with the villain, and the Indians were appropriately ferocious and aimed their arrows accurately. Then, in the nick of time, Alan Ladd rode up in his beautiful sparkling red uniform, on his black horse, and pointed his gun at Carillo, who cowered appropriately. The wagon and the mule harness were burning, the bad cowboys were being shot from their horses and the good Mounties were winning. Then Alan Ladd swept me onto the back of his horse. As I grabbed him tightly around the waist, my blonde wig became entangled in his epaulets. He struggled to free us, but my heavy skirts and I outweighed him, and we were thrown off-balance and plop, into the river.

Raoul Walsh screamed, "Cut!" and went slightly insane on the other bank. Vittorio was rolling on the ground, holding his stomach, not at all caring if I drowned in my heavy skirts. The cowboys and Indians were laughing hysterically, too. Alan Ladd and I waded back to Vittorio's side of the river. Alan Ladd was also laughing, but I was furious. I was soaking wet and shivering. Rivers in Canada are always just above freezing point. To get even, I lay down full length on top of Vittorio so he could share my discomfort and embarrassment. It didn't help. He was still laughing so hysterically he was in pain. The prop man had to throw a bucket of water on him and give him a glass of whiskey before he could stop.

I went into my trailer, where the wardrobe mistress dried me off and stopped my shivering; then they gave me a glass of whiskey, redid my makeup and dried my hair. Luckily they had another wig and double wardrobe, so I was fixed up and ready for a retake in less than an hour. The director sent Vittorio back to the hotel because he would be calm for ten minutes and then go into hysterics again. This went on more or less for the rest of his stay. Even when making love, he would be calm for the important part, then suddenly begin to laugh hysterically. It wasn't fair. I really wasn't that heavy. I had all those heavy clothes on and that damned long blonde wig, and Alan Ladd weighed about 120 pounds soaking wet, including his medals. Thank God we got the shot that afternoon and completed the close-ups before nightfall. But I have never seen such a giggly company in my life.

My perpetual gin rummy game had ceased during Vittorio's visit, and I went with him to the nightclub in the hotel that had an English band that played English waltzes circa 1938 and the weirdest jazz I've ever heard. One night Marilyn and Bob Mitchum joined us. Although we were working in films with 6:00 A.M. calls, we all obviously hated our escapist movies so much we didn't care if we had rings under our eyes. Mitchum never cared in *any* film.

Vittorio got a cable from his Italian lawyer saying that he was needed in Rome right away. So after posing for more innumerable romantic photographs and phoning to L.A. to hear Vittorina yell at us long distance, Vittorio asked me to make his plane reservations. He has always resisted the mundane things of life like getting tickets, answering the phone, shopping for groceries and taking clothes to the cleaners. Lisa and his mother did all those things for him. One of the worst fights we ever had was when he was in the living room, sitting right next to the phone while it was ringing, and I was in the nursery feeding the baby. "Shelley, come quick," he called. "The phone is ringing." I ran into the living room with Vittorina in my arms, the bottle clenched between her gums, and grabbed the phone with my other hand. It was his agent calling. Vittorio motioned to me to discuss whatever it was the agent wanted and that I would call back later with his decision. When I put the phone down, even Vittorina yelled at him. She was upchucking because I had rattled her around while feeding her. I've always been furious with him about his refusal to recognize the invention of the telephone. To this day he likes to talk to people only when he can see their faces.

The night before he was to leave Banff, we were in bed, and finally we both started to laugh at my unintentional swim with Alan Ladd. Then he said something very odd to me: "In my whole life, I never have or do I think I will ever have so much fun and laughter connected with love and sex." I decided that he was referring to that week because he often mixed his tenses when he was tired. Sunday morning I accompanied him to the airport two hours away and waved him off. He kissed me many times before he left and seemed to be looking at me as if he were memorizing my face. It frightened me. But after we waved good-bye, I told myself that it was only my imagination and perhaps he knew we were in for another long separation unless I went to Italy after *Saskatchewan* for a visit. But I didn't want to leave my child so soon after such a long film location.

Our gin rummy game resumed at a feverish pace, and by now I owed Hugh O'Brian $2,000, he owed Robert Douglas $3,000 and Robert Douglas owed me $4,000. When the game finally ended, we all owed each other about $3. But during the eight weeks of filming this intense gambling made our lives bearable.

Monday night, when I got back to the hotel, there were many phone messages for me from Vittorio from all over Canada. From every little town from its farthest north to its southernmost point. Why he had crisscrossed Canada this way I couldn't understand. The last message was from a Montreal hotel, and there was a return number. I returned the call at 7:00 P.M., which was his 11. I obviously woke him up. He was out of his mind with rage and practically inarticulate. He was even cursing at me in Italian, which he knew I didn't understand too well. But what I finally managed to gather was that he had been on a small mail plane that took only a few passengers. The plane that flew directly to Montreal left only twice a week, and not on Sunday. He was exhausted after spending twenty-four hours landing and taking off from glaciers, Eskimo villages and lumber camps. He accused me of having done the whole fucking thing on purpose! That really made me mad. I said, "Listen, King Farouk, from now on make your own reservations and buy your own tickets. Bon voyage." And I hung up.

The picture progressed slowly, and I got saddle sores even through my heavy petticoats. *River of No Return* was now shooting near the hotel, and late one afternoon, when I got through early, my limousine drove me over to a pier where Marilyn was shooting a scene on a raft, an optical illusion done with movie magic. The camera was on the pier, and she and a little boy were ostensibly floating down the river without any oars and only a tiller to guide them. It was a short scene with the little boy questioning her about what was going to happen when they got to the rapids. In those days B.A.S. (Before Actors' Studio), Marilyn was always a little vague about her intentions in a scene unless she had a kind and thoughtful director to guide her.

As I got out of the limousine to watch, there were about 300 tourists watching the filming and listening to what was going on. Otto Preminger was standing on a tall ladder with a bullhorn, directing her and the little boy. I immediately gathered that they'd been at this short scene all day, and by now Marilyn did what she always did when she was confused. She just opened her mouth and smiled her sexy smile at anything in sight. At the tiller, the little boy, the camera, whatever. Preminger was looking slightly crazed because he was losing the light, which meant the sun was setting; if he didn't get the scene in the next few minutes, it would be too dark to film, and that would add another day to his already hopelessly overscheduled picture. As they fixed Marilyn's makeup, he began to use dreadful language, implying to an imaginary friend that he had to use her in this picture because of pressure from the entire board of directors of Twentieth Century-Fox and that she was so untalented she should stick to her original "profession." Marilyn never looked up; her fixed smile just became more frozen. I don't know where the Society for the Protection of Children was, because never mind Marilyn, the child actor and the children among the tourists didn't miss a word.

They rehearsed the scene once more, and Marilyn was almost inaudible. Preminger added, "Well, we can always get someone else to dub her. Let's shoot. It'll be hopeless anyway." With that encouragement, of course, Marilyn got halfway through the next take and fluffed a line. The eight-year-old boy pretended it was his fault; even he understood the inhumanity of what was going on. Preminger yelled, "It's a wrap," and got down from his ladder, stepped into his limousine and drove away.

Marilyn climbed off the raft onto the pier, with many hands helping her. She too had on a long blonde wig and heavy skirts, a requisite for any film made in Canada at that time. I held her hand tightly, but she slipped a little as we walked toward my limousine. I knew she didn't want to wait for hers amid the crowd that had been watching her being humiliated all afternoon. I caught her other arm as she slipped, and just to make conversation, I said something like: "Watch your step, you can break a leg on this wet slippery pier." We both got into the limousine, and the chauffeur drove us quickly and silently back to the hotel. When we arrived, I got out first, but Marilyn just stayed where she was and said, "I can't get out. I've broken my leg."

"What?"

"Yes, I've broken my ankle, and they'd better put it in a cast as quickly as possible."

The chauffeur turned as white as Marilyn's hair and quickly ran to the Twentieth production office in the hotel to tell them what had happened. Two big crew members made a seat of their hands and carried Marilyn to her suite. Tears were finally rolling down her cheeks. They put her on the bed and I told them to get the house doctor as quickly as possible. Her stand-in arrived, and we got Marilyn out of her heavy skirts and waist cincher, the brown wool stockings and high-button shoes. I got her into a baby doll nightgown. She grimaced with pain and asked me to get her a Percodan out of her medicine cabinet. I wasn't sure what Percodan was, so I gave her one, then wrapped some ice in a towel and put it on her ankle. I asked her to move her toes, but she said she couldn't. She seemed quite comfortable, though, sitting up in bed.

The phone rang. It was Darryl Zanuck from Hollywood, and she explained to him that she might have to miss a day's shooting while a walking cast was put on her leg. Her long heavy skirts would cover it, and they could shoot around her the next day. And since the rest of her scenes in the film were mostly sitting down, the double could do any walking, and she would be able to finish the film, although she was in considerable pain. She didn't seem to be in pain to me; only her speech was slightly fuzzy from the Percodan and a double vodka she had washed it down with. Zanuck seemed greatly relieved but said he was sending Dr. Kenamer, the studio doctor, an orthopedic specialist and X-ray equipment up by a private plane but they couldn't land at the little airport till daylight. Marilyn tried to talk him out of it, insisting that all she needed was the local doctor to set her ankle and put a walking cast on it. But Zanuck insisted that he cared about her welfare—he didn't mention Twentieth Century-Fox's—and he had to do it because of the insurance on the film. Marilyn told him perhaps the film would make more money if they collected the insurance and didn't release the film. Then she hung up.

Then she called room service. Mitchum came in as she ordered dinner for the four of us: eight double martinis, four lobster cocktails, four huge steaks, four salads and four pieces of pecan pie with vanilla ice cream. And a partridge in a pear tree. Mitchum looked at me and said, "She must be in some pain, huh?" I told him about the Percodan and that I was a little worried about her having so much vodka on top of it. He just laughed and said, "She might as well be happy while the stock of Twentieth Century-Fox plunges."

Reporters and assistant directors were beginning to bang on the doors, but Marilyn's stand-in, Mitch and I told them she was in too much pain to talk to anyone until the Hollywood doctors arrived. And that her foot was now encased in ice, she was receiving medication, and this was the only statement for the waiting world. The reporters refused to leave and stood vigil outside the door, and what they thought when the enormous meal arrived from room service, I have no idea. Marilyn didn't seem to care. We four ate and got happily drunk.

The doctors arrived early the next morning. The famous orthopedic specialist X-rayed her foot, and the verdict was that perhaps she had sprained her ankle, but there was no break showing on the many X rays they took. Marilyn looked sweetly at them and said, "You know, doctors can sometimes be wrong, and I don't think I'm willing to go back to work on that dangerous slippery pier and river unless I have a walking cast on my ankle up to my knee." The doctors informed her that was the wrong treatment for a sprain, if she had one. Marilyn said in her sweet whisper, "That may be so, but I must have crutches and a walking cast on my ankle up to my knee if I am to finish the film. My long skirt will cover the cast." After several long-distance consultations with Darryl Zanuck about Marilyn's "obsession," the doctors put a walking cast on her left leg from the arch of her foot to her knee, with a steel heel so she could walk on it.

The day she reported back to work with Otto Preminger, I wasn't needed on the *Saskatchewan* set, so I went with her for moral support. Marilyn hobbled on her crutches to that same raft. No one on the crew, the newspapermen or even the whole world were exactly sure what had happened to Marilyn Monroe's beautiful leg. We all watched from the shore as she got back into position on the raft and the little boy took his place. They were going to rehearse first, so Marilyn handed me the crutches, pulled up her brown skirt to air her crippled leg with its heavy ugly cast and said sweetly, "Now, Mr. Preminger, what exactly is it you want me to do?"

If he had dared say one word out of line to this poor crippled girl, the crew would have torn him limb from limb, and he knew it. Most of them had worked for Fox for years and knew what a valuable box-office draw Marilyn had become and how much money her pictures made for the studio. So they just glared at Preminger and waited. With a great display of European manners, he politely explained the scene slowly and fully to her and the little boy. They rehearsed it once, then shot it. "That's wonderful, Marilyn," Mr. Otto Preminger said. "Cut and print." He obviously wanted Zanuck back home at Twentieth to hear his voice on the sound track complimenting Marilyn. No doubt the production reports had shown otherwise, and he was worried about his money and his job if she continued breaking things.

Dumb? Like a fox, was my young friend Marilyn. That night we celebrated at the nightclub, and at one point she was sort of doing a rumba with Mitch. "For God's sake, Marilyn, sit down!" I told her. "You're supposed to be crippled!"

"Oh, yes, I forgot." She giggled and sat down on Mitch's lap. They finished the film in three weeks.

My film, *Saskatchewan*, was beginning to appear as though it would never end, too, and the perpetual gin game was no longer helping me sleep. Even though I called Vittorina every night, I would lie awake, looking at the Canadian stars, wondering why my life always seemed to go in circles like a wire coil that keeps going nowhere, just that the circles repeat and repeat and repeat and seem to get smaller and smaller and smaller.

The film finally wrapped. When I at last arrived home and held my Vittorina in my arms, I found she had gained about six pounds and was crawling all over the place. And she was easily the most beautiful little girl in the world, no matter what any other mother says.

My seven-year UI contract was at last over, and the next day Herb Brenner called to say that Universal wanted to renew the contract for another seven years, starting at $7,000 a week. I said no. Herb also had a rather strange offer for a film called *Mambo*, to be shot in Italy and produced by Paramount and Dino de Laurentiis. I would star with Silvana Mangano, VITTORIO GASSMAN, Michael Rennie and the Katherine Dunham Dance Company. The film would be directed by Robert Rossen, who had directed *Body and*

Soul with John Garfield and Lilli Palmer, which had been nominated for a great many Oscars and had been a hugely successful film. A year later I was to costar with John Garfield in *He Ran All the Way*. Garfield was an inspiration to work with, and it was his last film.

I thought about *Mambo* carefully. I immediately suspected Vittorio's mother, Donna Luisa's, fine Italian hand involved in this some way. Here I was being offered $100,000 as a free-lance actress in Rome with my geographically and perhaps emotionally separated husband. Was somebody trying to get me and my daughter to come to Italy by hook or by crook and get me working in Italian films? I phoned my agent back and asked him to deliver the script to my house. I would read it on the weekend, and Dino de Laurentiis and Paramount would just have to wait while I considered the whole thing.

Herb Brenner didn't understand, and I didn't explain. He also told me a few other startling developments. Charles Laughton and United Artists were offering me $100,000 for six weeks to star with Robert Mitchum in *The Night of the Hunter*. There was another offer, for $50,000 for one week's work in the wonderful role of the feisty sad Hollywood call girl in *The Big Knife*, with Robert Aldrich producing and directing. RKO and Howard Hughes were discussing a film called *The Treasure of Pancho Villa* to be filmed in Mexico for a lot of American gold, as soon as I was available.

When I hung up, I sat in the middle of my bed and cried harder than I have ever cried in my life. I felt really insane. Here I had achieved ALL my goals. Every studio wanted me. Every big important male star wanted to act with me. All the good directors were sending scripts. I could soon buy myself a mansion with a pool. I hugged my sleeping baby and cried myself to sleep.

CHAPTER 32

Looking out at the gray English Channel, I thought about my baby, who was almost two years old, and what her father would do when he found out I had not brought her with me. My friend, Dawn Addams, had recently separated from Prince Vittorio Massimo, and the law in Italy then was that the children belonged to the father. He had taken their very young son, and Dawn was back in England, alone and practically suicidal. Knowing that, how could I bring our daughter to Italy? Dr. Rosen, my pediatrician, honestly felt the trip was not wise in the middle of winter.

I was at last to see Vittorio's *Amleto* in Genoa; then in a couple of weeks we would go on to Rome to start filming *Mambo*. There had been no letters exchanged between us, and few phone calls. I was beginning to feel as if I had a business partner, not a husband, but I was praying that our marriage could still somehow be saved. I resolved that whatever happened, our daughter would always know how much Vittorio loved her and how much I respected him.

I, who *always* fly, was approaching Genoa as slowly as possible. En route I had visited London, where I had taken part in a royal command performance and was presented to the young queen, Elizabeth II. I arrived in Paris between Christmas and New Year's but no one I knew was in town, so I spent a lonely day at the Louvre. I finally took the train to Genoa and had a bedroom on the Rapido, which got me into Genoa just in time to miss everything but the last few minutes of *Amleto*.

I rushed to the hotel where Vittorio had booked us and quickly changed into a formal gown for the "Gassman Cousins' Family Circle" New Year's Eve party, to be held in the swanky ballroom of one of Genoa's best hotels after his performance, with all his relatives and friends who were in town at the time. His mother was waiting for me in our suite and couldn't imagine why I hadn't flown, but she didn't speak English too well, so I just told her I had suddenly developed a fear of flying. I *think* she believed me.

We saw the fifth act of this Italian version of *Amleto*. The costumes and scenery and staging and Vittorio looked wonderful, from the little I saw. We went backstage quickly, and I told him so and

455

that I was sorry I had been so late coming from Paris. He thanked me for the compliment and said he was rather surprised to see me there at all; he thought I had figured out a way to get to Genoa by way of Kenya. When I explained why I hadn't brought the baby, he just stared at me and said nothing. Then he turned to his mother and in Italian gave her some complicated excuse about Vittorina's health. She *didn't* believe that one. He then showered and cologned with his wonderful lemon cologne. When he was dressed, I must say he looked fantastic in his Sy Devore dinner jacket with one of those new ruffled off-white shirts and a maroon cummerbund and tie and black velvet and gold embroidered "Pope's shoes."

When we all went out into the theater alley, there seemed to be a million photographers—I was blinded by the flashbulbs. Vittorio hurried me through the press corps. The only word I did catch was *divorzio,* followed by "Vittorio," with a question mark intonation. Vittorio practically threw me into the waiting Mercedes limousine and slammed the door in the faces of the press. This was very unlike him—he knew how important good press relations were, and we both looked great and were doing a film together, and this was my first return to Italy in more than three years. But he looked quite exhausted from having played two shows that day and was very hungry and angry, in just that order. I had never seen Vittorio drink very much, but the limousine had a bar in it, and starting that moment, I became aware that he was going through a phase where he was drinking a lot, especially whiskey. Rare for an Italian. As we rode to the hotel, I had a Campari, and he had a water glass full of whiskey. He had not kissed me hello yet. I reminded him of it and he gave me a fierce kiss. Then, to lighten the atmosphere, I showed him the latest snapshots of Vittoria.

At the hotel, about 200 of Vittorio's Genovese blood relatives greeted us. The band was playing, champagne corks were popping and the women were all attired in gorgeous bejeweled French designer gowns. There was only one thing that drove me into shock. Every female over thirteen in that room had black bushes of hair under her arms; this was the accepted custom in Italy then, and sometimes now, I think. In my strapless low-backed gown, I felt nude by comparison. I took Vittorio's white silk muffler and covered my shoulders and armpits so they wouldn't think I was an uncouth American.

When midnight came, we all had champagne, and tears were flowing down Vittorio's cheeks as he took me in his arms. I had never seen him cry before, not even in films when a scene demanded it and not even when he left his adored daughter to go back to Italy to work. I felt a cold hand around my heart. He kissed me and said, "Have a happy New Year, *carissima.*"

And clinging to him, I said, "I will try, Vittorio. You have a happy one, too," and we kissed briefly.

Everyone in the ballroom suddenly went insane and began throwing little pastel-colored balls, about the size of a large marble, at each other. They were made of compressed paper, and they really hurt—an old Italian sadistic New Year's custom. I suggested to Vittorio that we get the hell out of there. He took me out through the kitchen and found the rented limousine, which drove us back to our hotel. I felt very self-conscious with him, and I guess he did with me. So we *each* had a glass of whiskey, which I somehow got down with *acqua minerale* and sugar-coated almonds.

In our suite, I got into a beautiful blue negligee, and he into elegant gray silk monogrammed pajamas. (The flannel nightgown and the old red satin pajamas were better.) We made careful love, rather like acquaintances. When he was sleeping, I got up and took two sleeping pills; there was no chance of my sleeping that night otherwise. Vittorio was doing a special rather early New Year's Day show. All five acts of *Amleto* which I had to see, starting at two and ending at seven, with three five-minute intermissions.

New Year's Day dawned cold and rainy. Vittorio ordered cappuccino for breakfast, saying we would have a large early lunch so he could digest it all before he became Hamlet. I was so nervous about seeing the play that for a minute I thought about telling him that I had the flu and couldn't go out in the rain. But I had avoided seeing it for so long I was afraid to miss another performance for fear of the consequences. As it turned out, it would have been better if I'd avoided it forever.

At lunch in a nearby restaurant, with a kind of sixth sense, I pointed to a pretty but rather dowdy, very young girl with long brown hair and asked, "Is that your new Ophelia?" Vittorio said yes quickly and hurried to the phone to call his agent in Rome. I couldn't imagine what business he had to discuss on New Year's Day.

As I sat alone, stirring my pasta, I noticed that the new Ophelia was peeking at me while talking to a youngish redheaded woman sitting opposite her and an oldish woman who looked like the mother. As my dessert came, the redheaded woman rose, seemed to check that Vittorio was still on the phone and came over to my table and introduced herself. She spoke English quite well. In fact, she assured me she was not Italian, but Swiss. She sat down without being asked, helped herself to some wine and told me that she was Queen Gertrude's understudy and did a small role in the "actors' scene" as a favor to Vittorio, whom she had known "quite well" for many many years. She explained she was really a well-known variety artist. "I bet," I answered.

I detested her immediately but didn't want to be rude. She then asked me if I didn't think Anna Maria Ferrero, who was now playing Ophelia, wasn't brilliant last night. I told her I had unfortunately arrived for the last few minutes of the play and had not even seen Vittorio's death scene, much less seen Ophelia drown herself. She gave me a funny look and checked again to see if Vittorio was still on the phone, before replying, "You know Signorina Ferrero, although she is only sixteen, made a huge success in the film *The Sky Is Red.*" I remembered I had seen it three years ago, and this little girl, who was about thirteen then, had indeed been very good, and I told this busybody so.

She lit another of Vittorio's cigarettes, took a deep drag, her eyes shooting hatred at me in my lush blonde mink coat, and said, "We all know you are busy in Hollywood because you are such a big star there and that you couldn't manage to see your husband's *Amleto* until now. You will be amazed." I didn't know if I should slug her or leave. I have often wished I had done both. Instead, I said, "Signora, of course, I was busy in Hollywood, but primarily caring for Vittorio's baby, who was quite ill when she was born but now is very strong and healthy. You as a mother can probably appreciate my reluctance to leave my baby." She informed me icily that she wasn't a mother yet, that she was too young to consider having a family. She was thirty-five if she was a day. I said, "Too bad. I personally believe that for a woman to have the necessary humanity to be a fine actress, she must experience both the joys and agony of motherhood."

I guess I had pushed this witch too far because she then cast all caution to the winds and bitchily informed me that Anna Maria really hadn't been very good when she had started rehearsing Ophelia because she was so young. Vittorio had had to work with her day and night. In fact, he had moved into the hotel where she was staying and just yesterday had moved back to the hotel where we were staying. She had made her point.

Vittorio returned to the table, and Typhoid Maria said something saccharine in Italian to him and left. I sat there staring at him as he tried to find out exactly how much I knew. I can't remember if I answered his questions. Some part of me knew he was a normal man and very sexual, and because of our work, we had long, enforced separations. He had never inquired if I was faithful to him, which of course I was, and I had hoped, because I knew he loved me, that he was faithful, too. He looked across the room at Anna Maria Ferrero, who burst into tears and left with her mother. He paid the check and said, "Come, let's walk to the theater. I must digest my lunch. You can rest in my dressing room as I make up. And you can watch the matinee with my mother and some other relatives."

All 200 members of the Gassman family came to every performance when he played in Genoa. Lisa was also there, of course, taking care of his wardrobe. I tried to wipe out of my mind the information that bitch had given me in the restaurant. As I watched Vittorio make up, I asked him if I was disturbing his preparation for this performance of *Amleto*. He paused, looked at me and said, "Is that some of your Actors' Studio jargon?"

"Yes," I answered. "Preparation is what you think about before the play. A remembered trauma from your own life that is parallel to the problems of the play." He just sat there staring at me. I went on, "What I mean is that Hamlet's terrible dilemma concerns the death of his father, and you speak so little of your own father and his death that it must have traumatized you considerably when you were so young."

He took a deep breath. "You waited until I was playing this role for almost a year before you decided to tell me this?"

"Vittorio, you never asked me, and you saw Strasberg working with this technique."

He looked at me sadly, then said something loud in Italian, which I understood from his arrogant tone to be: "I don't need help from anybody. Especially from old-fashioned Stanislavskyites."

It was high time for me to go out front. His mother came in just then, kissed him, and I, like she, wished him, *"In bocca al lupo"* ("In the mouth of the wolf"), which is the Italian theater expression for "good luck."

It was a large theater with two balconies, and every seat was taken. The curtain went up, and I was amazed by the innovative beauty of the set. When Vittorio made his entrance, he got an ovation just like an opera star. I was soon to find out that his *Amleto* was, in fact, very close to grand opera. Vittorio can act in four octaves, and did. When the ghost of his father floated across the stage by some extraordinary special effect, he spoke to it from a basso profundo agony to a lyric tenor pleading. Vittorio faced the audience, and all the other actors faced him—we saw only their profiles. I squirmed with embarrassment at this style of acting, but the rest of the audience sat enthralled, even applauding various soliloquies as if they were arias. This, I believe, is called the Sacconi School of Acting.

When the play finally ended, at which time I thought it surely must be three in the morning, the audience ran down the aisles and threw flowers at Vittorio. He took about a dozen curtain calls, and I applauded as heartily as I could. I think his mother thought my dazed condition was the result of his superb acting. I didn't enlighten her. I stalled as long as I could getting myself together: my coat, my purse, my scarf, my binoculars, waking up my feet, which had gone to sleep, getting my shoes back on, and finding my gloves. During all this, hundreds of people were congratulating me for my husband's spectacular *Amleto*.

What could I say to him? Was I a good enough liar to tell him I thought it was great? Wouldn't it be a bigger disservice to him? Wouldn't it be better for his future artistic life if he was to be an International Actor if I told him this kind of performance was old-fashioned, superficial and phony? My quandary increased the closer we came to his dressing room. His mother was beginning to look at me strangely. I waited till all his well-wishers and relatives had left, then went into the dressing room with not the slightest idea of what I was going to say. He was sitting in an armchair dressed in a satin robe, still in the character of Prince Hamlet. I sat down on the dressing-room table and smiled brightly. He must have ordered everyone else out of the room because we were suddenly alone. The following dialogue ensued:

VITTORIO: Well, what did you think?
SHELLEY: It was a very unusual production, but you know I don't speak Italian.
VITTORIO: Don't give me that crap. You know the story of *Amleto*. What did you think of my interpretation?
SHELLEY: It was most unusual and interesting.
VITTORIO: Unusual and interesting, huh? You saw Laurence Olivier do it in England, didn't you?
SHELLEY: Oh, yes, a long time ago.
VITTORIO: Was mine better than his?
Pause.
SHELLEY: NO!

Ladies of the theater . . . if your husband ever does *Hamlet*, whatever you think of it, you must say it is the greatest *Hamlet* you have ever seen. I tell you this with great authority because I almost lost an eye for my foolish truth. In a rage, Vittorio swung at me. He probably was aiming for my jaw, but I ducked, and he connected with my left eye. I can't remember exactly because I hit him back with anything that came to hand. If I remember rightly, I saw blood on his satin robe, and it wasn't mine.

He was yelling at me in both Italian and English, and I was screaming at him in Brooklynese and English. The gist of our violent words was that he insisted that I was predisposed to hate his performance because I was jealous of poor little Anna Maria Ferrero, and I told him that he was an old-fashioned phony idiot actor who refused to learn anything new or listen to any criticism, constructive or otherwise, and would listen only to his flattering family and friends and use only his overtrained voice instead of his brain and heart. At one point he stood on the windowsill and threatened to jump and commit suicide. Even though the dressing room was on the ground floor, my deep survival sense warned me not to call his bluff. I turned and left the theater.

That miserably cold night in Genoa I took a taxi back to the hotel, where I immediately got an ice pack for my eye, started to pack and had the concierge make a reservation for me on the midnight train to Rome. I remembered that Farley was finishing *Senso* for Visconti in Rome, so I called him at the Residence Palace and asked him to meet my train the next morning.

I didn't have time yet to deal with the mental agony of the decision I had made. I was too busy with the physical pain of my left eye. As I was taking several Anacin tablets, Vittorio's mother arrived. Whether or not he had sent her, I never knew, but in her limited English she tried to dissuade me from leaving. She said that I had insulted Vittorio's artistic soul and that he was never a violent man. I kept right on packing and told her I was going to divorce Vittorio as soon as possible. She seemed completely bewildered by this information and said, "In God's name, why?"

"Because he is sleeping with that sixteen-year-old Ophelia."

Her answer bewildered me. She said, "Shhh. Italian wives *never* speak of such things. You have the name and the house and the money and the children. This is just a passing thing. You must not notice it. Besides, she was a bad Ophelia, so what could he do?"

I knew in my heart this was not the real reason. The truth was that Vittorio no longer wished to work and live in America, if he ever had, and I could not live and work in Italy. It seemed too stupid a thing to admit to myself that we had not settled this enormous life question before three years of engagement, marriage and baby, both of us pretending that we were going to live in the other's country. But that is what we had done. So Anna Maria Ferrero was as good an excuse as anything for the public breakup of our marriage.

Donna Luisa was very worried about my eye. The white had already turned red, and the left side of my face had turned black, blue and purple. She gave me the name of a specialist in Rome and insisted on taking me to the train. She also insisted that in a couple of days things would not seem so terrible. She gave me exact instructions on how to turn on the heat in Vittorio's apartment and made sure I had the keys to the outer and inner doors. She said she would phone the concierge, who would be expecting me, and I should phone her and Vittorio long distance as soon as I had seen the eye doctor. She smiled and said Vittorio was seeing a doctor just then because he thought I had broken his nose. With a twinkle in her eye, she said in broken English, "If you have, perhaps it will be an improvement." She made sure I had enough lire, and I kissed her and gave her some photos of Vittorina. Then we went to the train. I took three sleeping pills, got into my berth, with an ice pack on my eye, and was unconscious all the way to Rome.

The conductor had considerable trouble waking me when we arrived. Farley and Mickey Knox (who by now was a translator and screenwriter in Rome) had boarded the train and come to my berth. They were really worried when they saw my face and eye and thought I had been in some sort of accident. I had, but not the kind they thought. I had been sleeping in my clothes, covered by my enormous mink coat, so they collected me quickly, the conductor gave me three cups of that lethal Italian coffee which counteracted the pills very effectively, and they piled me and all my belongings into Farley's studio car.

We drove around Rome for an hour while we discussed the situation; then they insisted on taking me to an eye specialist, who was the same one Donna Luisa had recommended. The doctor said my eye had received a severe trauma, but with rest and almost complete darkness and medication, it would return to normal in six weeks. (Hence my characterization in *Mambo* was a woman who constantly wears huge dark glasses, especially at the beginning of the picture.)

When we left the doctor's office, the chauffeur, without being told, drove us to Vittorio's apartment. I could not go in; I especially did not want to see the flowers on the terrace or those god-damned green drapes. Farley tried to reason with me. "Since you've been married, Vittorio has made your apartment in Beverly Hills his home in America. Don't you think the least you can do is live in his apartment with him on your first trip back to Italy? For a little while anyway, until you decide the future of your marriage." I couldn't move from the car. Everything waited, including the suitcases. Mickey Knox said, "The son of a bitch is obviously very unstable. Who knows what else he's liable to do next?" My eye was hurting, and my vision was blurred, especially by the tears that were flowing again. Farley told Mickey to go take a walk for a few minutes, and that was fortunate because it looked as if the Italian chauffeur were going to slug Mickey.

We sat there in front of Vittorio's apartment, holding the keys. Farley and I got out of the car and sat on an outside wall. "Shelley," he said, "do you want to stay married to Vittorio?" And then I told him the truth. That I loved Vittorio and my baby more than anything, but I didn't see how he and I could have any life together, as I didn't think Vittorio wanted to come to America anymore. He hated the way most American directors worked, and his theater company was subsidized by the Italian government. And no matter how I tried, I could not seem to learn Italian. At heart I was an American, and Italy was a foreign country to me.

The chauffeur, who could hear us from the car, was weeping. He was a very young handsome Italian named Evo, who is now a middle-aged handsome Italian with a wife and two children and has always loved everything connected with the film and theater world. For all I knew back then, he might have been Vittorio's driver. "Well," Farley finally said, "I guess the best thing would be for you to go to a hotel and when he comes back, have another talk with him and his family." I gave the keys to the concierge with a note for Donna Luisa, and Mickey told us that all the rest of the *Mambo* company were staying at the Hotel de la Ville.

The hotel was almost full up, and they couldn't give me a suite, but they could give me a rather dark but large, beautiful room on the second floor. I took it. Farley gave the concierge 5,000 lire and told him I was ill and was not to be pestered by the press or anyone. Farley also called the Dino de Laurentiis company and told them I was in Rome and not feeling good, and they should wait as long as possible before having me do my fittings. It turned out that I would not be actually filming for ten days. The De Laurentiis people also seemed to be aware of everything that had gone on in Genoa and seemed pleased at the enormous publicity *Mambo* was getting by the reflected "gory" in the world press.

I took another couple of sleeping pills, put on my mink coat and my Italian electric heating pad and got back in bed. The maid tried to lecture me about all the pills on my nightstand. In her garbled English and dramatic gestures she tried to explain that when an Italian husband hits you, it is only because he loves you so much. I made a threatening gesture at her to get out of the room. She ignored me and kept pointing to the telephone, saying, *"Telefonata bambina* Vittorina," as she polished the silver frame of Vittorina's picture, then put it between me and the pillows. I knew her intentions were good, but when she left, I locked the door. What could I tell my family and baby?

When I awakened some hours later, I was very cold. Rome is damp in January, and the room felt like an icebox. As I took the Do Not Disturb sign off my door, I found that this second-floor room was near the bar and restaurant. It was very hard to see with my dark glasses on, but I could see that the bar was crowded with what seemed to be a lot of colorfully dressed black American actors. I kept going until I got into the restaurant and sat in the darkest corner. Without my ordering, the waiter brought me oatmeal and hot milk, tea and lemon, and soda crackers. I didn't understand his rapid Italian, but he was obviously encouraging me to eat slowly, and the oatmeal would be good for me. He also brought me a Campari and soda, explaining that it was a *digestivo*. His brisk manner helped me get almost everything down. I guess no one has ever died of a broken heart because the stomach still functions no matter what. But I also had acquired a severe cold, and I managed to ask this nice waiter in my limited Italian for an electric *stufa* ("stove") for my chilly room. He seemed to understand, picked up the house phone and yelled angrily at somebody. Then he put down the phone and smilingly assured me with gestures that that night there would be an electric heater in my room. I added a kiss to the tip.

A beautiful dark-skinned young Indian-looking girl whom I had met casually at a party in New York came over, sat down and re-introduced herself. Her name was Julie Robinson, and she was one of the lead dancers with the Katherine Dunham Dance Company and was also in *Mambo*. She didn't say a word about the condition of my eye or face but asked if she could join me for dinner. Grateful for her company, I said, "Of course." Her dinner consisted of a salad and a piece of toasted mozzarella cheese. She told me that this was what she always ate for dinner. No wonder she was a size three. She had a slim dancer's body and two long black braids, with her beautiful hair parted in the middle.

She told me all about the rehearsals of the film, and they sounded even crazier and funnier than the usual Italian picture. She was curious about my role. So was I. From the garbled script I had received in Hollywood, the nearest I could figure out was that I was the manager of a dance company she and Silvana Mangano were members of and that we were trouping through Italy performing in various cities. The emotional undercurrents of the picture were thus: I was in love with Silvana. Silvana was in love with Michael Rennie, who was secretly in love with Vittorio, and Vittorio was in love with Vittorio. But he previously had been in love with Silvana, whose boyfriend/pimp he had been. I thought that was the story, but I wasn't sure. As Julie laughed, I told her my Italian wasn't too good, and maybe I hadn't read it correctly. The dancers had not been given the script; they just knew that at the climax of the picture, which took place at a Mardi Gras in Venice, they were to do a very long and difficult ballet while the complicated emotions of the principals came to a head.

Little contradictions—like what was a modern American dance company doing in Italy in the middle 1950s, why was an Italian girl like Silvana in an all-black American dance company and what exactly was the relationship of the English prince, Michael Rennie, to this company?—were never explained. And why the picture was called *Mambo*, which implied a South American background, was never explained either. Julie reassured me on that point—the Dunham Company would definitely do one dance number that was a mambo.

What really reassured me was when a bellhop came up and handed me a cable on a silver tray. It was from Barney Balaban, informing me that my $100,000 salary was in escrow with MCA and would be paid into my account weekly, starting that morning, when I had reported for work in Rome. The figure $100,000 looked wonderful to me since now I didn't have to split it with UI (I momentarily forgot about the 10 percent to the agent, the 10 percent to the business manager and the 20 percent to the Italian government). It flashed through my mind that maybe I really didn't want to start this picture because once they had me on film, I knew I had to finish it. But the thought of returning to my family and explaining the failure of my second marriage terrorized me, so I just put the cable in my purse for future consideration, and Julie took me to the bar to meet the other members of the company.

I asked her if she would mind coming to my room for a minute, and she said of course not. She was surprised it was so close to the noisy bar. But once there, I quickly covered my black and blue face with Cover Mark and makeup, put on my bravest lipstick, gold earrings and a Gucci scarf over my hair. I put back on my huge dark glasses and mink coat. As we were going out the door, the phone rang. It was Vittorio calling from Genoa, practically inarticulate with rage. When he could calm down enough to speak English, I understood his questions, which were: Why had I left Genoa? If I was staying in Rome, why wasn't I in our apartment instead of the Hotel de la Ville, where all the well-paid hookers stayed? I answered that I was afraid that all my clothes would not fit in the same closet with Anna Maria's. And since being a hooker, especially a young one, paid so well, I was thinking of taking up the profession myself. (I knew, of course, that Anna Maria was an innocent young girl, but then, twenty years ago, I was so angry I would have said anything.) I slammed down the phone and got Julie to tell the operator in Italian that they were to announce all calls and not to take any more long-distance ones except from Hollywood, California. My electric heater had arrived, and Julie connected it because I was trembling so badly. I put on another heavy sweater under my mink coat and followed her to the bar.

Those were the days of "Hollywood on the Tiber." Richard Burton was doing *Alexander the Great*, and there were about 100 films shooting in Rome that winter. Actors, young directors and writers, in fact, everyone connected with the International Film Set, were in Rome, and most of them seemed to be staying at the Hotel de la Ville, or near it. I soon found out why this hotel was so popular. Italy being such a Catholic country, the assistant manager always took your passport when you registered at a hotel and, I presume, gave it to the police and the labor permit authorities for a couple of days before returning it. So it was impossible for unmarried couples to share a room in most Italian hotels. The advantage of the Hotel de la Ville, then and now, is that the bar is on the second floor, and you can go up to the bar, have a drink, and from there go to any room without dealing with the assistant manager. When I realized this, I understood what Vittorio's scurrilous remark had meant.

I came to know Bruno, the bartender, and to regard him as a dear friend over the months I was there. He was always busy waiting on celebrities, who were six deep around his bar, yelling their orders and screaming to be served. That first night Julie and I sat at a corner table, and one of her fellow dancers brought us double whiskeys with Coke chasers and sat down opposite us.

Through my dark glasses I saw that Richard Burton seemed to be waving at me from across the room; he was with a pretty little blonde girl, *not* Sybil, his wife, so I ignored him. Sitting next to us was a young screenwriter by the name of Roger Vadim, with one of the most beautiful girls I had ever seen. She had long, long light-brown hair, and her name was Brigitte Bardot Vadim. At that time she had no thought of being an actress; she just wanted to be her handsome young screenwriter's wife. I also met several French actors who have since died much too young: Gérard Philippe, a great actor and star; Henri Vidal, who was a fine actor as well as Michèle Morgan's husband; and Jean Gabin, who had always been an idol of mine.

In those days it was very inexpensive to make films in Italy, and there seemed to be a renaissance of European filmmakers, all centering on Rome. I heard many deals arranged in that bar for films that were made for whatever monies the producer could steal. But many were for art and turned out to be fine films.

Daniel Gelin, who was a friend of Julie's and could speak English, came over and joined us. I thought they were speaking a kind of English that I couldn't quite understand because he frantically explained to Julie that he was expecting his wife *and* mistress in a couple of weeks and was hoping to get finished with the most exhausting part of his film so he could entertain them while they were both in Rome . . . but he didn't know where to hide his nubile girlfriend, Ursula Andress. I gathered from his questions that Julie was expecting Harry Belafonte, to whom she was engaged. I then noticed she was wearing a large beautiful diamond engagement ring. Belafonte was separated from his wife and he was coming to Rome to stay with Julie for part of the time she was working on the film.

My own emotions being in such a precarious state, I began to feel that I was in a sexual Babylon and someone was playing some secret music, and when it stopped, everyone changed chairs. Except one person was always left without a chair. Unfortunately it was now my turn.

Suddenly a man sat down to my left, speaking English with one of the most enchanting French accents I'd ever heard. Daniel Gelin introduced him to me; his name was Raymond Pellegrin. He was holding three bottles of beer and three double shots of whiskey which he carefully placed on the table. At first I thought he was serving them to me, but I soon realized they were *all for him*. He said, "*Enchanté*," and kissed my hand, but before he could say another word or comfortably seat himself, I looked him right in the eye and said, "Monsieur, what exactly is your marital status?" He started to get up, but since I looked like death warmed over, he sat down again and answered my impertinent question. (Later on I found out he spoke Italian and had been keeping track of my three-ring-circus marriage in the Italian papers and magazines.) He answered me as truthfully as any French-Italian man could, confronted by a blonde in a mink who was still more or less sexy. Even with three sweaters and a black eye. He said he was separated from Dora Dorn (a famous French vaudeville soubrette), and they were in the process of getting a divorce which was just as complicated in France as in Italy. What he didn't tell me was that he was involved with Giselle Pascal who had been the mistress of the prince of Monaco for many years. Raymond told me he had a lovely little girl of about six, whom he loved very much, and we began to show each other our children's pictures. Meanwhile, I was polishing off my whiskey and, unconsciously, some of his; eventually Julie had to take me back to my room, where mercifully I passed out.

I woke at dawn, and the room was so dry from the little electric heater that I rushed to the bathroom and coughed and choked and drank water for half an hour. There was no room service at that hour, so I was grateful for the soda crackers and tea and lemon the maid had left next to my bed. The bathroom was too cold to take a bath, so I put on my thermal underwear and flannel nightgown, then got into bed with my heating pad, the feather bed and mink coat. I was still freezing. I had taken some aspirin and cold medicine for my chest and rubbed Vick's on my chest and forehead. But my sinuses hurt like hell, and I was very cold, especially my feet, even with Vittorio's heavy woolen tennis socks. The cold seemed to be coming from somewhere deep inside myself and going out, rather than from the outside coming in. There was just no way I could get warm. I felt as if even the tears rolling down my cheeks were freezing, and as I heard the dawn motor scooters of the Roman workers, I finally dozed off.

The telephone awakened me about eleven, and it was the De

Laurentiis company, saying it was sending a car at noon to take me to my first fitting. I tried to argue with the telephone operator, who spoke a little English, reminding her that I wasn't feeling well and had left firm instructions that I was to be disturbed only by overseas calls from California. She explained to me no less firmly that calls from the *produzione* were always put through, even if the recipient was dying. Then she disconnected.

The studio car, like Fate, arrived promptly at noon. I covered my discolored face as best I could with my huge dark glasses and a scarf and the collar of my mink coat, which became my uniform for the rest of my stay in Italy. I grabbed a tight girdle, a waist cincher and a pair of high heels, went down and got into the car. The chauffeur took me to a famous costume house where I was measured and fitted with cloth patterns. (This is done superbly in Rome.) Then the designer showed me sketches of about fifteen costumes. From his sketches I could tell that I was about to have very short blonde mannish hair, very man-tailored dark suits, complete with foulard blouses, slack suits and a fleece-lined black leather coat, obviously to wear in cold Venice. As a matter of fact, I wore the coat through most of the film because I could wear thermal underwear and sweaters underneath. There was also a sketch for a rather bizarre Turkish costume complete with turban and mask that I was to wear at the Venetian Mardi Gras. For some odd reason they were making me several pairs of beautiful riding boots, handmade and very expensive. What this had to do with my character I never did find out. I guess it was just the director's concept of a lesbian.

I must say I was very puzzled about how to go about playing this part. To my knowledge, the lesbians I had met in the theater or Hollywood up to then didn't dress or behave much differently from the heterosexual women I knew. The mannish clothes seemed very "cliché" to me, but I was so preoccupied with my emotional problems that I didn't give anybody any arguments about anything. Julie tried to help me with my character and told me that among dancers she knew many homosexual men and women, and the only visible difference she could tell was that they were perhaps more driven and neurotic than your average housewife. I lately have wondered about even that. I decided to play it that way and just pretend Silvana Mangano was a boy I was in love with. Now, that took some imagination! The riding boots did help, and I sort of walked like Gary Cooper and chain-smoked and talked out of the side of my mouth. I still couldn't inhale, so I choked, and at least that somewhat accounted for my teary eyes throughout the film.

In the middle of the fittings, Dino de Laurentiis paid me a call. He arrived with an English publicity man based in Rome, who worked for Paramount, and Stan Swinton, who was then head of Associated Press in Rome and whom I'd met the night before in the Hotel de la Ville bar. They waited until I was done with my fittings, then took me to lunch. They suggested that since the press of every country knew of Vittorio's and my separation, it would be wiser to have a joint press conference in order to get everybody off my and Vittorio's backs so we could continue the picture in peace. Vittorio would be interviewed on the phone in Genoa by the northern Italian reporters, and I would be in Rome with whomever Stan Swinton could round up from the press. Which turned out to be AP, UP, Reuters, the Middle East and Israeli press services and virtually every journalist in Rome. There were even members of the Chinese, Japanese and Indian press services present. Only the Russians seemed uninterested.

I reluctantly agreed to the press conference and said it would have to wait until the following Monday, when, the doctor assured me, most of the discoloration on my face would be gone. I told them at no time would I take off my huge dark glasses, and no one was to ask me to or I would get up and leave.

To this day I can't believe Vittorio and I were so stupid as to let ourselves be used this way, but I guess we both were so upset we couldn't think clearly, so we allowed our personal anguish to be used as publicity for a picture.

CHAPTER 33

If there was any hope of saving our marriage, this press conference killed it. The smart Shelley Winters—who had been trained by the UI Publicity Department—was no match for the Lucrezia Borgia tradition of the Italian press. After all, I had deserted one of their national heroes just because he had a little *passage* with a young Italian girl. To an Italian male's mentality, what the hell had that to do with a marriage? What I hadn't realized was that European women and, for that matter, women in most of the world at that time were beginning to rebel against the traditional double standard.

What looked like my public refusal to continue a marriage, even to such an extraordinary man as Vittorio Gassman, because he was unfaithful had somehow disturbed the fabric of Italian family life. Everyone was taking sides; even the church, which had never recognized our marriage in the first place, sent an Irish priest to the Hotel de la Ville to dissuade me from holding this press conference. In retrospect, I wish I had listened to him, but after this priest gave me all the Vatican opinions, I just told him that the Vatican newspaper had better attend and left him sitting in the bar, finishing his whiskey.

My hurt and pain turned to furious anger. Very true is that expression "Hell has no fury like a woman scorned." I had rearranged everything to turn myself into the scorned woman, how I'm not sure, but every time I looked in the mirror and saw my blood-red eye and knew that it would stay that way for another few weeks, I decided the following: (1) Vittorio's career had not been hurt by all the publicity of his trips to America and his many marriages to me. (2) He had not been there when Vittorina had been born. I'd been all alone. (3) Anna Maria Ferrero was a nobody. Couldn't he at least have been unfaithful to me with somebody famous? How did it look for a movie star like me? (4) He was so used to Lisa, his mother, his sister, his sister-in-law and whoever his resident *amante* was taking such care of him that he barely managed to brush his own teeth. (5) He had a seven-year contract with MGM, and although it was lending him to Paramount for *Mambo*, was he just going to ignore the five years he had left

471

on it? (His damned Italian pictures seldom played in America anyway and couldn't do anything for him in the world market.) Besides, what kind of artistic integrity was that? (6) He had never paid me for his damned ticket from Banff to Rome. (7) Although he had put a great deal of money into blue-chip stocks for Vittorina, he hadn't given me any. (In my rage I forgot about the duplex apartment house he had bought me.)

The day of the press conference irrevocably arrived. My hair was now blonde and very short, so I wore a very feminine black dress, black kid gloves, diamond earrings, my dark sables, black shoes and stockings, and with my huge dark glasses I managed, though not intentionally, to give the impression of a movie star in mourning. It suddenly popped into my mind that I should have bought myself some red patent leather sandals like the ones Magnani wore on that infamous night when she had pointed out Vittorio to me and she had been in mourning for Rossellini, who was then living with Ingrid Bergman.

The press conference began with each of us making a statement. Vittorio first, since it was his country. He said he did not understand why I was living in a hotel and had left his home. He loved me and his eighteen-month-old baby, Vittorina, very much, and since he preferred living and working in Italy, he felt that I, his wife, could and should slowly accommodate herself to his way of life and language.

There was a loudspeaker arrangement on the telephone so all the reporters with me in Rome could hear him in Genoa. The lousy *paparazzi* were taking pictures of me listening to him, although I didn't understand a word of his fancy Florentine Italian and a bilingual reporter was translating for me in Rome as quickly as he could.

Vittorio then must have recited a section of Dante's *Inferno* regarding Dante's feelings for Beatrice—he never could resist performing when a microphone was present—and concluded that he hoped I would bring our *bambina* to Rome and we would happily "act into the sunset" together in *Mambo*, also starring Silvana Mangano and produced by Dino de Laurentiis, directed by Robert Rossen and distributed by Paramount.

Now it was my turn. The first thing I said was: "If Vittorio loves his baby so much, he should know that she is twenty-two months old now and not eighteen months." (Every reporter there who was a father fell on the floor laughing.) I said that I had moved to a hotel where some English was spoken because Vittorio had teased me and made fun of me when I attempted to learn Italian, and had taught me improper words for everyday expressions, so that I had become afraid of speaking the language.

Julie, who was sitting next to me, was shaking her head, no, no, no, and the translator could hardly keep up with me. I was in a devil-take-the-hindmost mood and wouldn't look or listen. After all, I couldn't resist an audience either, especially one that was obviously enjoying my remarks so much.

I then informed the reporters that Vittorina had been born prematurely with congested lungs and I had been three days in labor. ALONE. And since she was still a delicate baby—what a lie!—and since we were shooting most of the film in Venice, which was notoriously cold and damp in the winter, my mother's heart would not allow me to take her out of warm, sunny California during the bitterest time of the Venetian winter. I could hear Vittorio trying to answer me in both English and Italian, and I told him to *stai zitto* ("shut up"). It was my turn. I then threw all caution to the winds and said that since Vittorio had found his sixteen-year-old Ophelia so attractive and amorous, he should be allowed to have her, and I wanted a divorce.

The conditions of the divorce were as follows: (1) He must put 10 percent of his earnings into a fund for Vittorina until she was twenty-one. (2) As soon as I filed for divorce in California, he must set up an educational fund for Vittorina. AND (3) he must *marry* Anna Maria Ferrero since she was still such a child and *educate her, too.* (Many years later Vittorio told me that shortly after this famous press conference, Anna Maria's mother had had a heart attack and died. She had no father. Anna Maria had to live with Vittorio and his family, and he had to support her until she was twenty-one, or he would have gone to jail.)

I finished the press conference with the information that although I wasn't as familiar with Dante's *Inferno* as Vittorio was, I believed that one of the requisites of his emergence from hell was fidelity and respect to one's wife and family.

The reporters were so awed by the intensity of my anger and hatred that they had no other questions for me, but we could hear a small riot going on in Genoa. A man who had been sitting in the shadows turned out to be someone from the lower echelons of the American Embassy, and he went over and turned off the loudspeaker. He ended the press conference with: "That's enough, gentlemen!" and escorted Julie and me from the room. I was beginning to shake, and whether this man was trying to cheer me up or was serious, I'll never know, but he said, "Italy may take this to the Security Council at the UN." And as he left us at my door, he whispered in my ear, "Don't bring your baby here just now. The beach is too far from Rome for the marines to land." I gave him a wary smile and thanked him as Julie took me into my room.

The next day the director, Robert Rossen, suddenly discovered a scene the scriptwriter had forgotten about. In it I was to sit near a piano, watching the dance company rehearse, and criticize Silvana because I suspected her of starting up her affair with her boyfriend (Vittorio) again. This scene was toward the end of the picture, but we were doing all the Roman filming first, obviously waiting until it got freezing cold in Venice before going there to film. I later understood that Barney Balaban wanted to establish me in the film quickly so I couldn't change my mind and walk off the picture and fly back to Hollywood (once I worked, I was committed). If I walked off, then it would be a breach of contract, and he could sue me for a lot of money. But in my very real anguish, physical pain and desperation, my usual quick-witted business sense had deserted me. I was even too ashamed to call my agent, Herb Brenner, and ask his advice.

Anyone who goes through a separation and divorce knows it is distressing enough without having to work daily for many months with the other partner of the marriage. Perhaps I went through with the film because despite the public spectacle of the press conference, deep inside I was still hoping that all the hurt and recrimination between Vittorio and me would magically disappear and we would reconcile somehow. Perhaps I was hoping that he would get an attack of "Americanism" and want to work on the New York stage in English and would finish his contract with MGM, and Anna Maria Ferrero would decide that he was an old man of thirty-two and leave him for some eighteen-year-old actor. I think I was hoping most of all that Vittorio would remember how much he had loved me and our baby and had wanted us to have more children and would again believe that was the top priority of his life. And we would somehow magically work out all our problems. So I didn't call my agent and discuss the pros and cons of doing this film. Brilliant.

By this time I had a permanent case of insomnia, and the one good thing about the Hotel de la Ville was the unwritten rule that no one in the gang that hung out in the bar was ever to go to sleep. You must sleep only on the producer's time. That is, during lunch, which in those days was between one and four, or between scenes while they were lighting, or while you were acting since it didn't matter much what you said as everyone was speaking different languages and they dubbed it all later in any language.

Raymond Pellegrin seemed to have taken me under his wing, and every evening as actors straggled in from their exhausting day at the studio, we all would have Camparis and soda spiked with vodka or gin and tell each other hilarious stories about the multi-lingual films we were shooting. Then, around nine or so, we would bathe and get dressed up, then go out and find gourmet restaurants and nightclubs that seemed to stay open till dawn. We all abided by this "no sleep" rule, plus the entire Katherine Dunham Company, Walter Chiari, Raf Vallone, Anita Ekberg and three or four gorgeous Italian starlets. We would troop through the darkened streets that always looked as if a blackout were in progress because of the blinds pulled down over every window. We went to the Hostaria dell' Orso, Tre Scalini, Piccolo Mondo, Sabatini's, the California, the Colony, and the Club Jicky, where one night, Prince Dado Ruspoli was so stoned that he burned a cigarette hole in my beautiful mink coat, and that damned millionaire prince never paid me for repairing it. At dawn we would go back to the hotel. Bruno would give us cappuccinos, and we would shower again and put on our working clothes; then the limos would pick up and deliver us to studios scattered all over the city.

So, in the middle of my personal agony, I managed somehow to have a lot of frantic fun, bouncing around Rome, often in very bare evening and cocktail dresses, and generally creating a scandal with Raymond Pellegrin as my escort. I hoped I was hurting Vittorio as much as he had hurt me with Anna Maria Ferrero.

I received a call from Vittorio's sister, Maria, who asked me if I had told my family and somehow informed the baby of my plans for divorcing Vittorio. "I haven't even telephoned them since I've been in Italy," I replied truthfully. "I just write funny postcards and wires and hope they don't believe the headlines. And I don't even want to think about what they must be reading in the scandal sheets. I've heard nothing from them either, although they know which hotel I'm staying at."

She sighed and said, "Vittorio is returning from Genoa tomorrow, Sunday, and he would like to meet you and have a talk." She mentioned the name of an unfashionable restaurant where the *paparazzi* never went, near the Colosseum. I agreed to meet him the next afternoon.

I dressed very carefully for this meeting, trying to live up to the respectable Italian wife image; with my mink coat and hat I looked like a typical well-to-do matron out for Sunday lunch. I even wore the little diamond and sapphire family heirloom pin he had given me. I brought along some new pictures of Vittorina my mother had sent in an envelope with no letter. What bothered me about the pictures was that her right hand was bandaged. When I received them, I immediately called my sister, who didn't ask any questions, though I sensed her disapproval. She told me that when they were roasting the turkey on New Year's Day, Vittorina had moved like lightning and put her little right hand into the open oven and touched the hot turkey pan before they could stop her. My mother had rushed her to a specialist, and luckily the burn was only second degree and would not leave a scar. They had sent me two of each photograph, so I brought a set to the restaurant to give to Vittorio, who had not seen the baby or any new pictures of her for several months. She now had quite a lot of blonde curls and was almost two years old and looked like three. In a couple of the photographs she was riding a tricycle; Vittorio had sent my father the money to buy it for her for Christmas, and also one for Alice. In that photograph her bandaged little hand could be seen.

Vittorio was already at the restaurant when I arrived, his face still scratched and bruised. When I said, "Hello," he stood to kiss my cheek, and I his, but we were so nervous we bumped our heads together. This, of course, knocked off my huge dark glasses, and when he saw my eye, he cried, "Oh, my God, Shelley, are you sure there is no permanent damage to it?"

"No, Vittorio, only to my pride."

We sat down, and the waiter attempted to get an order out of us but only got as far as prosciutto and melon. I looked so sick Vittorio said, "We'll order the rest later."

As I played with the first course, we made conversation that went something like this: "You look the thinnest I've ever seen you. Don't you like Italian food anymore?"

"I'm not sure I like anything Italian anymore. Was the rest of the engagement of *Hamlet* in Genoa successful?"

"Yes, as a matter of fact, even without my enormous family present. I even tried to use some of the Method work that I've heard you and Lee Strasberg talk about."

"It's very painful at first. Did you find you were able to do it?"

"Sometimes, but it was in and out. And when it would get too strong for me, I would forget my technique and become inaudible."

"Bravo. That means it's working for you."

"When I resume the tour after *Mambo*, I'm going to try to use it more and more."

"Good. But you'll find it very difficult because your other method of acting works so well for you and is ingrained, and you've rehearsed the role that way, so it's like trying to put a train on a whole new track."

"Well, next season I am going to attempt another role, *Prometheus Bound*. In fact, I'm doing it in Syracuse at a festival the government is having there this spring."

"I somehow knew you would always do that role on location." (The actual rock that Prometheus was bound to was probably somewhere off Greece near Sicily.)

Vittorio then laughed and said, "Shelley, I didn't realize until our infamous press conference what a lethal tongue you have. I had always thought of you as such a nice, sweet girl. Your barbs appalled the entire Latin male population of Europe."

"Well, I hope it also gave a little backbone to the female population." I pointed out to him that European women had been forced to live in ignominious situations because of custom and the necessity of security for their children.

After a pause Vittorio said, "I thought we were only having a personal discussion of our differences. I didn't know we were having an international protest rally on the subject of the rights of women under international law. You could at least have given me some warning."

To change the subject, I gave him the photographs of Vittorina. He too became terrified when he saw her hand bandaged, and quite angry. "With all those adults in the house, can't they keep their eyes on a little baby so she doesn't hurt herself?" I assured him it wasn't serious and then told him that Vittorina had almost deliberately burned herself the very night we were having that terrible fight in Genoa; even allowing for the time difference, it was almost the exact hour. He took a long look at me and said, "Shelley, it's impossible to be a mystic and a socialist at the same time." I told him I was neither one of those things. I was too much for Number One to be a true socialist. And I didn't mean to sound mystical—I was just reporting what my sister had said.

We started to argue again. The meeting seemed pointless so I went back to the hotel and got into bed without even washing off my streaked mascara. Mentally, physically and spiritually, I was defeated. My work call for the next day had been put under the door. There was no way I could be sick, so I called room service and ordered a triple hot whiskey and tea and lemon. I managed to get down the whiskey with some soda crackers, and then I took two or three sleeping pills.

What had Vittorio been trying to do? Did he want a reconciliation, with him living part time with Anna Maria Ferrero? Was he trying to say he would always need some other woman as his mistress? Whatever it was, I couldn't bear it. I called my family in California and Vittorina yelled at me and then gave me some kisses, which almost sent me off on another crying jag.

My worried mother got on the phone and, after assuring me that Vittorina didn't even have a bandage on her hand anymore, asked me what had happened. I didn't want to tell her about my emotional condition or that I seemed to have a nonstop sinus infection, so I told her some big lie, saying I had a sort of anemia because I'd been so busy I'd forgotten to eat. My tone seemed to convince her I was all right, so she laughed and said, "Shirley, of all the lies you've ever told me since you've been a little girl, that's the biggest one. You undernourished with anemia?"

"Whatever it is, Mama, I'll just have to examine the fact that I keep marrying men who go away to war or want to live in other countries."

My father, who was listening on the other extension, said, "Shirley, Paul only lived in Chicago. Vittorio lives in Rome! Please come home through New York, and don't fly east as you've always wanted to and stop in Hong Kong or India. You promise?" I promised and told them I would call the following week and write them in a couple of days, and they were to send me more pictures of Vittorina immediately.

That night the atmosphere in the bar was frantically hilarious as the "artistic gang" joked in many languages and played poker dice. Julie kept watching the door because she was expecting Harry Belafonte to arrive momentarily. Raymond was telling me jokes and teaching me French words—respectable ones, I warned him. Despite my supposed block about learning foreign languages, I was holding a simple conversation in French before Raymond got his second trio of whiskeys and beers. If Vittorio had heard me, I think he would have blacked my other eye.

Catherine Zago, Raymond's compatriot from Marseilles who was in his present film, had been having an affair with Michael Rennie and was still madly in love with him although he wanted to end the affair as his wife was about to arrive in Rome. She wept quietly, then paused in her sorrow to congratulate me on the press conference, because now I would get a lot more alimony from Vittorio. I was properly indignant and told her that the press conference had nothing to do with our divorce settlement, and I was confident Vittorio would see to it that I and our child would always have everything we needed. Catherine shrugged and said, "Better get it in writing. He is probably a very rich man by now, and his brother-in-law, Guido, is head of the Rome Electric and Gas Works, and I'm sure he invests Vittorio's money very wisely."

A cold Roman drizzle had started again, and that and Catherine's pessimism were making my sinuses ache with a vengeance. Bruno out of pity got me some hot salt in a napkin which I was to hold to my head. Daniel Gelin sat down at our table uninvited, much to Raymond's pique. Raymond had been really coming on with me and was charming and seemed to like to make me laugh. He was a very intelligent, attractive and muscular young man, a wonderful French actor with the most gallant manner of flirting—holding and kissing the hand that wasn't holding the hot salt to my head.

Gelin told me there was a marvelous new French cure for sinusitis, and when Raymond left to get another of his three beers and whiskeys, Gelin took me over to a mirror at the end of the room and opened a little gold box that had white powder in it. "Blow your nose," he told me, giving me a Kleenex. "Then I will give you a little bit of this powder which you sniff up each nostril as far as you can." With that, he took out a little silver espresso spoon.

Brooklynite me said, "This is really a new French sinus cure?"

"Absolument."

I did exactly as he instructed, and I must say my head felt clear immediately and the pain disappeared. But suddenly I heard someone screaming; then I realized IT WAS ME.

The next thing I remember is lying on my bed with Julie holding my hands as I stared upward, becoming aware of the color green. The ceiling was the most gorgeous shade of green I had ever seen. "Julie, have you ever 'felt' green?"

"No"—she laughed—"but I wish I felt like you do right now."

Then I looked at the crystal chandelier. Someone had strung all of Bulgari's diamonds in my room while I was at dinner. I felt they were so valuable that I'd better not tell Julie; she would get frightened. I knew I was lying on the quilt, but the bed felt like a cloud that had conveniently floated into my room. Though my nose was burning a little, I didn't mind it. The muted motorcycle sounds of the Via Sistina were rare ancient music. I smiled at Julie and asked if she liked the lilacs the perfume of which was permeating the room. She said, "Shelley, there's every flower in this room but lilacs." I looked at her pityingly and told her about my hot summer nights in St. Louis, and tonight this room was obviously crowded with St. Louis lilacs.

For some odd reason Julie was holding both my hands tightly, but I didn't mind. I loved her dearly, and if she wanted to hold my hands in this fashion, it was okay with me. In fact, at that moment everything was okay with me. Then she had to say, "Did you ever read Aldous Huxley's *The Doors of Perception*? You're having that sort of experience now." I didn't remember if I had read it, but I did remember I had met him once at Laughton's house and he was blind.

I began to moan with the injustices of the world. Julie took my shoes off, loosened my slacks and covered me with everything in the room. She placed the heater as close to the bed as she dared and put the heating pad on my chest, muttering all the while, "That Daniel Gelin must be crazy. You have a bad sinus infection." I told her I had to blow my burning nose, and when I did, it started a furious nosebleed. Understandably Julie was afraid to call a doctor. Then suddenly Raymond and Daniel were in my room, sat me up, put ice under my upper lip and plugged my nose with Kleenex. The bleeding stopped, but they wouldn't let me lie down. I must have presented a very romantic sight with my red eye, my bloody nose, my now bloody mink coat and melting ice sprinkled around. I wanted to tell them to be careful—the ice bucket was dangerously close to the electric heater—but I couldn't talk.

I must have gone to sleep then because when I woke up, it was dawn and the only light I saw was the glow of the electric heater. Someone was in bed with me, and I thought it was Julie, but it was Raymond, on top of the covers with his arm under my head. And lots of little bloody Kleenexes scattered around. Some sinus cure!

I got out of bed carefully and cleaned up the room as best I could, washed my face, drank a whole bottle of mineral water, then got back in bed under the covers. I didn't dare undress with that sexy Frenchman asleep on my bed. I fell asleep immediately.

I was awakened around 10:00 A.M. as Raymond reentered my room with three bottles of beer, which even in those Hollywood on the Tiber days seemed a strange breakfast. As he drank them, he sat at the foot of my bed and asked me how I felt. "Pretty good," I had to admit. I don't know if it was because it was now a beautiful sunny day or because the French sinus medicine had worked, but my head felt better than it had since I'd landed in Italy.

Raymond began to run a hot bubble bath for me, which I considered very nice of him. He also threw some rose petals in the water. Ah, the ideas the French have. He gave me a blue terry-cloth robe from my closet, and I went to bathe.

I was soaking in the enormous tub when in walked Raymond, wearing a bathrobe and carrying a large goblet of champagne with fresh strawberries floating on top. As I stared at him in astonishment, he sat on the edge of the tub and sang a lovely French song to me. I understood almost every word. Then he bathed me with a huge sponge as if I were a baby. It got to the point where I was hoping he wouldn't powder and diaper me afterward.

Instead, cut to:

The fountains at the Place de la Concorde . . .
The Seine flowing tenderly through the city of Paris . . .
And the fireworks of Bastille Day, blotting out Lautrec's sad dancers of Montmartre.

CHAPTER 34

Later, after a lovely breakfast of croissants with fresh butter, and *American* coffee—Raymond had a very authoritative manner when he chose to—we decided to walk down to the Piazza di Spagna. During our walk I found out he'd been an officer in the French underground, the maquis, and later had been in a concentration camp. By sheer strength of will he had managed to survive and his political convictions were still intact.

He invited me to lunch but said we had to go someplace inexpensive in Trastevere because he wouldn't be paid until the next day. Italian producers then and now are notorious for holding onto their lire and the actors' per diems as long as possible. Hotels were used to it, but restaurants couldn't care less for the actors' plight.

As we walked down the beautiful Spanish Steps, I looked at the many colored flower stalls and saw the little boys wading in Bernini's Boat Fountain, singing Puccini arias. My anger and hatred had left me, and my love for Italy and all things Italian returned with an emotional rush. I no longer even hated Vittorio very much. That day I was glad to be alive despite the chaotic nature of my personal life. I re-resolved to do the picture as well and as quickly as possible and get home to my baby, then come back with her someday and enjoy Italy—after all, she was half Italian.

Raymond and I jumped on a bus, something I hadn't done in years, and got off in Trastevere, the old quarter of Rome that has excellent, though modestly priced restaurants. We ate outdoors, and even though it was the end of January, the air was warm and balmy. With typical Latin authority, Raymond ordered for us. I noticed Brigitte Vadim sitting all alone, having lunch and reading a book, probably because her writer-husband was at the studio. I suggested to Raymond that she join us for coffee, and he looked annoyed and said he wanted to be alone with me. I doubt if anyone will believe it, but this Frenchman preferred being with ME to Brigitte Bardot. We had a very large delicious lunch, and then I invited Brigitte over to our table for coffee because she looked so lost and lonely.

When the bill came, I made a motion toward my purse, but Raymond had a look in his eye that warned me to sit still. He changed his last 100-franc notes into lire to pay the bill. We strolled back to the Hotel de la Ville and up the Spanish Steps, where a peddler was selling beautiful short white leather gloves for 100 lire—about 75 cents—a pair. Brigitte and I stopped to look at them, but Raymond tried to force me to continue up the steps. "Raymond," I pleaded, "they're only one hundred lire. In America these gloves are at least ten dollars!" Raymond stood aside and became very quiet. I should have paid attention to the odd look on his face. Brigette bought three pairs of gloves, but I bought only one. Raymond then escorted me back to my hotel room and gave me a final *au revoir*. His face was as white as a sheet. I closed my door sadly. For a lousy pair of gloves I had ended what promised to be a lovely romance which my bruised ego especially needed at that moment. Why had I not recognized his embarrassment at being unable to buy them for me?

There was a work call for the next day. Harry Belafonte had arrived, and I had dinner with Julie and him, and Julie thought my sad look was because of Vittorio. At that point I didn't know if it was because of Vittorio or Raymond, or a little of each. Raymond was not in the bar that night, although the joint was jumping as usual. Harry commented on the extracurricular activities of Julie's fellow hotel guests, and I assured him that up till then she had been very busy nursing me through my sinusitis and had barely had time to have her toasted mozzarella. Now *I* kept looking at the doorway, hoping Raymond would appear, but he didn't. I went back to my room early and studied my Italo-English dialogue for the next day. I was doing a scene with Silvana and had to know when she stopped talking in Italian so that I could say my lines in English. This cockamamie way of working drove everybody, especially the sound man, who couldn't speak English, bananas.

After a long dusty day's shooting, I returned to the hotel about 7:00 P.M., and as I was preparing to bathe, there was a knock on my door. I put on my blue bathrobe, hoping it was Raymond, but it was the bellboy with a BOUQUET of gloves. Expensive, well-made ones. There were white, pink and blue ones, black leather embroidered ones, and driving, golf and riding ones. Suede ones of every color imaginable. They all were tied together with a pink ribbon, like a bouquet of flowers. And from the bow dangled a little gold boxing glove, which I still have. There was also a note in French, which I translated with my recently acquired French-English dictionary: "Darling, I want to buy you anything you need. Forgive me for being so rude. I know you have enough troubles.

Your therapeutic lover, Raymond." I unwound the bouquet and hung the gold boxing glove around my neck on a gold chain. It was a good symbol for the coming months. I wondered what would be an appropriate gift to send Raymond for the comfort, love and understanding he was giving me during this most difficult time of my life.

He knocked on my door at eight o'clock, and complete with my eyelashes on my pink eye and diamond earrings and my new black embroidered gloves, I was ready to go to dinner. He kissed me, and we both laughed. He took out a huge wad of lire and said, "This is my per diem until next Friday. We must spend it all by then." We had a Campari at the bar, and he said, "I bet you would like a huge American steak."

I salivated and asked, "Is there such a thing in Rome?"

"Of course."

Harry and Julie came out of her room—they were obviously so in love they could barely answer when we asked them if they wanted to join us at Jerry's restaurant for American steaks and salad. Julie finally decided she needed the sustenance of a steak, and they would join us in a little while.

The evening was brisk, but I didn't feel cold as we walked up the Via Veneto where the ever-present *paparazzi* took several hundred pictures of Signora Gassman and the French matinee idol, Raymond Pellegrin. One of them was flashing bulbs a foot from my face, hurting my eye so Raymond shoved him aside. He fell into the gutter, in front of a *Topolino*, which was parking and which, thank God, had good brakes. Then the *paparazzi* literally chased us into Jerry's. Even behind my dark glasses, my eye was hurting from the flashbulbs.

We sat down at a table for two, and I asked Raymond if we didn't need a bigger table for Harry and Julie. He smiled. "I don't think they're hungry enough to leave the hotel. They are so in love and haven't seen each other for several months. I'll bet you a back scrub they won't show up. [It sounds better in French.]" He won the bet.

After dinner he took me to the Fiametta, an American movie theater, where we saw *On the Town*. I had seen it before, but I enjoyed it even more in Italian. There's a strange custom in Roman movie theaters. They have an intermission in the middle of the picture for fifteen or twenty minutes. Hawkers go up and down the aisles, selling ice cream, candy and popcorn, and all the lights of the theater are full up. After about five minutes I became aware that the entire audience was staring at Raymond and me. He was then quite a big new French film star and was also making a lot of good Italian films since he spoke the language perfectly. The women in the audience were staring at me disapprovingly, while the men stared at Raymond, smiling and making sexy clicking sounds out of the corners of their mouths. We both got very angry, but before Raymond could punch anybody, thank God the lights went out, the picture started again and we quickly left the theater. Raymond got us a taxi back to the hotel, although it was only a couple of blocks away, but the ever-present *paparazzi* were flashing away.

When we got back to the hotel, we reported to the bar. A band had been left over from somebody's wedding and was still playing in the large reception room. Raymond and I acquired a free bottle of champagne and a couple of brandies and joined in the tail end of the celebration. Raymond was a great jitterbugger—where he had learned this in the French resistance I'll never know. Maybe he took lessons from the same teacher as my first husband, Capt. Paul Miller.

I didn't have to be up until 7:00 the next morning, but I awoke at 4:00 A.M. and sat on my little balcony in my mink coat, looking at the picture of Vittorina in its silver frame. As I glanced over the roofs of the Piazza di Spagna, I wondered if my "husband" was now in bed somewhere in Rome with little Anna Maria Ferrero.

While I was sitting there, Raymond came out, and I felt his warm calloused hand on my cheek (an actor's hands calloused?). I looked up at him, and he brought me back into the room, and we sat on a green and gilt rickety sofa. I was quite chilled because I had not been able to find my slippers. He put his arms around me and said, "*Ma chérie*, in this too short life, one must learn to take the bitter with the sweet. When I was in the concentration camp, I resolved that if I was to live through the horrors of that experience, I would never again shed one tear of regret for whatever Fate gave me, but for the rest of my life enjoy the fun and love and even the pain that each day brought me." His English was inadequate to the nuances of what he was trying to tell me, but I understood. He had been raised in the toughest section of Marseilles, and during the war had exploded trains of ammunition in the very teeth of the Nazis. He was trying to give me some of his courage and will to love life no matter what. He had learned this in a much harder school than I had. We went back to bed, and he warmed my feet and my soul. And we made lovely, friendly love, and I didn't once think of Vittorio and his young girlfriend. I think.

The next day I had a big scene with Michael Rennie, and the only other people involved were a bartender and some of the dancers. The director was asking where Julie was, and I told him that I felt that since she was so young and pretty, it would be better if she weren't in this very emotional scene I had with Michael. Robert Rossen, knowing that I wasn't that kind of actress, looked at me rather strangely. Then he had the assistant call the hotel, and he caught Julie just as she was getting into the studio car and told her that she didn't have to come to work that day. Later she told me she was so disappointed she went right back to bed with Harry.

At lunchtime my stand-in showed me the daily Italian papers. Raymond Pellegrin and I had our pictures three columns wide on the front pages of all of them. The titles underneath were: "Shelley mourns for Vittorio"; "Is Raymond Shelley's next husband?"; "At least Shelley is faithful to the Latin countries"; "Raymond fights for Shelley's love" (with the picture of Raymond throwing the rude photographer into the street). Alongside one was a photograph of Vittorio doing *Amleto* with this classic: "Amleto's indecision has been decided by the French."

That afternoon, when I went back to the scene with Michael Rennie, in my mannish suit and with my cigarette holder, the camera was shooting over Michael's shoulder onto me. Vittorio walked onto the stage, dragging little Anna Maria Ferrero by the hand. Her hair was done up on her head, and she was wearing diamond earrings exactly like the ones Vittorio had bought me from Bulgari for Christmas. The entire crew, Robert Rossen and Dino de Laurentiis— who had come down quickly onto the set—looked very nervous. But Vittorio wouldn't move. It was one of the few times in my life when an icy sort of calm took hold of me. I was beyond anger. One who has experienced this feeling never forgets it.

I rehearsed the scene calmly a couple of times while Vittorio stood next to the camera watching, with his arm around Anna Maria. As we got ready to shoot, the makeup man handed me his mirror and a lipstick brush for me to check my makeup. Without warning, especially to myself, I suddenly threw the mirror with all my force at Vittorio's head. It missed by an inch and smashed against the wall. Luckily no one was killed. But from that day on, Vittorio and I met twice a week in the eye specialist's outer office. He had gotten a scratch in his right eye from a sliver of glass. I was terribly sorry about it.

Unsurprisingly Robert Rossen decided to eliminate all scenes in the film that he possibly could between Vittorio and me. I informed De Laurentiis that if he ever let Vittorio come on the set again to watch me act—although I knew he needed the instruction—I would walk off the set and the picture and sue *him*, De Laurentiis, for community property under California law. Consequently, I had a great many scenes with Michael Rennie that I'd previously had with Vittorio. Neither Vittorio nor I cared very much how quickly they had done this rewrite; we just wanted to get the picture the hell over with, get our money and go our separate ways. And Rennie was pleased at the way his part had grown.

One day in the eye doctor's outer office, Vittorio and I discussed our personal problems thoroughly. He agreed that Jerry Giesler should draw up the divorce papers and send them to us. He didn't seem in a terrible hurry for the California divorce, but I wasn't sure if we were married in Italy anyway. I wondered if he knew about community property in California and if I had to give him one of my diamond earrings and half my Cadillac. But I wasn't about to suggest it. As Vittorio went out the door, he said something rather strange: "France has the same Catholic rules about divorce as we do here. And if you think Italian men are unfaithful, the accepted *modus vivendi* in Paris is for men to spend their four hours of lunch in the afternoon with their established and recognized mistresses and go home to their families in the evening. In Italy we just reverse the hours." Then he went out. I sat there and wondered about what he had just said. He came back in again. "On second thought, there's an *avvocato* in Venice who is a relative of that Genovese *avvocato*, and we'll talk to him when we get to Venice because I should pay for Vittorina's education, the nurse's salary, and things like that. And I want to make sure I see my baby every year. Meanwhile, let's *try* not to hate each other so much."

Recently Vittorio was in New York publicizing the Robert Altman film *A Wedding*, and on the *Dick Cavett Show* he was asked quite a few questions about his personal life. With Italian dexterity he avoided answering most of them. Then Cavett slipped in, "Of all the women you've been involved with in your life, which one do you think you really loved the most?" Vittorio got that blank but revealing Monty Clift look in his black eyes and said, "Shelley and I probably loved each other the most because we hated each other the most afterwards and tried to hurt each other in every way possible for a couple of years. When you don't love someone very much, you're not interested in hurting them and don't need to cause them pain. During this period Shelley and I figured out many Machiavellian tortures for each other. I must say, although she isn't Italian, she often bested me." He paused, then said, "In a way it's sad, because Shelley had a great deal to give me artistically in her Method technique, and I think I had a great deal to give her in my disciplined vocal and theater technique. But we have been good friends for many years now and have a grown-up, beautiful and intelligent daughter." When I saw that program, although it had been almost twenty-five years or so, the "*Mambo* sadness" overcame me again, and I used up half a box of Kleenex. But not a full box.

But back then in Rome, I kept on my very red lipstick, my diamond earrings, wrapped myself in my mink coat, and thanked God for Bruno's lively bar and for my lovely, funny, hard-drinking Raymond. Michael Rennie's wife finally arrived from England and he had ended his affair with Catherine Zago. She sat around the bar, weeping and drinking interminable Pernods, and putting a damper on everyone else's frantic fun. We tried to console her, and there were many other handsome, famous international actors ready to help her do this. But the "true love of her life" had been destroyed and she was inconsolable.

About 3 A.M. one morning, she suddenly got up, dramatically threw off her coat, and with tears streaming down her face, announced that she was going to end it all. She ran up a little circular iron stairway that led to a high landing. I pleaded with Raymond to go help his countrywoman; after all, she was from Marseilles, and she was suffering. He finished his three whiskeys and three beers and then, with great reluctance, followed her up the stairs. I waited five, ten minutes. Everyone in the bar listened, waiting. Nothing. I finally followed them up the stairs.

I shall never forget the sight that greeted me. Raymond was pushing Catherine out the full-length window high above the Spanish Steps. Her feet were off the sill and he was trying to loosen her grip as she clutched for dear life to the steel blinds, the drapes, the window sash, anything. "If you want to go, go! But stop making everybody else miserable. You want so much to go? Get out of here!"

I grabbed her, pushed Raymond aside and pulled her back inside. She fled down the stairs.

"Raymond, would you really push her out the window?" I was almost afraid to ask.

"No," he laughed, "I was holding her around the waist . . . I was just calling her self-deceiving emotional bluff."

From that day, Catherine Zago was very thoughtful and the

picture of charm, boring no one with her troubles. Two days later she was running around with Henri Vidal, another French actor, and was again having a very good time with the gang. No discussions of suicide ever again.

Dino de Laurentiis hurried into my dressing room one morning with the wardrobe woman carrying six or seven Marilyn Monroe-type sequined dresses and took away my expensive mannish wardrobe. When I tried to fight him about this, saying that I had already established a lesbian character, he said, "No, no, no. You have misunderstood the script. You are very female and are in love with Michael Rennie." What?

I found out from Raymond that night that the Italian Parliament had had a big discussion—as if it didn't have more important problems—about the homosexual picture Dino de Laurentiis was making. And the newspapers, especially the Vatican paper, were demanding that the Italian government take away from De Laurentiis the usual film subsidy. That accounts for the confusion in my characterization in *Mambo*—if anyone saw it.

I had successfully avoided Vittorio and sleep in that order for days, and I had begun to join Raymond in his boilermaker activities. I had a scene in the film in which I tell the Dunham Dance Company they are not getting enough rest or the proper food for dancers, and since Italy is so damp in the winter, it is dangerous. In the middle of the scene I developed a terrible pain in my chest and collapsed, and before you could say "Anna Maria Ferrero," I was under an oxygen tent in the Salvatore Mundi Hospital. I had been burning the candle at both ends and melting the middle. I had been over-dieting, overpartying and over in Italy too long.

CHAPTER 35

After several lovely days in which oblivion enveloped me, I was awakened early one morning, or perhaps it was late dusk, by a peculiar clicking sound. I was in a bed in a strange room and was no longer cold. Sitting next to me rocking and knitting was a strange creature in a medieval blue gown covered with a long white apron and in a white-winged headdress. As I peeked at her, I decided through the dusky light that she must be an angel and I had died and gone to heaven. I mean, she had a lovely face, and it made me very happy to think that although I had led a somewhat promiscuous life, God had forgiven me, and I was up there where I belonged. After all, I had tried to do my best for my fellowman, when I had time.

The angel suddenly noticed I was awake and gazing at her. She smiled sweetly and said serenely, "It's all right, Miss Winters." This angel obviously spoke English, so I was no longer in Italy. "You can go on and have your nervous breakdown. I've spoken to your mother in California, and your baby is very well taken care of. She doesn't need you there at all." I would have slugged the angel, but my arms were taped to the protective bars at the side of the bed, and a syringe was in the vein of my right arm because I was getting intravenous feeding. The angel kept rocking and clicking her needles. She continued, "We were afraid you were going into double pneumonia because your lungs were so congested, but we've given you a great deal of penicillin and vitamins, and you're physically in pretty good shape now. So you can go ahead and have your nervous breakdown."

I began to notice that this angel had a decidedly British accent and was wearing a rosary at her waist, as well as a white collar. Wrong heaven. And as she kept rocking and knitting away, she assured me that Salvatore Mundi Hospital had the most modern equipment for nervous disorders. Ice baths, hot and cold hoses and electric and insulin shock treatments. "Go ahead and let go," she encouraged me. "Lots of celebrities come here to have their nervous breakdowns."

With that a jovial chubby priest came in, with a brogue you could cut with a knife. "Well now, Miss Winters, so it's awake we are at last." I informed him that I didn't know about him, but I was very awake. And hungry. I wished to be unstrapped from this bed immediately and have the needle that was hurting my arm taken out.

It turned out to be 6:00 A.M., and the doctor wouldn't arrive until 7:00. But I had been so terrorized by the nun's description of what had been prescribed for my impending nervous breakdown that all I could think of was to get some food, get dressed and get the hell out of there. While I waited for the doctor, the beaming sinister clerics let me use the phone and untied both my arms when I promised not to move the right one until the doctor ordered the intravenous stopped.

I called Julie at the Hotel de la Ville, waking her up and begging her to come get me before they locked me in a cell forever. She was overjoyed that I was recovering from the mental and physical coma I had sunk into for three days and said she would visit me after work because the film company was leaving for Venice the next morning.

A serious young Swiss doctor came in and told me that I'd had a slight nervous breakdown—I was both emotionally and physically exhausted, and if I wanted to get well, I had better relax, think happy thoughts and stay in the hospital for two more weeks. This was his firm medical opinion. I was disturbed by this information, but by now I didn't care what happened to that cockamamie picture.

Julie and Raymond came to see me at about seven that night and brought a mink coat and some of my warmest clothes. Julie said she would take the rest of my things to Venice to the Hotel Danieli, and when I was well enough to travel, she would have a nice warm room ready for me there. Raymond kissed my hand and cheek and cheered me, bringing me a little phonograph with records of French lessons and a knockout record of Doris Day singing "April in Paris." He told me to get well quickly, and he planned to visit me in Venice his first free weekend. In fact, he hoped to be able to take me to France when we finished filming, and we would spend April in Paris together. I was to listen to the record and remember that. And he was going to show me a Paris right out of a storybook from my childhood dreams. I had already told him it was my favorite and the most beautiful of cities.

When he left, he gave me a little box which he told me to open later, and be careful with it because it really was his heart. I think I will love that man all my life in a very special way. I opened the box and saw that it contained a beautiful chocolate Valentine.

I realized then it was my daughter's second birthday. Before she was old enough or had a chance to know her father's warm arms, I was divorcing him. This guilt stayed with me for years. In fact, until Vittoria was five, I let her play only with children whose mothers were divorced or widowed. I was so mixed up that I thought in this way she would not notice there was such a thing as fathers and wouldn't feel deprived of hers at such an early age. But as I held Raymond's chocolate heart in the Salvatore Mundi Hospital, I knew then I had no choice. Again, I had not looked before I leapt and would never be able to give her a stable home like that of many of her friends.

The next morning Dino de Laurentiis's huge, tough production man arrived at the hospital. The nurse took my temperature, and it was normal. After an exchange of rapid-fire Italian with our visitor, the doctor completely reversed his diagnosis and suggestions for treatment. I believe this production man had been one of Mussolini's top officers and still had great persuasive powers. So in a few minutes I found myself all bundled up in my mink coat and blankets and in a berth on the way to Venice with the rest of the *Mambo* company.

As soon as I checked into my room at the Hotel Danieli, I telephoned Vittorio at the Grünwald Hotel, reminding him it was our daughter's second birthday and for him to cable flowers. Then I hung up. He cabled flowers and $2,000—$1,000 for each year. He kept up this lovely tradition for many years. I then phoned the Toy Bazaar in Beverly Hills and had it send Vittorina a doll. It was bigger than she was, and she would sit in its lap and call it Mommy (until I got home and straightened her out). When I phoned her, she was strangely silent, then said, "Love Mommy, where Papa?" The ache in my chest returned, and I reassured her that Papa would telephone *subito*. I hardly talked to the rest of my family because I didn't want them to catch on to how sick I was in the freezing Venice winter. I telephoned Vittorio's hotel again and asked his concierge to have him phone his daughter immediately. I couldn't bear to talk to him myself again.

My room was very modern, and the lovely lilacs Raymond had sent cheered me up. I put Doris Day's "April in Paris" on my little phonograph and managed somehow to escape into my old fantasy world with the help of the music.

Vittorio and I had gotten to the point where we were pretending we were invisible to each other and would look the other way and not even say good morning. We were to film an indoor scene at the Lido, in which the character Vittorio was playing suddenly turned into a dealer at the gambling casino. And I had what appeared to be a long, involved love scene with Michael Rennie. Since up to that point in the picture both Michael and I had been playing homosexuals, this scene was rather difficult to justify. We racked our actors' intellects to try to figure out how to act this passionate love scene in full view of everyone in the casino. We finally decided secretly it was a desperate attempt on Michael's part to make Vittorio jealous, and on my part to make Silvana jealous. What else could we do?

Complete with a blonde curly postiche stuck on the back of my head, long eyelashes and a bosom-revealing sequined gown, I stood near Vittorio's gambling table with Michael, and we sipped champagne from the same glass and smooched and nuzzled while the Dunham Company, including Silvana, did a number on the nearby dance floor. We rehearsed the scene a few times, and then finally Mr. Rossen caught on to our secret motivations because I kept glancing at Silvana to see if she noticed, and Michael kept glancing at Vittorio to see if he cared. Rossen was amused but pleased that the nonsensical rewrite now had some relation to the original script. And the Italian Parliament could dissolve once again, for all we cared.

The director told all the extras to mime their speech so he could shoot this very amusing but painful scene with direct sound. When he said, "Action!" we started doing the scene. The dancers danced without music, and the extras at the gambling tables mouthed their words and kept the chips as quiet as possible. Only Vittorio, the dealer, clicked his dice and chips noisily and gave his instructions to the gamblers loudly in French, as he would have in a noisy casino.

Halfway through the scene I stopped—something I had never done since the days when George Stevens had taught me that only the director says, "Cut." I asked the director politely if, since Vittorio was so used to dubbing, he too could speak silently while Michael and I did this delicate scene. Vittorio informed Robert Rossen in careful English that although Italian actresses weren't noted for their training, he wasn't used to working with an actress who couldn't concentrate on her scene and walk and talk at the same time. The prop men who understood English—remembering the mirror incident—immediately grabbed everything throwable in sight. I did nothing, although I was white with anger. The director asked me if this muted talking bothered me that much, and I haughtily replied, "Mr. Rossen, I am a *Method*-trained actress. This is a difficult scene, and I act with my inner feelings. Superficial Italian actors don't understand this, but a quiet set is helpful." They immediately broke for lunch, and Dino and the director changed the camera angle so Vittorio was no longer in the shot.

It wasn't until sometime later that I found out why Vittorio had been so ornery that day. It turned out that this was the morning his lawyer had informed him that he'd better support Anna Maria Ferrero until she was twenty-one, or her family would denounce him and possibly send him to jail.

Vittorio was not the only person I knew who had reservations about the Method technique. I once shared a platform in New York's garment center with Myrna Loy and Melvyn Douglas, waiting for Senator John Kennedy to arrive and make a speech after an introduction by David Dubinsky. It was lunch hour, and Kennedy's car seemed to be waiting at Forty-second Street. Literally a million people were hanging out of the windows of all the skyscrapers and jamming the streets, waiting for Kennedy's speech. The police were almost unable to control the crowd, and I began to fear for *our* safety on the podium. After what seemed an eternity, Kennedy's car drove up, and to a wild ovation he joined us in front of the microphone. He was looking through his notes while Dubinsky introduced him. "What took him so long to drive two blocks?" I whispered to Melvyn Douglas. "Why did his car just wait on Forty-second Street?"

I didn't think John Kennedy had overheard me, but he looked up from his notes, leaned over and said, "Now, Shelley, what does a *Method* actress know about an entrance?" Wise and fast, that President was, and seemed to understand everything.

Back then, during that freezing Venice winter Rossen was going crazy and sending wires back to Barney Balaban in Hollywood that something had to be done or he would never be able to finish the picture, much less do it on the present budget. As for me, *non mi frega niente.*

The next day the sun was shining brightly, and the Production Department decided to do the gondola scene. It went very well until they called *"Pausa"* for lunch. Michael Rennie got out of the gondola first, then helped Silvana. But somehow I had so much trouble balancing while getting out that Vittorio, despite all his athletic ability, fell into the canal. To this day I don't know if I pushed him accidentally or if I was grabbing onto him for support. Shades of *A Place in the Sun!* Naturally the *paparazzi* were taking pictures. Vittorio managed to climb back onto the pier quickly with fire in his eyes. Since the air was quite chilly, I can imagine how cold the water was. He yelled Genovese curses at me as they rushed him to his dressing room. I knew he had doubles of his wardrobe and could work after lunch because he had a scene where he got shot and blood would have to be splattered all over his clothes. Incidentally, Vittorio absolutely refused to do his death scene until I *left* Italy; he was somehow positive that I would manage to change the blanks in the gun to real bullets. Why would he think that?

When I got back to the hotel that evening, I was thoroughly chilled from *his* dip in the canal. I drank some whiskey, turned on the electric heater that Julie had borrowed from the Hotel de la Ville and went to bed in my "uniform." I felt very stupid and guilty for having caused, accidentally or on purpose, Vittorio's unscheduled swim; I knew the canal was dangerous. Luckily there were no bad aftereffects. (Katharine Hepburn told me years later that she had gotten an eye infection from a scene in *Summertime* when she was required to fall into the canal, and it has been very persistent and is still with her.)

At dinnertime that night Julie insisted that I get out of bed, collect myself and go with the gang to Harry's Bar, which, for the last half century, had been the hangout for American and English writers who lived in Venice. There was something there that Julie especially wanted to show me. Besides, they had very good steaks. As we sat down at a table in the bar to have an American martini, she pointed to a famous sign stuck up against the mirror. It said in English: "No Jews or dogs allowed in this bar." On the mirror under it was written: "The Nazi who put up this sign is now at the bottom of a Venetian canal." The original Harry is long gone, but the Italian Harry who now owns the bar has kept that sign up there as a reminder of the brutality of the Nazi occupation of Venice. German tourists who wandered into the bar then usually left quickly.

The whole cast and crew of *Mambo* seemed to be at Harry's that night, having American martinis and enjoying the huge steaks and baked potatoes. And they all were laughing about Vittorio's unexpected dip that day. I wasn't laughing because I was now truly angry at myself for my inexplicable and childish behavior. Since Vittorio was usually so concentrated, dignified and remote on the set, and since the Italian crews are great pranksters, they secretly were delighted at his undignified swim. They all had worked with him on many films, and although he was very accommodating and friendly, no one ever got to know him very well. He was a very reserved person, and I believe that is as true now as it was then. He makes his own decisions and carries them out in his own way. I think his daughter has inherited this quality from him.

But that night so long ago, when her father entered Harry's Bar he was accompanied by Princess Alessandra Something Or Other, who was one of the local aristocracy of the church. She was very chic and beautifully dressed, bejeweled and coiffed, and very aristocratic in manner. Vittorio and she sat down at a table next to Julie and me and two of the handsome black dancers from the Dunham Company. And since we all were eating in such close proximity, we had to address a word to each other once in a while.

Vittorio presented his princess with her full title, but the black dancers with me said, "Hi there, Princess. Hi there," as if she were a bitch dog that had wandered into the bar; she had been looking at me and my "uniform" with disdain, as if to say, "How in the world could Vittorio Gassman have ever married THAT?" I was huddled in my by now shabby mink coat, with a wool muffler wrapped around my head covering my sinuses as much as possible, my usual three sweaters, leotards, baggy flannel slacks and fleece-lined galoshes. I hated her on sight. She looked as if she'd just stepped out of *Vogue*, and although she wasn't really pretty, she had that aristocratic slim look that *some* men find attractive.

Vittorio was kissing her hand openly, as if daring me to do some-thing. He had placed a sharp steak knife on his table, the blade facing toward me. He didn't seem at all put out by his unexpected plunge that morning, and my attempts to apologize sincerely were thwarted by the princess's remarks, one of which was something like: "Vittorio told me you majored in klutzery at your so-called Method drama school in New York. What exactly is that?"

The idea that he had dared discuss our marriage or relationship or anything about me with that Venetian bitch made me shut up and quietly eat my steak, although I could hardly swallow. As in all good Italian restaurants, there was a cat wandering around, so I surreptitiously slipped the meat under the table and gave it to the cat when I thought no one was looking. Julie, of course, realized what I was doing but said nothing. I wondered what had happened to Anna Maria Ferrero but didn't really care.

One of the black dancers said in a loud voice, "According to the new World Health Organization, beautiful Venice has one of the highest rates of syphilis and TB in the world." Then, looking right at Vittorio, he added, "So all we dancers are going to be real careful while we're shooting here." Vittorio gave him a blank look; I think he didn't understand his Harlem English. But the princess, who had been raised in British schools, did.

Unfortunately we all finished eating together, and as we had early calls, we began traipsing back to our hotels, more or less in a group. As we passed in front of the Piazza San Marco, I stupidly felt I had to say something to break the deathly tension, so although I knew the square was named for it, I said inanely, "What a beautiful church that is. What's the name of it?"

The princess looked at me pityingly and said loudly, "You Americans really are barbarians, aren't you?" She laughed, and Vittorio seemed to be laughing with her and said nothing in my defense. They turned off toward the Grünwald, and Julie and the other dancers put their arms around me, and cold tears of rage started to stream down my face.

My only moments of joy those days were Doris Day singing "April in Paris," the letters from my family, Raymond's phone calls and the news that he was coming up the next weekend. He had to fly to Paris first to talk with a director about his next film, in which he was to play Napoleon in a big French Technicolor epic, his most important role since starring in *The Wages of Fear* with Yves Montand. I was to meet him at the train station on Friday night.

Since Vittorio was being very uncooperative about the divorce papers Jerry Giesler had sent him, Giesler warned me that my conduct should be very circumspect until Vittorio signed the settlement giving me Vittorina's custody and his support. So I did not get Raymond an adjoining room at the Hotel Danieli.

The few days until Raymond arrived dragged slowly. Vittorio was bringing his princess on the set just so the *paparazzi* could photograph her watching us acting. Such behavior was not Vittorio's usual *modus operandi* because he had always been very sensitive to the nuances of my feelings in the past and, for that matter, of the feelings of anyone he was working with.

It was a bitterly cold night as I waited at the station for Raymond, but I had managed to glamor myself up as much as possible, considering my permanently watering red eyes. I saw him approach, coming out of the steam the engine generated, carrying his suitcase and some peonies he had brought from Paris, and my sad heart jumped. He dropped his possessions as I did my purse, and we hugged each other the way drowning men must hug a life preserver. I knew he had seen his little girl in Paris. He loved her very much, and the knowledge that when he finished this film, he would be moving into a new apartment away from her must have been very difficult for him. We kissed and hugged, which was the norm for an Italian train station, and no one noticed. Then we grabbed our belongings and took a water taxi to the Hotel Danieli.

On the way, Raymond told me that he and his about-to-be-ex-wife, Dora, had signed all the papers necessary to commence the divorce proceedings in England. His wife was to file there, and it would take three years before it was final and one of the partners could marry again. I didn't ask anything about these arrangements, but he was weeping because he had had to give up custody of his child. He explained, "I am a film actor and away on location a great deal. Dora works mostly in the theater or television in Paris, so she can give our little girl more security than I can."

When we arrived at the hotel, he was surprised at the "lack of adjoining rooms" situation, but when I explained, he understood immediately. I had twelve bottles of Heineken's beer and a bottle of Jameson's Irish whiskey for him, and he put his beautiful flowers in a big water glass. (Why do French flowers have more color and perfume than those from the rest of the world, or does it just seem that way?) I put on "April in Paris," and he said, "My God, Doris Day sounds like she has a sore throat."

"I know, I've played the record almost constantly since I left the hospital. The thought of Paris in the spring is the only thing that has kept me sane throughout this nightmare picture with Vittorio."

Raymond sat me down on the bed and took a velvet jeweler's box out of his pocket. "I was going to wait and give this to you after dinner over champagne, with lovely music in the background. But I think you need it now." He gave me the box, and with very, very ambivalent feelings, I opened it. Thank God it didn't contain a ring. What it did contain, though, was the most beautiful heart-shaped antique diamond necklace I had ever seen. The central heart was made of antique-cut diamonds, and the delicate chain had diamonds in a floral design going up to the clasp. I was stunned by the beauty, craftsmanship and obvious value of this gift. Raymond showed me the thick crystal at the back of the heart, which could be opened. Inside was a sort of reddish brown curl tied with pink thread. He kissed me and said, "This is the necklace that Napoleon gave to Josephine when they were bethrothed. That is Napoleon's hair in the back of the heart." I was aghast and told Raymond I couldn't possibly accept it. "Yes, yes," he insisted. "I bought it especially for you in Paris, and I think it is very fitting for us. Napoleon and Josephine's alliance was made out of loneliness and despair, and it grew into a great love that gave strength to both of them."

He was frightening me, and he soon realized it. I was not yet disentangled from one foreign relationship. How could I commit myself to another? He kissed me reassuringly. "Shelley, I will not be free for three years, and you certainly not for a year under California law, and we have our children and our careers to think about. I purposely did not buy you a ring. This locket just represents a hope, not a commitment. *Ça va?*"

I said, "Okay," and he clasped the locket around my neck. I did not take it off until I had to show it to the customs officer in New York. He looked at it carefully and said, "Just a minute, Miss Winters, I have to call French customs before you can bring that into the country." The French customs officer came down from some secret cubbyhole and examined my locket with a jeweler's loupe. He then looked at me rather sadly and said, "Miss Wintaires, this locket is a very beautiful antique and quite valuable. But that is not Napoleon's hair in the back. The diamonds are not cut the way French jewelers of that period cut them. It is more Italian. It is the kind of work they did in Florence around the middle of the seventeenth century."

"Oh."

Then this charming French customs official twirled his little mustache, took my hand and said, "Mademoiselle, you simply must stop believing everything those Latin lovers say. If you are going to continue making international films, you must take everything you are told with a few large grains of salt."

"Couldn't you have given me this advice a few years ago?"

"We live and learn," he said with a Gallic shrug, "and, with any luck, we enjoy the process."

Raymond and I had a lovely loving night, but we sensed it was a little sad and final. He understood that as soon as I got home, I wanted to concentrate on being a mother, and I had no plans to come back to Europe for a long time. And he now had to work much harder since he would have to support two households.

I got a notice the next morning that I had to report to the set at once to do a scene in the Piazza San Marco in which Vittorio would also be involved. Raymond seemed a little doubtful about coming on the set with me, but I told him that it was quite all right as Vittorio and I had reached an official agreement and he always had his new love, this Venetian princess, on the set with him. So Raymond came along. There were many photographers around, and although Vittorio saw nothing wrong with his "old friend" Princess Alessandra sitting with him, he became highly incensed at the presence of Raymond waiting with me for my scenes to be done.

By afternoon Dino de Laurentiis and the Production Department, the *polizia* and the assistant directors, the Prop Department, the Special Effects Department, and even the male hairdresser all looked ready in case anything physical started. Vittorio kept arguing with Robert Rossen that Raymond must leave the set. I understood enough Italian to tell Rossen that in that case I wanted Princess Bitch off the set and that she could go back to her kennel. Vittorio, who obviously had had a lot of wine to drink at lunch, was beginning to get rambunctious, and Raymond was getting that white, scary look on his face, and I was never quite sure that he didn't carry a Marseilles kind of rope brass knuckles or a knife with him. I reminded Vittorio that we still had to finish this film, and Vittorio immediately reminded me that we still had a child together, whom he was planning to support, and there were boats in the canal whose motor blades were very dangerous, and also that the canals were beginning to be full of rats. "In that case," I retorted, "the canal is your natural habitat."

"IT'S A WRAP!" Robert Rossen yelled. "We'll continue Monday morning with only the members of this company present."

Raymond was due back on his picture in Rome. When I took him to the train, it was sleeting for a change in Venice. He made me stay in the station and say good-bye from there and tenderly kissed me *au revoir*. I slipped into his pocket a package containing a beautiful carved gold Venetian cigarette case. I had had an odd thing engraved inside. It was a slogan of the Spanish people I had heard from the returning soldiers of the Abraham Lincoln Brigade. It said: "For Raymond, who knows 'It is better to die on your feet than live on your knees. But better still to stand firmly on your feet and survive amid the chaos of life.' Your friend in love, Shelley."

As I watched Raymond walk away from me through the steam, I wondered for a second what would have happened if Anna had had her little shop in Paris instead of Rome. But there is no going back, and I was grateful for the company and fun this lovely man had given me through the worst period of my life.

When I got back to my room, I decided that I was being a fool. They had enough film on me to complete the picture, and there was no earthly reason why I had to put myself through any more of this hell. I went down to the concierge and dictated a cable to my agent in Hollywood, telling him that I was leaving the picture and Paramount could have its money back, and it was necessary for my life and health for me to go home immediately. I made a reservation on the morning train to London, then started to pack. I called Julie to tell her I was leaving in the morning, and if I didn't see her, I would call her in New York.

The next morning I phoned for my breakfast and asked for a bellboy to come up and get my suitcases. *Nothing happened.* I ate an orange and called room service again, and they said, "*Sì, sì,*" but after fifteen or twenty minutes *still nothing happened.* Then I realized the maid hadn't come into my room, as she usually did by ten. I went to the door, and *it was locked from the outside.* I couldn't believe it. I just couldn't believe it. When I phoned down and screamed at the assistant manager, he immediately gave me that huge production man of De Laurentiis's who had put me on the train right from the hospital in Rome. He spoke very little English, and all he said was, "You wait. Cable comes from Barney Balaban soon." I screamed at him that I would miss my train. He said, "You wait. Cable comes from Barney Balaban soon," and hung up. From that moment on my phone was blocked, and I couldn't reach anyone.

I have cried often in this book and in my life, but the feeling of being helpless and locked in a hotel room in a foreign country where you cannot even call the American Embassy for help is terrifying.

Finally, about three in the afternoon, a thick cable was shoved under my door. It was a twelve-page message from Barney Balaban, president of Paramount Pictures. For eleven of those pages he told me how he sympathized with me and understood my agony, suffering and misery, and being away from my baby, and my having pneumonia, and how cold it was in Venice, and I was one of their favorite actresses at Paramount. On the twelfth page it said, in very clear type, "But if you leave the film *Mambo* before your role is completed, we will be forced to sue you for every cent you have or will probably ever have. Yours sincerely, Barney Balaban and the Legal Department of Paramount Pictures."

I read the cable three times, then began to laugh and cry at the same time. Then the phone rang. It was Julie. She had finally been let through to tell me that De Laurentiis had suggested I call my agent and Jerry Giesler before leaving the film. But it wasn't necessary; my spirit was broken.

Julie came up immediately and said, "Those Fascist bastards! How dare they lock you in your room and not let you leave the hotel! Let's call the American Embassy in Rome and tell them." But I was too tired now. I called Jerry Giesler in California, and he thought about it for a while, then said, "They are businessmen, Shelley. They have invested several million dollars in this film, and if they cannot complete the film, they lose their completion bond and all the money they invested in it. Unless you come right back here and check into a hospital, they have a very good case. But if we prove that you *are* having a mental breakdown, it'll be very difficult to get insurance for you on your next picture."

I said, "Jerry, I can't win for losing, can I?"

"This too will pass," he said. "Have you received the papers I mailed for you and Vittorio to sign in the presence of a notary or one of their *avvocatos*? It guarantees you custody of Vittoria and other things. I think Vittorio will agree to it, although he's obviously very hurt and miserable right now. You realize, Shelley, that this is the second child he's had to give up. His life right now must seem a shambles. It would be very easy for him to live in Los Angeles, be a movie star, get lots of publicity and make a lot of money. I'm sure that somewhere underneath he loves you and Vittoria very much. He too made a mistake in thinking his life could follow your average Hollywood pattern. Why don't you see if my papers have arrived and try to talk less bitterly to him, and for God's sake stop hurting each other, physically and mentally? Your family is terrified that you're going to literally kill each other."

I thanked this wise man, then went down to the lobby and found that his legal documents had arrived. I phoned Vittorio at the Grünwald, and he said he didn't want to read them. I said I didn't want to either. He then asked, "How is my little baby, Vittorina?"

I started to cry and said, "I miss her so much I can't stand it. Will this insane picture ever be over?"

There was a pause, and he said, "Soon, Shelley, I am sending you over an Italian doctor, and although he is not an American, believe it or not, he is a very good doctor. You sound terrible, and there is a special vitamin C we have here in Italy that you dissolve in water, and if you take a lot of it, perhaps you will not get pneumonia again and you will finish this damned picture. Then you can go home to your beloved California and Vittorina."

"I hope so," I told him.

He said, "Tomorrow at lunchtime bring the papers, and we will go to an *avvocato*'s office and show them to him. If he thinks they're all right, we'll both sign them. I guess there is nothing else to do, is there?"

"No, I don't think so."

And that is what we did. The *avvocato* read the papers. The only hitch came when he saw what Giesler had listed as the various expenses that Vittorina had, including Kathy's salary. He stared at it in amazement and said, "Vittorio, you think I can go to America and be a baby nurse?" We both tried to laugh, but couldn't. Vittorio signed all the papers automatically, as did I. They gave me custody of Vittorina except for summer holidays, and he agreed to pay all her educational and living expenses and to put 10 percent of his earnings in a trust fund for her.

The *avvocato* then asked me to sign a couple of documents which, if I had known exactly what they were, I'm not sure I would have signed them. But they were something Vittorio had to publish in the paper. Later I found out they said in Italian that Vittoria Gina Gassman was the child of an unknown mother adopted by Vittorio Gassman. At that time he had to do that in order for her to have his name legally.

That night Julie insisted upon taking me to the La Fenice Opera House to hear Gigli sing *Pagliacci*. I still felt sick and cold, and it was sleeting again, but I remembered Gigli's beautiful record of "O Paradiso" that I had listened to so often. With his artistry, Gigli had recorded man's longing for paradise as he looks over the mountains of his difficulties and finally sees it.

So, huddled in my mink coat and "uniform," I let Julie drag me to the Venetian opera house. That winter in Venice, I think even my soul was cold. As I sat in a box in that beautiful little gold and green theater, which until recently had been lit only by gas, I heard one of the most fantastic artists in the world. I was glad Julie had made me come. Gigli very seldom, if ever, performed in America, so I would have missed seeing and hearing a great artist.

Afterward Julie insisted we go backstage and meet and congratulate Signor Gigli. I whined that I was too cold, and it was getting late and too dangerous to walk all the way across slippery Piazza San Marco, and if I stayed outdoors another minute, I would freeze to death. She ignored my protests.

The chorus singers had obviously known I was there, and since I had become infamous in Italy as the deserter of their great matinee idol, I was self-conscious as I attempted to congratulate them in my halting Italian.

Only that morning, *Europa*, one of the weekly magazines, had carried a heart-rending story about "the deserted mother" whose baby was so far away from her on the other side of the world and the tempestuousness of Vittorio's and my relationship. I think Italy has two sports it never tires of discussing: soccer and the convoluted love affairs of its movie stars. Since I was indeed sick and lonely and in despair, I wasn't taking kindly to this national pastime.

When we finally got back to Gigli's dressing room, I saw a little unassuming fat man in an orange terry-cloth bathrobe. I managed to tell him, with Julie translating, what a great experience his *Pagliacci* had been and how much I had appreciated his records and artistry for many years.

He was obviously pleased, and as he looked into my tear-reddened eyes, he complimented me in return, through Julie, and told me he and his wife had seen *Un Posto nel Sole* (*A Place in the Sun*) twice. I thanked him. He then suggested we join him and some friends and walk across the Piazza San Marco quickly and have dinner with Maria Callas. Of course, I could do nothing but accept, but all I really wanted to do was get back to the hotel, take a couple of sleeping pills and sink into oblivion.

Julie and I waited in the green room while Gigli and four of his chorus sponged each other off with cold alcohol and then dried and dressed warmly. As I sat there waiting, I thought of "O Paradiso" and wondered why that special land of happiness had never been mine. Not with Paul, certainly not with Burt, and now not with Vittorio, whom I had loved totally, the only man whose children I'd ever really wanted. And now I seemed to hate him.

As all seven of us crossed the Piazza San Marco on that late winter night, the hundreds of lamps and the many arches were mirrored on the sleet-covered square. It was an extraordinarily beautiful optical illusion. We were halfway across when something happened that I know I will treasure all my life. Singers are notoriously careful of their throats and muffle them with woolen scarves and wear woolen hats pulled down over their ears. I had been shuffling slowly along with my head bowed, thinking of how I could possibly get through the rest of my life now, when suddenly Gigli put out his hand and stopped me. He opened his muffler and coat and began to sing the great tenor aria from *Tosca*. The four young men with him began to harmonize, using their voices as accompanying instruments. I began to shiver, but not with cold. Gigli was holding my hands and looking straight into my eyes, and although he spoke not one word of English, my actor's antenna interpreted his meaning: "Life, even with its misery, is still life. You must relish and fight through its pain and conquer it, grow, and then the joy will come again." When the echo of Tosca's last note faded from that beautiful square, he said, "*Shelli, tu capito?*"

"*Sì,*" I answered. "*Io capito.*" I was so moved I could not even say thank-you. He had made me understand with his music that life's immediate purpose is often hidden from us, but if we take care of each day, whatever it brings, and insist on living and experiencing it fully, the future will become a vision of hope.

As Gigli wrapped up his throat again, Julie looked at my face and said, "Thank God." I just stood there. "Shelley, do you want to wait here a little and then meet us in the restaurant?"

"Yes, and please thank him."

She kissed my cheek. "He knows he's thanked."

As I watched them walk toward the lighted restaurant across the shimmering square, a line of Serafina's came into my mind. (She is the young Italian widow in Tennessee Williams's *The Rose Tattoo*.) When asked where are her tears, she answers, "Why? I had the best. Not the second best . . . not the third best . . . but the best. So my pillow is never wet." I thought about what Gigli had tried to communicate to me with his great artistry. I knew he was right. So from here on in, everything else in my life was gravy, and I would try to live it to the fullest—with my work, my child, my intellect. I suddenly no longer felt vengeful and sad. In examining my feelings, I realized I was at last content and maybe even proud.

As I stood there in the sleet, a group of Venice's poor people came toward me. In those days they would wander around the city, especially at night, and ask tourists to sign petitions to the government demanding they remedy the terrible unemployment and medical problems. Of course I signed their petition and gave them all the lire I had, just keeping enough for dinner.

When they left, I noticed a young woman still standing under an archway about thirty feet away. As I approached her to give her the last of my money, she looked somehow familiar. In halting Italian I offered her my lire, but she seemed to be asking for my autograph. Then she took off her kerchief and she had kinky dirty blonde hair. She said something in rapid Italian which I did not understand. Perhaps it was an optical illusion, but she looked to me exactly like the adolescent Shirley Schrift. So I had a conversation with her, although we could not speak each other's language. But inwardly I understood it as:

"Isn't this movie star business enough already?" she seemed to ask.

Amazed, I said something silly like, "What are you doing in Venice?"

"You don't think you left me in Group Theatre's office fifteen years ago, do you? I'm always around somewhere with you, even though we don't have fun and march in May Day parades anymore, or organize strikes at Woolworth's. But I still give you the business every once in a while, like when you spent that five hundred dollars for that dumb Dior dress in Paris."

I said, "Yes, Shirley, I know. I guess you do."

With that I took her hand and as I did, I experienced, in some deep mysterious way, a merging of that long buried part of my self with the rest of me. I ran then into the warmth of the Taverna Fenice. I sat down next to Maria Callas and Gigli and the rest of the fine artists at the table. At one with myself, at last I felt I belonged there.

TO BE CONTINUED, I HOPE . . .

P.S. Shelley Winters A.K.A. Shirley Schrift are now firmly fused together. In this life journey, perhaps I'm sometimes vague about what took place in which year, but conversations of long ago have come back almost word for word. All the things I've written about are exactly as they happened. Some things are even exactly as I wished they *hadn't* happened. Perhaps a few things are exactly as I *wished* they had happened. However, I will never know the difference . . . nor will you.

PICTURE CREDITS

Photographs are from the author's collection unless otherwise indicated.

Page 397: Four sons—© American International Pictures, 1970. All Rights Reserved.
With Ralph Richardson—© American International Pictures, 1972. All Rights Reserved.

Page 398: Palm tree—Don Elson.
Emmy—courtesy of the National Academy of Television Arts and Sciences.
Foreign Press Award—Don Elson.
David of Donatello Award—Don Elson.
Academy Award—Don Elson.